PERSPECTIVES

The timeless way of wisdom

The Intellectual-Principle is a self-intent activity, but Soul has the double phase, one inner, intent upon Intellectual-Principle, the other outside it and facing to the external; by the one it holds the likeness to its source; by the other, even in its unlikeness, it still comes to likeness in this sphere, too, by virtue of action and production.

THE NOTEBOOKS OF PAUL BRUNTON

PERSPECTIVES

The timeless way of wisdom

Vol. 1

PAUL BRUNTON
(1898-1981)

A survey of categories 1-28
compiled by students at
Wisdom's Goldenrod, Ltd.

New Age Books

ISBN: 978-81-7822-338-4

First Indian Edition: Delhi, 2009
Originally published in USA

This edition is published by arrangement with Paul Brunton Philosophic Foundation, NY, USA

Published by
NEW AGE BOOKS
A-44 Naraina Phase-I
New Delhi-110 028 (INDIA)
Email: nab@vsnl.in
Website: www.newagebooksindia.com

For Sale in Asia Only

Printed in India
at Shri Jainendra Press
A-45 Naraina Phase-I, New Delhi-110 028

§

THIS BOOK IS MADE DEDICATE

to that Sage of the Orient at whose behest these pages were written: to one incredibly wise and ceaselessly beneficent. And, further, I have wrapped this book in the bright orange-chrome coloured cloth even as you have wrapped your body in cloth of the same colour—the Sannyasi's colour—the mark of one who has renounced the world as you have. And if the dealings of the cards of destiny bid me wear cloth of another hue, command me to mix and mingle with the world and help carry on its work, be assured that somewhere in the deep places of my heart, I have gathered all my desires into a little heap and offered them all unto the Nameless Higher Power.

—P.B.

CONTENTS 1–28

EDITORS' INTRODUCTION

Perspectives is a representative survey of more than 7,000 pages of notes withheld by Paul Brunton for posthumous publication. It introduces a much larger work that Dr. Brunton spoke of as his "Summing up."

Our original plan was to initiate this project with a boxed set of seven to ten volumes. Thousands of unsolicited letters from throughout the world, however, have urged us to accelerate publication—and much work remains to be done on our side before the rare breadth, depth, and beauty of the material in these notebooks can be adequately presented to the public. While we are happy to comply with so many sincere requests, we want to do so in a way that will best serve the larger project still in hand. A few introductory remarks should help to minimize the risk that the notebooks will be judged improperly because of being presented early in too brief a form.

To reap the greatest spiritual harvest from these "seed thoughts"—particularly those written after April of 1963—we should try to appreciate a condition of mind and heart which is rare in any century. Plotinus gives one of the best reports of this attainment when he writes:

> The Intellectual-Principle is a self-intent activity, but Soul has the double phase, one inner, intent upon Intellectual-Principle, the other outside it and facing to the external; by the one it holds the likeness to its source; by the other, even in its unlikeness, it still comes to likeness in this sphere, too, by virtue of action and production; in its action it still contemplates, and its production produces forms—detached intellections, so to speak—with the result that all its creations are representations of the divine Intellection and of the divine Intellect, moulded upon the archetype, of which all are emanations and images, the nearer the more true, the very latest preserving some faint likeness of the source. —v.3.7, MacKenna translation

It would be an error to think even of a sage as operating with the omniscience of the Divine Mind (Intellectual-Principle). But we can think of a sage—insofar as he does at times speak the thoughts of that Divine Mind with which he has become inwardly attuned—as producing these "detached intellections" or spiritual intuitions and translating them into contemporary language. The World-Mind (Intellectual-Principle, God) uses such purified, ennobled, and spiritually matured individuals as vehicles through which it can fashion representations of itself in our world. The aphorisms and philosophical maxims which such sages present us give us some dim reflection, at least, of what is going on in the depths of the Mystery—depths of which we are aware, but which we are unable to penetrate without the help of superior wisdom.

Whenever such writings have been produced, the task of "organizing" them proves insurmountable. Thousands of truly great and inspired minds have discovered in reading the Hindu *Upanishads*, for example, that it is impossible to reduce the entirety of the spiritual intuitions "captured" in them to any single kind of systematic whole. Anyone who has sincerely tried has given up the task as a hopeless one, though some have found through their effort to do so that the mind that coldly systematizes is on a lower plane than that which discovers in moments of awe. The kind of logical and coherent order which we find so important to the preservation of our sanity in the world of the senses is out of place in the realm of such discovery: it is transcended—though certainly *not* contradicted—by the unimaginably grand Divine Order of which our own best thoughts are but meager representations. To demand that the greater conform to the laws of the lesser is to deprive ourselves of our own Best.

The stilled, introverted, and receptive mind of the sage perfectly mirrors the powers of the Divine Mind which unfold temporally as all that is true or real in our world. When appropriate conditions exist, the sage may find himself being used to announce outwardly what is being thought in an indivisible way in the undivided larger Mind, with which he is inwardly at one and outwardly in harmony. The Divine Mind's ideation remains indivisible and whole, but its representation in our world—through the sage who writes or speaks with its inspiration—conforms to the laws of temporality and contemporary language. Though what the sage gives us through his speech or writing is not to be *equated* with the undifferentiated Intelligence of the living universal Consciousness, it is in truth an accurate reflection of it in terms more accessible to our spiritually younger minds. A *functioning* Wisdom that cannot be fathomed becomes dimly available to us; something of its master plan becomes available to guide our daily aspirations.

Such a sage, as you will read in section 25, remains—or more accurately *becomes*—fully human and verifies in his being and life the attainability for ourselves of such ennoblement and self-completion. In one sense the simplest, in another the most complex of human beings, the fully developed sage fashions a legacy which is much more than an intellectual one—though it of course includes that as well. It is not a hard-and-fast, tightly formulated, systematic doctrine all on one level but rather a multi-faceted and open-ended Way of Seeing and Being—a Vision unfolding and completing itself within us as our own best selves becoming Actual. In fulfilling their spiritual birthright, such pioneers of Humanity affirm the eventual fulfillment of a similar seed within each one of us. We can feel all that is good and noble within us being nourished by the inner Knower affirming itself in their written and spoken words.

A few remarks are also required concerning both the form of these writings and the structure of their organization by category. Throughout the thirty years during which he refrained from publishing new material, P.B. deepened and broadened his research into spiritual matters and wrote daily. His method of writing involved a minimum of three well-defined stages for a given piece of material. His custom throughout the years was to first jot down brief notes while an intuition was fresh and vital. These handwritten notes were later organized by topic, typed, and filed as "Rough Ideas." He regularly returned to the material in this stage and revised many of the notes there into more literary form. The revised versions were then typed afresh and filed by topic in notebooks entitled "Middle Ideas." A second review and literary revision followed, after which the "final" material was typed and then put into notebooks titled simply "Ideas." At any given time, new material for each stage could be found in his workroom.

P.B.'s preference for this form of writing is best expressed in one of his own entries, written probably in 1980:

> Poetry is at its best when it leads man towards spiritual beauty. This indeed is the mission of all the other arts also. To write a book that will sustain a single theme through three hundred pages is an admirable intellectual achievement, but it is not really my way; I have done with it since long ago. A man must express himself in his own way, the way which follows the nature he is born with. I prefer to write down a single idea without any reference to those which went before or which are to follow later, and to write it down in a concentrated way. The only

> book I could prepare now would be a book of maxims of suggestive ideas. I have not the patience to go on and on, telling someone in a hundred pages what I could put into a single page.

By the time the present editors were invited to the project, more than 7,000 single-spaced pages of such "detached intellections" had been produced—along with approximately 3,000 pages of related research material. During his last two years, P.B. conceived the present system of classification and began training a few students to bring the existing notes into conformity with his new categories. Since his death July 27, 1981, we have been carrying out the reclassification to the best of our ability in keeping with his guidelines. The reader should be fully aware that, while the writings themselves are those of a sage, the "organization" is largely the work of students. Often a passage will fit more than a single category, and we have had to choose what seems to us the most fitting one. The placement in some cases is admittedly arbitrary and should be recognized as such.

The same is true with respect to the contents of this survey. A work for general publication must always deal with the difficulty of anticipating the level of its audience, and there is little doubt that other people would have selected different writings from the voluminous array of possible choices. The notebooks consist of "paras," as P.B. called them, addressing a variety of *types* of people and many different levels of *development* within similar types. In the same spirit, we have tried to be representative of the actual material: advice is offered for many different types and many different levels. Where apparent contradictions surface, consider first that the advice may be for someone at a different level or of a different type than yourself. Take what is relevant and valuable for you: others may benefit from what does not appeal to you or apply to your present level.

Punctuation and capitalization are almost entirely as in the notebooks. Whereas standard stylebooks would dictate many required "improvements," we have left the vast majority of the paras untouched. In general, we have opted for authenticity rather than to impose our own stylistic preferences. We have introduced minor modifications only in those relatively few cases where—particularly in the "rough" and "middle" stages—we are agreed among ourselves that P.B. would approve our changes as clarifying his meaning or expressing it more smoothly—a process each of us worked on with him frequently during his last two years. Wherever there is disagreement among us, the paras stand as written for readers to debate among themselves what P.B. would have done.

We have made three useful concessions to the "hobgoblin" of consistency. British spelling has been maintained and made conformable with the Oxford English Dictionary, with the following exception: when O.E.D. lists two correct spellings of which only one appears in Webster's Third International, we have chosen the entry common to both. Also, we have applied the University of Chicago serial comma rule to those series in which commas already appeared in the notebooks. Finally, we have established consistent hyphenation in compound words.

We hope that P.B.'s readers will forgive our personal shortcomings that find expression in this and forthcoming volumes, and that they will sympathize with our sincerity in trying to do the best and most thorough job that we can do. We are grateful to P.B. for his grace and guidance, and for the opportunity to work with this material. We are also deeply grateful for the extensive clerical and moral support being given to us by many friends at Wisdom's Goldenrod Center for Philosophic Studies.

Further information about progress with these notebooks can be obtained by writing:

Paul Brunton Philosophic Foundation
P.O. Box 89
Hector, NY 14841

PERSPECTIVES

§

The way to use a philosophic book is not to expect to understand all of it at the first trial, and consequently not to get disheartened when failure to understand is frequent. Using this cautionary approach, he should carefully note each phrase or paragraph that brings an intuitive response in his heart's deep feeling (not to be confused with an intellectual acquiescence in the head's logical working). As soon as, and every time, this happens, he should stop his reading, put the book momentarily aside, and surrender himself to the activating words alone. Let them work upon him in their own way. He is merely to be quiet and be receptive. For it is out of such a response that he may eventually find that a door opens to his inner being and a light shines where there was none before. When he passes through that doorway and steps into that light, the rest of the book will be easy to understand.

—P.B.

If you feel that the principles touched on in these pages are true, then remember that the greatest homage you can pay to Truth is to use it. Spiritual peace is given as a prize to those who wisely aspire, and who will work untiringly for the realization of their aspiration.

—P.B.

1

THE QUEST

Its choice—Independent path—Organized groups —Self-development—Student/teacher

The Quest of the Overself is none other than the final stage of mankind's long pursuit of happiness.

§

When a man feels imperatively the need of respecting himself, he has heard a faint whisper from his Overself. Henceforth he begins to seek out ways and means for earning that respect. This begins his Quest.

§

The central point of this quest is the inner opening of the ego's heart to the Overself.

§

It is not for those who feel the want of a social meeting every Sunday morning, where they can display their good clothes and listen to good words. It is for those who feel the want of something great in life to which they can give themselves, who cannot rest satisfied with the business of earning their bread and butter alone or spending their time in pleasures. What cause, what mission can be greater than fulfilling the higher purpose of life on earth?

§

We are here on earth in pursuit of a sacred mission. We have to find what theologians call the soul, what philosophers call the Overself. It is something which is at one and the same time both near at hand and yet far off. For it is the secret source of our life-current, our selfhood, and our consciousness. But because our life-energy is continuously streaming outwards through the senses, because our selfhood is continuously identified with the body, and because our consciousness never contemplates itself, the Overself necessarily eludes us utterly.

§

There are four goals which philosophy sets before the mind of man: (1) to know itself; (2) to know its Overself; (3) to know the Universe; (4) to know its relation to the universe. The search for these goals constitutes the quest.

§

It is this Ideal that gives a secret importance to every phase of our life-experience. It is this goal that invests unknown and unnoticed men and women with Olympic grandeur. It is this Thought that redeems, exalts, and glorifies human existence.

§

A humble life dedicated to a great purpose, becomes great.

§

This is not merely a matter for a small elite interested in spiritual self-help. It is a serious truth important to every man everywhere.

§

There is a great tendency on the part of students of mysticism, practitioners of Yoga, and seekers after spiritual truth to regard their Quest as something quite apart from life itself, just as the stamp collector and the amateur gardener regard their special hobby as something which can be added to their routine of living. This is a fundamental error. The Quest is neither a serious hobby nor a pleasant diversion from the dullness of prosaic everyday living. It is actually living itself. Those who do not understand this fall as a result into eccentricities, self centerednesses, superiority complexes, sectarianism, futile proselytizing of the unready or antagonistic, and attempting to impose upon others what is not suited to them.

Those who separate the Quest from their day-to-day existence shut out the most important field of their further growth. They tend to become dreamers and lose their grip on practicalities. Yet, when any of these faults is mentioned to a seeker, he rarely realizes that it applies to him personally but usually believes that it applies only to other seekers. This is because he regards himself as being more advanced than he really is.

§

The work starts with you—with some impulse arising in you, or with some feeling, thought, idea, or some object seen, or with a person, teacher, or with a book or with a lecture or with Nature or with an artistic creation. But whether it be outside or inside you it has to be accepted by ***you***. But if you ask why it happens just then, the answer can only be the Source of all things willed it.

§

The intuition which brought you to the gates of this quest is, like all authentic intuitions, a spark which you may contract by doubt, hesitation, and accepting negative suggestion from outside sources or which you may expand by faith, obedience, and accepting positive suggestion from those who have already followed and finished this quest.

§

His journey starts from the place in consciousness where he finds himself. He may repeat the history of some other travellers who seek here and there in this cult and that one for the food that will allay their inner hunger. Years may be spent in such search but whether it ends inside one of these cults or outside all of them, one day something happens to him. His mind is suddenly lit up with understanding and his heart filled with peace. The experience soon passes but the memory of it lasts long. It made him so happy that he yearns to repeat it. But alas! This is one thing that he seems unable to do at will. If it happens again, he will take up the Quest where it really belongs—inside himself. He will cease looking here and there and set to work in real earnestness on himself. He will have to purify his character, practise meditation regularly, and study inspired works.

§

When this vague yearning for something that worldly life cannot satisfy becomes unendurable, it may be a sign that they are ready for this Quest.

§

We may first take to this quest to find a way of escape from our sufferings, whether mental or physical; but gradually we become aware that this negative attitude is not enough, that we must also realize positively the mysterious purpose of human existence.

§

He may arrive at a true appraisal of life after he has experienced all that is worth experiencing. This is the longest and most painful way. Or he may arrive at it by listening to, and believing in, the teachings of spiritual seers. This is the shortest and easiest way. The attraction of the first way is so great, however, that it is generally the only way followed by humanity. Even when individuals take to the second way, they have mostly tried the other one in former births and have left it only because the pain proved too much for them.

§

Man's main business is to become aware of his true purpose in life; all other business is secondary to this primary concern.

§

After the work done to gain livelihood or fulfil ambition, there is usually a surplus of time and strength, a part of which could and should be devoted to satisfying higher needs. There is hardly a man whose life is so intense that it does not leave him a little time for spiritual recall from this worldly existence. Yet the common attitude everywhere is to look no farther than, and be content with, work and pleasure, family, friends, and possessions. It feels no urge to seek the spiritual and, as it erroneously thinks, the intangible side of life. It makes no effort to organize its day so as to find the time and energy for serious thought, study, prayer, and meditation. It feels no need of searching for truth or getting an instructor.

§

Is the inner life irreconcilable with the world's life? Religio-mystical disciplines and practices are usually based on such a fundamental irreconcilability. Traditional teaching usually asserts it too. Yet if that be true, "Then," as Ramana Maharshi once sceptically said to me, "there is no hope for humanity."

§

Anyone who is willing to make an earnest endeavour may arrive by his own intelligence, helped if he wishes by the writings of those who have more leisure and more capacity for it, at a worthwhile understanding of these abstract subjects. The intermittent study of these writings, the regular reading of these books will help him to keep his thinking close to true principles. He will get inspiration from their pages, comfort from their phrases, and peace from their ideas. These statements spark the kinetic mental energy of a responsive few and inspire them to make something worthwhile of their lives. What it writes in their minds is eventually written into their activities.

§

The highly strung nervous, mental, and artistic temperaments that largely throng these spiritual paths are of all others predisposed to go astray. They become fascinated by the wondrous worlds of study and experiment which open out for them. They are apt to ignore the vital potency of living out these teachings, as opposed to talking about them. For the opposition of having to work in heavy matter brings out the real power of the soul. Its resistance makes accomplishment more difficult but more enduring.

§

Procrastination may be perilous. Later may be too late. Beware of being drawn into that vast cemetery wherein men bury their half-born aspirations and paralysed hopes.

§

The quest is not an enterprise of fits and starts, not something to be started today and left off tomorrow, but is the most durable undertaking in a man's life. This is to be his most sacred life-purpose, the most honoured ground of his very existence, and everything else is to be made to subserve it.

§

We do not approach God through our knees, or through the whole body prostrate on the ground, but deep in our hearts. We do not feel God with our emotions any more than we know him with our thoughts. No! —we feel the divine presence in that profound unearthly stillness where neither the sounds of emotional clamour nor those of intellectual grinding can enter.

§

In that sacred silence he will dedicate his life to the Quest. And although no one except himself will hear or know that dedication, it will be as binding and obligatory as any solemn pledge made in full assembled lodge.

§

Its chief enemy is indecision. The world is packed with people who suffer from this fault. So our greatest dramatist took this as his theme for his wonderful play, *Hamlet*. A little more decision on the part of the Prince of Denmark, and the series of tragedies which close the play would have been averted. But in that case the play would not have carried the lesson Shakespeare wanted it to give—how Hamlet was tortured by his own indecisiveness. Wise Faith wins. The fool of today is the wise man of tomorrow—if he lets his mistakes teach him. Not what he can do, but what he *does* do, matters. The bird of victory finally perches on the shoulders of the man who dares.

§

No one who feels that his inner weakness or outer circumstances prevent him from applying this teaching should therefore refrain from studying it. That would not only be a mistake but also a loss on his part. For as the *Bhagavad Gita* truly says, "A little of this knowledge saves from much danger." Even a few years study of philosophy will bring definite benefit into the life of a student. It will help him in all sorts of ways, unconsciously, here on earth and it will help him very definitely after death during his life in the next world of being.

§

Those who decline to search for ultimate truth because they believe it to be unattainable, because they despair of ever finding it, betray it.

§

The higher truth can properly be given only to those who are eligible for it, whose minds are ripe enough to receive it without bewilderment, and whose judgement is developed enough to see its worth.

§

There must be a certain ethical maturity before a man will even be willing to listen to such a teaching, and there must be a certain intellectual maturity before he will be able to learn it. There must be the will to analyse, the capacity to take an impartial attitude, the strength to renounce the vulgar view of things, and the desire to travel the road of truth inexorably to its last and logical conclusion. The fount of seeking must not be consciously or unconsciously muddied by selfish motive. It is not suggested that these preliminary qualifications must be present in their perfection and fullness—such will be the final result and not the first attempts on the quest—but that they should be present to a sufficient degree to make a marked disciplinary contribution to one's inner life.

§

It is not only a path to be followed but one to be followed with good humour and graciousness.

§

Those whose emotions are strongly held by personal psychological problems would be better prepared for the quest if they first got their lives straightened out or first underwent personal re-adjustment. Where their attitudes are neurotic, hysteric, or psychopathic, it is rash impertinence to dare to consider themselves as candidates for probing the divine mysteries.

§

The sacrifice demanded of the aspirant is nothing less than his very self. If he would reach the higher grades of the path, he must give up the ego's thinking and desiring, must overcome its emotional reactions to events and persons and things. Every time he stills the restless thoughts in silent meditation he is giving up the ego; every time he puts the desires aside in a crucial decision he is giving up the ego; every time he disciplines the body, the passions, the activities, he is giving up the ego. It demands the utmost from him before it will give the utmost to him; it forces him to begin by self-humbling and, what is worse, to end by self-crucifixion. Every aspirant has to pass through these ordeals—there is no escape from them. They are what *Light on the Path* refers to as "the feet being bathed in the blood of the heart." Thus, the Quest is not for weaklings.

§

There is only one Duty for men: it is to realize the divinity within. Slavish adherence to any personal, social, or racial duties, set us from outside, must bend and go whenever it comes into conflict with this higher Duty. At the call of this compelling inner voice, the Prince Gautama Buddha trampled down the gilded "duties" of his royal position and walked out into the wilderness a homeless wanderer.

§

Entering upon this Quest is neither a pleasant nor an easy affair. The aspirant has to begin with the belief that he is a very imperfect person, that before he can penetrate into the spiritual realms he must first prepare himself for such an entrance by working hard to separate himself from these imperfections. Before he entered on the Quest, he liked himself most —now he discovers that he hates himself most. Before he entered on the Quest, he had different enemies here and there—now he has only one enemy, and that is himself. Hitherto he supported the ego by identifying himself with it—henceforth he must deny the ego, and try to affirm the higher self.

§

He will not be the first aspirant, nor the last, who continues to worship the ego under the delusion that he has begun to worship the Overself.

§

This wrong self-identification is not only a metaphysical error but also a mental habit. We may correct the error intellectually but we shall still have to deal with the habit. So deeply ingrained is it that only a total effort can successfully alter it. That effort is called the Quest.

§

When a man becomes tired of hearing someone else tell him that he has a soul, and sets out to gain firsthand experience of it for himself, he becomes a mystic. But, unfortunately, few men ever come to this point.

§

You may be familiar with the contents of a hundred books on mysticism and yet not be familiar with mysticism itself. For it concerns the intuition, not the intellect.

§

My Webster defines a mystic as "one who relies chiefly upon meditation in acquiring truth." This is a good dictionary definition, but it is not good enough because it does not go far enough. For every true mystic relies also on prayer, on purificatory self-denial, and on a master.

§

That the soul exists, that it is something other than his ordinary self, and that it abides within himself, are affirmations which remain basic and common to authentic mystical experience of every school and religion.

§

It must be clearly understood that it is only the philosophical quest, the path of the Bodhisattva, which we advocate here, which is threefold. The mystical quest is not. It is simpler. It requires only a single qualification—meditation practice. But it gives only a single fruit—inner peace—whereas the threefold quest yields a threefold fruit: (1) peace, (2) the intellectual ability to instruct others, (3) service. If therefore philosophy calls for a greater effort than mysticism, it compensates by its greater result. And whereas the mystical result is primarily an individual benefit, the philosophical result is both an individual and social one.

§

If this benevolent ideal has been set up from the start, then he will not swerve from it at the end. He will draw back from the very verge of the eternal Silence and resume his human garb, that he may compassionately guide those who still seek, grope, blunder, and fall.

§

Be not afraid!
This very hour begin
To do the Work thy spirit glories in;
A thousand unseen forces wait to aid,
Be not afraid,
Begin! Begin!

§

Some have the illusion that the Path is heavily trodden. It is not. "Many are called but few are chosen." The traveller must learn to walk resignedly in partial loneliness. The struggle for certain truth and the quest of the divine soul are carried on by every man and must be carried on in an austere isolation when he reaches the philosophic level. No crowd progress and no mass salvation are possible here.

There is and could be no such thing as a sect in philosophy. Each of its disciples has to learn that there is only one unique path for him, dependent on his past history and present characteristics which constitute his own individuality. To attempt to forego that unique individuality, to impose the spiritual duty of other persons upon himself is, as the *Gita* points out, a dangerous error. Philosophy tries to bring a man to realize his own divinity for himself. Hence it tries to bring him to independent thinking, personal effort, and intuitive development. This is not the popular way nor the easy one; it offers no gregarious comfort or herd support. But it is the only way for the seeker after absolute truth. Though the solitary student may suffer from certain disadvantages, he also enjoys certain definite advantages.

In any case, man never really escapes from his essential loneliness. He may push his social efforts at avoidance to extremes and indulge his personal ones to the point of creating illusions, but life comes down on him in some way or other and one day forces him back on himself. Even where he fancies himself to have achieved happiness with or through others, even in the regions of love and friendship, some physical disharmony, some mental change, some emotional vacillation may eventually arise and break the spell, driving him back into isolation once more.

§

Does this mean that the aspirant should seek no guide, should take no friendly hand in his own at all? No! It simply means that if he realizes that his choice of a teacher might well change his whole life for better or for worse, and if he seeks well-qualified guidance, he must be discriminating, which means that he must not rush into acceptance of the first guide he meets. He should take his time over the matter and give it the fullest thought. It is quite proper and sound practice for him to be prudent before signing away his life to a teacher or his mind to a creed. It is not the first teacher he meets or the first doctrine he hears that he should accept. Rather should he follow Confucius' practical advice to shoppers: "Before you buy, try three places." Nay, he might have to try thirty places before he finds a really competent teacher or a completely true doctrine. Such a search calls for patience and self-restraint, but the longer it continues the likelier will its goal be reached.

§

It is true that the higher self can guide and even teach the aspirant from within and that in the end it is the only real guide and teacher. But it is also true that a premature assumption of self-sufficiency may lead him dangerously astray. Indeed, the higher self will direct him to some other human agent for help when he is sufficiently ready. Self-reliance and independence are valuable qualities but they may be pushed too far and thus turned into failings. The student who remains self-guided and self-inspired without making missteps or wasting years, is fortunate.

§

There is no contradiction between advising aspirants at one time to seek a master and follow the path of discipleship, and advising them to seek within and follow the path of self-reliance at another time. The two counsels can be easily reconciled. For if the aspirant accepts the first one, the master will gradually lead him to become increasingly self-reliant. If he accepts the second one, his higher self will lead him to a master.

§

That there are perils on this path of self-guidance, is obvious. It is easy to fall into conceit, to breed arrogance, even to imagine an inner voice. Here the saving virtue of balance must be ardently sought, and the protective quality of humbleness must be gently fostered.

§

The truth is that nearly all aspirants need the help of expert human guides and printed books when they are actively seeking the Spirit, and of printed books at least when they are merely beginning to seek.

§

Is it really necessary to travel to some holy land, some sacred place, some distant guru? The true answer is that none of these things is necessary. What you seek is precisely where you now are. Holiness and teaching can meet you there. Is it too hard for you to believe this?

§

But one can only have the right to exercise such self-reliance if one pays for it in the coin of self-discipline.

§

No seeker should be so foolish as to reject the proffered hand of a worthy master. Indeed, such is his weakness and ignorance that he needs all the help he can get from all the strong and wise men of his own times and, through their writings, of past times. But the basis of his relation to such a master should not therefore be one of complete servitude and intellectual paralysis, nor one of totalitarian prohibition from studying with other masters or in other schools. He should keep his freedom to grow and his independence to choose if he is to keep his self-respect.

§

This injunction to be oneself is to be followed discriminatingly, not blindly. Why should I not follow the procession of another man's thoughts if they be good and true and beautiful?

§

A small group of sincere students meeting together may be of great help to each participant provided there is a basic spiritual affinity among them. If this is lacking even in one of the group, such a meeting may well lead to more confusion than enlightenment or may cause some or all to forget that on the quest each walks alone.

§

A school should exist not only to teach but also to investigate, not to formulate prematurely a finalized system but to remain creative, to go on testing theories by applying them and validating ideas by experience.

§

True spirituality means applying the knowledge got from learning and heeding the laws of the inner life in the differing degree that each individually can do so. It does not mean joining a group or a society and chattering fruitlessly about it or gossiping inquisitively about spiritual leaders.

§

The moral re-education required by philosophy is not a mere Sunday-school pious hope. It is a practical necessity because of the psychological changes and nervous sensitivity developed by the meditation practices. Without it these exercises may prove dangerous to mind, character, and health. The virtues especially required are: harmlessness in feeling and deed, truthfulness in thought and word, honesty with oneself and with others, sexual restraint, humility.

§

No amount of travel will arrive at truth, or bring one into contact with an Adept, if the other conditions are lacking.

§

It is a grave misconception to regard the mystical progress as passing mostly through ecstasies and raptures. On the contrary, it passes just as much through broken hearts and bruised emotions, through painful sacrifices and melancholy renunciations.

§

That same light which reveals his spiritual importance reveals also his personal insignificance.

§

When the sublime light of the Ideal shines down upon him and he has the courage to look at his own image by it, he will doubtless make some humiliating discoveries about himself. He will find that he is worse than he believed and not so wise as he thought himself to be. But such discoveries are all to the good. For only then can he know what he is called upon to do and set to work following their pointers in self-improvement.

§

You will not be able to understand the world better than you understand yourself. The lamp which can illumine the world for you must be lighted within yourself.

§

He begins by an unthinking and immature religious attitude, proceeds to the meditational experiments and personal experience of mysticism or the rational abstractions of metaphysics, and ends in the integral all-embracing all-transcending life of philosophy.

§

The practice of yoga as a psychological discipline and the study of philosophy as a mental re-education are two essentials in the equipment of the man who would explore the highest. None may be left out without leaving the seeker like a one-legged man trying to ascend a difficult mountain. The ultimate goal cannot be found by the yogi because he is concerned only with himself and not the entire universe. It cannot be found by the philosopher because he is concerned only with the *theoretical* knowledge of its meaning of all existence. It can be found by him alone who has mastered both yoga and philosophy, and who is then willing to take the next step and sacrifice his ego on the altar of ultimate attainment. For the final stage of this climb demands that the insight gained by philosophic knowledge into the ego's true nature be applied to the entire life of thought, feeling, and conduct—not by some sudden dramatic gesture but by *working* incessantly during every moment of every day. Such a perpetual vigil is really a form of continuous concentration, that is, of yoga, and it is impossible for those who have not successfully trained their minds in the yogic discipline. These are the reasons why we must view yoga and philosophy as the two legs needed to support a man who would then enter into the ever-renewed practice to attain realization. This is the final climb to the summit.

§

He must purify his heart of egoism, his bodily instincts of animalism, and then a favourable atmosphere will be available *for the truth to make itself known to him*. This statement presupposes that it is already present and only waiting to reveal itself. Such is philosophy's contention, and such is the philosopher's own experience. It first comes to him as "The Interior Word," the Logos within, and later as "the second birth."

§

There are two paths laid out for the attainment, according to the teaching of Sri Krishna in the *Bhagavad Gita*. The first path is union with the Higher Self—not, as some believe, with the Logos. But because the Higher Self is a ray from the Logos, it is as near as a human being can get to it anyway. The second path has its ultimate goal in the Absolute, or as I have named it in my last book, the Great Void. But neither path contradicts the other, for the way to the second path lies through the first one. Therefore, there is no cleavage in the practices. Both goals are equally desirable because both bring man into touch with Reality. It would be quite proper for anyone to stop with the first one if he wishes; but for those who appreciate the philosophic point of view, the second goal, because it includes the first, is more desirable.

§

The stages of the quest are fairly well defined. First, the aspiration toward spiritual growth manifests itself in a man's heart. Second, the feeling of repentance for past error and sin saddens it. Third, the submission to an ascetic or self-denying discipline follows as a reaction. Fourth, the practice of regular exercises in meditation is carried on.

§

He will know what both the fullness and the fulfilment of life mean only when the consciousness that the Spirit is his own very self comes to life within him.

§

The path requires an all-round effort. It calls for the discipline of emotions as well as the purification of character from egoism, the practice of the art of meditation as well as religious devotion and prayer, constant reflection about the experiences of life to learn the lessons behind them, and constant discrimination between the values of earthly and spiritual things. This self-development crowned by altruistic activity will in time call forth the grace of the Overself and will bring blissful glimpses occasionally to encourage his endeavours. As pointed out in my *Wisdom of the Overself*, not only one but all the functions of one's being must unite in the effort to reach the spiritual goal.

§

If the quest is to be an integral one, as it must be to be a true one, it should continue through all four spheres of a man's being: the emotional, the intellectual, the volitional, and the intuitional. Such a fourfold character makes it a more complicated affair than many mystics believe it to be.

§

Anyone who can find a direct teacher in the Overself needs no other. But because the ego easily inserts itself even into his spiritual explorations and its influence into his spiritual revelations, he may still need an outer teacher to warn him against these pitfalls in his way.

§

The *need* of a spiritual guide is nearly as great as ever today and remains but little changed, but the character of the *relation* between the disciple and the guide has to change. The old following in blind faith must give place to a new following in intelligent faith.

§

It is not the human thoughts which the teacher sends out, so much as the spiritual power within the disciple which is aroused by those thoughts, that matters.

§

Do not pretend to be other than you are. If you are one of the multitude, do not put upon yourself the proud robes of the Teacher and pretend to be able to imitate him; unless you stick to the Truth, you can never find it. To put yourself upon the pedestal of spiritual prestige before the Master or God has first put you there, is to make the first move towards a humiliating and painful fall.

§

Few aspirants are sufficiently developed to justify receiving the personal attention and tuition of a master. All aspirants may, however, seek for his blessing. He will not withhold it. But such is its potency that it may at times work out in a way contrary to their desire. It may bring the ego suffering in the removal of inner weakness as a prelude to bringing it inner light. They should therefore pause and consider before they ask for his blessing. Only a deep earnestness about the quest should motivate such an approach.

§

It is next to impossible to ascertain the Truth without the guidance of a Teacher. This is the ancient tradition of the East and it will have to become the modern tradition of the West. There is no escape. The explanation of this statement lies in the subtle nature of the Truth. Thus, in the West, men of such acute intelligence and such high character as Spinoza, Kant, Hegel, and Thoreau came close to the verge of Truth. They could not fully enter because they lacked a Guide. Even in India, the greatest mind that land of Thinkers ever produced, the illustrious Shankara, publicly acknowledged the debt he owed to his own Teacher, Govindapada.

§

If an opportunity seems to occur to become the disciple of a master, be sure first to test whether he is fit to hold such a position. Do not test his supposed possession of occult powers or healing gifts; check rather whether he is master over himself before he plays the role over the lives of others. Is he free from the lust of sex, the greed of money, the itch for fame, the passion of wrath, and the desire for power? If not, he may be remarkable, unusual, clever, fluent, psychic, friendly, or anything else, but be sure that he is not competent to guide disciples to the kingdom of heaven.

§

Six are the duties of such a teacher: (1) to instruct the student in new knowledge, (2) to correct the errors of his existing knowledge, (3) to develop his mentality in a balanced way, (4) to restrain him from committing evil, (5) to encourage him compassionately, and (6) to open the mystical path to him by active help in meditation.

§

Three qualifications at least are required in a spiritual teacher: thorough competence, moral purity, and compassionate altruism. Only he who has triumphed over the evil in himself can help others do the same for themselves. Only he who has discovered the divine spirit in himself can guide others to make their own discovery of it. Teaching that does not stem forth from personal experience can never have the effectiveness of teaching that does.

§

It is essential that a spiritual preceptor live up to the lofty precepts he hands out; if he is unable to do this, he ought to come down from his high seat and take his place among the pupils—preferably in the back row. The Western student of divine mysteries is very eager and very apt to rush out and attempt to teach his fellows before he has completed his course of studies, and before he has quite realized their truth by experience. The obvious reasons are many: a love of the limelight and a sense of superiority are but two of them. How different, this, from that lowly humility of Lao Tzu, whose followers increased from a single person in his lifetime to many millions after his death. "The Sage wears a coarse garment, but carries a jewel in his bosom" is his beautiful announcement. "To know, but to be as though not knowing, is the height of wisdom" is another of his spirit-realized utterances.

§

Truth cannot be got without a master. That the Buddha did get it without such help does not disprove the truth of this principle. For the arisal of a Buddha is a rare phenomenon on this earth. Mortals who are struggling in mental darkness compose the mass of mankind, not Buddhas sent to enlighten them and therefore destined to be self-enlightened.

§

That man is most likely to become and is best fitted to become your teacher to whom you are drawn not so much by his experience and wisdom, his goodness and power, as by some intuitional attraction. For this is a sign of an earlier relationship in other lives on earth. The personal trust and intellectual dependence which it generates are themselves signs that you have been teacher and disciple in former reincarnations. It is best to accept the leading of this attraction, for the man under whom you have continuously worked before is the man whom destiny will allot you to pick up the same work again. You may postpone the opening up of such a relationship again but in the end you cannot avoid it. Destiny will have the last word in such a matter.

§

Either at acceptance or later, the disciple experiences an ecstatic reverie of communion with the teacher's soul. There is a sensation of space filled with light, of self liberated from bondage, of peace being the law of life. The disciple will understand that this is the real initiation from the hands of the teacher rather than the formal one. The disciple will probably be so carried away by the experience as to wish it to happen every day. But this cannot be. It can happen only at long intervals. It is rather to be taken as a sign of the wonderful relation which has sprung up between them and as a token of eventual attainment.

§

When a man has at last found himself, when he has no longer any need of an outside human Symbol but passes directly to his own inner reality, he may stand shoulder to shoulder with the teacher in the oldest, the longest, and the greatest of struggles.

§

2

PRACTICES FOR THE QUEST

Ant's long path—Work on oneself

If he is not too proud to begin at the point where he finds himself rather than at some point where he once was or would now like to be, if he is willing to advance one step at a time, he may realize his goal far more quickly than the less humble and more pretentious man is likely to realize it.

§

The Long Path represents the earlier stages through which all seekers after the higher wisdom will have to pass; they cannot leap up to the top. Therefore those stages will always remain valuable.

§

The aspirant for illumination must first lift himself out of the quagmire of desire, passion, selfishness, and materialism in which he is sunk. To achieve this purpose, he must undergo a purificatory discipline. It is true that some individuals blessed by grace or karma spontaneously receive illumination without having to undergo such a discipline. But these individuals are few. Most of us have to toil hard to extricate ourselves from the depths of the lower nature before we can see the sky shining overhead.

§

An intellectual understanding is not enough. These ideas can be turned into truths only by a thorough self-discipline leading to liberation from passions, governance of emotions, transformation of morals, and concentration of thoughts.

§

He has to develop religious veneration, mystical intuition, moral worth, rational intelligence, and active usefulness in order to evolve a fuller personality. Thus he becomes a fit instrument for the descent of the Overself into the waking consciousness.

§

Many a yogi will criticize this threefold path to realization. He will say meditation alone will be enough. He will deprecate the necessity of knowing metaphysics and ridicule the call to inspired action. But to show that I am introducing no new-fangled notion of my own here, it may be pointed out that in Buddhism there is a recognized triple discipline of attainment, consisting of (1) *dyhana* (meditation practice), (2) *prajna* (higher understanding), (3) *sila* (self-denying conduct).

§

It is a fault in most of my writings that I did not mention at all, or mentioned too briefly and lightly, certain aspects of the quest so that wrong ideas about my views on these matters now prevail. I did not touch on these aspects or did not touch on them sufficiently, partly because I thought my task was to deal as a specialist primarily with meditation alone, and partly because so many other workers had dealt with them so often. It is now needful to change the emphasis over to these neglected hints. They include moral re-education; character building; prayer, communion, and worship in their most inward, least outward, and quite undenominational religious sense; mortification of flesh and feeling as a temporary but indispensable discipline; and the use of creative imagination in contemplative exercises as a help to spiritual achievement.

§

There is a point of view which rejects the attitude that destitution and dire poverty are the only paths to spirituality and replaces it by the attitude that a simple life and a small number of possessions are better. The poverty-stricken life is usually inadequate and unaesthetic. We need a sufficiency of possessions in order to obtain efficiency of living, and an aesthetic home in order to live the beautiful life. How much more conducive to success in meditation, for instance, is a well-ordered home, a refined elegant environment, a noiseless and undisturbed room or outdoor spot! But these things cost money. However much the seeker may saturate himself in youthful years with idealistic contempt for the world's values, he will find in time that even the things important to his inner spiritual life can usually be had only if he has enough money to buy them. Privacy, solitude, silence, and leisure for study and meditation are not free, and their price comes high.

§

To live a simpler life is not the same as to live an impoverished life. Our wants are without end and it is economy of spiritual energy to reduce them at certain points. But this is not to say that all beautiful things are to be thrown out of the window merely because they are not functional or indispensable.

§

What earlier scholars translated as "nonacceptance of gifts" in Patanjali's *Yoga Sutra*, Mahadevan has translated as "non-possession." The difference in meaning is important. The idea clearly is to avoid burdens which keep attention busy with their care.

§

What is really meant by renunciation of the world? I will tell you. It is what a man comes down to when confronted by certain death, when he knows that within an hour or two he will be gone from the living world—when he dictates his last will and testament disposing of all his earthly possessions.

§

It is not the world that stands in our way and must be renounced but our mental and emotional relationship with the world; and this needs only to be corrected. We may remain just where we are without flight to ashram or convent, provided we make an inner shift.

§

There is something crazy in this idea that we were put into the world to separate ourselves from it!

§

The inability to believe in or detect the presence of a divine power in the universe is to be overcome by a threefold process. The first part some people overcome by "hearing" the truth directly uttered by an illumined person or by other people by reading their inspired writings. The second part is to reflect constantly upon the Great Truths. The third part is to introvert the mind in contemplation.

§

He must be observant, must understand the heights and depths of human nature, human motives, and human egoism. He should do this because it will help him to know both others and himself, to serve them better and to protect his quest.

§

He who enters upon this quest will have plenty to do, for he will have to work on the weaknesses in his character, to think impartially, to meditate regularly, and to aspire constantly. Above all, he will have to train himself in the discipline of surrendering the ego.

§

Show me a man who is regular and persistent in his practice of daily study, reflection, and meditation, and you will show me a man determined to break the bonds of flesh and destined to walk into the sphere of the spirit, though years may elapse and lives may pass before he succeeds. He has learned to ask, to seek, and to find.

§

As a preface to this reflective reading, he should put his heart in an attitude of humility and prayerfulness. He needs the one because it is the divine grace which will make his own efforts bear fruit in the end. He needs the other because he must ask for this grace. And however obscurely he may glimpse the book's meaning at times, his own reflective faith in the truth set down in its pages and in the inner leading of his higher self, will assist him to progress farther. Such a sublime stick-to-it-iveness brings the Overself's grace in illuminated understanding.

§

From the first moment that he sets foot on this inner path until the last one when he has finished it, he will at intervals be assailed by tests which will try the stuff he is made of. Such trials are sent to the student to examine his mettle, to show how much he is really worth, and to reveal the strength and weakness that are really his, not what he believes are his. The hardships he encounters try the quality of his attainment and demonstrate whether his inner strength can survive them or will break down; the sufferings he experiences may engrave lessons on his heart, and the ordeals he undergoes may purify it. Life is the teacher as well as the judge.

§

Every act is to be brought into the field of awareness and done deliberately.

§

The discipline of the self, the following of ethical conduct, the practice of mystical meditation—all these are needed if the higher experience resulting in insight is being sought.

§

Aspiration alone is not enough. It must be backed by discipline, training, and endeavour.

§

He who wishes to triumph must learn to endure.

§

From the intuitions that are the earliest guides of the seeking mind to the ecstatic self-absorptions that are the latest experiences of the illumined mystic, there are certain obstructions which have to be progressively removed if these manifestations are to appear. They can be classified into three groups: those that belong to the unchecked passions of man, those that belong to his self-centered emotions, and those that belong to his prejudiced thinking. By a critical self-analysis, by a purificatory self-denial, and by an ascetic self-training, the philosophic discipline generates a deep moral and intellectual earnestness which wears down these obstructions and prepares the seeker for real advance.

§

The neophyte may stumble and fall, but he can still rise up again; he may make mistakes, but he can still correct them. If he will stick to his quest through disheartening circumstances and long delays, his determination will not be useless. If it does nothing else, it will invite the onset of grace. When moods of doubt come to him, as they do to most, he must cling steadfastly to hope and renew his practice until the mood disappears. It is a difficult art, this of keeping to the symbol in his serene centre even for a few minutes. It can be learnt by practice only. Every time he strays from it into excitement, egotism, or anxiety, and discovers the fact, he must return promptly. It is an art which has to be learnt through constant effort and after frequent failure, this keeping his hold on the spiritual facts of existence. He should continue the quest with unbroken determination, even if his difficulties and weaknesses make him unable to continue it with unshaken determination. It implies a willingness to keep the main purpose of his quest in view whatever happens. He must resolve to continue his journey despite the setbacks which may arise out of his own weaknesses and undeflected by the misfortunes which may arise out of his own destiny. The need to endure patiently amid difficult periods is great, but it is worthwhile holding on and hoping on by remembering that the cycle of bad karma will come to an end. It is a matter of not letting go. This does not mean lethargic resignation to whatever happens, however. He has got to maintain his existence, striving to seize or create the slenderest opportunities.

§

The Quest is not to be followed by studying metaphysically alone or by sitting meditatively alone. Both are needful yet still not enough. Experience must be reflectively observed and intuition must be carefully looked for. Above all, the aspirant must be determined to strive faithfully for the ethical ideals of philosophy and to practise sincerely its moral teachings.

§

Even though he learns all these truths, he has only learnt them intellectually. They must be *applied* in the environment, they must be deeply felt in the heart, and, finally, they must be established as the Consciousness whence they are derived.

§

Make it a matter of habit, until it becomes a matter of inclination, to be kind, gentle, forgiving, and compassionate. What can you lose? A few things now and then, a little money here and there, an occasional hour or an argument? But see what you can gain! More release from the personal ego, more right to the Overself's grace, more loveliness in the world inside us, and more friends in the world outside us.

§

It is not merely undesirable for others' sake for a man to engage in spiritual service prematurely and unpurified, but positively dangerous to his own welfare.

§

The only authentic mandate for spiritual service must come, if it does not come from a master, from within one's Higher Self. If it comes from the ego, it is then an unnecessary intrusion into other people's lives which can do little good, however excellent the intention.

§

When he came down into reincarnation, he came with the responsibility for his own life, not for other people's. They were, and ever afterwards remained, responsible for their own lives. The burden was never at any time shifted by God onto his shoulders.

§

To understand the mysterious language of the Silence, and to bring this understanding back into the world of forms through work that shall express the creative vitality of the Spirit, is one way in which you may serve mankind.

§

He must examine himself to find out how far hidden self-seeking enters into his altruistic activity.

§

It is futile for anyone who has muddled his own life to set out to straighten the lives of others. It is arrogant and impertinent for anyone to start out improving humanity whilst he himself lamentably needs improvement. The time and strength that he proposes to give in such service will be better used in his own. To meddle with the natural course of other men's lives under such conditions is to fish in troubled waters and make a fool of himself. Only when he has himself well in hand is there even a chance of rendering real service. A man whose own interior and exterior life is full of failure should not mock the teaching by prattling constantly about his wish to serve humanity. Such service must first begin at the point nearest to him, that is, his own self.

§

If he can keep his motives really pure and his ego from getting involved, he may find the way to render service. But few men can do it.

§

It is not that he is not to care about other people or try to help them, but that he is to remember that there is so little he can do for them while he is so little himself.

§

Help given, or alms bestowed, out of the giver's feeling of oneness with the sufferer, is twice given: once as the physical benefit and once as the spiritual blessing along with it.

§

Philosophic service is distinguished by practical competence and personal unselfishness.

§

I must cut a clear line of difference between helping people and pleasing them. Many write and say my books have helped them when they really mean that my books have pleased their emotions. We help only when we lift a man's mind to the next higher step, not when we confirm his present position by "pleasing" him. To help is to assist a man's progress; to please is to let his bonds enslave him.

§

The seeker must live primarily for his own development, secondarily for society's. Only when he has attained the consummation of that development may he reverse the roles. If, in his early enthusiasm, he becomes a reformer or a missionary much more than a seeker, he will stub his toes.

§

If he begins to think of himself as the doer of this service, the helper of these people, he begins to set up the ego again. It will act as as barricade between him and the higher impersonal power. The spiritual effectiveness of his activity will begin to dwindle.

§

Because the ultimate issue lies with the grace of the Overself, the aspirant is not to prejudge the results of his Quest. He is to let them take care of themselves. This has one benefit, that it saves him from falling into the extremes of undue discouragement on the one hand and undue elation on the other. It tells him that even though he may not be able, in this incarnation, to attain the goal of union with the Overself by destroying the ego, he can certainly make some progress towards his goal by weakening the ego. Such a weakening does not depend upon grace; it is perfectly within the bounds of his own competence, his own capacity.

§

Such inward invulnerability seems too far away to be practicable. But the chief value of seeking it lies in the *direction* which it gives to thought, feeling, and will. Even if it is unlikely that the aspirant will achieve such a high standard in this present incarnation, it *is* likely that he will be able to take two or three steps nearer its achievement.

§

3

RELAX AND RETREAT

Intermittent pauses—Tension and pressure—
Relax body, breath, and mind—Retreat centres—Solitude—
Nature appreciation—Sunset contemplation

Let us accept the invitation, ever-open, from the Stillness, taste its exquisite sweetness, and heed its silent instruction.

§

Let him withdraw once a day at least, not only from the world's outer activities but also from his own inner conflicts.

§

In these periods of retreat we are to live with Principles, to get our minds cleansed and hearts pure, to straighten the crooked thoughts and to be where hurry and pressure are not.

§

Such a retreat is not to be regarded as a holiday, although it accidentally serves that purpose too, but as a way of life. It is not just a means of filling idle time or of inertly resting in an interval between activities, but is a creative endeavour to transmute oneself and one's values.

§

To practise retreat in the philosophical manner is very different from the escapist manner. In the first case, the man is striving to gain greater mastery over self and life. In the second case, he is becoming an inert slacker, losing his grip on life.

§

What philosophy prescribes is neither a life solely given up to monastic retreat nor a life entirely spent in active affairs, but rather a sensible and proportioned combination of the two, a mixture in which the first ingredient necessarily amounts to less than the second.

§

Wisdom demands balance. Yet the modern man leads an unbalanced life. He is engaged in ceaseless activity, whether of work or pleasure, without the counterbalance of quiet repose and inner withdrawal. His activity is alright in its place, but it should be kept there, and should not overrun these precious moments when he ought to take counsel of his higher being. Hence the periodic practice of mental quiet is a necessity, not a luxury or hobby. It is called by the Chinese esoteric school "cleansing the mind."

§

If these occasional retirements from the world benefit him, if he comes out of them with a stronger will and a clearer mind and a calmer heart, if they enable him to collect his thoughts about deeper matters and to gather his forces for the higher life, then it would be foolish to dub this as escapism.

§

If he is to find the highest in himself, a man can best begin this search by retiring to the country and by working at some occupation where he does not have to fight selfishly and compete fiercely with others. By thus working less ambitiously and living more plainly, he will have a better chance to cultivate the tender plant of aspiration. By thus separating himself from the agitated atmosphere of cities, what he loses in outer fortune he will gain in inner fortune. Yet, if he faithfully follows his ideals, he will find that the same inner voice which prompted him to dwell apart will at times urge him to return for a while also and learn the missing part of his lesson. Most of the needful lessons of life can be learnt in obscure retreat, in small rural communities, but not all. The others are to be gained only in the large bustling cities and societies of men.

§

Because most of us have to pass our lives on this earth and in human society, we cannot travel the fugitive way. We cannot enter monasteries or sit in ashrams. And because some of us prefer philosophy to escapism we do not want to do so. For we believe that the real thing ascetics seek escape from is not the world, not society, but themselves; that our chief work in life is to remake ourselves. When we go into occasional and limited retreat we do so to quieten the mind, to detach the heart, to extend our perspectives, and to reflect upon life—not to run from it and squat the years idly away.

§

He who lives a noble life in the midst of the world's business is superior to him who lives a noble life in the midst of a monastery.

§

We need to take these occasional retreats to cleanse ourselves inwardly, to find fresh strength and gather new inspiration, to study ourselves, meditate, and understand truth.

§

There is a real need to balance our extreme tendency to activism with something of quietism, to offset our excessive doing with deeper being.

§

The fast pace of modern living and the busy clamour of modern cities prevent us from meeting ourselves. We have to sit down as if we were in the desert all alone surrounded by silence and slow the pace of thoughts until in the gaps between them we begin to see who the thinker is. But we must give it time, we must be patient. It is not out there right in front, but hidden deep inside. Inside there is a light at the end of the dark tunnel.

§

How many of us find ourselves worn out by the physical anxieties, the frequent nerve-tensions, and the jittery tumultuousness of our period! We tend to get entrapped in our own activities, to multiply them by the dozen, to be everlastingly busy with this and that. We are, in a sense, the unwitting victims of our surface-life, the unconscious slaves of its activities and desires, the dancing marionettes of its interests and possessions. There is no real free movement of our wills, only an apparent one. We have only to look at the faces of the men and women in our big cities to realize how desolate of spiritual repose most of them are. We have become so extroverted that it has become unnatural to turn the mind upon itself, artificial to direct the attention inwards for a while. All this causes us to miss the most important values, keeps us on the plane of being merely higher thinking and mating animals and little more.

Everyone wants to live. Few want to know how to live. If people permit work to take up so much of their time that they have none left for their devotional prayer or mystical meditation or metaphysical study, they will be as culpable for this wastage of life as they will be if they permit transient pleasures to do so. Those who have no higher ideal than to chase after amusement and to seek after pleasure may look upon religious devotion as senseless, metaphysical studies as boring, mystical meditations as time-wasting, moral disciplines as repulsive. Those who have no such inner life of prayer and meditation, study and reflection, will necessarily pay, in emergencies or crises, the high price of their hopeless extroversion. The needs of external life are entitled to be satisfied in their place, but they are not entitled to dominate a man's whole attention. The neglected and unnoticed needs of internal life must also receive their due. It is quite true that man must eat, find shelter, wear clothes, and amuse himself. And it is also true that if a fortunate fate has not relieved him of the necessity, he must work, trade, scheme, or gamble to get the money for these things. But all this is insufficient grounds for him to pass through life with no other thoughts in his head than those of bodily needs or financial strivings. There is still room there for another kind of thought, for those concerning the mysterious elusive and subtle thing that is his divine soul. The years are passing and he cannot afford such a wastage of time, cannot afford the luxury of being so extroverted at the cost of having lost touch with the inner life.

It is bad enough to be a sick person, but it is worse to be sick and believe you are well. Yet the complete extroverts are in this condition, because they regard complete extroversion as the proper state for normal healthy living! The fact is that to let ourselves be swept into the whirlpool of unending act without intervals of inner rest and physical quiet is not only unworthy but also unhealthy. Such a complete suppression of the inner life and such a complete immersion in the outer upsets Nature's balance and may express itself in disease. Unfamiliar and irksome, unpractical and inconvenient as it mostly is, exercise in meditation does not attract the modern man. In former times it was a kind of pleasant duty. In present times it is a kind of bitter medicine. Yet his need of it still remains, indeed it is even larger than the medieval man's need. The more we suffer from the psychic and physical sicknesses bred by our incessant extroversion and by our disequilibrated materialism, the more does it become imperative to swallow this valuable medicine. Here we ought to be guided by the importance of effecting a cure rather than by the importance of pleasing our taste. Meditation provides men with a sanctuary from the world's harassments, and those who would not enter this sanctuary of their own accord are being driven by the harsh experience of contemporary life itself to do so. They are being forced to seek for new sources of healing peace. They need it greatly. There is only one safe retreat for the harassed emotions in these turbulent times and that is within themselves, within the beautiful serenity which the mystical can find at will. The world will inevitably witness a large-scale reaction against its own excessive extroversion and an inward search for mental detachment will then arise. For it there is waiting the message and the panacea of modern meditation.

Meditation must be restored to its rightful place in the human program. Only those who have tasted its wonder know how bare, how poor, is a life from which it is always absent. Only those who have become expert in the art know the major pleasure of lying back on its velvet couch and letting their burdens fall from them. The benefits of meditation apply both to mundane life and to spiritual seeking. Think what it means to be able to give our mental apparatus a complete rest, to be able to stop all thoughts at will, and to experience the profound relief of relaxing the entire being—body, nerves, breath, emotions, and thoughts! Those whose nerves cannot endure the extreme tension of modern existence will find ample healing by resorting to mental quiet.

The need to practise meditation is an obligatory one upon us as beings who have become conscious that we are human and not merely animal beings. Yet few men ever recognize this obligation. Most men either do not perceive its importance or, perceiving it, they try to establish an alibi by suggesting to themselves that they are too busy fulfilling their other obligations and consequently have no time for meditation. But the fact is that they are too lazy to disengage themselves from the common state of complacent indifference towards the soul. We must strike a healthy balance between work and retirement, activity and contemplation, pleasure and reflection, and not remain victims of prevailing conventions. A few minutes invested every day in meditation practice will more than pay for themselves. We must not only introduce it as a regular feature of the human day but also as an important one. We must reorganize our daily lives so that time can be found for the leisurely cultivation of the soul through study, reflection, and meditation. Such periodical intervals of withdrawnness from the endless preoccupation with external affairs are a spiritual necessity. We must learn to bring in the new factor of introversion and turn inwards, tapping our finer reflective resources and liberating our profounder possibilities. To know that man has a sacred soul and to know this fact with invulnerable certitude, is the first reward of right prayer and philosophic meditation. The true soul of man is hidden and concealed from his senses and from his thoughts. But it is possible for him by these methods to awaken a higher faculty—intuition—whereby he may reach, know, and be lovingly received by this soul.

§

We daily dissipate our mental energies and throw our thoughts to the fickle winds. We debauch the potent power of Attention and let it waste daily away into the thousand futilities that fill our time.

§

The ego ceaselessly invents one "duty" after another to keep him so involved in activities, often trivial, that he is never still enough to attend to the Overself's presence and voice within. Even many so-called spiritual duties are its invention: they are not asked of him by the Overself.

§

Because all his meditation exercises can succeed only to the extent that he succeeds in becoming utterly relaxed, the importance of this ability must be noted.

§

We truly relax from strains and strivings only when we relax in the inward stillness of the divine presence. Silently to declare the metaphysical truths about our personal life, quietly to affirm them in the midst of our active life, and deliberately to recognize them above the swirl of our emotional life is to achieve true repose.

§

It is wiser to go to the fountainhead, to the source of all energies directly. There our fatigued mind or body can find its most life-giving recuperation.

§

The stress of modern existence has made the need for regular mental rest not merely advisable, but vital. Unless our excessive external activity is counter-balanced by a little inward orientation, we shall be devastated by neurasthenic disease.

§

The external segregation of spiritual aspirants for a whole lifetime is impracticable today. It is also undesirable. The ashram ideal suited a primitive society, but does not suit our complex one. What is really needed now is the establishment of "Houses of Retreat" where men of the world may pass a weekend, a week, or even a month, in a holy atmosphere under the helpful guidance of an experienced spiritual director.

§

Ashram existence fails to impose any real test of character other than childish ones. Exposure to the corrosive acids of the world's tensions and temptations, conflicts and perils, would soon test the unworldliness of an ashramite's character and soon show the real worth of his pious attainments. A monastic life which possesses no perils, struggles, and constructive activity also possesses no intrinsic value, no ultimate worth apart from the temporary rest it gives. It takes no risks but gains no prizes.

§

Having obtained a place where he may rest for a period, an environment suited to prayer and meditation, let him begin and end each day by a solemn silent call to the Overself for guidance, for enlightenment, and for help in overcoming the ego. Then let him give as much time as his capacity allows to meditation repeated twice and even thrice during the day.

§

The need today is for philosophic retreats rather than monastic communities, for semi-retirement from the world rather than complete abandonment of the world, for limited and temporary periods of relaxation from personal activities.

§

The true place of peace amid the bustle of modern life must be found within self, by external moderation and internal meditation.

§

Ram Gopal: "At many of the ashrams I visited in India I could plainly see that the vast majority of people milling around the central figure of the particular sage, all had the timid and cowardly expressions of escapists, running away from life. They were taking the easy way out by sitting at the feet of these holy ones. Such a negative attitude helped them merely to postpone what the true seeker faced boldly."

§

There is a need for spiritual retreats where laymen and laywomen, who do not wish to become monks or nuns, may come for a day or weekend or month or two, to search for truth, to study, and to meditate in an undistracting atmosphere.

§

There are some exceptions to this precept, of course. An old man, for instance, who feels he has done his principal work in life, is quite entitled to rest, to withdraw from the world and make his peace with God in solitude and repose.

§

The heart is my ashram. The higher self is the master who dwells within it.

§

The deepest solitudes do not always contain the divinest men. Renunciation of the world works most when it works in the heart, which unfortunately is not a visible thing. It is not always necessary to permit one's dress-suit to become covered with cobwebs in order to become a true devotee.

§

Alone and silent, with body and mind quiet, it would be unlikely and even difficult to become nervous, unstable, fidgety, and restless.

§

But a man cannot profit by this lonelier life, nor find it pleasurable, unless he has more inner reserves than most others or unless he actively seeks to gain them.

§

While he is still struggling to attain the light, the larger his acquaintance with people and the more they crowd his life, the less time and chance he has to know and find himself—if his relationship with them is the ordinary egoistic one. If it is not, but involves rendering them some sort of altruistic service which thins down his ego, the result will be better and more favourable to this purpose. Even so, it is an unbalanced existence and a day will come when he will *have* to take a vacation from them and make solitude and time for his own inner need of meditation, reflection, or study.

§

It is not because he finds the company of most people disagreeable that he seeks solitude, that he separates himself from society, not because he is soured, vinegary and cynical in his attitude toward them, but because this inner work requires intense uninterrupted undisturbed and undistracted concentration.

§

There is only one real loneliness and that is to feel cut off from the higher power.

§

There is a vast difference between idle morbidly introspective solitude and the inwardly active creative solitude advocated here.

§

"Let him be devoted to that quietude of heart which springs from within, let him not drive back the ecstasy of contemplation, let him look through things, *let him be much alone.*" Such is Buddha's counsel to the student of the higher life.

§

The man who does not learn how to be alone with himself cannot learn how to be alone with God.

§

A man has to make his own inner solitude wherever he goes.

§

There is always some feeling of mystery in the deep silent haunts of the forest. There is always some eerie sense of strangeness in its leaf-strewn shady paths. There is great age in its green bowers and mossy trunks, grave peace in its secluded recesses. There is great beauty in the tiny flowers set on their couches of grass and in the cheerful song which comes down from the boughs. It is a satisfying place, this home of dignity and decrepitude, this forest.

§

The wise will turn to the mountains for rest as they will return to them from the ends of this earth when they are world-weary. For they are ancient souls of many births and their Methusalean propensities will find fit neighbour in those aged heights. And then they will sit upon the craggy stones and gaze up at the peaks' defiant heads and suck in peace as a bee sucks the pollen from a flower.

§

They whose emotions can respond to the grandeur and sublimity of Nature in all her manifold expressions, in forest and mountain, river and lake, in sea and sky, and the beauty of flowers, are not materialists even though they may so call themselves. Unconsciously they offer their devotion to the Divine Reality, even though they may call it by some other name.

§

Saint John of the Cross, whenever he stayed at the monastery of Iznatoraf, would climb to a tiny attic room in the belfry and there remain for a long time looking out fixedly through a tiny window at the silent valley. When he was prior of the Hermitage of El Calvario, in Andalusia, one of the exercises he taught the monks was to sit and contemplate where there was a view of open sky, hills, trees, fields, and growing plants and to call on the beauty of these things to praise God. We know from his writings that he made imageless contemplation the last stage in all such exercises.

§

The evening sunfall brings its own beauty, declaims its own poetry. It is worth the waiting in the short period before Nature's holy pause, when one can share her peace with one's soul, her mystery with one's mind, and feel her kinship with one's self. As the dusk deepens there is a shift of standpoint and basic truths come into sight or become more clear. The heart and its feelings are affected, too—purified, ennobled, enriched.

§

As he gazes, the more attention gets concentrated, the more he sinks into finer and finer thought, honouring not only the visible sun outside but also the invisible soul inside.

§

I let time unfold and pass away into its source as, minute after minute, in the gathering dusk, the mountains slowly vanish, the room too, eyes close, contemplation ends, the Void takes over, and there is no one left to report.

§

4

ELEMENTARY MEDITATION

Place and conditions—Wandering thoughts
—Practise concentrated attention—Meditative thinking
—Visualized images—Mantrams—Symbols
—Affirmations and suggestions

The truth needed for immediate and provisional use may be learned from books and teachers but the truth of the ultimate revelation can be learned only from and within oneself by meditation.

§

Meditation is not to be regarded as an end in itself but as one of the instruments wherewith the true end is to be attained.

§

Among the values of meditation is that it carries consciousness down to a deeper level, thus letting a man live from his centre, not his surface alone. The result is that the physical sense-reactions do not dominate his outlook wholly, as they do an animal's. Mind begins to rule them. This leads more and more to self-control, self-knowledge, and self-pacification.

§

It is a principle of philosophy that what you can know is limited by what you are. A deep man may know a deep truth but a shallow man, never. This indeed is one of its reasons for taking up the practice of meditation.

§

Meditation is merely a form of simple practice most Western people are too unfamiliar with to understand. What could be simpler than saying this: if you will look into your heart and mind, deep enough and long enough to penetrate beneath the tumult of desires that daily distract your attention, you may then discover peace.

§

It is a means of severing attention from its ever-changing objects, and then enabling the freed mental force to study its own source.

§

When the mind is distracted by its surroundings, it is prevented from perceiving itself. This is easy to understand. When it is distracted by the body, it is also prevented from gaining such perception. This is harder but still possible to understand. But when the mind is distracted from attending to itself by its own thoughts, this is the hardest of all its situations to understand.

§

The true state of meditation is reached when there is awareness of awareness, without the intrusion of any thoughts whatever. But this condition is not the ultimate. Beyond it lies the stage where all awareness vanishes *without the total loss of consciousness that this normally brings*.

§

The meditation has been successfully accomplished when all thoughts have come to an end, and when the presence of Divinity is felt within this emptiness.

§

Philosophy does not teach people to make their minds a blank, does not say empty out all thoughts, be inert and passive. It teaches the reduction of all thinking activity to a single seed-thought, and that one is to be either interrogative like "What Am I?" or affirmative like "The godlike is with me." It is true that the opening-up of Overself-consciousness will, in the first delicate experience, mean the closing-down of the last thoughts, the uttermost stillness of mind. But that stage will pass. It will repeat itself again whenever one plunges into the deepest trance, the raptest meditative absorption. And it must then come of itself, induced by the higher self's grace, not by the lower self's force. Otherwise, mere mental blankness is a risky condition to be avoided by prudent seekers. It involves the risk of mediumship and of being possessed.

§

Meditation in one sense is an effort. It seeks first to approach, by actively cutting a way through the jungle of irrelevant thoughts, and second to enter, by passively yielding to its outraying influence, the very core of oneself, the very centre of one's psyche, which is indeed the divine spirit. In the first stage, a resolute will is required to overcome and banish the eager intruders who would destroy his chances of success. In the second stage, the exercise of will would itself be just as destructive, for an opposite attitude is then called for—total surrender of the ego.

§

The mere making one's mind a blank, the mere stopping of thoughts for a few minutes, is not by itself, unaccompanied by the other endeavours of the fourfold quest, sufficient to bestow any mystical state. A high official of a mystical order who practised this mental blackout of several years standing, confessed privately that he has not had any higher consciousness as a result. The general effort in meditation should not be to make the mind a blank but to make it concentrated, poised, and still. If blankness supervenes sometimes, as it may, it should do so of its own accord, not as a result of our striving. But then this would mean the cessation of thinking, which is a very advanced stage at which few arrive. A positive attempt to induce blankness might induce the wrong kind, which is negative and mediumistic and has nothing spiritual about it. If, however, it comes by itself as a by-product of correct meditation, then it will not be mere emptiness but rather an utter serenity which is satisfied with itself and regards thoughts as a lower disturbance.

§

The novice must be warned that certain ways of practising concentration, such as visualizing diagrams or repeating declarations, as well as emptying the mind to seek guidance, must not be confused with the true way of meditation. This has no other object than to surrender the ego to the Overself and uses no other method than prayerful aspiration, loving devotion, and mental quiet.

§

None of the elementary methods of yoga such as breath control and mantram lead to a permanent control of the mind, but they prepare the way and make it easier to take up those practices which do lead to such a result.

§

If in meditation he goes down sufficiently far through the levels of consciousness, he will come to a depth where the phenomenal world disappears from consciousness, where time, thoughts, and place cease to exist, where the personal self dissolves and seems no more. If there is no disturbance caused by violent intrusion from the physical world, this phase of complete inner thought-free stillness may continue for a long period; but in the end Nature reclaims the meditator and brings him back to this world. It is only an experience, with the transiency of all experiences. But it will make its contribution to the final State, which is permanent establishment in the innermost being, whether in the depth of silent meditation or in the midst of worldly turmoil and activity.

§

He needs to remember the difference between a method and a goal: the one is not the same as the other. Both meditation and asceticism are trainings but they are not the final goals set up for human beings.

§

It would be a serious error to believe that he is to continue with any particular exercise or chosen theme, with any special declaration or analysis or question, no matter what happens in the course of a session. On the contrary; if at any moment he feels the onset of deeper feelings, or stronger aspirations, or notable peace, he ought to stop the exercise or abandon the method and give himself up entirely to the interior visitant. He ought to have no hesitation and no fear in considering himself free to do so.

§

The only way to learn what meditation means is to practise and keep on practising. This involves daily withdrawal from the round of routine and activity, of about three-quarters of an hour if possible, and the practice of some exercise regularly. The form which such an exercise should take depends partly upon your own preference. It may be any of the set formal exercises in books published, or it may be a subject taken from a sentence in some inspired writing whose truth has struck the mind forcibly; it may be a quality of character whose need in us has made itself felt urgently, or it may be a purely devotional aspiration to commune with the higher self. Whatever it is, the personal appeal should be sufficient to arouse interest and hold attention. This being the case, we may keep on turning over the theme continually in our thoughts. When this has been adequately done, the first stage (concentration proper) is completed. Unfortunately most of this period is usually spent in getting rid of extraneous ideas and distracting memories, so that little time is left for getting down to the actual concentration itself! The cure is repeated practice. In the next stage, there is a willed effort to shut out the world of the five senses, its impressions and images, whilst still retaining the line of meditative thinking. Here we seek to deepen, maintain, and prolong the concentrative attitude, and to forget the outside environment at the same time. The multiplicity of sensations—seeing, hearing, etc.—usually keeps us from attending to the inner self, and in this stage you have to train yourself to correct this by deliberately abstracting attention from the senses. We will feel in the early part of this stage as though we were beating against an invisible door, on the other side of which there is the mysterious goal of your aspiration.

§

During this brief period he is to undertake a strange task—to separate himself from the petty and the passional, from the affairs of his personal career and family relationship, and to seek to unite himself with the grand truths, the impersonal principles of spiritual being.

§

He should fully understand and accept the importance of being punctual in keeping his unwritten appointment when the meditation hour comes round. If he is careful to honour his word in social or professional engagements, he ought to be at least not less careful in honouring it in spiritual engagements. Only when he comes reverently to regard the Overself as being the unseen and silent other party with whom he is to sit, only when he comes to regard failure to be present at the prearranged time as a serious matter is the practice of these exercises likely to bear any of the fruits of success. It is a curious experience, and one which happens too often to be meaningless, that some obstacle or other will arise to block the discharge of this sacred engagement, or some attractive alternative will present itself to tempt him from it. The ego will resent this disturbance of its wonted habits and resist this endeavour to penetrate its foundations. He must resist this resistance. He must accept no excuse from himself. The decision to sit down for meditation at a stated time is one from which he is not to withdraw weakly, no matter what pressure falls upon him from outside or arises from inside. It may require all his firmness to get away from other people to find the needed solitude or to stop whatever he is doing to fulfil this promise to himself, but in the end it will be worthwhile.

§

You begin your meditation by remembering its spiritual purpose and consequently by putting away all thoughts of your own affairs or of the world's affairs and paying attention only to the single thought of the Overself.

§

No matter how limited the period available may be, whether five or fifty minutes, approach it with the deliberately induced feeling of complete leisureliness. Bring no attitude of haste into the work, or it will thwart your efforts from the start.

§

It is not possible to master the art of meditation without acquiring the virtue of patience. One has to learn first how to sit statue-still without fidgeting and without changes; second, how to endure the waiting period when the body's stillness is mocked by the mind's restlessness.

§

In theory the best time for meditation would be after sleep because the mind is then at its calmest. In practice, it may not be so if dreams have disturbed it, or if a very early start to activity is necessary or unavoidable. Further, there may be individual affinity with particular times, such as sunset or midnight, which render meditation more attractive then.

§

The aspirant who is really determined, who wants to make rapid progress, must make use of the early hour of morning when dawn greets the earth. Such an hour is to be set aside for meditation upon the Supreme, that ultimately a spiritual dawn may throw its welcome light upon the soul. By this simple initial act, his day is smoothed before he starts. Yet of the few who seek the highest Truth, fewer still are ready to make this sacrifice of their time, or are willing to forego the comfort of bed. Most men are willing to sacrifice some hours of their sleep in order to enjoy the presence of a woman and to satisfy their passion for her; but exceedingly few men are willing to sacrifice some hours of their sleep to enjoy the presence of divinity and to satisfy their passion for God-realization.

§

But on another plane of being there is a curious and more elevated quality during the meditations practised before the early hours of dawn while it is still dark. This is a period recommended in certain schools of Sufic and Hindu mysticism.

§

It is a common mistake to believe that because no fruit seems to grow out of the exercise, no feeling and no experience result from it, the time given to it is wasted. This is why so many abandon it after a short or long trial. But how can the ego know that even the simple act of sitting like a beggar at the Overself's door, in resigned humility and patience and perseverance, is an act of faith for which the reward is certain, even though the form of this reward may not be?

§

To sit down for meditation with the secret expectation, the half-hidden hope, or the fully conscious desire for a dramatic glimpse, a sudden transformation, or a speedy result is to introduce the ego and thus block the way to the egoless plane of the Overself.

§

For meditation or worship it is a fitting posture to face the east where the sun rises, the west where it sets or the south where it is strongest. But the north is less desirable, not only because it is sunless but because it is the direction whence come the powers active in the body during sleep.

§

The body's position is not without its influence upon the beginnings of meditation. All muscles should be relaxed, all limbs at ease, all fingers at rest, and the jaw unclenched. Any physical tenseness hinders the onset of contemplation.

§

Because of inferior auric magnetism of other persons picked up during the day, the washing of hands and feet and face is prescribed in Islamic religion before prayer and recommended in philosophic mysticism before meditation.

§

What shall they do with their eyes during meditation? It is best for beginners to shut them entirely and thus avoid distracting sight-impressions from the outer world. For moderately advanced practisers it is better to begin with shut eyes and at an appropriate point sometime later in the meditation, to half-open them, directing the gaze downwards and some feet beyond, and to keep it so until the meditation period is ended. But it is easiest for highly advanced proficients to pass quickly through the earlier positions of shut and half-shut and then, at a time prompted for them by inward guidance to keep their eyes open fully until the practice period is over, or until the guidance reverses itself. These are the general rules governing the three chief degrees.

§

There are four chief points in the body which may be used to hold the attention of the eyes if the latter are to be kept open or partly open during meditation. They are: first, the navel; second, the tip or the end of the nose; third, the space between the eyebrows, or the root of the nose; and fourth—which is rather a Chinese exercise—on the ground a little in front of the feet, which sights the eyes somewhere between the second and third exercise.

§

It is not enough to lull the mind: the heart's feeling must be stimulated and directed in aspiration and devotion, warm and strong toward the Overself, which by reaction, arouses a certain force, the Spirit-Energy, which acts for a short time to prepare him for deeper, more concentrated contemplation.

§

An aid is *bhakti*, love. Love is essential to meditation; it is a binding force comprised of devotion and reverence. The aim is to become united. Success in meditation is to become one with the Higher Self (unity). Meditation should be a yearning to come home to one's place in the universe.

§

He need not get either perturbed or puzzled if, after a certain period of the session has elapsed and a certain depth of concentration reached, there is a momentary disappearance of consciousness. This will be a prologue to, as well as a sign of, entrance into the third state, contemplation. The immediate after-effect of the lapse is somewhat like that which follows deep dreamless sleep. There is a delicious awakening into a mind very quiet, emotions gently stilled, and nerves greatly soothed.

§

Meditation can be misused. It is then no longer a help toward the spiritual liberation of man but another captivity to keep him from it. It is misused when the object is to gain occult powers. These merely cater to the ego's aggrandizement. It is misused when the object is to become a prophet, teacher, or reformer who will influence or lead people. This merely caters to the ego's spiritual ambition, which is the same force as worldly ambition working on a higher level.

§

The ego is so taken up with itself that the time of meditation, which ought to be its gradual emptying-out, remains merely another field for its own activity.

§

It is necessary to warn the beginner in meditation against the mistakes and perils into which he is liable to fall. The greatest mistake is to fail to realize the contributions of the ego to his own mystical experience; the greatest peril is to let himself be overcome by a mediumistic passivity under a belief that it is a mystical passivity.

§

There are certain persons who belong by birth and temperament to the type of spiritistic medium. Until they have strengthened their higher nature, purified their feelings, and obtained sufficient knowledge, they should avoid meditation. The risk of being used by inferior spirits, even of obsession, is present.

§

Those whose minds are neurotically or psychotically disordered, will do better to take some treatment first before embarking on a meditation course.

§

Too much attention is too often put upon the role of meditation itself. It is a necessary practice but it is only a part of the total work to be done. Balance, reverence, knowledge, virtue, and awareness despite or during activities are also parts.

§

It is necessary to pronounce certain words of caution to the novice in meditation. He is trying to penetrate the unknown parts of his being with a vehicle not only fashioned by himself but also fashioned out of himself. If the material is defective or the method inaccurate, the result will be disappointing and may even be harmful. Moreover, the journey itself is beset with certain risks and dangers for the man whose emotions are undisciplined, whose passions are ungoverned, whose ambition is to exploit other persons, whose critical judgement is poor, and whose knowledge is small. Therefore the traveller must safeguard himself by sufficient preparation and adequate equipment before beginning his journey, by a preliminary discipline to fit his mind and character for the effort.

§

If he can enter the state of contemplation at any time he wishes to do so, and can sustain it as long as desired, he is said to be an adept in meditation.

§

The first part of the exercise requires him to banish all thoughts, feelings, images, and energies which do not belong to the subject, prayer, ideal, or problem he chooses as a theme. Nothing else may be allowed to intrude into consciousness or, having intruded by the mind's old restlessness, it is to be blotted out immediately. *Such expulsion is always to be accompanied by an exhaling of the breath. Each return of attention to the selected theme is to be accompanied by an inhaling of the breath.*

§

When thoughts are restless and hard to control, there is always something in us which is aware of this restlessness. This knowledge belongs to the hidden "I" which stands as an unruffled witness of all our efforts. We must seek therefore to feel for and identify ourself with it. If we succeed, then the restlessness passes away of itself, and the bubbling thoughts dissolve into undifferentiated Thought.

§

Exclude all thoughts other than the one which is the point of concentration. If, as is likely, you weaken and permit them to intrude, renew the battle and drive them out by will. Return again and again if necessary to your focus.

§

It is not enough to seek stillness for the body and mind alone: the attention and intention must be directed at the same time to that Overself which transcends body and mind.

§

He must lock himself in a room for a few minutes every day with the fierce determination to tame this mind which jumps about like a monkey. He must choose a topic and then keep his thoughts rigidly fixed on it. He should concentrate all his attention on it and try first to provoke and then to develop a sequential logical line of thought about it. He must wear down its resistance by unremitting daily practice of this kind.

§

If the wandering characteristic of all thoughts diverts attention and defeats the effort to meditate, try another way. Question the thoughts themselves, seek out their origin, trace them to their beginning and reduce their number more and more. Find out what particular interest or impulse emotion or desire in the ego causes them to arise, and push this cause back nearer to the void. In this way you tend to separate yourself from the thoughts themselves, refuse to identify with them, and get back nearer to your higher identity.

§

This work of pushing attention inwards, back to its very source, and the sense of "I-ness" back with it, is to be accompanied by thinking only until the latter can be stopped or itself stops. This work is then continued by a stilled and steady search. When the need of search comes to an end, the searcher vanishes, the "I" becomes pure "Being," has found its source. In these daily or nightly sessions, it is his work to turn away from the diffused attention which is his normal condition to the concentrated attention which is indispensable for progress, and to sustain it.

§

The state of concentration acquired during a worldly pursuit differs from that acquired during mystical meditation in that the first is usually directed toward outward things and the experience of sense-pleasures, whereas the second is directed toward inward being and rejects sense-pleasures. Thus the two states are at opposite poles—one belonging to the ego-seeking man, and the other to the Overself-seeking man.

§

Others know the condition in which the yogi is, when they are so absorbed in the story of a book as not to hear when spoken to; when they are so lost in a line of thought that the immediate surroundings are banished; when the imagined is the real; when tranced feeling and held mind alone exist, separated from the physical actuality. But there is this vital difference—that their total absorption usually concerns a personal or a worldly matter, whereas the yogi's concerns That which transcends both.

§

Stefan Zweig, the Austrian novelist, when still a youth, visited the sculptor Rodin and watched him at work in his Paris studio. He wrote of this visit: "I learned more that afternoon at Meudon than in all my years at school. For ever since then I have known how all human work must be done if it is to be good and worthwhile.

"Nothing has ever so moved me as this realization that a man could so utterly forget time and place and the world. In that hour I grasped the secret of all art and of all earthly achievement—concentration, the rallying of all one's forces for accomplishment of one's task, large or small; capacity to direct one's will, so often dissipated and scattered, upon one thing."

§

When concentration attains its effective state, the ever-tossing mental waves subside and the emotional perturbations become still. This is the psychological moment when the mystic naturally feels exaltation, peace, and super-earthliness. But it is also the psychological moment when, if he is wise, he should turn away from revelling in personal satisfaction at this achievement and, penetrating yet deeper, strive to understand the inner character of the source whence these feelings arise, strive to understand pure Mind.

§

The disciplined use of imagination will promote the attainment of ideals through imagination but the wild use of fancy will retard it.

§

Thinking must stop, but if it stops at the level of the little ego only a psychical experience or a mediumistic possession may result. If, however, it stops at a deeper level after right preparation and sufficient purification, the mind's emptiness may be filled by a realization of identity with the Overself.

§

Getting intensely absorbed in a true spiritual idea may, if it penetrates to a sufficient depth, put one into communication with the Universal Mind. This in turn enables him to receive, intuitively, what could not be found intellectually.

§

This habit of persistent daily reflection on the great verities, of thinking about the nature or attributes of the Overself, is a very rewarding one. From being mere intellectual ideas, they begin to take on warmth, life, and power.

§

The Overself takes his thoughts about it, limited and remote though they are, and guides them closer and closer to its own high level. Such illumined thinking is not the same as ordinary thinking. Its qualitative height and mystical depth are immensely superior. But when his thoughts can go no farther, the Overself's Grace touches and silences them. In that moment he *knows*.

§

It may be easy to get the worldly, the practical message of particular experiences, but it is not so easy to get the higher, the spiritual message they contain. This is because we habitually look at them from the ego's standpoint, especially when personal feelings are strongly involved. Truth calls for a transfer of the inner centre of gravity.

§

In *The Wisdom of the Overself* there was given a meditation exercise to be practised just before sleep. It consists of a review, undertaken in a particular way, of the previous day's events and thoughts and deeds. Here is a further exercise which is akin in character and yields equally important results but which may be practised either before sleep or at any other time of the day. The student should select episodes, events, or whole periods out of his past experience and personal conduct, and he should review them in the same detached impartial lesson-seeking manner. They may pertain to happenings many years distant or to those of the same week. A particularly valuable part of this exercise is the analytic dissection of moral errors and mistaken conduct with a view to their clearer understanding and future correction. The ego is to be sharply and critically examined throughout these reviews.

Let it not be forgotten, however, that he should remember his faults of character and mistakes of conduct not to moan over them but to get rid of the one and correct the other. For beneath most of his misfortunes lie faults of character and defects of temperament which are largely their hidden causes. Dispassionate observation of other people's present experience, together with impersonal reflection upon his own past experience, provides the best practical wisdom for future guidance. But such wisdom is only of limited value if it ignores the working of karma and the impetus of spiritual evolution; all these different elements must therefore be brought into an integral union.

The exercise here given does not seek, like ordinary yoga, to blot out thoughts as its final aim. Rather does it kindle them into vigorous life as it proceeds through its philosophical reflections and retrospective imaginations. But their character will gradually become unusually impersonal and profound, whilst their truth will become remarkably undistorted by emotional or passional deflections. Even this virtue, however, does not exhaust the advantages of the exercise. For there will also develop an interiorization of awareness which brings the practitioner ever closer to his spiritual self until his entire outlook on life is reorientated in a marvelous manner.

§

Whatever he has experienced, thought, or done in the years which have been lived through can afford a subject for this kind of meditation—reflective, analytic, and finally philosophic.

§

We must get to the very source of those deep-seated karmic, mental, and emotional tendencies if we would attain the Real which they obscure. When this is done a tremendous sense of liberation is experienced, an inner revolution undergone, and then follows the "lightning flash" of insight into the nature of the Real.

§

Is the experiment too difficult? How can a man stop thinking? I remember now that it is not suggested that one should deliberately stop thinking. No, it is taught, "pursue the enquiry, 'What am I' relentlessly." Well, I have pursued it up to this point. I cannot definitely pin down my ego either to the body or the intellect. Then who am I? Beyond body and intellect there is left only—nothing! The thought came to me, "Now pay attention to this nothingness."

Nothing? . . . Nothing? . . . Nothing? . . . I gradually and insensibly slipped into a passive attitude. After that came a sense of deepening calm. Subtly, intangibly, quietness of soul invaded me. It was pleasant, very pleasant, and soothed nerves, mind, and heart. The sense of peace which enveloped me while I sat so quiet gently swelled up into bliss ineffable, into a marvellous serenity. The bliss became so poignantly keen that *I forgot to continue thinking*. I simply surrendered myself to it as ardently as a woman surrenders herself to the man she loves. What blessedness was not mine! Was it not some condition like this to which Saint Paul referred when he mentioned "the peace which passeth understanding"? The minutes trickled by slowly. A half hour later found my body still motionless, the face still fixed, the eyes still indifferent to, or oblivious of their surroundings. Had I fathomed the mystic depths of my own mind? Impatience might have reared its restless head and completely spoilt the result. I saw how futile it was to attempt always to impose our habitual restlessness in such unfamiliar circumstances.

§

Now the ultimate use of a mental image, whether of God or guru, is only to help him do without it altogether in the end. For the ultimate aim of a true seeker must always be to become aware of God for himself, to perceive the Real with his own insight, and to understand the truth with his own intelligence. Therefore when he has reached this stage of meditation, when he is able easily to enter into rapport with the presence of the Guide or guru, it has accomplished its work and he must take the next step, which is to let go this presence, or the image which carries this presence, altogether. If he clings unduly to it, he will defeat the very purpose of his practice. The Overself will, of its own accord, eventually complete the work, if he does not so resist, by banishing the image and the presence and itself stepping into the framework of his consciousness. He will then know it as his own very soul, his true self, his sacred centre. He will then feel God within his own being as the pure essence of that being. Any other feeling of any other individual would be sacrilege.

§

If he trains himself until he can see with the mind's eye a picture exactly like the one he saw with his physical eyes printed or drawn on paper, he will have achieved the object of this (visualization) exercise.

§

The practice of mantram yoga is well known throughout India as a method of suppressing the wandering tendencies of the mind. A mantram, usually given by a guru or adapted by oneself from a book, is a word or phrase or even a whole sentence which the practitioner chants to himself or whispers or even mentally utters again and again. Some Sanskrit mantrams are quite meaningless sounds whereas others are full of metaphysical or religious meaning. Which one is used does not matter from the point of view of acquiring concentration, but it does matter from the point of view of developing any particular quality of character or devotional homage which the mantram symbolizes. This mental or vocal repetition is to be done periodically and faithfully.

§

The mantram becomes of best worth when it is heard deep, deep down in the practiser's being. It will then produce the effect of profound inner absorption.

§

The first revelation of the divine world is sound. Before beholding it, one hears it with an inner ear. The name of God has not only the power of easily washing away all sin, but can even untie the knot of the heart and waken love of God. To be severed from God is the only real sin.

§

Mantram consists of repeating a selected word over and over, soaking oneself in it. There are three stages: (a) chanting the word out loud; (b) whispering it; (c) repeating it mentally. Then, when repetition ceases, all thoughts cease. Through this constant concentration, the mantram becomes a backdrop to one's daily life. Just as one can hum a tune while attending to other affairs, so the mantram becomes an ever-present accompaniment. When one turns full attention onto it and concentrates fully upon it and then stops—all thoughts stop. This is the purpose of the mantram. This result may take weeks or months.

§

The Spiritual Symbols are given to pupils who are highly intellectual, professional, or active-minded as a means of (1) allaying mental restlessness; and (2) constructively working on the inner bodies, since these forms are in correspondence with the actual construction of (a) an atom, and (b) the universe.

§

It is easier to meditate on Reality through a symbol than directly.

§

Concentrate on each symbol for seven minutes. (1) Think of a cross in a light blue colour, as pertaining to the crucifixion of the physical or bodily nature. Regular concentration may lead to a psychological change. (2) Picture a triangle of golden colour as representative of harmony and intellectual balance. (3) Picture a five-pointed Star of silver colour, as a symbol of the perfect man.

§

A flower is as good an object to concentrate on as any other. Indeed it is better, for he may also try to make his own heart one with the flower's heart.

§

The use of short statements, often strangely worded, made by a master to a disciple as a means of getting the flash of enlightenment flourished in China during the Tang dynasty. It was taken up later by the Japanese, among whom the method's original name "kong-an" changed slightly to "ko-an." Despite extravagant claims made for it, the successful practiser got a glimpse only, not a permanent and full result. It is not the same as, and not to be confused with, the method of meditating upon affirmations, pithy condensed truth-statements (called ***Mahavakyas*** in India) since these openly possess a meaning whereas koans are often illogical and always puzzling.

§

To hold any idea in the mind during meditation, and to hold it with faith, sympathy, and pleasure, is to make it a part of oneself. If care is taken that these ideas shall be positive, constructive, and elevating, then the profits of meditation will show themselves in the character and the personality.

§

The restless, ever-active intellect may turn its overactivity to good account by turning to this practice. When that is done, the very quality which seemed such a formidable antagonist on the quest becomes a formidable ally. If instead of constantly thinking of his personal affairs, the man will constantly think of his mantra or his master or of God's infinitude and eternity, the trick is done.

§

If a thought enters his mind or a desire stirs his feelings of which he is ashamed but too weak to resist, let him repeat at once an appropriate declaration, or his familiar habitual one, or any pertinent word, and go on repeating it until mind or feelings are again clear.

§

The effectiveness of a Declaration depends also upon its being repeated with a whole mind and an undivided heart, with confidence in its power and sincere desire to rise up.

§

A friend told me some years ago of an interesting and useful method of using these Declarations which had been taught her by a celebrated holy man and mystic in her country, when he gave her the "Prayer of Jesus." This is a Declaration which was widely used several hundred years ago in the old Byzantine monasteries and even now is used to a lesser extent in Balkan and Slavonic monastic circles in exactly the same way as in India. The method is to reduce the number of words used until it is brought down to a single one. This reduction is achieved, of course, quite slowly and during a period covering several months. In this particular instance, there are seven words in the Prayer: "Lord Jesus Christ, have mercy on me." They are all used for the first few weeks, then the word "Christ" is omitted for the next few weeks. The phrase is again shortened by detaching from it, after a further period has elapsed, the word "Lord." Then "have" is taken out and so on until only one word is left. The Declaration as finally and permanently used is "Jesus–Jesus–Jesus–Jesus." This method can be applied to almost any Declaration. The selected last word should be a name, if addressed to God or to a Spiritual Leader, or, if that is not part of it, a desired quality.

§

Declarations:

1. "I am becoming as free from undesirable traits in my everyday self as I already am in the Overself."
2. "In my real being I am strong, happy, and serene."
3. "I am the master of thought, feeling, and body."
4. "Infinite Power, sustain me! Infinite Wisdom, enlighten me. Infinite Love, ennoble me."
5. "My Words are truthful and powerful expressions."
6. "I see myself moving toward the mastery of self."
7. "May I co-operate more and more with the Overself. May I do its will intelligently and obediently."
8. "I co-operate joyously with the higher purpose of my life."
9. "O! Infinite strength within me."
10. "O! Indwelling Light, guide me to the wise solution of my problem."
11. "I am Infinite Peace!"
12. "I am one with the undying Overself."
13. "Every part of my body is in perfect health; every organ of it in perfect function."
14. "In my real self life is eternal, wisdom is infinite, beauty is imperishable, and power is inexhaustible. My form alone is human for my essence is divine."
15. "I am a centre of life in the Divine Life, of intelligence in the Divine Intelligence."
16. "In every situation I keep calm and seek out the Intuitive that it may lead me."
17. "I look beyond the troubles of the moment into the eternal repose of the Overself."
18. "My strength is in obedience to the Overself."
19. "O Infinite and impersonal Bliss!"
20. "I am happy in the Overself's blissful calm."
21. "God is ever smiling on Me."
22. "God is smiling on me."
23. "The Peace of God."
24. "I dwell in the Overself's calm."
25. "I smile with the Overself's bliss."
26. "I dwell in Infinite peace."
27. "I am a radiant and revivified being. I express in the world what I feel in my being."

§

What is newer than a new dawning day? What a chance it offers for the renewing of life too! And how better to do this than to take a positive affirmative Declaration like, "I Am Infinite Peace!" as the first morning thought, and to hold it, and hold on to it, for those first few minutes which set the day's keynote? Then, whatever matters there will be to attend, or pressing weighty duties to be fulfilled, we shall carry our peace into the midst of them.

§

Never introduce any particular problem or personal matter for prayer or for consideration until after you have gained the peak of the meditation, rested there for a while, and are ready to descend into the deserted world again.

§

When his last thought at night and first thought in the morning refers to the Overself, he may appraise his progress as excellent.

§

In the earlier periods of his development, the higher self will become accessible to him under the form of some mental image registering on his human senses. In the later periods, however, it will be discerned as it is in itself and consequently as pure Being without any form whatever.

§

5

THE BODY

Hygiene and cleansings—Food—Exercises and postures —Breathings—Sex: importance, influence, effects

This work must begin with a discipline of the body because it is the servant of the ego. To the extent that we bring it to follow the Ideal, to that extent is the ego's path impeded and obstructed.

§

The tendency to neglect the body in the zeal to attain to the spiritual self is often seen among aspirants. Yet the two cannot rightly be separated and must be considered together if a successful result is to eventuate. Every man—and the aspirant is no exception to this rule—lives on both planes of being. The body's neglect cannot be justified by the assertion that there is no interest in it because all interest has been elevated above it. Whatever mental assertion or vocal pretext the aspirant delivers himself of, he still remains housed in the flesh and is still responsible for what he does—or fails to do—for the house itself. If he lets it deteriorate, clog with poisons and no longer carry on its organic functions properly, there will come a reaction upon mind and a rebound upon the feelings that must inevitably penetrate his view of things and force him to recognize that his feet are planted on earth, whatever his eyes may be gazing at.

§

The body is as much a divine projection as the planet on which it dwells. It is not demoniacal, nor even a symbol of man's sad downfall. Every tissue cell, bone cell, nerve cell, and muscle cell of which it is constructed is itself an expression of divine intelligence and purpose. It is a miniature copy of the universe.

§

Solicitude for the body to the extent of learning how to care properly for it, how to keep it in good health, how to keep up its strength, will only help and not obstruct solicitude for the soul. The person whose body is breaking down, whose organs are unable to work properly, whose vitality is poor, is likely to become more worried and preoccupied about his body than the person who is free from these troubles. How can he forget the flesh under such conditions? He will be miserably conscious of it far too often. Lofty advice which pays no heed to it and tells him nothing about how to deal with it may sound elevating to his ear but will not be alleviating to his problem. Any teaching which ignores the body, which leaves it an ever-present worry, must inevitably be a one-sided, incomplete one. Such indifference to the body's welfare cannot be the teaching of true wisdom and therefore cannot be defended.

§

A healthy asceticism which is in pursuit of sane self-mastery will always be harmonious with Nature; but an unhealthy, morbid, and twisted asceticism will always be conflicting with Nature.

§

It is as blasphemous to ignore, decry, or dismiss the physical side of human life as unimportant as it is to deny that the universe is a divine projection.

§

Bodily instincts concerning food have become so perverted by lifelong artificial habits, so deadened by old civilized so-called custom, that the bodily system no longer reacts to foods as it should. To regain the proper instincts and find out what really is a natural diet for man, a fast or series of fasts is necessary.

§

Fasting gives the body a chance to clarify its dietetic reactions and to regain its true instincts. It need not be extreme or long except in the worst and most hopeless chronic cases. It is easier, more comfortable, and just as effectual to take short fasts, each ranging from one to four days and spaced apart at intervals of a week to a month. A teaspoon of unsweetened lime juice in a tumbler of warm water may be drunk whenever thirsty to help dissolve the toxic deposits lining the internal organs.

§

The practice of meditation is undesirable when fasting as it may easily lead to a mediumistic condition or hallucinations. But, on the other hand, prayer can and should be increased when fasting. Usually, excellent results may follow.

§

Those first meals following a period of fasting are excellent for the purpose of learning what foods are really undesirable or harmful to one's own body. At such a time its instinct is much clearer and unperverted, while the ability to respond to its advice is much greater. Bad habits of feeding or living, such as gluttony or excessive smoking, can then be broken more easily. But it is necessary to concentrate all one's attention very carefully to note physical responses to each mouthful.

§

He who enters upon this renovating regime should first equip himself with enough knowledge about it, for he is likely to run into difficulties and complications, become disheartened, and even abandon it. He ought to know what course it usually takes and what he may expect. He should particularly learn about the alternations of feeling, the rise and fall of vitality, the appearance of different symptoms, and the correct ways in which to meet them. At certain times, healing crises will manifest themselves and these will constitute his hardest problem. The process of dissolving and eliminating the fermenting and decaying materials from the cellular tissues will become very potent at such times, and its outer indications may well frighten him into belief that the whole system is wrong, that he ought never to have tried to follow it. It is then that he will need the hand of reassurance from those who have travelled the whole course and have realized with joy the incredible benefits that wait at its end—the cure of their ailments and the rejuvenation of their organs. Therefore it is better that before he begins such a radical changeover from conventional regimes, and especially before a fast, he ought to learn more about the experiences of others who have followed this new course. This he can do by reading the literature on the subject. He will not be groping in the dark but will know where he is going and what he is doing.

§

Those who really aspire towards a higher kind of life will have no alternative than to bring about a higher quality of the body in which they have to dwell and whose nerves and brain condition their very thinking. Such aspirants will have to stop being careless about the material that is fed to the body.

§

The intolerance of some aggressive and fanatical opponents of meat-eating, smoking, and alcohol-drinking is itself a vicious attitude which harms them in a different way as much as those bad habits harm their addicts.

§

It is not enough to eat sparingly: he must also eat consistently, if he would keep well. He should not eat rightly for several months or years and then suddenly plunge into wrong eating for a while. For then he may lose in a few days or weeks the good health he has gained, so powerful may the reaction be. To stay faithful to his regular regime in diet is one of the basic rules he must follow. Yet friends and relatives may insist on such a departure from what experience has taught him is best for his own body and mind, and he will need much strength of will to resist them. It will require from him an obstinate adherence to his initial resolve that nothing and no one may be allowed to make him break it.

§

The banishment of flesh from a correct diet has a thoroughly scientific basis. This kind of food has far too much poisonous uric acid in it, far too much toxic purine to make it a healthy constituent of such a diet. Moreover, it deteriorates the intestinal flora. This will not affect healthy manual-worker types who have enough resistance to throw it off, but it will affect sedentary weaker types.

§

Thomas Jefferson's "Letters": "I fancy it must be the quantity of animal food eaten....which renders their characters insusceptible of civilization. I suspect it is in their kitchens and not in their churches that their reformation must be worked, and that missionaries of that description from hence would avail more than those who should endeavour to tame them by precepts of religion or philosophy."

§

If men believe that they must eat meat because it is necessary to life, let them at least first remove the blood from it, as the first Bishop of the earliest Christian church, St. James, ruled to be a Christian duty, and as Moses, wise and powerful leader of those who escaped from Egyptian slavery, ruled to be a Hebrew duty. In this way they will reduce their chance of physical sickness and improve their chances of moral progress. Those who must have further authority for this bloodless diet from a Biblical text may consult their Genesis, I:29. Not for nothing is it that so many rites of black magic call for the use of blood, a sacrificial offering fit only for the dark principle of the universe but not for the maintenance of the human body. Still worse is it for the purpose of such maintenance when the blood is permeated with psychic horror, fear, and anguish generated during first the waiting period at the slaughterhouse and, more intensely, at the actual bloodstained spot itself.

§

Just before an animal meets its death in a slaughterhouse, it finds itself surrounded by the frightening cries and fear-raising scenes of past, present, and impending murder. Its own dread then mentally permeates the body with harmful influences while the subsequent shock of its own slaying causes an involuntary passage of some urine into the body itself. This uric acid is spread by the blood and then *physically* permeates the body with poisonous material.

§

The eating of flesh foods and, to a lesser degree, animal products tends to keep the human consciousness limited to an outlook which is influenced by the animal propensities. If it is to become truly human, it must free itself from dependence on such foods and such products whose cellular substance is naturally impregnated with such propensities.

§

The killing instinct in man is kept *indirectly* alive by the meat-eating appetite of man.

§

They beseech the Lord with whining prayers for compassionate help or gracious mercy, yet never for a moment ever think of themselves granting mercy to the innocent creatures which are bred and slaughtered for their benefit.

§

So long as the slaughter of animals is really unnecessary for human food, so long does it remain a moral crime, an ancient shame upon whole nations, against which prophets and saints, seers and teachers have inveighed and warned. For under the Law of Recompense, the guilty —however unconscious—have had to suffer penalty. If they find their own prayers for mercy to the Higher Power remain unanswered, let them remember how they themselves showed no mercy.

§

We do not deny but on the contrary fully accept the ingenuity and effectiveness of hatha yoga methods. They are cleverly designed to achieve their particular aims and are capable of doing so. But what we do deny is first, their suitability for modern Western man and second, their safety for modern Western man. And we make these denials both on the ground of theory and on the ground of practice. These methods are extremely ancient; they are indeed remnants of Atlantean systems. The mentality and physique of the races for whom they were originally prescribed are not the same as the mentality and physique of the white Eur-American races. Evolution has been actively at work during the thousands of years between the appearance of the ancients and the appearance of the moderns. Important changes have developed in the nerve-structure and brain-formations of the human species. According to the old texts which have come down to us from a dateless antiquity, the trance state constitutes the pinnacle of hatha yoga attainment. But it is an entirely unconscious kind of trance. This we have learnt from the lips of hatha yogis who had perfected themselves in the system. It is indeed nothing more mentally than an extremely deep sleep brought on deliberately and at will, although physically it bestows extraordinary properties for the time being on the body itself. Even where the trance is so prolonged that the yogi may be buried alive under earth without food or drink for several days or weeks, he is throughout that period quite inactive mentally and quite unaware of his own self. His heartbeat and respiration are then extremely low, in fact imperceptible to human senses although perceptible to delicate electric instruments like the cardiogram.

In what way does this condition differ from the animal hibernation? In northern climates certain types of reptiles, rodents, bears, lizards, marmots, and bats retire to secluded places, mountain caves or sheltered holes under the ground, when the cold weather arrives and when food becomes scarce, and pass the whole winter in a state of deep-sleeping suspended animation. In tropical climates certain kinds of snakes and crocodiles do exactly the same when the hottest months arrive. It is particularly interesting to note that birds like the tinamou fall into a rigid cataleptic trance under the shock of terror and then become as immune to pain as the hatha yogis do in the same state. In both cases there is only a hypnotic and not a spiritual condition. Its value for mental enlightenment, let alone moral improvement, is nil.

Twentieth-century man has better things to do with his time and energy than to spend several years and arduous efforts merely to imitate these animals and birds. Such a trance benefits the animals who cannot get food and it is therefore sensible procedure for them to enter it. But how does man demonstrate his spiritual superiority over them if he follows the bat to its cave in the hills, lets the same torpor creep over him as creeps over it, and permits every conscious faculty to pass into a coma? In terms of consciousness, of spiritual advance, the hatha yoga hibernation has nothing to offer man in any way comparable with what the higher systems of yoga have to offer—unless of course he disdains the fruits of mental evolution and takes pleasure in atavistic reversion to the state of these wide-winged yogis, the bats, and those four-footed mystics, the rodents! We should therefore remember that there are different types of trance state and should seek only the higher ones, if we wish to make a real rather than illusory progress.

§

We witness today that all over Europe and America there have sprung up schools of hatha yoga. This is to be welcomed for several reasons. Most of the teachers are Westerners who have studied, usually for short periods, under an Indian guru who has come to the West and, in a few cases, under one in India itself. It is worth repeating, in this context, that the principal medical officer of the hospital at Rishikesh (which, situated at the foot of the Himalayas, is the greatest centre for practising yogis in India) informed me that more than three hundred cases had passed through his hands of yogis—or rather, would-be yogis—who had damaged their health or become insane through practising a particular breathing exercise connected usually with hatha yoga but also with elementary raja yoga. I refer to the exercise known as "Holding the Breath." Those who practise this exercise imprudently risk damaging their lungs or bursting blood vessels or irreparably injuring the brain—quite apart from the possibility of going out of their mind at least temporarily. The question therefore arises, why was this exercise incorporated in the yoga system? And why has it attracted so many to it? The answer to the second question is that most of those who have attempted it have done so because they have read or heard that it is a quick way to spiritual achievement or, more frequently, that it leads to the acquisition of occult powers. The answer to the first question is that properly performed by the proper person under competent supervision, the danger is eliminated. Since these conditions are not often present, the perils exist. There is no doubt that in the course of the next ten or twenty years we shall be hearing of several cases of self-injury in the West to these students of the yoga schools which have arisen here, unless they are fortunate enough to have a thoroughly responsible and well-informed teacher.

Even apart from the breathing exercises there are dangers in the postures of hatha yoga. The American vice-consul in Calcutta, for example, told me that for a year and a half he had suffered from a crick in the neck which caused his head to be half turned to the left. This was caused by his attempting to practise one of the hatha yoga contortions, but he was doing it under the tuition of an Indian guru! And when the crick happened, his guru was quite unable to rectify the injury, nor were the doctors he was able to contact at the time.

But to return to the breathing exercise: the holding of the breath is beneficial if one has experienced a visitation of grace and an uplift of consciousness. This retention enables one to prolong the glimpse which results from the visitation or which may come from meditation. Conversely, the holding of the breath leads almost directly to the holding down of the thought movement, which of course is also one of the goals of yoga. But since Nature forces the man to recover his breath after some time, the thoughts begin to move again. No doubt, if the exercise is repeated many times, the control of the thoughts becomes easier. Now, the yoga texts which have come down from ancient times give precise figures for the period of retention. With the in-held breath, it should be four times the period taken to breathe in. With the emptied lungs, it should be only twice that period.

Ah! First, people vary in their capacities, and exercises must be adjusted accordingly. For instance, the mountain-dwelling Gurkas of Nepal have broad shoulders and wide lungs and can take in much more air than the half-stooped office worker of a western city. Secondly, the yoga textbooks which were written in the days before printing were intended to be expounded by a competent guru. Hence, they were highly condensed and the present-day reader must pick his way through them very circumspectly if he is working alone.

Now, to return to this holding of the breath. It was not intended to be played with. The eager enthusiast of today plunges into the work quite drastically. He tries to perform the full exercise as he reads it in the translated text. He tries to perform it immediately, and this is where the terrible risk comes in. No beginner should attempt the full exercise of *any* of the hatha yoga breathings or postures. They should be spread out over a period of three months where the increase is measured in seconds each day so that the full exercise is only reached after daily work—very, very slowly increasing the development. The full exercise is only reached after ninety or one hundred days. This is a necessary precaution.

§

It will help to empty the mind of its tumult and the nerves of their agitation if he will breathe out as fully as possible, inhaling only when the first feeling of discomfort starts. He should then rest and breathe normally for several seconds. Next, he should breathe in as deeply as possible. The air is to be kept in the lungs until it is uncomfortable to do so. This alternation completes one cycle of breathing. It may be repeated a number of times, if necessary, but never for a longer period than ten minutes.

§

The other breathing exercise which is dangerous—not physically so much as mentally—is that which prescribes breathing through alternate nostrils so that one nostril is closed by a finger and only the other used until the changeover is made to the other nostril. This exercise is the one that threatens sanity. I would enforce as a rule that everyone who sets up to teach hatha yoga to others should be compelled to go through a course of at least one year in the anatomy of the body and then in the physiology of the body. The work must have a scientific basis because it encroaches on the medical domain.

§

Revitalizing Breath Exercise: (1) Stand at an open window, spine erect, body straight, hands tightly holding hips. (2) Expel all stale air through the mouth. (3) Take three short sharp sniffs of air and expel the total quantity in one long-drawn exhalation. Pause and breathe normally. Repeat three times. (4) Breathe in deeply through the nose, starting as low in the abdomen as possible, rising upward in the lungs until the upper part is filled. (5) The mind should concentrate on the solar plexus behind the navel. Imagine a stream of golden-white energy being drawn from there and radiated throughout the body. (6) Pucker up the lips and let all the air out as vigorously as possible. Tighten the diaphragm muscle while doing so, and move it upwards. Pause and breathe normally. Repeat three times.

§

The would-be-illumined person must conform to the double action of nature in him: to the outgoing and incoming breaths. So his illumination, when it happens, must be *there* and *here*: in the mind and in the body. The two together form the equilibrium of the double life we are called upon to live: that is, being in the world and yet not being of it. In the prolongation of the expiring breath we not only get rid of negative thought but also of the worldliness, the materialism, of keeping to the physical interests alone. With the incoming breath we draw positive, inspiring remembrance of the divine hidden in the Void. Hence we are there in the *mind* and here in the *body*. We recognize the truth of eternity, the act in time. We see the reality of the Void, yet know that the entire Universe comes forth from it.

§

The experience of human love between the two sexes is the nearest thing, perhaps, apart from artistic creativity, to the experience of divine love between the heart and soul. Therefore it should be regarded with an elevated and respectful mind, not with a degraded and coarse one. The cheap exploitation and cynical animalization of sex in the contemporary world of entertainment, as well as the deliberate stimulation of it in the contemporary worlds of commercial art, light literature, and the press, are evil things with evil results. To centre the attention of young impressionable people on the physical side of love as if it were the whole of love, to influence them to ignore the needs of the mind and cry of the heart when coupling for marriage or for passion, is to spread personal unhappiness and promote social wreckage.

§

The religious sham, which offers mere prudery as if it were real purity, is closely followed by the social sham, which rejects both.

§

Appetites of the body which are derived from merely physical habits tend to get mixed with emotions, which are of a different and higher kind. This is particularly true of one physical appetite—sex. If a man is to know and master himself, he will need to be clear as to the difference between a sexual affection, which is emotional, and sexual desire, which is physical. This knowledge is important to all Questers.

§

The lowest kind of sexual drive is concerned solely with finding, by any means and through any person, momentary release and physical satisfaction. It is biological, what man shares with the animals for continuing the race; yet it is often rendered obscene in him by its combination with cunning or fancy. In a superior kind of drive, it is mingled with emotional, aesthetic, and romantic feelings and begins to free itself from confinement to the crude animal attraction alone. This is the specifically human stage of sex life, where not any kind of woman, but only certain kinds, allure: love of two human beings for each other, emotional response between them, now complements the lust of two animals for each other. In the sexual union of two human beings who have reached this second level, each is called upon to receive the other into himself or herself, *that is, to fall in love once again* and quite afresh. The experience may be and usually is quite a fleeting one. But it will always arouse much ecstatic feeling and tender conduct. It is egoistic, and therefore subject to the vacillations and selfishnesses, the illusions and exploitations which the personal ego shows in its social relations generally. With evolutionary growth, the third stage marks a further change in the kind of satisfaction the sexual drive desires. Intellectual, moral, and cultural affinity is the attraction at this level. The highest aims of the egos must harmonize.

§

His passage from the common animality to a spiritualized humanity will necessarily involve a raising of force from the generative organ to the thinking organ. What was heretofore exteriorized must now be interiorized; what was wasted must be conserved, and what was physically spent must be spiritually transformed.

§

At the time when a child is conceived, two factors contribute powerfully towards its physical nature and physical history. They are the state of the father's thinking and the mother's breathing.

§

Philosophy recognizes that there are different stages on the path of dealing with sex, different needs which must be allowed for. But since those stages and needs are graded ones, it does not compromise on the rules for the last grade. Here, for those who are willing to do everything necessary and make every sacrifice required, it is not enough to discipline the sexual cravings, however severely. They must be brought to an end by a process of complete sublimation. Whereas it allows the young in years or the spiritually unready to abide by simple rules and lighter disciplines, it recommends to older persons or to the spiritually ready of any age to be the master of their animality in every sense. This applies whether they are married householders or not. It does not enforce a rule but simply makes a recommendation. Everyone has a perfect right to choose the stage which lies within his strength. But he must accept the results of his choice, which are governed by law.

§

The man who struggles with the passion of sex within his nature and conquers it, not merely physically but also mentally, finds that his very nature becomes bi-sexual. For he finds within himself the woman whom he had formerly sought outside himself. She who was to complement his mind and companion his body, and whom he could only find in an imperfect form or not find at all, is then discovered within his own spirit, in that which is deeper than body and mind. The mysterious duality which thus develops corresponds to the last stage but one of his mystical progress, for in the last stage there is absolute unity, absolute identity between his own ego and his Overself; but in the penultimate stage there is a loving communion between the two, and hence, a duality. Such a man is in need of no fleshly woman, and if he does marry it will be for reasons other than the merely conventional ones. In achieving this wonderful liberation from the drawbacks which accompany the delights of sex and from the shortcomings which modify its promises, he achieves something else; he enters into love in its purest, noblest, most divine, and most exalted state. Thus his nature is not starved of love as shallow observers may think or as the sensual minded may believe, but only he, rather than the others, knows what it means. Seemingly he stands alone, but actually he does not. He is conscious of a loving presence ever in him and around him, but it is love which has shed all turmoils and troubles, all excitements and illusions, all shortcomings and imperfections.

It is hard to overcome sexual desire, and neither ashamed repression nor unashamed expression will suffice to do so. Hunger and surfeit are both unsatisfactory states. The middle way is better, but it is not a solution in the true meaning of this term.

§

Why did so many primeval cultures in Asia, Africa, and America worship the serpent? A full answer would contain some of the most important principles of metaphysics and one of the least known practices of mysticism—raising the force symbolized under the name of the "serpent fire." The advanced occultists of Tibet compare the aspirant making this attempt to a snake which is made to go up a hollow bamboo. Once aroused, it must either ascend and reach liberty at the top or it must fall straight down to the bottom. So he who seeks to play with this fiery but dangerous power will either reach Nirvana or lose himself in the dark depths of hell. If a man seeks to arouse kundalini before he has rid himself of hate, he will only become the victim of his own hatreds when he does raise it from its sleeping state. He would do better to begin by self-purification in every way if he is to end in safety and with success. The uprising of the penis closely resembles the uprearing of the cobra. Both become erect and stiff by their own innate force. When the serpent fire passes from the root of the penis up the spinal cord, the latter also becomes upright and stiff. Yet sex is not the serpent power but the chief one of its several expressions. The advanced yogis of India symbolize by the pent-up hissing of the serpent the aggressive energy of this sex power. They picture the threefold character of the process in their texts as a triangle with a serpent coiled up inside it. The intense fire of love for the higher self must be kindled in the "mystic" heart, kindled until it also shows a physical parallel in the body, until the latter's temperature rises markedly and the skin perspires profusely. Deep breathing is an important element in this exercise. It provides in part the dynamism to make its dominating ideas effective. The other part is provided by a deliberate sublimation of sex energy, through its imaginative raising from the organs in the lower part of the body to a purified state in the head.

The strange phenomena of a mysterious agitation in the heart and an internal trembling in the solar plexus, of sex force raised through the spine to the head in intense aspiration toward the higher self accompanied by deep breathing, of a temporary consciousness of liberation from the lower nature, are usually the forerunners of a very important step forward in the disciple's inner life. A twofold trembling may seize him. Physically, his diaphragm may throb violently, the movement spreading like a ripple upward to the throat. Emotionally, his whole being may be convulsed with intense sobbing. It is this same bodily agitation, this nervous repercussion of a higher emotional upheaval, which developed in the meetings of the early members of the Society of Friends and got them the name of Quakers. The agitation of his feeling will come to an end with the calm perception of his Soul. The kundalini's activity being primarily mental and emotional, the diaphragmatic tremors and quivers are merely its physical reactions. The necessity for keeping the back erect exists only in this exercise, not in the devotional or intellectual yogas, for such a straight posture permits the spinal column to remain free for the upward passage of the "serpent fire." The latter moves in spiral fashion, just like the swaying of a cobra, generating heat in the body at the same time. If the trembling continues long enough and violently enough, a sensation of heat is engendered throughout the body and this in turn engenders profuse perspiration. But all these symptoms are preliminary and the real mystical phenomena involving withdrawal from the body-thought begin only when they have subsided. This exercise first isolates the force residing in breath and sex, then sublimates and reorients it. The results, after the initial excitement has subsided, are (a) a liberating change in his consciousness of the body, (b) a strengthening development of the higher will's control over the animal appetites, and (c) a concentration of attention and feeling as perfect as a snake's concentration on its prey. It is a threefold process yielding a threefold result. In those moments when the force is brought into the head, he feels himself to be liberated from the rule of animality; then he is at the topmost peak of the higher will. Power and joy envelop him. The attainment of this state of deep contemplation and its establishment by unremitting daily repetition bring him finally to an exalted satisfied sense of being full and complete and therefore passion-free and peace-rooted.

§

The attempt to gain all or nothing and to gain it at once might succeed on the stock exchange but is hardly likely to succeed here. He cannot leap abruptly to this great height across the intervening stages but must travel laboriously step by step upwards to it. Nevertheless there exists a way of taking the kingdom by violence, a way which can be finished in six months. It is the arousal of the serpent fire. But unless the nature has been well purified, it may prove a highly dangerous way. Few are yet ready for it, and no teacher dare incur the responsibility of plunging into such a risky gamble with his pupil's health, sanity, morality, and spiritual future unless there is sufficient sexual stability and hardness of will in him. There is a slower way, the yoga of self-identification with the Guru. Practised once or twice daily, and combined with Mantramjapa practised continuously, it leads to the same goal in a period twelve times as long and is perfectly safe. He should understand that the goal both ways lead to is not the philosophic one. Yet to attain the latter it is indispensable to pass through the mystic's goal. From all this we may gather not only how long is the road, but also how grand is the achievement with which philosophy is concerned.

§

At opposing ends of the spine, the human and the animal oppose each other.

§

The vital forces are dissipated unreasonably and stimulated excessively by turns, until the hapless victim mistakes for normal use what is really abnormal and unintended by Nature. The penalty has to be paid at some time and, spiritually, consists in his being blinded to the finer truths —metaphysical and mystical.

§

The power to control sex lies partly in the mind, where the media for this control are the imagination and the will united on the intuitive level, and partly in the body, where the media are dietetic restrictions, fasting, internal and external cleansings, and physical exercises.

§

An important part of the technique of redirecting perverted, vicious, or excessive sexual energies is active bodily exercise regularly done. Lack of it will not be sufficiently substituted for by dieting, fasting, or bathing.

§

"As a result of these experiments, I saw that the celibate's food should be limited, simple, spiceless and, if possible, uncooked. The ideal is fresh fruit and nuts. The immunity from passion that I enjoyed when I lived on this food was unknown to me after I changed this diet." —Gandhi

§

The masculine element in a woman and the feminine element in a man need to be as well developed and as actively expressed as the physical sex poles already are developed and expressed. And not only do these inner poles need this, but they need it to be done to the point of balancing the outer poles.

§

In the properly developed person, the strength of a man will be united with the tenderness of a woman.

§

If some people have found their way to God through the acceptance of sex, many more people have found their way through the rejection of it.

§

6

EMOTIONS AND ETHICS

Uplift character—Re-educate feelings
—Discipline emotions—Purify passions
—Refinement and courtesy—Avoid fanaticism

We begin and end the study of philosophy by a consideration of the subject of ethics. Without a certain ethical discipline to start with, the mind will distort truth to suit its own fancies. Without a mastery of the whole course of philosophy to its very end, the problem of the significance of good and evil cannot be solved.

§

The pursuit of moral excellence is immeasurably better than the pursuit of mystical sensations. Its gains are more durable, more indispensable, and more valuable.

§

The philosophical discipline seeks to build up a character which no weakness can undermine and from which all negative characteristics have been thrown out.

§

There are five ways in which the human being progressively views his own self and consequently five graduated ethical stages on his quest. First, as an ignorant materialist he lives entirely within his personality and hence for personal benefit regardless of much hurt caused to others in order to secure this benefit. Second, as an enlightened materialist he is wrapped in his own fortunes but does not seek them at the expense of others. Third, as a religionist he perceives the impermanence of the ego and, with a sense of sacrifice, he denies his self-will. Fourth, as a mystic he acknowledges the existence of a higher power, God, but finds it only within himself. Fifth, as a philosopher he recognizes the universality and the oneness of being in others and practises altruism with joy.

§

The moral precepts which it offers for use in living and for guidance in wise action are not offered to all alike, but only to those engaged on the quest. They are not likely to appeal to anyone who is virtuous merely because he fears the punishment of sin rather than because he loves virtue itself. Nor are they likely to appeal to anyone who does not know where his true self-interest lies. There would be nothing wrong in being utterly selfish if only we fully understood the self whose interest we desire to preserve or promote. For then we would not mistake pleasure for happiness nor confuse evil with good. Then we would see that earthly self-restraint in some directions is in reality holy self-affirmation in others, and that the hidden part of self is the best part.

§

We have begun to question Nature and we must abide the consequences. But we need not fear the advancing tide of knowledge. Its effects on morals will be only to discipline human character all the more. For it is not knowledge that makes men immoral, it is the *lack* of it. False foundations make uncertain supports for morality.

§

This grand section of the quest deals with the right conduct of life. It seeks both the moral re-education of the individual's character for his own benefit and the altruistic transformation of it for society's benefit.

§

If you want to obtain a good objective, you must use a good means as no other will bring the same result.

§

Such study of the ethics of philosophy will not, of course, give the student the power to be able to practise those ethics completely. He cannot always govern his own complexes or control his own desires or rule his own compulsions. Nevertheless, to know what he is expected to do and what he ought to do is a valuable first step towards doing it.

§

Disinterested action does not mean renouncing all work that brings financial reward. How then could one earn a livelihood? It does not mean ascetic renunciation and monastic flight from personal responsibilities. The philosophic attitude is that a man shall perform his full duty to the world, but this will be done in such a way that it brings injury to none. Truth, honesty, and honour will not be sacrificed for money. Time, energy, capacity, and money will be used wisely in the best interests of mankind, and above all the philosopher will pray constantly that the Overself will accept him as a dedicated instrument of service. And it surely will.

§

He may look at what has happened in five different but equally valuable and equally necessary ways: (a) as a test, (b) as opposition of adverse force, (c) as a problem to adjust himself to psychologically, (d) as a temptation or tribulation to be met and overcome morally, (e) as the outworking of past karma to be intelligently endured or impersonally negotiated.

§

But, after all, these qualities are only the negative prerequisites of spiritual realization. They are not realization itself. Their attainment is to free oneself from defects that hinder the attainment of higher consciousness, not to possess oneself of true consciousness.

§

The longer he lives the more he discovers that real peace depends on the strength with which he rules his own heart, and real security depends on the truth with which he rules his own mind. When he leaves his emotions in disorder they bring agony—as the accompaniment or the follower of the happiness they claimed at first to be able to give. When he lets his thoughts serve the blindnesses of his ego, they deceive, mislead, or trouble him.

§

Men ask, "What is truth?" But in reply truth itself questions them, "Who are you to ask that? Have you the competence, the faculty, the character, the judgement, the education, and the preparation to recognize truth? If not, first go and acquire them, not forgetting the uplift of character."

§

The act must illustrate the man, the deed must picture the attitude. It is thus only that thought becomes alive.

§

The philosophic attitude is a curious and paradoxical one precisely because it is a complete one. It approaches the human situation with a mentality as practical and as cold-blooded as an engineer's, but steers its movement by a sensitivity to ideals as delicate as an artist's. It always considers the immediate, attainable objectives, but is not the less interested in distant, unrealizable ones.

§

The discovery of moral relativity gives no encouragement however to moral laxity. If we are freed from human convention, it is only because we are to submit ourselves sacrificially to the Overself's dictate. The unfoldment of progressive states of conscious being is not possible without giving up the lower for the higher.

§

Buddha did not go into deeper problems before he had gone into practical ethics. He taught people to be good and do good before he taught them to venture into the marshy logic of the metaphysical maze. And even when they had emerged safely from a territory where so many lose themselves utterly, he brought them back to ethical values albeit now of a much higher kind because based on utter unselfishness. For love must marry knowledge, pity must shed its warm rays upon the cold intellect. Enlightenment of others must be the price of one's own enlightenment. These things are not easily felt by the mystic, who is often too absorbed in his own ecstasies to notice the miseries of others or by the metaphysician who is often too tied by his own verbosity to his hard and rigorous logic to realize that mankind is not merely an abstract noun but is made up of flesh-and-blood individuals. The philosopher however finds these benign altruistic needs to be an essential part of truth. Consequently the salvation which he seeks—from ignorance and the attendant miseries that dog its steps—is not for himself but for the whole world.

§

The more I travel and observe the more I come to believe that the only men who will make something worthwhile of philosophy are the men who have already made something worthwhile of their personal lives. The dreamers and cranks will only fool themselves, the failures and alibi-chasers will only become confirmed in their fantasies.

§

Each person who enters our life for a time, or becomes involved with it at some point, is an unwitting channel bringing good or evil, wisdom or foolishness, fortune or calamity to us. This happens because it was preordained to happen—under the law of recompense. But the extent to which he affects our outer affairs is partly determined by the extent to which we let him do so, by the acceptance or rejection of suggestions made by his conduct, speech, or presence. It is we who are finally responsible.

§

Unless he passes through the portals of this discipline, he cannot receive truth, but only its parodies, distortions, and imitations.

§

It is quite true that moral codes have historically been merely relative to time, place, and so on. But if we try to make such relativity a basis of nonmoral action, if we act on the principle that wrong is not worse than right and evil not different from good, then social life would soon show a disastrous deterioration, the ethics of the jungle would become its governing law, and catastrophe would overtake it in the end.

§

The first and immediate consequence of perceiving philosophic truth is a moral one. There is a strong appeal to the intellect and an equally strong appeal to the heart. These two viewpoints are not opposed to each other.

§

It is not enough to wish to better one's character. One must also know how to begin the task aright and how to continue it correctly. Otherwise he gropes blindly and falls into the old weaknesses, the old errors, even if they take new forms.

§

He has to find out what unwise tendencies are operative in his character without his knowledge, what wrong impulses arise from his subconscious self and lead to harmful actions.

§

It is true that thought precedes action, that actions express thoughts, and that to rule mind is to rule the entire life. But it is also true that man's battles with himself proceed by progressive stages, that he exerts will more easily than he changes feeling. Therefore, the discipline of inward thinking should follow after—and not before—it. To counsel him to take care of his inner life and that then the outer life will take care of itself, as so many mystics do, is to be plausible but also to show a lack of practicality. Man's heart will feel no peace as his mind will know no poise until he abandons the lower instincts and gives himself up to this unearthly call. First, he must abandon them outwardly in deeds; later he must do it inwardly even in thoughts. This will inevitably bring him into inner struggle, into oscillation between victories and defeats, elations and despairs. The way up is long, hard, rugged, and slow to tread. It is always a stage for complaints and outcries, battles and falls. Only time—the master power—can bring him to its lofty end. Only when the lessons of birth after birth etch themselves deeply and unmistakably into his conscious mind through dreadful repetition can he accept them co-operatively, resignedly, and thus put a stop to the needless sufferings of desire, passion, and attachment.

§

Many people talk mysticism or play with psychism so long as either promises them wonderful powers which most other people haven't got or wonderful experiences which most people do not have. But when they come to philosophy and find that it demands from them a renovation of their entire character, they are seized with fear and retreat. Philosophy is not for such people, for it does not conform to their wishes. It tells them what they do not like to hear. It disturbs their egoistic vanity and troubles their superficial serenity when it throws a glaring spotlight on their lower nature, their baser motives, and their ugly weaknesses.

§

At the beginning of each temptation there is a choice offered, as though one stood at the crossroads and must take one which leads upward to peace and well-being or the other which leads downward to hell. In the offering, the chance to escape from the oncoming temptation is given. If the chance is taken *immediately*, it can be escaped; but if there is the slightest dallying with the luring picture, then the chance is lost. Therefore, there should be instant rejection of it.

§

From Lord Beaconsfield's novel: "Ah," said Coningsby, "I should like to be a great man." The stranger threw at him a scrutinizing glance. His countenance was serious. He said in a voice of most solemn melody, "Nurture your mind with great thoughts. To believe in the heroic makes heroes."

§

While the aspirant fails to take an inventory of his weaknesses and consequently fails to build into his character the attributes needed, much of his meditation will be either fruitless or a failure or even harmful.

§

The fundamental test and final measure of anyone's spirituality is provided by his character. And his character is tested and measured by his actions.

§

Those who underrate the difficulty of self-changing, who promise a simple and easy path to a successful result, render the flock of gullible aspirants only a disservice. Wishful thinking may bring such aspirants to this path but eventual disappointment will throw them off it.

§

The key to right conduct is to refuse to identify himself with the lower nature. The hypnotic illusion that it is really himself must be broken: the way to break it is to deny every suggestion that comes from it, to use the will in resisting it, to use the imagination in projecting it as something alien and outside, to use the feelings in aspiration towards the true self and the mind in learning to understand what it is.

§

The disciple who wishes to make real progress must attack, weaken, and ultimately destroy certain bad traits of character. Among them is the trait of jealousy of his fellow disciples. It is not only an unpleasant thought but may also end in disastrous consequences. It often leads to wrathful moods and raging spells. It not only harms the other disciple but always does harm to the sinner himself. It is caused by an unreasonable sense of possessiveness directed towards the teacher which does not understand that love should give freedom to him, not deny it to him.

§

If a man becomes cold, pitiless, impenetrable, if he sets himself altogether apart from the life and feelings of other men, if he is dead to the claims of music and the beauties of art, be sure he is an intellectualist or a fanatical ascetic—not a philosopher.

§

The forming of a good character is the beginning, the middle, and the end of this work.

§

He who is jealous does not thereby show he loves the one on whose account he shows this emotion. He shows only that he loves himself. What he feels is selfish possessiveness. It is the same feeling which he manifests for his bank account. This is not love in any sense.

§

That it is not enough for men to think truth, that they must also feel it, is a statement with which most scientists, being intellect-bound, would disagree. But artists, mystics, true philosophers, and religious devotees would accept it.

§

What did Jesus mean when he enjoined his disciples to love their neighbours as themselves? Did he mean the sentimental, emotional, and hail-fellow-well-met attitude which the churches teach? How could he when in order to become what he was, he had once to hate and turn aside from that part of himself, the lower part—that is, the ego and the animal nature—which is mostly what neighbours show forth? If his disciples were taught to hate, and not to love, their egos, how then could they love the ego-dominated humanity amidst which they found themselves? The injunction "Love thy neighbour" has often led to confusion in the minds of those who hear or read it, a confusion which forces many to refuse to accept it. And they are the ones who do not understand its meaning, but misinterpret it to mean "Like thy neighbour!" The correct meaning of this age-old ethical injunction is "Practise compassion in your physical behaviour and exercise goodwill in your mental attitude towards your neighbour." Everyone can do this even when he cannot bring himself to like his neighbour. Therefore this injunction is not a wholly impracticable one as some believe, but quite the contrary.

Whoever imagines that it means the development of a highly sentimental, highly emotional condition is mistaken; for emotions of that kind can just as easily swing into their opposites of hate as remain what they are. This is not love, but the masquerade of it. Sentimentality is the mere pretense of compassion. It breaks down when it is put under strains, whereas genuine compassion will always continue and never be cancelled by them. True love towards one's neighbour must come from a level higher than the emotional and such a level is the intuitive one. What Jesus meant was "Come into such an intuitive realization of the one Infinite Power from which you and your neighbour draw your lives that you realize the harmony of interests, the interdependence of existence which result from this fact." What Jesus meant, and what alone he could have meant, was indicated by the last few words of his injunction, "as thyself." The self which they recognized to be the true one was the spiritual self, which they were to seek and love with all their might—and it was this, not the frail ego, which they were also to love in others. The quality of compassion may easily be misunderstood as being mere sentimentality or mere emotionality. It is not these things at all. They can be foolish and weak when they hide the truth about themselves from people, whereas a truly spiritual compassion is not afraid to speak the truth, not afraid to criticize as rigorously as necessary, to have the courage to point out faults even at the cost of offending those who prefer to live in self-deception. Compassion will show the shortcoming within themselves which is in turn reflected outside themselves as maleficent destiny.

When the adept views those who are suffering from the effects of their own ungoverned emotion or their own uncontrolled passion and desire, he does not sink with the victims into those emotions, passions, and desires, even though he feels self-identity with them. He cannot permit such feelings to enter his consciousness. If he does not shrink from his own suffering, it is hardly likely that the adept will shrink from the sufferings of others. Consequently it is hardly likely that the emotional sympathy which arises in the ordinary man's heart at the sight of suffering will arise in precisely the same way in the adept's heart. He does not really regard himself as apart from them. In some curious way, both they and he are part of one and the same life. If he does not pity himself for his own sufferings in the usual egoistic and emotional way, how can he bring himself to pity the sufferings of others in the same kind of way? This does not mean that he will become coldly indifferent towards them. On the contrary, the feeling of identification with their inmost being would alone prevent that utterly; but it means that the pity which arises within him takes a different form, a form which is far nobler and truer because emotional agitation and egotistic reaction are absent from it. He feels with and for the sufferings of others, but he never allows himself to be lost in them; and just as he is never lost in fear or anxiety about his own sufferings, so he cannot become lost in those emotions or the sufferings of others. The calmness with which he approaches his own sufferings cannot be given up because he is approaching other people's sufferings. He has bought that calmness at a heavy price—it is too precious to be thrown away for anything. And because the pity which he feels in his heart is not mixed up with emotional excitement or personal fear, his mind is not obscured by these excrescences, and is able to see what needs to be done to relieve the suffering ones far better than an obscured mind could see. He does not make a show of his pity, but his help is far more effectual than the help of those who do.

The altruistic ideal is set up for aspirants as a practical means of using the will to curb egoism and crush its pettiness. But these things are to be done to train the aspirant in surrendering his personal self to his higher self, not in making him subservient to other human wills. The primacy of purpose is to be given to spiritual self-realization, not to social service. This above all others is the goal to be kept close to his heart, not meddling in the affairs of others. Only after he has attended adequately—and to some extent successfully—to the problem of himself can he have the right to look out for or intrude into other people's problems.

This does not mean, however, that he is to become narrowly self-centered or entirely selfish. On the contrary, the wish to confer happiness and the willingness to seek the welfare of mankind should be made the subject of solemn dedication at every crucial stage, every inspired hour, of his quest. But prudence and wisdom bid him wait for a more active altruistic effort until he has lifted himself to a higher level, found his own inner strength, knowledge, and peace and learnt to stand unshaken by the storms, passions, desires, and greeds of ordinary life.

Hence it is better for the beginner to keep to himself any pretensions to altruism, remaining silent and inactive about them. The dedication may be made, but it should be made in the secrecy of the inmost heart. Better than talk about it or premature activity for it, is the turning of attention to the work of purifying himself, his feelings, motives, mind, and deeds.

Just as the word compassion is so often mistaken for a foolish and weak sentimentality, so the words egolessness, unselfishness, and unself-centeredness are equally mistaken for what they are not. They are so often thought to mean nonseparateness from other individuals or the surrender of personal rights to other individuals or the setting aside of duty to ourself for the sake of serving other individuals. This is often wrong. The philosophical meaning of egoism is that attitude of separateness not from another individual on the same imperfect level as ourself but from the one universal life-power which is behind all individuals on a deeper level than them all. We are separated from that infinite mind when we allow the personal ego to rule us, when we allow the personal self to prevent the one universal self from entering our field of awareness. The sin lies in separating ourselves in consciousness from this deeper power and deeper being which is at the very root of all selves.

§

Jesus' preachment of love of one's neighbour as oneself is impossible to follow in all fullness until one has attained the height whereon his own true self dwells. Obedience to it would mean identifying oneself with the neighbour's physical pain and emotional suffering so that they were felt not less keenly than one's own. One could not bear that when brought into contact with all kinds of human sorrow that shadow life. It could be borne only when one had crushed its power to affect one's own feelings and disturb one's own equilibrium. Therefore, such love would bring unbearable suffering. By actively identifying oneself with those who are sorrowing, by pushing one's sympathy with them to its extreme point, one gets disturbed and weakened. This does not improve one's capacity to help the sufferer, but only lessens it. To love others is praiseworthy, but it must be coupled with balance and with reason or it will lose itself ineffectually in the air. Not to let his interest in other matters or his sympathy with other persons carry him away from his equilibrium, his inner peace, but to stop either when it threatens to agitate his mind or disturb his feelings, is wisdom.

§

Love of the divine is our primary duty. Love of our neighbour is only a secondary one.

§

Regard, affection and friendliness, sympathy, fellow-feeling and love are not feelings to be thrown away because he has taken to the philosophic quest. On the contrary, they may become valuable stepping-stones in his progress if he treats them aright, if he evaluates them correctly, purifies them emotionally, and ennobles them morally.

§

One consequence of this compassionate habit is that an immense comprehension of human nature floods his whole being.

§

"Loving your neighbour as yourself" needs a careful interpretation. The verb "to love" holds widely different meanings for different people. It does not mean that he will feel very much more affectionate to everyone he meets, no matter who it be, than he formerly was. Its fundamental meaning is that one will so identify himself with another person, thing, or idea as to feel emotionally one with it and selflessly surrendered to it. This has little to do with his liking or disliking the object of his love. They affect the conditions under which his love operates, for liking makes the operation easier and disliking harder, but its essential attribute is self-identification with the beloved and selfless response to it. Loving starts and ends with giving up the ego to another.

§

Compassion is the highest moral value, the noblest human feeling, the purest creature-love. It is the final social expression of man's divine soul. For he is able to feel with and for another man only because both are in reality related in harmony by the presence of that soul in each one.

§

He who can detach himself from emotion even while he continues to feel it, becomes its true master.

§

It is not that he is asked to rise above all emotions to attain the serenity and blessedness of such a life; it is rather that he is asked to rise above the lower emotions. For it is indispensable to cherish the higher ones. Indeed, it is in the complete overturn of his seat of feeling that the passage from earthly to spiritual life will most show itself. Without it, with a merely intellectual overturn alone, the Overself can never be realized.

§

He will rise above personal emotion into perfect serenity rather than fall below it into dull apathy.

§

The same human characteristic of emotion which enslaves and even harms him when it is attached to earthly things alone, exalts and liberates him when it is disciplined and purified by philosophy.

§

Those who talk of liberating themselves from the moral repression of conventional society are right in some cases but wrong in most. For they chiefly mean that they want to be free to follow sensual desires without imposing any self-discipline. They do not see that to overcome those desires is the true self-liberation.

§

When a man's desires and yearnings, thirsts and longings are so strong as to upset his reasoning power and block his intuitive capacity, he is stopped from finding truth. In this condition he shuts his eyes to those facts which are displeasing or which are contrary to his desires and opens them only to those which are pleasing or agreeable to his wishes. Thinking bends easily to desires, so that the satisfaction of personal interest rather than the quest of universal truth becomes its real object.

§

The obligation is laid upon him to respond to the Overself's demand that he shall make an endeavour to rise above the animal level of his being. And this cannot be done upon a basis of mere emotion alone. It calls for an exercise of the higher will. He has indeed to engage in a holy war.

§

Refinement of the way one lives, thinks, speaks, and acts is not only a positive value but in its indirect result actually contributes to the spiritual quest. Those who decry it as a mere superficiality confuse the imitated action with the real one.

§

A high degree of refinement in morals, manners, and mind shows not merely human quality but also spiritual sensitivity.

§

In practising this large forbearance towards others, we need not allow them to practise imposition towards us. We should consider the circumstances and decide by wisdom how far it is wise to go and at what point to stop; in short, we should use discrimination.

§

His goodness, forgiveness, and comprehension should go out to those who seem to have misjudged him. What they feel about him seems to them to be the truth about him. It is the best they know—why blame them if appearances deceive them? If he continues to send them such kind thoughts, he actually lifts himself out of his own ego, he vanquishes his own egoism.

§

To the degree you keep ego out of your reaction to an enemy, to that degree you will be protected from him. His antagonism must be met not only with calmness, indifference, but also with a positive forgiveness and active love. These alone are fitting to a high present stage of understanding. Be sure that if you do so, good will ultimately emerge from it. Even if this good were only the unfoldment of latent power to master negative emotion which you show by such an attitude, it would be enough reward. But it will be more.

§

If some people regard him as a peculiar character and others as an eccentric individual, that will only be because he has failed to disguise his philosophic interests sufficiently in an unphilosophic world.

§

The idea that perfectly harmonious human relations can be established between human beings still dominated by egoism is a delusional one. Even where it seems to have been established, the true situation has been covered by romantic myth.

§

We need not become less human because we seek to make ourselves better men. The Good, the True, and the Beautiful will refine, and not destroy, our human qualities.

§

If he is to keep his inward peace unruffled he must live above the level of those who have it not. This can be done only if he obeys the practical injunctions of Jesus and Buddha, only if he keeps out of his emotional system all the negatives like resentment, bitterness, quarrelsomeness, jealousy, spite, and revenge. These lower emotions must definitely be outgrown if philosophic calm is to be the supreme fact and philosophic wisdom the guiding factor in his life. When other men show their enmity and meanness toward him, he is to retaliate by showing his indifference and generosity. When they falsely assail his character or enviously calumniate his work, he is to forbear from harsh feelings and not let them forfeit his goodwill. He is not to succumb to the human temptation to retaliate in kind. For he is engaged on a holy ascent, and to succumb would be to slip grievously back. Indeed, out of the base actions of others, he may kindle noble reactions which assist his upward climb.

§

In his own heart he has no enemies and is always ready to make his peace with those who have acted as such. However, even those who treat him as an enemy but whom he does not regard as such, as well as those who turn the basilisk glance of envy upon him, will be useful tutors of the values of existence, and after every kind of onslaught he can sit quietly beneath a friendly tree and understand better why fame is a gift of doubtful value, a sword with two edges whose sharper and crueller edge is jealousy; why it is as satisfying to have malignant enemies as to have benevolent friends, for they afford practical instruction in non-attachment and self-purification, priceless tuition which no friend is ever likely to give him; why a man is sometimes indebted to his bitterest opponents for the favour of a useful criticism which has somehow crept in among their ugly lies, while his best friends injure him by being silent; why he must be content to walk alone with truth and refrain from asking of the world that understanding which it is incompetent to give; why most warm human longings for a happiness dependent upon others inevitably end in the dismal dust and cold ash; and why the finite ego affords too narrow a life for the infinite Mind, of which, as Jesus told his wondering hearers, we know neither whence it cometh nor whither it goeth.

§

Justice often demands that force be used in order to implement its decisions. Philosophy sets up justice as one of the guiding principles of personal and national conduct. Therefore philosophy has no use for pacifism or nonviolence.

§

The goodness which one man may express in his relation to another is derived ultimately from his own divine soul and is an unconscious recognition of, as well as gesture to, the same divine presence in that other. Moreover, the degree to which anyone becomes conscious of his true self is the degree to which he becomes conscious of it in others. Consequently, the goodness of the fully illumined man is immeasurably beyond that of the conventionally moral man.

§

The resistance of evil is a social duty. Its strongest expression heretofore has been defensive war against a criminally aggressive offending nation. If resistance is itself an evil, war is the most evil form of that evil. The appearance of the atomic bomb is a sign that a new approach must be found today, that the old way of defensive war will not meet the new problems which have arisen. If man is to end war once and for all and find peace, he must do so both internally and externally. He can do the one by ending the rule of the animal aggressive emotions within himself such as greed, anger, revenge, and hatred, and he can do the other by abandoning the slaying of his fellow creatures, whether human or animal. He may take whatever defensive preparations he pleases, but he must stop short at the point of killing other men. The refusal to slaughter would then evoke powerful spiritual forces, and if enough persons evoke them the end of war would be assured. However it is unlikely that such an idealistic course would appeal to more than a small minority of mankind, so that if the end of war is to be brought about in another way it can only be by the political method of an international policing army operated by a world federation of peoples. Since such a federation does not exist today, its only possibility of coming into existence is through the hard lessons learnt out of the appalling destructiveness of an atomic war. There is no other alternative to such a war than the renunciation of the right to kill.

§

If what is right for the masses, with their limited standards, is not right for the disciple, with his loftier ones, then the reverse is also true. The code which he must apply to life is well beyond the understanding and reach of the masses. To attempt to impose it on them is to create moral or social confusion and to unbalance their minds.

§

7

THE INTELLECT

Nature—Services—Development
—Semantic training—Science—Metaphysics
—Abstract thinking

Most of us move from one standpoint to another, whether it be a lower or a higher one, because our feelings have moved there. The intellect merely records and justifies such a movement and does not originate it.

§

The work done by original deeply penetrative thinking can go far, can uncover much not yet known; but it cannot solve the mystery of the thinker himself, unless it renounces its right to do so and lets the diviner Self take over in utter silence.

§

Intellect, reason, and intelligence are not convertible terms in this teaching. The first is the lowest faculty of the trio, the third is the highest, the second is the medial one. Intellect is logical thinking based on a partial and prejudiced collection of facts. Reason is logical thinking based on all available and impartially collected facts. Intelligence is the fruit of a union between reason and intuition.

§

A training in logic may guard us against transgressing the rules of right thinking but it cannot guard us against ignorance.

§

Logic is always beset by the serious charge that its so-called truths are fallacious ones. For instance, it insists on the law of contradiction, the law which says that a statement of facts cannot be true and false at the same time. But the careful study of illusions produces conclusions which falsify this law. We do not mean by this criticism to declare logic to be useless. We mean only what we have elsewhere written, that it is a good servant but a bad master.

§

Just as the path of return from body-ruled intellect to divine intuition is necessarily a slow one, so the descent into matter of man's originally pure mind was also a slow process. The "Fall" was no sudden event; it was a gradual entanglement that increased through the ages. Pure consciousness—the Overself—is required even for the intellect's materialistic operations. We may say, therefore, that the Overself has never been really lost, for it is feeding the intellect with necessary life. All this has been going on for untold ages. At first man possessed only a subtle body for a long period; but later, *as his intellect continued more outward bent than before*, the material body accreted to him. This curious position has arisen where intellect cannot indeed function in the absence of the Overself, yet deceptively arrogates to itself the supremacy of man's being. Pretending to guide and protect man, it is itself rebelliously and egotistically blind to the guidance of the Overself, yet enjoys the protection of the latter. The intellectual ego-self is thus propped up by the Overself and would collapse without it, but pretends to be self-sufficing.

§

Right thinking is not only an intellectual quality; it is almost a moral virtue.

§

Intelligence is inspired intellectuality. It yields well-reasoned and divinely prompted ideas.

§

But with stronger thinking power there comes also intellectual pride and egoistic conceit. He must offset them by humbling himself deliberately before the higher self. He must not hesitate to pray daily to it, on bended knees and with clasped hands, begging for its grace, offering the little ego as a willing sacrifice and asking for guidance in his darkness.

§

Shallow thought, superficial reasoning, is the means to bondage, but hard thinking, deep reasoning, is the means to freedom.

§

Reasoned thinking may contribute in two ways to the service of mystical intuition and mystical experience. First and commonest is a negative way. It can provide safeguards and checks against their errors, exaggerations, vagaries, and extravagances. Second and rarest is a positive and creative way. It can lead the aspirant to its highest pitch of abstract working and then invite its own displacement by a higher power.

§

"Thinking," said Hegel (when his landlady worried about his absence from church service), "is also Divine Service."

§

The intellect's finest function is to point the way to this actual living awareness of the Overself that is beyond itself. This it does on the upward path. But it has a further function to perform after that awareness has been successfully gained. That is to translate that experience into its own terms, and hence into ordinarily comprehensible ones, both for its own and other people's benefit.

§

The intellectual study of these truths is not without great value. It prepares him for their eventual realization, nourishes his soul, strengthens his higher will, and encourages his finer hopes. Moreover, holy reverence is born of itself as he meditates on the picture of universal intelligence which thus unfolds before his gaze.

§

In this little head we must first conquer the larger world. From this obscure corner we may master life.

§

The philosophical aspirant turns these intellectual studies into acts of devotion.

§

Because philosophy aims to develop a fully rounded psyche, it does not share the fanatic and extreme points of view of some medieval Western mystics and modern Indian yogis who banish every intellectual pursuit from the aspirant's path and who regard study as not merely being useless but as even being harmful. It is true that if a student is forever reading and never digesting what he reads, or never acting on it, he will make little progress. Nevertheless he cannot be said to be entirely wasting his time, for he will be gaining information. And if his reading includes works by the great masters, he will also be gaining inspiration. If, moreover, he has learned to read properly, he will be gaining yet a third thing and that is stimulation in thinking and reflecting for himself. Yes! An inspired book and a good reader if brought together are not necessarily an unspiritual combination, but the qualifications which we earlier made should be remembered. What he reads should be digested. He should learn to think, to create his own ideas under the stimulus of what he reads. Otherwise the more he reads, the more bewildered he may become with contradictory ideas and doctrines. And again reading and thought must lead to action and not leave him uselessly suspended in the world of dreams and theories.

Philosophy does not adopt the anti-intellectual attitude of so many medieval ascetics and their modern inheritors. For it declares that metaphysical thinking can lead the thinker to the very threshold of mystical intuition. It asserts that by persevering in abstract reflection he may earn the grace of the higher self and be led nearer and nearer to the highest truth. But there is one qualifying condition for such a triumphant achievement. The thinker must first undergo a self-purificatory discipline. His thoughts, his feelings, and his actions must submit themselves to a prolonged training and a constant regulation which will eliminate or at least reduce those factors which falsify his thinking or prevent the arisal of true intuition. Therefore his character has to be improved, his egoistic instinct has to be struggled against, his passions have to be ruled, his prejudices have to be destroyed, his biases have to be corrected. It is because they have not undergone this discipline that so many people have been led astray by the thinking activity into a miserable materialism. For philosophy asserts that the ordinary man's thinking is corrupted by his lower nature, with which it is completely entangled. Therefore he must free that thinking to a large extent from the thraldom of the lower nature if it is to lead to true conclusions, if it is to lead to the recognition of its own limitations, and if it is to invite intuition to arise and replace it at the proper moment. Just as education of intellect and practice of courtesy lift a man from a lower class of society to a higher one, so purification of thought, feeling, and will lifts his mind into a realm of higher perception than before. So philosophy welcomes and includes metaphysical activity into its scheme of things.

§

It is fallacious to believe that clear and precise intellectual expression is inimical to, and hence unable to accompany, inspired and flashing mystical experience. It is true that many mystics have been intellectually hindered and limited and that this simplicity made their ascent easier. But it is not true that such a one-sided development will be the end of man's story. It is the whole of life which has to be experienced, and which the universal laws force everyone to experience in the end. The growth of intelligence—of which intellect is a limited but necessary part—can only be put aside or avoided for a time, not for all time.

§

We do not overcome our doubts by suppressing them, we do not meet our misgivings by denying them, and we do not refute falsehood by shirking questions which happen to be inconvenient.

§

If a man will constantly think about these metaphysical truths, he will develop in time the capacity to perceive them by direct intuition instead of by second-remove reflection. But to do this kind of thinking properly the mind must be made steady, poised, concentrated, and easily detached from the world.

§

When intelligence is applied so thoroughly as to yield a whole view and not merely a partial view of existence, when it is applied so persistently as to yield a steady insight into things rather than a sporadic one, when it is applied so detachedly as to be without regard to personal preconceptions, and when it is applied so calmly that feelings and passions cannot alter its direction, then and only then does a man become truly reasonable and capable of intellectually ascertaining truth.

§

Like the two sides of the same coin, so it is that a thing thought of is thought of always by comparison with something not itself, that all our thinking is therefore always and necessarily dualistic, and that it cannot hope to grasp Oneness correctly. Hence the logical completion of these thoughts demands that it must give up the struggle, commit voluntary suicide, *and let Oneness itself speak to it out of the Silence*. But this must not be done prematurely or the voice which shall come will be the voice of our own personal feelings, not of That out of which feeling itself arises. Thinking must first fulfil, and fulfil to the utmost, its own special office of bringing man to reflective self-awareness, before it may rightly vacate its seat. And this means that it must first put itself on the widest possible stretch of abstract consideration about its own self. That is, it must attempt a metaphysical job and then be done with it. This is what the average mystic rarely comprehends. He is rightly eager to slay his refractory thoughts, but he is wrongly eager to slay them *before* they have served him effectively on his quest.

§

There is nothing new in this requirement of philosophy. It has been voiced since antiquity by some of those who gave out publicly what they could or would from their philosophic initiation. Socrates spoke of the "incoherent notions" which filled human minds and which had to be cleared away before diviner ones could replace them. So he called for adequate statement of the definitions of general and abstract terms. Confucius, who was always the practical man rather than the pedant, said nevertheless: "It is most necessary to rectify names of things. If names are not correct, language will not be in accordance with the truth of things; if language is not in accordance with the truth of things, administration will not be successful." The untiring search for clearer meanings and more articulate definitions should not be confused with mere academic purism. It makes use of verbal precision only as a means of achieving truthful valuation.

§

The philosopher must ask each word to yield thoroughly a definition which possesses an exactitude that may well terrify the ordinary man. He must become a hunter and wander through the forests of verbal meaning to track down real meaning. He will not rush prematurely into utterance. Words are cheap for the ordinary man but dear for him. His studied hesitation leads however closer to truth. This interpretational discipline must be vigorously applied until it leads to a thorough understanding of all concepts which are the essential counters in philosophical research. For when men go astray in their definitions of these highly important terms, they will surely go astray in their thinking and thence be led astray altogether from truth.

§

The analytical study of certain metaphysical conceptions such as God, the soul, and the ego, is necessary.

§

Unless he brings into his metaphysical studies a passionate appreciation of ultimate values and a profound feeling of reverence, they will not bear either a sound or a full fruit. In short, his thinking must be given a rich emotional, ethical, and intuitional content.

§

The unsatisfactoriness of most Vedantic metaphysics is that it limits itself to ontology. The unsatisfactoriness of most Western metaphysics is that it limits itself to epistemology. Both are one-legged creatures. A satisfying full-limbed system must first begin with epistemology and then end with ontology.

§

Intellect can perceive what belongs to reality, not reality itself. The metaphysician deludes himself into thinking that he has seen the world in all its varied aspects, but what he has really seen is the world in all its *intellectual* aspects only. Moreover when he thinks that he has put together the results of one science with another, uniting them all into a harmonious whole, he omits to reckon that such are the limitations of human capacity and such is the rapidly growing vastness of scientific knowledge, that no man could ever combine all the multitudinous results. He could never acquire an intimate knowledge of them during a single lifetime. Therefore he could never develop a complete philosophy of the universe as a whole.

The intellect fulfils itself practically when it discovers that each idea it produces is incomplete and imperfect and therefore passes on to replace it by a further one, but it fulfils itself metaphysically when it discovers that every idea which it can possibly produce will always and necessarily be incomplete and imperfect.

Now so far as they are almost entirely metaphysical works, these two volumes[1] have no option but to make their appeal chiefly to reason alone. And expounding the special and unique system called the ***metaphysics of truth*** as they do, they have to start where possible from verifiable facts rather than mere speculations. But whatever other importance they ascribe to reasoning as an instrument of truth-attainment applies only to the particular stage for which it is prescribed, which is the stage of metaphysical discipline and certainly not beyond it. Although the status bestowed on reason in every metaphysical system beginning with science must necessarily be a primary one, its status within the larger framework of the integral hidden teaching can only be a secondary one. This teaching possesses a larger view and does not end with science or limit itself to the rational standpoint alone. How can it do so when metaphysics is merely its intermediate phase? We must rightly honour reason to its fullest extent, but we need not therefore accept the unreasonable doctrine that the limits of reason constitute the limits of truth.

Our senses can perceive only what they have been formed to perceive. Our reason similarly cannot grasp what it was never formed to grasp. Within their legitimate spheres of operation, the deliverances of both sense and reason should be acceptable to us, but outside those spheres we must seek for something that transcends both.

But the basic cause why reason is insufficient exists in the fact that intellect—the instrument with which it works—is itself insufficient. Reason is the right arrangement of thinking. Each thought thus arranged depends for its existence on another thought and is unable to exist without such a relation, that is, it suffers from relativity. Hence a thought cannot be considered as an ultimate in itself and therefore reason cannot know the absolute. The intellect can take the forms of existence apart bit by bit and tell us what they consist of. But such surgical dissection cannot tell us what existence itself is. This is something which must be experience, not merely thought. It can explain what has entered into the composition of a painting but, as may be realized if we reflect a little, it cannot explain why we feel the charm of the painting. The analytic intellect describes reality sufficiently to give some satisfaction to our emotions or our intelligence, but it does not touch this baffling elusive reality at all. What it has dissected is not the living throbbing body but the cold dead image of it.

When reason tells us that God *is*, it does not actually know God. The antennae of intellectual research cannot penetrate into the Overself because thinking can only establish relations between ideas and thus must forever remain in the realms of dualities, finitudes, and individualities. It cannot grasp the whole but only parts. Therefore reason which depends on thinking is incompetent to comprehend the mysterious Overself. Realization is to be experienced and felt; thought can only indicate what it is likely to be and what it is not likely to be. Hence Al Ghazzali, the Sufi, has said: "To define drunkenness, to know that it is caused by vapours that rise from the stomach and cloud the seat of intelligence, is a different thing from being drunk. So I found ultimate knowledge consists in experiences rather than definitions." The fact that metaphysics tries to explain all existence in intellectual terms alone and tries to force human nature into conceptual molds, causes it to suppress or distort the non-intellectual elements in both. The consequence is that metaphysics alone cannot achieve an adequate understanding. If it insists upon exalting its own results, then it achieves misunderstanding.

Metaphysics proves the existence of reality but is unable to enter into it. Indeed, metaphysics must in the end criticize the desert-sand dryness of its own medium of thinking and not make the mistake of regarding thought-activity as the ultimately real, when it is itself only a section cut from the whole of human experience and existence. The intellect offers a reality which can never be a felt reality but only a described one and then only in negative terms. Intellectual work can only paint the picture of reality; we have then to verify this picture by realizing it within our own experience. The final office of reasoned thought is to reveal why reason is not competent to judge reality and why thinking is not competent to know reality.

The moment we attempt to understand what reality is, we get out of our depth because our own thinking must move in a serial sequence which itself prevents us from escaping the particular space-time form which confines us to a particular world of appearance. Just as, because it has entered our space-time experience, we can take hold of an artist's production but not the mind behind it, so and for the same reason we can take hold of the screen which cuts us off. This is because we can think of existence only in a particular shape or relative to a particular thing, not of existence that is formless, bodiless, and infinite. We have to localize it somewhere in space. Because space and time are forms taken by rational knowledge, because they are only conditions existing within personal consciousness, they do not enter into the knowledge of consciousness of that which is beyond both rational thinking and personal selfhood.

§

No idea is ever really outside another, nor is any idea ever outside the mind, and all ideas, all that which is seen, can only *theoretically* be separated from the thinking seeing mind. As psychologists we have had in thought to separate seer from seen, so that we might learn at length what the nature of pure mind really is; but as philosophers we must now merge them together. It is because thinking must always have an object with which to occupy itself that it can never penetrate the Overself, for here there is only the One. We must renounce thoughts and things if we would enter into the Absolute. Because in this ultimate state there is no more awareness of an individual observer and an observed world, the distinction between individual mind and individual body also ceases. Everything, including our *separate* selfhood, is voided out, as it were. The resultant nothingness however is really the essence of everything. It is not the nothingness of death but of latent life. Human thought can proceed no farther. For when "not-two-ness" is established as the Real, the logical movement from one thought to a second can only prolong the sway of "two-ness" over the mind. In this pure being there can be no "other," no two, hence it is called non-dual. The integrity of its being cannot really be split. If the Overself is to be actually experienced, then it must be as a realization of the Infinite One. To divide itself into knower and known is to dwell in duality. The antithesis of known and knower cannot enter into it just as the opposition of reality and illusion is meaningless for it. The oneness of its being is absolute. The return to this awareness, which regards the world only under its monistic aspect, is the realization of truth possessed by a sage. When rational thinking can perceive that it cannot transcend itself, cannot yield more than another thought, it has travelled as far as it can go and performed its proper function. Metaphysical truth is the intellectual *appearance* of reality, the rational knowledge of it; but it is not reality itself, not realization. For knowing needs a second thing to be known; hence metaphysical knowledge, being dual, can never yield realization which is non-dual.

Reality must stand grandly alone, without dependence on anything and without relation to anyone; it ever was, is, and ever will be. It is this inability of human reason to grasp the super-rational, the divine ineffable, that Omar Khayyam tried to express in his beautiful quatrains which have been so widely misunderstood by Western readers. If the *Rubaiyat* of Omar is only a drunken refrain from a wine-shop, then the New Testament is a mere scribble from an out-of-the-way corner of the Roman Empire. The cup of language is too small to hold the wine of the Absolute. A thought of Mind as the Void is still a "something" no less than a thought of great mountains and therefore prevents us from realizing the Void.

Now when we grasp the basic nature of human thinking, that it is possible only by forming two opposing ideas at the same time as the concept of black is formed by the contrast against white, we can then grasp the fundamental reason why such thinking can never rise to awareness of the Absolute unity. We cannot think of eternity without thinking of time too. For our conception of it either prolongs time until imagination falters and ceases or negates time altogether into timelessness. In neither case do we really comprehend eternity. Why? Because intellect cannot lay hold of what lies beyond itself. We humans know a thing by distinguishing it from other things, by limiting its nature and by relating it to its opposite. But the infinite has nothing else from which it can be distinguished or to which it can be related, whilst it certainly cannot be limited in any way.

Our earlier division into a dualism of observer and observed must now come to an end. But let us not make the error of mistaking it for the final stage. There still lies a path beyond, a path which leads to the ultimate where both observer and the observed become one.

The Real can never be stated because it can never be thought. Therefore it is quite clear that ordinary means of knowledge are unable to grasp it. But such knowledge is not useless. For if religion can give us a symbolic idea and mysticism an intuitive idea of the Infinite, metaphysical knowledge can give us a rational idea of it. And to possess such an idea keeps us at least from falling into errors about the reality behind it. If metaphysics can never perform the task it sets itself—to know reality—it can perform the task of knowing what is *not* reality. And such a service is inestimable. The function of reason is ultimately a negative one; it cannot provide a positive apprehension of the Overself, but it can provide a clear declaration of what It is not. Reason can demonstrate that the Overself can possess no shape and can in no way be imagined.

Nevertheless we may have both the assurance and the satisfaction that our thinking is correct but we have neither the assurance nor the satisfaction of consciously embracing that with which this thinking deals. We may have formed a right mental image of God but we are still not in God's sacred presence. We must not mistake the image for the reality which it represents. Whatever discoveries we have hitherto made have been made only within the limited frontiers of reasoned thinking. Exalted and expanded though our outlook may now be, we can still do no more than think the existence of this reality without actually experiencing it. The mere intellectual recognition of this Oneness of Mind is no more sufficient to make it real to us than the mere intellectual recognition of Australia's existence will suffice to make Australia real to us. In the end all our words about the Overself remain but words. For just as no amount of telling a man who has never touched or drunk any liquid will ever make properly clear to him what wetness is unless and until he puts his finger in a liquid or drinks some of it, so every verbal explanation really fails to explain the Overself unless and until we know it for ourself within ourself and as ourself.

§

Metaphysics is ordinarily concerned with the criticism of superficial views about the experienced world and the correction of erroneous ones, whilst it seeks to construct an accurate systematic and rational interpretation of existence as a whole. This is good in its own place because we shall be all the better and not worse for finding a metaphysical base for our beliefs. It is quite clear however that metaphysical systems cannot alone suffice for our higher purpose, for being based on personal assumptions, reasoning, or imaginations, if they partially enlighten mankind they also partially bewilder by their mutual contradictions. Hence philosophy steps in here and offers what it calls "the metaphysics of truth." This is an interpretation in intellectual terms of the results obtained from a direct mystical insight concerned with what is itself incapable of intellectual seizure. Through this superior insight it provides in orderly shape the reasons, laws, and conditions of the supersensuous experience of the Overself, unifies and explains the experiences which lead up to this consummation, and finally brings the whole into relation with the practical everyday life of mankind. It is the sole system that the antique sages intellectually built up *after* they had actually realized the Overself within their own experience. *Such a point needs the utmost emphasis for it separates the system from all others which carry the name of metaphysics or philosophy.* Whereas these others are but intelligent guesses or fragmentary anticipations of what ultimate truth or ultimate reality may be and hence hesitant between numerous "ifs" and "buts," this alone is a presentation from firsthand knowledge of what they really are. It bars out all speculation.

Just as science is a rational intellectualization of ordinary physical experience, so the metaphysics of truth is a rational intellectualization of the far sublimer transcendental experience. It is indeed an effort to translate into conventional thought what is essentially beyond such thought. As expressed in intellectual language, it is scientific in spirit, rational in attitude, cautious in statement, and factual throughout. It is devoted to the relentless exposure of error, the fearless removal of illusion, and the persevering pursuit of truth to the very end—irrespective of personal considerations. It seeks to understand the whole of life and not merely some particular aspects of it.

§

Metaphysics points to a higher consciousness but cannot itself touch it. It provides the truest concepts of that consciousness, but being concepts only, they merely symbolize it. We must not confuse two entirely different things: the *feeling* of fundamental unity which the realized sage possesses and the *concept* of fundamental unity which the metaphysical thinker possesses. The sage will make use of the metaphysician's concept when he seeks to make the content of this felt unity articulate and intelligible in communication to others. The metaphysician cannot get beyond his concept, do what he may, unless he rises beyond metaphysics altogether. For when he tries to determine the indeterminable he merely fumbles through a series of empty words and finally fails in his attempt, his last words being purely negative ones. The metaphysician is utterly helpless when confronted by the problem of realizing his own ultimate concept of reality, for he can only express it in negative terms, which is tantamount to a failure in expressing it at all. The moment he endeavours to determine it in affirmative thoughts is the moment when he destroys its reality altogether, for it then becomes a mere thought among the numerous others considered by his mind. Just as cold scientific analysis deprives the warmest artistic emotion of its content and thus destroys the emotion itself, so the process of thinking deprives the profoundest mystical experience of its actuality and effaces its transcendental character. For reality is beyond the demonstration and inaccessible to the grasp of reason. Metaphysical reasoning is a self-destructive process for it can only reveal its utter inadequacy to grasp the Real other than as a thought. Consequently the Vedantic metaphysicians who claim that their path of discriminative reasoning is *alone* sufficient to gain God-realization without any kind of yoga practice at all always fail in their attempt. They can offer nothing more than mere sounding words, empty talk which leaves its victims as much in the realm of illusion as they were when they first sat at the feet of these babbling gurus.

The final work of metaphysics, after it has finished its corrective and disciplinary work upon the personal emotions and mystical experience, is to abolish itself! For it must then show that all intellectual questioning and all intellectual responses are dealing with a level of reference which is mere appearance. When metaphysics realizes that it cannot touch the Real, it silences its own agitations and disdains its own edifice. A genuine metaphysics will thus always be self-destructive. Metaphysical thinking strenuously manufactures isolated and fragmentary patterns of the Real and then puts them together to make a harmonious whole. But both in the method which it uses to attack the problem of the Overself and in the result which it reaches it never gets beyond mere representations, that is, it never gets to the Real itself. It runs away within the range of a circumference which limits it in the end. Every effort is like the effort of a man seeking to lift himself up by his shoestrings—it cannot be done. The Overself of an unvivified metaphysics will always remain a mere mental construction.

§

Most systems of metaphysics being really systems of *speculation*, often involving much logical hair-splitting, it must be reiterated that the system of "metaphysics of truth" alone seeks to direct the movement of thinking along the lines which it *must* take if it is to attain truth and not, like most other systems, along the lines which it wishes to take. The truth of a metaphysical system must be guaranteed by the mystic experience out of which it is born. No other assurance can offer the same certitude and the same satisfaction in the end. Whereas every man may hold whatever metaphysical opinion pleases him, this alone holds him to face up to the inescapable necessities imposed by the severe facts brought to light by the highest mystic experience. This alone is impersonally constructed in conformity with the *hidden* pattern of life, whereas speculative metaphysics is constructed in conformity with the limited experience and personal bias of its builders. It may tersely be said that metaphysics is based on logic whereas the "metaphysics of truth" is based on life.

§

The metaphysics of truth is set out in such a way that the student believes he is proceeding step by step purely by logical deduction from ascertainable facts, that his reasoned thinking upholds the findings of transcendental experience, whereas not only is he doing this but at the same time proceeding upon a path which conforms to his own latent insight. It kindles a higher intelligence in its students. Consequently the sense either of sudden or of growing revelation may often accompany his studies, if he be sufficiently intuitive. The *authentic* metaphysics of truth can bring him close to the mystical experience of reality. Then the trigger-pull which will start the experience moving need only be something slight, perhaps a printed inspired sentence, perhaps just a single meeting with one who has learnt to live in the Overself, or perhaps a climb in the mountains. For then the mind becomes like a heap of dry wood, needing only a spark to flare up into a blazing pile. The close attention to its course of thought then becomes a yoga-path in itself.

§

Because the metaphysics of truth deals with root ideas, and because in a mentalist universe such ideas are naturally more potentially powerful and more important than materialist ones, the metaphysics of truth becomes the most worthwhile study in which man's intellect can engage. For these ideas provide him with the right patterns for shaping physical existence.

§

The metaphysics of truth must not only be rightly grasped but also reverently grasped.

§

The conclusions to which reason comes can only have obligatory force upon the reason itself, not necessarily upon the whole integral being of man. We are finally to decide the problems of life by the integration of all our human nature and not merely by the judgement of a particular part of it. To make life a matter only of rational concepts about it is to reduce it, is to make a cold abstraction from it, and thus to fall into the fallacy of taking the part for the whole. Metaphysical concepts may fully satisfy the demands of reason but this does not mean that they will therefore satisfy the demands of the totality of our being. They satisfy reason because they are the products of reason itself. But man is more than a reasoning being. His integral structure demands the feeling and the fact as well as the thought. Hence it demands the experience of nonduality as well as the concept of it, the feeling as well as the idea of it. So long as he knows it only with a limited part of his being, only as empty of emotional content and divorced from physical experience, so long will it remain incompletely known, half-seized as it were. It is at this crucial point that the seeker must realize the limitations of metaphysics and be ready to put aside as having fulfilled its particular purpose that which he has hitherto valued as a truth-path.

§

Our advice is—study metaphysics to its bottom and then make good your escape from it before you become a mere metaphysician! Once you start using metaphysical jargon you are lost.

§

[1] We assume that *The Hidden Teaching Beyond Yoga* and *The Wisdom of the Overself* are meant. —ED.

8

THE EGO

What am I?—The I-thought—The psyche

Everything we do or say, feel or think, is related back to the ego. We live tethered to its post and move in a circle. The spiritual quest is really an attempt to break out of this circle. From another point of view it is a long process of uncovering what is deeply hidden by our ego, with its desires, emotions, passions, reasonings, and activities. Taking still another point of view, it is a process of dissociating ourselves from them. But it is unlikely that the ego could be induced to end its own rule willingly. Its deceptive ways and tricky habits may lead an aspirant into believing that he is reaching a high stage when he is merely travelling in a circle. The way to break out of this circle is either to seek out the ego's source or, where that is too difficult, to become closely associated and completely obedient to a true Master. The ego, being finite, cannot produce an infinite result by its own efforts. It spins out its thoughts and sends out its desires day after day. They may be likened to cobwebs which are renewed or increased and which never disappear for long from the darkened corners of a room, however often they may be brushed away. So long as the spider is allowed to live there, so long will they reappear again. Tracking down the ego to its lair is just like hunting out the spider and removing it altogether from the room. There is no more effective or faster way to attain the goal than to ferret out its very source, offer the ego to that Source, and finally by the path of affirmations and recollections unite oneself with it.

§

The practice of the impersonal point of view under the guidance of mentalism leads in time to the discovery that the ego is an image formed in the mind, mind-made, an image with which we have got inextricably intertwined. But this practice begins to untie us and set us free.

§

All your thinking about the ego is necessarily incomplete, for it does not include the ego-thought itself. Try to do so and it slips from your hold. Only something that transcends the ego can grasp it.

§

If the ego is to perpetuate itself it must enter into all the mind's activities, not merely in the baser ones. This is exactly what does happen. The spiritual aspirations, the moral ideals, and even the mystical experiences are themselves inverted projections of the ego. Through them the "I" is able to expand itself into an "I" greater, grander, happier, and stronger than before. If they are not its own creations, providing shelter or disguise for it, then they are soon infiltrated and betrayed, undermined or permeated, until they feed and nourish the very self they were supposed to lead away from.

§

The highest goal of the quest is not illumination gained by destruction of the ego but rather by perfection of the ego. It is the function of egoism which is to be destroyed, not that which functions. The ego's rulership is to go, not the ego itself.

§

If he is willing to look for them, he will find the hidden workings of the ego in the most unsuspected corners, even in the very midst of his loftiest spiritual aspirations. The ego is unwilling to die and will even welcome this large attrition of its scope if that is its only way of escape from death. Since it is necessarily the active agent in these attempts at self-betterment, it will be in the best position to take care that they shall end as a seeming victory over itself but not an actual one. The latter can be achieved only by directly confronting it and, under Grace's inspiration, directly slaying it; this is quite different from confronting and slaying any of its widely varied expressions in weaknesses and faults. They are not at all the same. They are the branches but the ego is the root. Therefore when the aspirant gets tired of this never-ending Long Path battle with his lower nature, which can be conquered in one expression only to appear in a new one, gets weary of the self-deceptions in the much pleasanter imagined accomplishments of the Short Path, he will be ready to try the last and only resource. Here at long last he gets at the ego itself by completely surrendering it, instead of preoccupying himself with its numerous disguises—which may be ugly, as envy, or attractive, as virtue.

§

Nothing that his own will can do brings about this displacement of the ego. The divine will must do it for him.

§

Your handicap is the strong ego, the "I" which stands in the path and must be surrendered by emotional sacrifice in the blood of the heart. But once out of the way, you will feel a tremendous relief and gain peace.

§

What or who is seeking enlightenment? It cannot be the higher Self, for that is itself of the nature of Light. There then only remains the ego! This ego, the object of so many denunciations and denigrations, is the being that, transformed, will win truth and find Reality even though it must surrender itself utterly in the end as the price to be paid.

§

Egoism, the limiting of consciousness to individual life as separate from the one infinite life, is the last barrier to the attainment of unity with the infinite life.

§

As the snake is never killed by its own poison, the Overself has never been deceived by this image-making power of its own ego, although the ego itself almost continually is.

§

The ego's self-flattery keeps out most suggestions that its motives may be tainted, its service not so disinterested as it seems, and its humility a pretentious cloak for secret vanity.

§

The obstacles which prevent the spread of philosophy amongst the masses are not only the lack of culture, the lack of leisure, and the lack of interest. The most powerful of all is one which affects all social classes alike—it is the ego itself. The stubborn way in which they cherish it, the passionate strength with which they cling to it, and the tremendous belief which they give to it combine to build a fortress-wall against philosophy's serene statements of what is. People demand instead what they desire. Hence it is easier to tell them, and easier for them to receive, that God's will decides everything and that the patient submission to this will is always the best course, than to tell them that their blind attachment to the ego creates so large a part of their sufferings and that if they will not approach life impersonally there is no other course than to bear painful results of a wrong attitude. This is the way of religion. Philosophy, however, insists on telling the full truth to its students even if its detached, still voice chills their egos to the bone. Acceptance of the philosophic standpoint involves a surrender of the selfish one. This is an adjustment that only the morally heroic can make. We need not therefore expect any rush on people's part to become philosophers.

§

Although the ego claims to be engaged in a war against itself, we may be certain that it has no intention of allowing a real victory to be achieved but only a pseudo-victory. The simple conscious mind is no match for such cunning. This is one reason why out of so many spiritual seekers, so few really attain union with the Overself, why self-deceived masters soon get a following whereas the true ones are left in peace, untroubled by such eagerness.

§

Until he learns that his enemy is the ego itself, with all the mental and emotional attitudes that go with it, his efforts to liberate himself spiritually merely travel in a circle.

§

When the ego is brought to its knees in the dust, humiliated in its own eyes, however esteemed or feared, envied or respected in other men's eyes, the way is opened for Grace's influx. Be assured that this complete humbling of the inner man will happen again and again until he is purified of all pride.

§

In all human activity the ego plays its role, and so long as this activity continues the ego continues. There is much confusion and much misunderstanding about this point. We are told to kill out the ego; we are also told that the ego does not exist. The fact is it must exist if activity exists. What then is to be done by the spiritual aspirant? He can bring and eventually must bring the ego into subjection to the higher Power. It is still there, but it is put in its proper place. Now why are we told to kill out the ego if it is not possible? The answer is that it is possible, but only in what is the deepest point of meditation, called *nirvikalpa* in Sanskrit, where all thoughts are blotted out, all sense reports cease to exist, and a kind of trancelike condition comes into being. In this condition, the ego is unable to exist; it becomes inoperative, but it is certainly not killed or it would not return again after the condition ends as it must end. It does not really help to assert that the ego does not exist or if it does exist that it must be killed. The fact is it must be taken into account by everybody who seeks the higher life; whatever theories he entertains about the ego, it is there, must be reckoned with, must be confronted. Some of the confusion is due to the fact that the ego is a changing thing; it changes with time and experience, whereas the Infinite Being, the Ultimate, is changeless. In that sense reality cannot be ascribed to the ego, but only in that ultimate sense. We however are living down here, in time and in space, and to ignore that fact is to cultivate intellectual deaf and dumbness.

§

The illusion of the ego stands behind all other illusions. If it is removed, they too will be removed.

§

The Sufis talk of an experience which they call annihilation (*fana* in Persian), meaning annihilation of the personal self. There is no doubt that in the Sufi mystic experience this is what is felt to happen, but if this really happened utterly and completely, would not the characteristics of the person disappear? We find that this disappearance does not in fact take place; the characteristics continue. What then has really happened, for it must have been a tremendous happening to have been likened to annihilation or death? The secret is that what took place was a change in the attitude towards the personal self. The personal self remained, but the attitude towards it was changed. The tyranny of the ego vanished, which is not the same thing as saying that the ego itself has vanished.

§

The ego is not really killed—how without body and intellect, emotion and will, could anyone act in this world?—but the centre of being is moved out of it to the Overself.

§

Remove the concept of the ego from a man and you remove the solid ground from beneath his feet. A yawning abyss seems to open up under him. It gives the greatest fright of his life, accompanied by feelings of utter isolation and dreadful insecurity. He will then clamour urgently for the return of his beloved ego and return to safety once more—unless his determination to attain truth is so strong and so exigent that he can endure the ordeal, survive the test, and hold on until the Overself's light irradiates the abyss.

§

The ego not only obligingly provides him with a spiritual path to keep him busy for several years and thus keeps him from tracking it down to its lair; it even provides him with a spiritual illumination to authenticate that path. Need it be said that this counterfeit illumination is another form of the ego's own aggrandizement?

§

I am dubious whether anyone can be perfectly sincere if his actions do not come from this deeper source. He may believe that he is, and others may believe the same of him, but since his actions must come from his ego, which is itself spawned by deception and maintained by illusion, how can they achieve a standard which depends on complete truth and utter reality?

§

The ego is arrogant, haughty, conceited, and self-deceived.

§

That crafty old fox, the ego, is quite capable of engaging in spiritual practices of every kind and of showing spiritual aspirations of every degree of warmth.

§

If the ego can trick him into deviating from the central issue of its own destruction to some less important side issue, it will certainly do so. Its success in this effort is much more common than its failure. Few escape being tricked. The ego uses the subtlest ways to insert itself into the thinking and life of an aspirant. It cheats, tricks, exalts, and abases him by turns, if he lets it. Anatole France wrote that it is in the ability to deceive oneself that the greatest talent is shown. It is a constant habit and an instinctive reaction to defend his ego against the testimony of its own activity's unfortunate results. He will need to guard against this again and again, for its own powers are pathetically inadequate, its own foresight conspicuously absent.

§

It is both true and untrue that we cannot take up the ego with us into the life of mystical illumination. The ego is after all only a reflection, extremely limited and often distorted, of the Higher Self . . . but still it *is* a reflection. If we could bring it into correct alignment with, and submission to, the Higher Self, it would then be no hindrance to the illumined life. The ego cannot, indeed, be destroyed so long as we need its services while in the flesh; but it can be subjugated and turned into a servant instead of permitting it to remain a master. When this is understood, the philosophical ideal of a fully developed, mastered, and richly rounded ego acting as a channel for the inspiration and guidance of the Higher Self will be better appreciated. A poverty-stricken ego will naturally form a more limited channel for the expression of the Higher Self than would a more evolved one. The real enemy to be overcome is not the entity ego, but the function of egoism.

§

The ego lies to itself, lies to the man who identifies himself with it, and lies to other men.

§

The ego constantly invents ways and means to defeat the quest's objective. And it does this more indefatigably and more cunningly than ever when it pretends to co-operate with the quest and share its experiences.

§

§

Most aspirants will submit themselves to all sorts of disciplines for the body, the passions, and the mind but they will not submit to the one discipline that really matters. They cling to their precious ego like barnacles to a ship and will let everything else go except that.

§

He will advance most on the Quest who tries most to separate himself from his ego. It will be a long, slow struggle and a hard one, for the false belief that the ego is his true self grips him with hypnotic intensity. All the strength of all his being must be brought to this struggle to remove error and to establish truth, for it is an error not merely of the intellect alone but also of the emotions and of the will.

§

The Overself-consciousness is reflected into the ego, which then imagines that it has its own original, and not derived awareness.

§

We draw the very capacity to live from the Overself, the very power to think from the same source. But we confine both the capacity and the power to a small fragmentary and mostly physical sphere. Within this confinement the ego sits enthroned, served by our senses and pandered by our thoughts.

§

If we analyse the ego, we find it to be a collection of past memories retained from experience and future hopes or fears which anticipate experience. If we try to seize it, to separate it out by itself, we do not find it to exist in the present moment, only in what has gone and what is to come. In fact, it never really exists in the *NOW* but only seems to. This means that it is a phantom without substance, a false *idea*.

§

The ego-self is the creature born out of man's own doing and thinking, slowly changing and growing. The Overself is the image of God, perfect, finished, and changeless. What he has to do, if he is to fulfil himself, is to let the one shine through the other.

§

If we have written of the ego as if it were a separate and special entity. a fixed thing, a reality in its own right, this is only because of the inescapable necessities of logical human thinking and the inexorable limitations of traditional human language. For in FACT the "I" cannot be separated from its thoughts since it is composed of them, and them alone. The ego is, in short, only an idea, or a trick that the thought process plays on itself.

§

The persona, the mask which he presents to the world, is only one part of his ego. The conscious nature, composed of thoughts and feelings, is the second part. The hidden store of tendencies, impulses, memories, and ideas—formerly expressed and then reburied, or brought over, from earlier lives, and all latent—is the third part.

§

It is as hard for the ego to judge itself fairly, to look at its actions with a correct perspective as for a man to lift himself by his own braces. It simply cannot do it; its capacity to find excuses for itself is unlimited—even the excuse of righteousness, even the excuse of the quest of truth. All that the aspirant can hope to do is to thin down the volume of the ego's operations and to weaken the strength of the ego itself; but to get rid of the ego entirely is something beyond his own capacity. Consequently, an outside power must be called in. There is only one such power available to him, although it may manifest itself in two different ways, and that is the power of Grace. Those ways are: either direct help by his own higher Self or personal help from a higher man, that is, an illumined teacher. He may call for the first at any time, but he may not rightly call for the second before he has done enough work on himself and made enough advance to justify it.

§

If we could pin down this sense of "I-ness" which is behind all we think, say, and do, and if we could part it from the thoughts, feelings, and physical body by doing so, we would find it to be rooted in and linked with the higher Power behind the whole world.

§

One day he will feel utterly tired of the ego, will see how cunningly and insidiously it has penetrated all his activities, how even in supposedly spiritual or altruistic activities he was merely working for the ego. In this disgust with his earthly self, he will pray for liberation from it. He will see how it tricked him in the past, how all his years have been monopolized by its desires, how he sustained, fed, and cherished it even when he thought he was spiritualizing himself or serving others. Then he will pray fervently to be freed from it, he will seek eagerly to *dis*-identify himself and yearn ardently to be swallowed up in the nothingness of God.

§

We all think, experience, feel, and identify with the "I." But who really knows what it is? To do this we need to look inside the mind, not at what it contains, as psychologists do, but at what it is in itself. If we persevere, we may find the "I" behind the "I."

§

This is effected by voluntarily and deliberately regarding his person as the earth which is occupied with these space-time movements and the hidden observer as the sun which remains stationary all the while. This is the higher individuality which he shall always preserve whereas he will preserve the personality only intermittently. Thus the "I" is not excluded in the end but reinterpreted in a manner which completely transforms it. When a man has advanced to this Witness's standpoint, he understands the difference between the descriptive phrase, "I am the great Caesar" and the terse statement "I am."

§

It would be wrong to believe that there are two separate minds, two independent consciousnesses within us—one the lower ego-mind, and the other, the higher Overself-mind—with one, itself unwatched, watching the other. There is but one independent illuminating mind and everything else is only a limited and reflected image within it. The ego is a thought-series dependent on it.

§

Only the deepest kind of reflection or the most exciting kind of mystical experience or the compelling force of a prophet's revelation can bring man to the great discovery that his personal ego is not the true centre of his being.

§

The true self of man is hidden in a central core of stillness, a central vacuum of silence. This core, this vacuum occupies only a pinpoint in dimension. All around it there is ring of thoughts and desires constituting the imagined self, the ego. This ring is constantly fermenting with fresh thoughts, constantly changing with fresh desires, and alternately bubbling with joy or heaving with grief. Whereas the centre is forever at rest, the ring around it is never at rest; whereas the centre bestows peace, the ring destroys it.

§

Every discussion which is made from an egoistic standpoint is corrupted from the start and cannot yield an absolutely sure conclusion. The ego puts its own interest first and twists every argument, word, even fact to suit that interest.

§

If his egoism is too strong, the highest part of the Overself's light will be quite unable to get through into his consciousness, no matter how fervent his aspiration for it may be.

§

An ego we have, we are; its existence is inescapable if the cosmic thought is to be activated and the human evolution in it is to develop. Why has it become, then, a source of evil, friction, suffering, and horror? The energy and instinct, the intelligence and desire which are contained in each individualized fragment of consciousness, each compounded "I," are not originally evil in themselves; but when the clinging to them becomes extreme, selfishness becomes strong. There is a failure in equilibrium and the gentler virtues are squeezed out, the understanding that others have rights, the feeling of goodwill and sympathy, accommodation for the common welfare—all depart. The natural and right attention to one's needs becomes enlarged to the point of tyranny. The ego then exists only to serve itself at all costs, aggressive to, and exploitive of, all others. It must be repeated: an ego there must be if there is to be a World-Idea. But it has to be put, and kept, in its place (which is not a hardened selfishness). It must adjust to two things: to the common welfare and to the source of its own being. Conscience tells him of the first duty, whether heeded or not; Intuition tells him of the second one, whether ignored or not. For, overlooked or misconstrued, the relation between evil and man must not hide the fact that the energies and intelligence used for evil derive in the beginning from the divine in man. They are Godgiven but turned to the service of ungodliness. This is the tragedy, that the powers, talents, and consciousness of man are spent so often in hatred and war when they could work harmoniously for the World-Idea, that his own disharmony brings his own suffering and involves others. But each wave of development must take its course, and each ego must submit in the end. He who hardens himself within gross selfishness and rejects his gentler spiritual side becomes his own Satan, tempting himself. Through ambition or greed, through dislike or hate which is instilled in others, he must fall in the end, by the Karma he makes, into destruction by his own negative side.

§

When he begins to see that passion is something which arises within him and with which he involuntarily associates his whole selfhood, he begins to see that the metaphysical study of "I" and the mystical discipline of thought can help greatly to free him from it.

§

His first mental act is to think himself into being. He is the maker of his own "I." This does not mean that the ego is his own personal invention alone. The whole world-process brings everything about, including the ego and the ego's own self-making.

§

§

When his own ego becomes intolerable to him with increasing frequency, he may take this as a good sign that he is moving forward on this road.

§

The ego turns ceaselessly around itself.

§

What a ridiculous psychological spectacle it is to see the ego preening itself at its spirituality!

§

The ego is hard at work all the time—either blatantly and obviously or secretly and insidiously.

§

The desire to continue life in the ego contains all possible desires. This explains why the hardest of all renunciations for which a man can be asked is that of his ego. He is willing even to suffer mortifications of the flesh or humiliations of his pride rather than that last and worst crucifixion.

§

Even irreproachable conduct and impeccable manners belong to the ego and not to the enlightenment.

§

He believes he is surrendering to his higher self when all the time he is only surrendering to his own ego.

§

The ego will creep even into his spiritual work or aspiration, so that he will take from the teaching only what suits his own personal ends, and ignore the rest, or only what suits his own personal comfort, and be averse to the rest.

§

Everyone is crucified by his own ego.

§

The ego does not rule men through their animalistic and materialistic desires only. It takes charge, and actively manages, their spiritual aspirations also!

§

He must learn to face the startling fact that the human ego carries itself even into his loftiest aspirations for the Divine. Even there, in that rarefied atmosphere, it is seeking for itself, for what it wants, and always for its own preservation. This is merely to enlarge the area of the ego's operations and not, to use Aurobindo's word, to divinize it.

§

It would be an error to believe that it is the Overself which reincarnates. It does not. But its offspring—the ego—does.

§

The ego is defiant, cunning, and resistant to the end.

§

The ego worships no other God than itself.

§

The ego is by nature a deceiver and in its operations a liar. For if it revealed things as they really are, or told what is profoundly true, it would have to expose its own self as the arch-trickster pretending to be the man himself and proffering the illusion of happiness.

§

9

FROM BIRTH TO REBIRTH

Experience of dying—After death—Rebirth —Past tendencies—Destiny—Freedom—Astrology

A time comes when the prudent person, feeling intuitively or knowing medically that he has entered the last months or years of his life, ought to prepare himself for death. Clearly an increasing withdrawal from worldly life is called for. Its activities, desires, attachments, and pleasures must give way more and more to repentance, worship, prayer, asceticism, and spiritual recollectedness. It is time to come home.

§

All humans pass through the portals of death but which of them pass through it *knowingly*, consciously, and calmly?

§

What sort of a death experience is he likely to have? What if he dies, as Ramana Maharshi died, as Ramakrishna died, as heroes of the Spirit—some anonymous and obscure, others famous—known to this author died, of that dreadful and contemporary malady, cancer? I can only tell what I have seen and heard when present during the last days as privileged co-sharer of the unbelievable atmosphere. To each there came a vision, a light seen, first far off, later all around; first a pinpoint, later a ray, then a wide shaft, lastly filling the whole room. And with the Light came peace; it came as an accompaniment to the cancer's pain, a compensation that as it grew made the peace grow and gave detachment, until to the amazement of doctors, nurses, family, the triumphant words were uttered before the final act, Spirit's victory over matter proclaimed. This is not to say that it makes no difference whether one dies quietly in sleep through nothing worse than age, or whether one dies through cancer, that peace and pain are equally acceptable to the emotions of an illumined man. I do not write here of the extreme fanatical ascetic. To him it may be a matter of indifference.

§

If there is any loss of consciousness during the change called death, it is only a brief one, as brief or briefer than a night's sleep. Many of the departed do not even know at the time what has really happened to them and still believe themselves to be physically alive. For they find themselves apparently able to see others and hear voices and touch things just as before. Yet all these experiences are entirely immaterial, and take place within a conscious mind that has no fleshly brain.

§

We think that birth is the beginning and death the end of all for us. Theologians and metaphysicians have argued and disputed over this as far back as the memory of man can go, so who are we to say "yea" or "nay" to them? But when the noise and din of their jarring voices fade into the distance, when the quieter hours of evening wrap us around, fold upon fold, then it is that a strange and sublime sense steals upon us, if we will but permit its coming, and says: "My child, what they think and what they say does not really matter. I am by your side and I shall never fail you. Smile at Death if you wish, or fear it—but I am with you always."

§

The dying man should cross his arms over his chest with interlaced fingers. He should withdraw the mind from everything earthly and raise it lovingly in the highest aspiration.

§

This is the way a man may best die—while resting on a chair or couch or sleeping in a bed, a peaceful expression on his face as if seeing or hearing something of unusual beauty, a pleased expression around the mouth.

§

What better death than to be drawn into the divine being, lost in its peace and radiance! What more miserable than to be wrenched away from earthly attachments while trying to clutch them!

§

It is a teaching in both India and China that by concentrating his thoughts during his dying moments on the name of his spiritual leader with full faith, undivided ardour, and sincere deep attention, a man saves himself some or all of the post-mortem purificatory torments that he would otherwise have to undergo. It is also written that if he prefers to concentrate on the kind of environment in which his next birth is to appear, he contributes toward its possible realization.

§

Our habitual trend of thinking on earth will necessarily be the habitual trend of thinking with which we shall start spirit-life although we shall not end that life with it.

§

If you want to know where you will go after you are dead, I shall tell you for I have been there. You go nowhere, no place. As awareness of this earth and the earthly body fade away, soon after dying, you will simply enter the condition of awareness to which your character entitles you.

§

It is said death levels all. This is true only on the visible side of it, for on the other side each goes to his own state of consciousness—what he has fitted himself for. Untied from the body, he enters the atmosphere to which he belongs.

§

One must develop wisdom and self-control in this life, for if he does not, he may suffer after death. He may be full of animal appetites but have no body with which to satisfy them. Wisdom and discipline will enable him to find a relatively easy adjustment.

§

The human mind is compelled by its own particular characteristics to create a picture of the outside world in a certain way and in no other way. The kind of world it experiences follows naturally from the kind of perceptions it exercises. Many different planes of existence would therefore be open to it were these characteristics to be altered abruptly in many different ways. We may be—indeed we are—living alongside of millions of other human minds of whom we are totally unaware merely because they do not come within the present restricted range of our perceptions. Life after death in another world is not merely a theological possibility but a scientific probability and a philosophic actuality.

§

Death is the entrance to a new kind of being, a renewed form of life, another period in which old experience is assimilated and the next phase (reincarnation) prepared for.

§

The first experience of death is not the last, for it is followed, after the due interval of appropriate experience in another condition of being, by a second death.

§

Cremation is a definite and emphatic challenge. If one really believes that the soul of man is his real self, or even if one believes that the thinking power of man is his real self, then there can be no objection to it, but, on the contrary, complete approval of it. The method of burying dead bodies is fit only for one who believes that this thinking power is a product of the body's brain, that is, for a materialist.

§

We need not always deplore the fact that we have to die. As Goethe remarked, "Nature is bound to give me another form of existence when the present one can no longer sustain my spirit." What we should deplore is dying without having known these best moments of living, these glimpses of the Overself.

§

For those who have made sufficient progress with the Quest, death is not a frightening experience. Once the exit from the body has been made, the rest is pleasant and peaceful.

§

The man who has lived quite selfishly and without care for the rights of others will suffer from strange visions in the after-death state. Those whom he has seriously wronged will appear before him repeatedly, reproaching him in some cases or denouncing him in others. This will continue until it becomes a kind of ghost-haunted torment, at first fatiguing him and later wearing him out to such an extent that he will fall into a sickly, wretched, fear-ridden state. At the lowest point of his misery, some other discarnate being will be sent to help him, to lead him to recognize his sinfulness and persuade him to repent. This entity may be a loving relative, an advanced mystic out of the body temporarily in sleep, or the man's own guardian angel. When this change of heart is effected, when the man confesses, repents, and resolves to mend his character, his persecution will stop.

§

The after-death condition of certain rare men like Jesus, Buddha, and Krishna is necessarily a rare one. They continue the beneficent work of urging and helping men to rise above their lower natures which was inaugurated when manifest in the flesh whilst on earth, albeit it must be understood that it will necessarily fail to achieve the same degree of sharp effectiveness which the use of a physical body would have given it. Nevertheless, what it loses in depth it gains in width, for although personal attainment is swift among their disciples during their lifetime, popular influence among the masses is able to spread like ripples only after their death. Only a materialistic outlook of the universe will fail to understand that such a man does not ever die and that his true existence continues, even when he is not in incarnation, and that his saving power is still made available for others even then. So long as men call earnestly upon their name or cherish their memory with reverence, so long will they continue their spirit-existence. They do not die, do not really disappear.

§

Heredity can answer for a man's face and form and nervous type but it cannot answer for his genius. Here it is necessary to bring in something quite different—the development of his talent through repeated earth lives.

§

There is no need for anyone to seek to know what his previous incarnations were. If the memories should come, they represent something abnormal. Nature does not desire that we should be hampered in the present by the memory of the past, when the past itself stretches away for such a long time. You need not trouble yourself therefore about previous incarnations, but concentrate fully on your present one so as to make it as worthy as you can.

§

We come back to this earth of ours and not to some other earth because it is here that we sow the seeds of thought, of feeling, and of action and therefore it is here that we must reap their harvest. Nature is orderly and just, consistent and continuous.

§

There is no direct and incontrovertible proof of reincarnation, but there is logical evidence for it. Why should there be certain abilities almost without previous training? Why should I be possessed at an early age of the mental abilities of a writer, or someone else of a musician? Heredity alone cannot account for it. But it is perfectly accounted for if we consider them to a subconscious memory. I am unwittingly remembering and using again my own capabilities from a former birth. This is possible only because I am *mind*. Mind alone can continue itself. Capacities in any field cannot appear out of nothing. The individual who shows them forth is repeating them out of his own deeper memory. There is the evidence of Nature. When I wake up in the morning, I pick up all that I had the day before. I remember my own individuality and use the same literary talents as before. Otherwise, I could never write again, or someone else could never sing. The basis of this reminiscence is not a physical occurrence, but a mental one.

§

We travel from one body to another, with suitable and necessary rest-periods in between them. From each we gather experiences; in each we learn and unlearn, sin and suffer, act aright and benefit. In the end, amid advance and relapse, there is the fullness and satisfaction of ripened manhood, cleaned, leaving behind more animality.

§

Freud's postulate of the Unconscious mind as a structure of forgotten unrecoverable memories is a precursor of the rebirth theory. It prepares the way for scientific acceptance of the latter and should inevitably lead to it. In turn, it throws light on the doctrine of karma. For the ego which revives out of apparent nothingness is the conscious mind which reappears out of the unconscious. When the production of these idea-energies (that is, tendencies, *samskaras*) is brought to rest, then they can never again objectify into a physical environment, a fresh rebirth, and thus man becomes karma-free and enters Nirvana. As long as he believes that he is the body he must reincarnate in the body.

§

If the teaching of rebirths is false then the justice of God is false too. There is no other way in which tragic situations of human life can be equitably adjusted or reasonably explained in the human mind.

§

Each reincarnation unfolds its story largely prewritten though it may be and is weighted by the unseen past. Yet some fresh possibilities come with it also through the introduction of fresh environments, scenes, acts, and happenings.

§

We return to birth so long as the ego is still our master and we tenant a form that is good or bad, whole or maimed, healthy or sick, in conformity with our just deserts under the law of Recompense.

§

The official alliance of a single Christian group with the Roman Empire in the reign of Constantine was fatal first to the so-called Pagans and later to nearly all the other groups of Christendom. The latter were persecuted, imprisoned, or killed and their writings burnt. The Emperor Magnus Maximus even put the Bishop of Avila to death for his beliefs. The Emperor Theodosius made death the prescribed penalty for all believers in Manichean Christianity which taught reincarnation. The vigour with which the Emperor Justinian proscribed and destroyed heretical books and documents left little record for later generations to know what other Christians had taught and believed on this tenet of rebirth. Justinian slew more than a million heretics in the Near East alone. Several canons in the service of Orleans cathedral in France were, some centuries later, burnt alive for embracing these doctrines. The diffusion of this single idea in the Western lands is likely to start questioning and inquiry into its background, history, and doctrinal ramifications. This may lead in turn to startling discoveries about what really happened not only to this tenet but to others of Oriental derivation which were stamped out ruthlessly.

§

The ego's desires, habits, and ways of thought have been established through many earth lives.

§

When he looks back upon the long series of earth lives which belongs to his past, he is struck afresh by the supreme wisdom of Nature and by the supreme necessity of this principle of recurring embodiment. If there had been only one single continuous earth life, his progress would have been brought to an end, he would have been cluttered up by his own past, and he could not have advanced in new directions. This past would have surrounded him like a circular wall. How unerring the wisdom and how infinite the mercy which, by breaking this circle of necessity, gives him the chance of a fresh start again and again, sets him free to make new beginnings! Without these breaks in his life-sequences, without the advantages of fresh surroundings, different circumstances, and new contacts, he could not have lifted himself to ever higher levels, but would only have stagnated or fallen to lower ones.

§

We are given one life, one day, one present time, one conscious space-time level to concentrate on so that Nature's business in us shall not be interfered with. Yet other lives, other days, other times, other levels of consciousness already exist just as much at this very moment, even though we do not apprehend them, and await our meeting and experience by a fated necessity.

§

The personal development and mental discoveries which have been made in past incarnations do not have to be repeated afresh in the same way with each new one. What happens however is a swift recapitulation or distillation of the whole historic previous experience during the first half of the new incarnation.

§

The tendencies brought over from earlier births determine his character and conduct but the impact of his present surroundings upon his personality, the influence of his latest race, religion, education, and class upon his psyche, the suggestions absorbed from this historical period, newspaper reading, and artistic culture modify or colour both.

§

What we were in the past is not important. What we are now is important. What we intend to make of ourselves in the future is vitally important.

§

The unity between our character and our destiny is inseparable; the connection between our way of thinking and the course of events is unerring.

§

Sufficient unto the day is the evil thereof say the apathetic, the sluggish, the inert, and they refuse to look forward. They experience the evil alright. If time is simultaneous and the future already exists, what is the use of making any effort? This despairing but plausible objection overlooks the parallel fact that the future is not fixed for all eternity; it is always fluctuating because it is always liable to modification by the intrusion of new factors, such as an intense effort to alter it or an intense interference by another person. The future exists, but the future changes at the same time.

§

The unexpected events which happen to us apparently without cause or connection in our conduct constitute fate. The tendencies by whose influences and the circumstances by whose compulsion we act the way we do, constitute necessity. The results of those actions constitute Karma (recompense).

§

What man really dominates his destiny? The great person may succeed in modifying it, but the psychological and physical factors with which the ordinary person starts the course of life are already in his genes and predicate both character and fortune. He is at the mercy of events until he learns this secret of modifying and influencing them.

§

Both the benign and the malefic are already concealed in destiny's decrees for the child at birth. To the extent that outer fortunes are directly traceable to inner tendencies, to that extent they are controllable and alterable. How large or how small a part of its life is quite beyond its free choice and direction is itself a matter of fate.

§

There are cosmic compulsions which none escape and which permeate human destiny, for they are part of the World-Idea.

§

Those who are unaware of the penalties they incur by misuse of the power to think and the will to act are in urgent need of the teaching of karma.

§

Fate is what an outside will imposes upon us, irrespective of our merits or demerits. Karma is what unconsciously our own will has imposed upon us through the come-back of our actions.

§

What a higher power has decreed must come to pass. But what a man has made for himself he can modify or unmake. The first is fate, the second destiny. The one comes from outside his personal ego, the other from his own faults. The evolutionary will of his soul is part of the nature of things but the consequences of his own actions remain, however slightly, within his own control.

§

The Law of Karma makes each man responsible for his own life. The materialist who denies karma and places all the blame and burden upon the shoulders of environment and heredity denies responsibility. He begins and ends with an illusion.

§

Karma's will could not prevail in one special part of our life and not in any other parts, nor in one special event of our life and not in the others. It could not be here but not there, in the past but not now. Nor going even farther still, could it confine itself only to major items and not to minor ones. It must be ever present or never present at all. If it puts more destiny into the happenings we experience than lets the Westerner feel comfortable, we must remember that other facet of truth, the creative and godlike intelligence in our deeper humanity and the measure of freedom which accompanies it.

§

Nobody succeeds in extinguishing karma merely because he intellectually denies its existence, as the votaries of some cults do. If, however, they first faced up to their karma, dealt with it and used it for self-cultivation and self-development, and then only recognized its illusoriness from the ultimate standpoint, their attitude would be a correct one. Indeed, their attempt to deny karma prematurely shows a disposition to rebel against the divine wisdom, a short-sighted and selfish seeking of momentary convenience at the cost of permanent neglect of the duty to grow spiritually.

§

Whereas fate (in the original and Greek sense of the word) is decreed by whatever Powers there be, karma is the result of our own doing.

§

The correct meaning of the word "karma" is willed action through body, speech, and mind. It does not include the results of this action, especially those which produce or influence rebirth. Such inclusion has come into popular concepts, but shows a loose use of the term. Karma is cause set going by the will, not effect at all. The phrase "Law of Recompense" is therefore not satisfactory and a better one is needed.

§

If he accepts this tenet of karma coupled with rebirth, then his awakening to a sense of responsibility for his life and the course it takes should lead in turn to a feeling of the need for self-discipline.

§

The law of recompense is not nullified nor proved untrue by the objector's proffered evidence of hard ruthless individuals who rose to influence and affluence over the crushed lives of other persons. The happiness or well-being of such individuals cannot be properly judged by their bank account alone or their social position alone. Look also into the condition of their physical health, of their mental health, of their conscience in the dream state, of their domestic and family relations. Look, too, into their next reincarnation. Then, and only then, can the law's presence or absence be rightly judged.

§

If philosophy accepted the doctrine of complete fatalism, it could hold out no hope to mankind. If it said that every event in the history of the world was predestined from the very beginning; that each event in a man's life was preordained from before his birth; that no thought, no word, and no deed could have been avoided, then its mystical teaching would have been unnecessary, its metaphysical teaching would have been falsified, and its moral teaching would have been in vain. But philosophy has never been shipwrecked upon the rocks of such foolish fatalism. It says that what happens inside you is intimately connected with what happens outside you, that thought, feeling, will, intuition, or character makes its secret contributions towards the events of your life, and that to the extent to which you begin to control yourself, you will begin to control your personal welfare.

§

If we look at men in the mass, we *must* believe in the doctrine of fatalism. It applies to them. They are compelled by their environments, they struggle like animals to survive precisely because they are not too far removed from the animal kingdom which was the field of their previous reincarnational activity. They react like automatons under a dead weight of karma, move like puppets out of the blind universal instincts of nature. But this is not the end of the story. It is indeed only its beginning. For here and there a man emerges from the herd who *is* becoming an individual, creatively making himself into a fully human being. For him each day is a fresh experience, each experience is unique, each tomorrow no longer the completely inevitable and quite forseeable inheritance of all its yesterdays. From being enslaved by animality and fatality, he is becoming free in full humanity and creativity.

§

Many Orientals put all happenings under the iron rule of karma. There is no free will, no individual control over them. One has to accept them fatalistically and, if dismayed by their evil, turn to the Spiritual Source for the only real happiness. In mental attitude, in personal inward response to events, lies one's chief freedom of will.

It might, however, be questioned how far such freedom is illusory, since the response, the attitude, are themselves conditioned by the past and many other things. It is quite correct to state that the past inclines us to think and act in a certain way. But it is also admitted that we can grow, can improve our lives and change in the course of time. So this is an admission that we are free to choose to grow or to remain exactly as we were. A man who commits robbery with violence may say that he is fated to act violently. With each offense, he is arrested and suffers imprisonment. After this has happened several times he begins to change his course. Eventually he fears imprisonment so much so that he resists temptation and ceases to be a criminal. This change of mental attitude was an act of free will. His past inclined him to the old direction but it did not compel him.

One of my readers claims that "the decision he makes is the only one he can make at the time." But the real situation is that it is the only decision he was *willing* to make. A man may not be conscious at first of conflict between two impulses inside himself. It is the presence of the Overself behind the ego which sets up the conflict. At first it remains in the subconscious, then in a dim vague way it becomes conscious. He may dismiss the alternative choice, but it was there all the time. Jesus said: "What you sow, you shall reap." The criminal chooses not to believe it, because he does not want to believe it. Inclinations from the past do not compel a man, but he unconsciously uses them as an excuse and claims he can do nothing else. The will is being expressed even when the man thinks he is, and seems to be, compelled to act in a certain way. It is expressed in the mental attitude adopted towards the situations in which he finds himself. Whenever he accepts the ordinary materialistic, negative, egoistic view of a situation, he is actually choosing that view. He *is* choosing even though he believes the contrary is true.

§

"We ought to exert our efforts in all (things) as though they were absolutely free, and God will do as he sees fit." —Maimonides

§

Karma compels us so long as we do not anticipate the direction of its course by intelligence, nor endeavour to divert its flow by self-determination.

§

It is tendencies and dislikes which among other things stand in the way of perceiving and receiving truth. It is being bound to these things at the deepest level of personal thought and feeling which keeps the aspirant ignorant. If instead of being held by them he would shift his position and simply hold them quite loosely, he would then be freer in himself for the truth. Because he is a person, an individual, he possesses certain colourings peculiar to himself. He is an ego functioning in the body and in the world. He has various possessions because he has to live among and use the various objects needed for his life in the world. The change which enlightenment brings is not necessarily to throw them out. He can not throw his body out, he can not throw the personal colouring out, but he can—and this is what enlightenment does—free himself from being bound to them. This is what nonattachment really signifies. Too often an aspirant misunderstands this point. If he lets himself be deceived by books, however ancient and authoritative, or by gurus, however knowledgeable, reputed, or esteemed, into pursuing inner freedom in the wrong way, he may end either in disappointment and frustration or in self-deception and deception of others. The conditions under which he lives have been dictated by karma in the largest possible meaning of the word. Those conditions can be modified and perhaps changed only to a limited extent, for there are limitations within himself and within the karma which prevent his going any farther. In understanding this and in accepting the actualities of life and self, he can claim and find the only true freedom that is findable. All else is clamour or illusion.

§

In the final chapter of *A Search in Secret India*, I provided some hints of the cyclic nature of life, writing of how "every life has its aphelion and perihelion" (paraphrase). Now the time has come to particularize this statement and cast some light on the great mystery of fate and fortune. The knowledge of this truth renders a man better able to meet all situations in life, both pleasant and unpleasant, in the right way. "With an understanding of the auspicious and inauspicious issues of events, the accomplishment of great Life-tasks becomes possible," taught a Chinese sage. According to the Chinese wisdom, Tao, in its secondary meaning, is the divinely fixed order of things; under this there are four cycles of history. The first two are "yang" and the last two are "yin." This law of periodicity refers to individual lives no less than to cosmic existence. Every human life is therefore subject to periodical changes of destiny whose inner significance needs to be comprehended before one can rightly act. Hence the method of grappling with destiny must necessarily vary in accord with the particular rhythm which has come into the calendar of one's life. Every situation in human existence must find its appropriate treatment, and the right treatment can only be consciously adopted by the sage who has established inner harmony with the law of periodicity.

The sage seeks to do the right thing at the right moment, for automatic adjustment to these varying fortunes. This is called, in the Chinese Mystery School teaching, "mounting the dragon at the proper time and driving through the sky." Hence I have written in *The Quest of the Overself* that the wise man knows when to resist fate and when to yield to it. Knowing the truth above of the ebb and flow of destiny, he acts always in conformity with this inner understanding. Sometimes he will be fiercely active, other times completely quiescent, sometimes fighting tragedy to the utmost, but at other times resigned and surrendered. Everything has its special time and he does not follow any course of action at the wrong time. He is a free agent, yes, but he must express that freedom rightly, because he must work, as all must work, within the framework of cosmic law. To initiate the correct change in his activities at the incorrect time and amid wrong environing circumstances would be rash and lead to failure; to start a new and necessary enterprise at the wrong moment and amid the wrong situation of life, would also lead to failure. The same changes, however, if begun at another time and amid other conditions will lead to success. The sage consults his innermost prompting which, being in harmony with truth, guides him to correct action in particular situations accordingly. We can neither dictate to him as to what he should do, nor prescribe principles for his guidance, nor even predict how he is going to respond to any set of circumstances.

The proper course of action which anyone should adopt depends ultimately upon his time and place both materially and spiritually. In short, human wisdom must always be related to the cosmic currents of destiny and the divine goal. Man must be adaptable to circumstances, flexible to destiny, if his life is to be both wise and content. Unfortunately, the ordinary man does not perceive this, and creates much of his own unhappiness, works much of his own ruin. It is only the sage who, having surrendered the personal Ego, can create his own harmony with Nature and fate and thus remain spiritually undisturbed and at peace. As Kung-Fu-Tze, (Confucius, in Western parlance) pithily says: "The superior man can find himself in no situation in which he is not himself." The wise man defers action and waits if necessary for the opportune and auspicious moment; he will not indulge in senseless struggles or untimely efforts. He knows how and when to wait and by his waiting render success certain. No matter how talented he be, if his circumstances are unfavourable and the time inopportune to express them, he will resign himself for the while and devote his time to self-preparation and self-cultivation and thus be ready for the opportunity which he knows the turn of time's wheel must bring him. He puts himself into alignment with the hidden principle which runs through man and matter, striking effectively when the iron is hot, refraining cautiously when it is cold. He knows the proper limits of his activity even in success and does not go beyond them. He knows when to advance and when to retreat, when to be incessantly active and when to lie as still as a sleeping mouse. Thus he escapes from committing serious errors.

§

Whether he enters birth in penurious squalor or in palatial grandeur, he will come to his own SPIRITUAL level again in the end. Environment is admittedly powerful to help or hinder, but the Spirit's antecedents are still more powerful and finally INDEPENDENT OF IT.

§

One important use of an astrological horoscope is principally to detect the presence of new opportunity, and to warn against the presence of dangerous tests, snares, and pitfalls. It is often hard to make a decision, when an important crossroad presents itself, if one of the roads leads to disaster and the other to good fortune. At such a time a correct horoscope will be helpful in arriving at a right decision.

§

Astrology was given by the primeval sages as a revelation to early mankind. No human being on earth could have created out of his own head this mysterious science of astrology. It was given to help human beings who still were far from spiritual attainment, as a concession to their human nature. But when man has come by spiritual advancement, under the grace of God, directly, or through a teacher, it is not possible to construct a horoscope that will perfectly fit him because his testimony will always be liable to modification and alteration.

§

10

HEALING OF THE SELF

Karma, connection with health—Life-force in health and sickness —Drugs & drink in mind-body relationship —Etheric and astral bodies in health and sickness —Mental disorders—Psychology and psychoanalysis

After he has felt the divine power and presence within himself as the reward of his meditative search, he may turn it towards the healing of his body's ailments. This would be impossible if he were less than relaxed, peaceful, assured, if either fear or desire introduced their negative presence and thus obstructed his receptivity to the healing-power's penetration. When the contact is successfully made, he should draw the power to every atom of his body and let it be permeated. The cure could be had at a single treatment, if he could sit still and let the work go on to completion. But although the power is unlimited, his patience is not. And so he must treat himself day after day until the outer and physical result matches the inner and spiritual achievement.

§

There are no miracles in Nature, but there are happenings to which science possesses no key. The human consciousness, for instance, is capable of manifesting powers which contradict psychological knowledge, just as the human body is capable of manifesting phenomena which contradict medical knowledge. Both powers and phenomena may seem miraculous, but they really issue forth from the hidden laws of man's own being. The processes take place in the dark only to us.

§

It is the routine activity of the brain, and especially the mental tendency toward anxiety and fear which is expressed through it, which interferes with Nature's healing processes—whether these be spiritual or physical or both—or obstructs them or delays them or defeats them completely. This anxiety arises through the sufferer's confinement to his personal ego and through his ignorance of the arrangements in the World-Idea's body-pattern for the human body's protective care. The remedy is in his own hands. It is twofold: first to change from negative to positive thinking through acquiring either faith in this care or else knowledge of it; second, to give body and brain as total a rest as his capacity allows, which is achieved through fasting and in meditation. The first change is more easily made by immediately substituting the positive and opposite idea as soon as the negative one appears in his field of consciousness. He trains himself not to accept any harmful thought and watches his mind during this period of training. This constructive thought must be held and nourished with firm concentration for as long as possible. The second change calls for an abstinence from all thoughts, a mental quiet, as well as an abstinence from all food for one to three days.

§

In a broad general division, philosophy finds three causes of sickness. They are wrong thinking, wrong living, and bad karma. But because karma merely brings back to us the results of the other two, we may even limit the causes of disease to them. And again because conduct is ultimately the expression of thought, we may limit the cause of disease finally to a single one of wrong thinking. But this is to deal with the matter in a metaphysical, abstract, and ultimate way. It is best when dealing with sickness in a practical way to keep to the threefold analysis of possible causes. Yet the matter must not be oversimplified as certain schools of unorthodox healing have oversimplified it, for the thinking which produced the sickness may belong to the far past, to some earlier reincarnation, and not necessarily to the present one, or it may belong to the earlier years of the present incarnation. In those cases, there is the fruit of an unknown earlier sowing, not necessarily of a known present one. Therefore, it may not be enough merely to alter one's present mode of thought to insure the immediate obliteration of the sickness. If we shoot a bullet in the wrong direction, we cannot control its course once it has left the gun. But we can change the direction of a second shot if we realize our error. We can continue our efforts, however, to change our first thinking, to get rid of negative harmful thoughts and feelings and thus improve our character. For if we do this, the type of physical karma manifesting as the sickness which they create will at least not come to us in the future, even if we cannot avoid inheriting it in the present from our former lives. Study of this picture would reveal what sickness as a karma of wrong thinking really means and why it often cannot be healed by a mere change of present thought alone. The proof of this statement lies in the fact that some people are born with certain sicknesses or with liability to certain diseases, or else acquire them as infants or as children before they have even had the opportunity to think wrongly at all and while they are still in a state of youthful innocence and purity of thought. Therefore it is not the wrong thoughts of this present incarnation which could have brought on such sickness in their case. Nor can it be correct to suggest that they have inherited these sicknesses, for the parents may be right-thinking and high-living people. By depriving themselves of faith in the belief in successive lives on earth, the Christian Scientists deprive themselves of a more satisfactory explanation of the problem of sickness than the one they have. They say that it was caused by wrong thinking, and yet they cannot say how it is that a baby or a child has been thinking wrongly to have been born with or to have acquired at an early age a sickness for which it is not responsible and for which its parents are not responsible.

§

Iconoclastic science came into the world and in a few short centuries turned most of us into sceptics. It may therefore surprise the scientists to be told that within two or three decades their own further experiments and their own new instruments will enable them to penetrate into, and prove the existence of, a superphysical world. But the best worth of these eventual discoveries will be in their positive demonstration of the reality of a moral law pervading man's life—the law that we shall reap after death what we have sown before it, and the law that our own diseased thoughts have created many of our own bodily diseases.

§

The theoretical basis of this teaching about the physical manifestation of mental sickness lies in mentalism. The practical basis lies in observation and experience.

§

The psychological causes of disease have only recently come under investigation by the strict methods of modern science, but the general fact of their existence was known thousands of years ago. Plato, for instance, said: "This is the great error of our day, that physicians separate the inner being from the body."

§

It would be just as wrong to argue that *every* physical disease proves a moral fault or mental deformity to exist, as it would be to argue that the absence of such disease proves moral or mental perfection to have been attained. Many animals are quite healthy too!

§

It might be said that most *organic* physical disease is karmically caused and most functional physical sickness is mentally caused.

§

Healing Exercise and Meditation: (1) Lie flat on back on flat surface (for example, rug on floor). (2) Let body go completely limp. (3) Relax breathing with eyes shut, that is, slow down breathing below normal. Slowly exhale, then inhale; hold breath two seconds, then exhale slowly again. Repeat for three to five minutes. Whilst inhaling, think that you are drawing in curative force from Nature. Whilst exhaling, think that there is being taken out of your body the ill conditions. (Note that on the inhaled breath, you—the ego—are referred to as the active agent, whereas in the exhaled breath this is not so and the change is being effected spontaneously.) (4) Let go all personal problems. (5) Reflect on the existence of the soul which is you, and on the infinite life-power surrounding you and in which you dwell and live. (6) Lie with arms outstretched and palms open, so as to draw in life-force either through palms or through head. (This makes contact with higher power through silent meditation, and it draws on the reconstructive and healing life-force attribute of this power.) Draw it into yourself. Let it distribute itself over the entire body. Let its omni-intelligence direct it to where it is most needed, whether that be the affected part or some other part that is the first cause of the sickness. (7) Place hands on affected part of body and deliberately direct force through hands to body. A feeling of warmth should be noticeable in palms of hands. (8) Recollect through imagination the all-pervading sense of God and his infinite goodness.

§

Where physical laws of hygiene have been broken and continue to be broken, where gluttonous or ill-informed eating and intemperate living have led to bodily disturbance, the sufferer must rectify his physical errors still whether his spiritual healing is successful or not.

§

Strong alcohol paralyses the brain centre controlling spiritual and intuitive activity for two hours, and so nullifies meditation, which should not be practised within two hours of drinking it. Those who take such stimulants and still want to unfold spiritually should restrict their drinks to light wine or beer.

§

Smoking not only harms the body but also depresses the mind. The cumulative and ultimate effect of the poison which it introduces is to lower the emotional state by periodic moods of depression.

§

A great rage or an overwhelming fear affects the heartbeat until it slows down or quickens dangerously. A sudden tremendous fright can cause syncope, even death. Such is the known power of emotion over functions of the body's organs. When living habits are reformed and brought to conform to the requirements of hygienic laws so that the patient stops doing those things which gave his disease the requisite conditions for it to take hold, and when the different systems of physical therapy are applied as required without prejudice against or favouritism for any particular one, and when this is combined with faith in the spiritual healing power invoked by a practitioner or by the patient himself, the chances of a cure are raised to the highest.

§

Behind, within, and around the physical body there is another and invisible body which we may call the vital body. This is a kind of archetype or pattern for the physical body. On several points they coincide, but not on others. This subtler etheric body comes into existence before actual birth and remains for a while after actual death. During incarnation it is closely connected with the physical body and especially with its vitality, health, and sickness. The part of it which surrounds the physical body and which we may call the vital aura should not be confused with the other and larger aura wherein emotions and thoughts are reflected. During experiments which I made with a group of London physicians before the war, it was found that this vital aura extended for about forty-five centimeters beyond the physical body. When the vital aura was in a devitalized, fatigued condition, there was less resistance to sickness; but when it was energized the resistance increased. The life-force which we draw from the universal life-force enters into the vital body. Resistance can be increased by deep breathing, by exercise, and by imagining the life-force as a white light entering through the head and penetrating downwards into every cell of the physical body. This also helps the healing process in sickness. Not only are the cells permeated by these methods, but they are also purified.

§

It is more prudent and more conducive to a successful result if he is prepared to make necessary changes of thought and feeling and character. The greater the healing asked for, the greater the sacrifice he may in turn be asked to make. When, for instance Jesus asked the distressed sufferers to believe, they were not being asked to believe merely superficially, but rather so deeply that they would at least try to make the changes called for. Having contributed so much to the disease, they ought to contribute something to the cure.

§

When plague broke like a wave over the heads of mankind in the fifteenth century and spread with startling rapidity through the nations of Europe, the obvious physical causes were in themselves but agents of the less obvious soul-causes, defects in the very character of humanity. Insomnia and cancer, to take but two of the representative illnesses of our own epoch, are no less plaguelike in their menace to people of today, no less the products of causes inherent in imperfect human character, habit, or environment.

§

The art of healing needs all the contributions it can get, from all the worthy sources it can find. It cannot realize all its potentialities unless it accepts them all: the homeopath along with the allopath, the naturopath along with the chiropractor, the psychiatrist along with the spiritual ministrant. It does not need them all together at one and the same time, of course, but only as parts of its total resources. A philosophic attitude refuses to bind itself exclusively to any single form of cure.

§

Another extremely fanatical attitude of which we must beware is the belief that mental healing displaces all other systems and agencies for curing disease or keeping health; that its advocates may totally discard every branch of medicine and surgery, hygiene, and physical treatment. Sanity and balance call for the acceptance in its proper place of whatever Nature and man can contribute. With these preliminary warnings, we venture to predict that as the principles and practices of mental healing come to be better, namely more rationally understood, it will establish for itself a firm place in therapeutics which will have to be conceded—however grudgingly—by the most materialistic and most sceptical of medicos.

§

The services of a physician skilled in the knowledge of diseases and in the care of their sufferers should never be slighted. Orthodox allopathic medicine deserves our highest respect because of the cautiously scientific way it has proceeded on its course. It has achieved notable cures. But it also has many failures to its debit. This is in part due to the fundamental error which it accepts in common with other sciences like psychology—the materialist error of viewing man as being nothing more than his body. Only by setting this right can it go forward to its fullest possibilities. Its deficiency in this respect has forced the appearance and nourished the spread of unorthodox healing methods, of which there are many. Most of these have something worthwhile to contribute but unfortunately—lacking the caution of science—make exaggerated claims and uphold fanatical attitudes, with the result that they too have their failures and incur public disrepute. The extreme claims made by credulous followers and unscientific leaders of mental healing cults revolt the reason of those outside their fold and lead to distrust of the justifiable claims that should be made. But they have enough successes to justify their existence. Only by a mutual approach and interaction will they modify each other and thus bring a truly complete system of healing. They are already doing this involuntarily and therefore far too slowly. They have to do it willingly and quickly if the world of sick and suffering patients is to benefit by the full extent of present-day human knowledge.

§

My basic conclusion is that healing exists on all these different levels, which means its power comes from different sources. But this said, I feel that all healers should know their limits, their limitations, and I fear that many of them do not simply because they are carried away by their enthusiasm. Secondly, I feel that all healers would not only be none the worse for some knowledge of anatomy and physiology and the commoner maladies, but they should even attempt to acquire some of this knowledge. Otherwise many errors, many false or exaggerated claims, are made by the healers. I am not questioning their honesty; I believe most of them are honest. But I am questioning their lack of knowledge, I mean accurate knowledge and fuller knowledge. On the other hand, I criticize the medical profession for failing to enter into dialogue with the healers, for they would learn much to their own profit and to the improvement of their professional help if they adopted a humbler attitude towards the unorthodox healers.

§

Those who are born with healing skills, probably brought over from former births, function on different levels. The commonest is that which radiates life-force and energizes the cells of the sick person. This kind of healer must first put himself into a passive mood and then, when he feels the vibratory force of the life-force active within him, let it pass, with or without touching the patient, into the latter. The vibrations of the life-force are universal; they are not the healer's own personal property. He simply possesses a skill in letting himself be used as a channel, and it is usually concentrated in his hands. A healer like Saswitha, who says he is merely drawing the therapeutic power from his patient and redirecting it or returning it back to the patient, forgets that if this is so the patient himself gets it from the cosmic forces. It is not his own personal property.

§

An informed friend asked me to warn against egoistic healing; it is dangerous for people still *in* the ego to heal others, and safe only in self-healing.

§

The New Thought mental healing cults do not understand the difference between those occult powers (healing is one of them) performed *by* the ego deliberately and those occult powers performed *through* the ego spontaneously at the Overself's bidding. The first kind are on an inferior level and keep the practitioner still enchained within egoism. But of course, by contrast to the orthodox church teaching, this New Thought teaching is certainly broader.

§

The Theosophical denunciation of hypnotism as a black art is too sweeping. Hypnotism can be good or evil. That depends partly upon the intentions with which it is practised, the depth of knowledge of the operator, and partly upon the methods used. In the field of healing it may offer useful although often merely temporary relief. The same is true of the field of psychological and moral re-education. If the hypnotist is more than that, if he is also an advanced mystic, it is possible for the alleviations which he brings about to be of a durable nature. Thus the vice of alcoholism can be and has been at times cured instantaneously. The changes are brought about by the impact of the hypnotist's aura upon the patient. When this occurs and when the hypnotist places his will and mind upon the suggestion which he gives, there is a discharge of force dynamically into the patient's aura. It is this force that brings about the change, provided the patient has been able to fall into a passive, sleepy condition. In the case of an advanced mystic, the various physical techniques which bring about this condition are not required. It is then enough if the patient has sufficient faith and is sufficiently relaxed. The mystic can then accomplish the discharge of force merely by gazing intently into the patient's eyes.

§

The mild use of tobacco and the mild indulgence in alcohol are better in the end than the sudden breaking away from them under the spell of a hypnotic "cure." For in the one case the addict still has some room left for the development of self-control, whereas in the other, not only has he none but he is liable either to relapse again or else to divert his addiction into some other channel which may be not less harmful and may even be more.

§

Mrs. Eddy, I regret to say, made these and other errors but it is not my purpose to evaluate either the merits or demerits of her cult. She had her part to play in the spiritual instruction of the Western world, and if she made serious mistakes, she nevertheless brought to birth a widespread movement which, as she says, has done much good. The system which she founded contains elements of the highest truth, and if her followers will only have the courage to remove the fetters which have been placed upon their independent thought, if they will not hesitate to utilize the powers of free inquiry which God has bestowed upon them, and if they will not shut their eyes but adopt an attitude of wider sympathy and less intolerance towards other systems, they may avoid the fate which overtakes most spiritual movements, when growing numbers kill the spirit and adhere to the letter. I have introduced Mary Baker Eddy's name into this book to render some small service of correction for the sake of her large following, if not for the benefit of the world at large. I cannot conceal a certain admiration for the dignified way in which Christian Science is doing its work in the world, much as I deplore its fanatical narrowness and intellectual mistakes. It contains truths which are sorely needed by ignorant humanity today.

§

Even if Christian Science and New Thought sects produce healings, they are still not truly "divine." They use some lower force—some vital force, as the Indians say. For they are all attached to the ego, which is itself a consequence of their unconscious belief in its reality. The ego has cunningly inserted itself even into these highly spiritual teachings and is still the hidden source behind both their prophets and their followers. This explains Mary B. Eddy's and so many New Thought teachers' commercialism as well as the errors which are contained in the teachings of Emmet Fox, which led to his own mental-physical breakdown and death.

§

Lord Lothian was for many years deeply interested in Christian Science and ardently devoted to its study and practice. Yet when the supreme test came in December, 1940—that is to say, when he was entrusted with the most important mission of his life time as British Ambassador to the United States at the most critical period of the relations between the two countries—he suddenly died from a form of blood poisoning known as uraemic infection. That is to say, at the time when it should have justified itself most, Christian Science completely failed to cure him. Not only that, but he died at the comparatively early age of fifty-eight. The proof of every theory is its consequence in practice. We hear much about the success of Christian Science, but nobody ever takes the trouble to inform us about its failures which must outnumber the former by hundreds to one at least. If it were really scientific, it would not be afraid, as it is, to publish the record of its failures. The discrepancy between exaggerated claim and modest result, between far-fetched theory and defective practice, is as noticeable here as in most other cults.

§

The psychoanalysts work busily on the ego all the time, thus keeping the poor patient still imprisoned in it. But a reference to the Overself might help him really to get rid of some complexes.

§

The mistake of the analysts is to treat lightly what ought to be taken seriously, to regard as a parental fixation or sex repression what is really the deep spiritual malady of our times—emptiness of soul.

§

Psychoanalysis is primarily a search for what is wrong with man; philosophic analysis is a search for what is right with him. Psychoanalysis seeks to correct the false self; philosophy to reveal the true one that is underneath it. Psychoanalysis probes the dead past of childhood; philosophy the living present of maturity.

§

We need also to remember that the attitude of the advanced soul towards personal suffering is not the same as the common one. His standpoint is different. So far as we know human history on this globe, all the facts show that sickness, pain, disease, and death are parts of the conditions governing the physical body's experience because they are inescapable and inevitable parts of all physical plane experience for highly organized forms, whether human or otherwise. That is, they are part of the divine plan for man. We humans resent such experiences, but it may be that they are necessary to our rounded development and that the Illuminated who have approached closer to the infinite wisdom perceive this and drop their resentment. Here we may recall Sri Ramakrishna's attitude towards the cancer in the throat from which he died, Saint Bernadette of Lourdes' attitude towards her painful lingering and fatal disease of consumption, Ramana Maharshi's fatalism about his bodily pains and ailments, and Sri Aurobindo's reply to the physician who attended him for a broken knee after a fall: "How is it that you, a Mahatma, could not foresee and prevent this accident?" "I still have to carry this human body about me and it is subject to ordinary human limitations and physical laws."

§

Deep down within the heart there is a stillness which is healing, a trust in the universal laws which is unwavering, and a strength which is rock-like. But because it is so deep we need both patience and perseverance when digging for it.

§

The attunement of man's mind to the Universal Mind, of his heart to the fundamental love behind things, is capable of producing various effects. One of them may be the healing of bodily ills.

§

That Power which brought the body into existence originally maintains its involuntary functions, cures its diseases, and heals its wounds. It is within the body itself; it is the life-force aspect of the Soul, the Overself. Its curative virtue may express itself through various mediums—as herbs and foods, hot, cold, or mud baths, and deep breathings, exercise, and osteopathy—or it may express itself by their complete absence as in fasting, often the quickest and most effective medium. Or, disdaining physical methods entirely, it may act directly and almost miraculously as spiritual healing.

§

Those who seek healing only to be restored to sensual courses and selfish designs, may commit further errors and be worse off in the end.

§

To pray for a bodily cure and nothing more is a limited and limiting procedure. Pray also to be enlightened as to *why* this sickness fell upon you. Ask also what *you* can do to remove its cause. And above all, ask for the Water of Life, as Jesus bade the woman at the well to ask.

§

Those who do not understand the Overself's workings expect it always to manifest—if it manifests at all—in all its naked purity. If they desire healing, they think that the Overself's help can show itself only in a direct spiritual healing, for instance. The truth is that they may get the cure from a purely physical medium, like a fast, a diet, or a drug; yet that which roused them to seek this particular medium or gave it its successful result *was* the Overself.

§

The basis of higher healing work is the *realization* of man as Mind. But the latter is a dimensionless unindividuated unconditioned entity. It is not *my* individual mind. The field of Mind is a common one whereas the field of consciousness is divided up into individual and separate holdings. This is a difference with vast implications, for whoever can cross from the second field to the first, crosses at the same time from an absurdly limited world into a supremely vital one. Consequently, genuine and permanent healing is carried on without one's conscious association and can be effected by dropping the ego-mind and with it all egoistic desires. Hence the first effort should be to ignore the disease and gain the realization. Only *after* the latter has been won should the thoughts be allowed to descend again to the disease, with the serene trust that the bodily condition may safely be left in the hands of the World-Mind for final disposal as It decides. There should not be the slightest attempt to *dictate* a cure to the higher power nor the slightest attempt to introduce personal will into the treatment. Such attempts will only defeat their purpose. The issues will partly be decided on the balance of the karmic and evolutionary factors concerned in the individual case. And yet there are cults which do not find it at all incongruous to suggest to the Infinite Mind what should thus be showered upon one, or to dictate to karma what exactly it should do! Once surrender is truly made, the desires of the self go with it and peace reigns in the inner life whether illness still reigns in the external life or not. Thus there is a false easy yielding of the will which deceives no higher power than the personal self, and there is an honest yielding which may really invoke the divine grace.

§

Humbled by feelings of personal littleness and moral unworthiness, he is awed by this discovery that he has become a channel through which a power that is not his own, and is indeed beyond his own, flows out for the helping and healing of other men.

§

Jesus' primary intention was to heal the inner man, to promote a directional change in his thought and feeling, to divert him from a sinful to a righteous attitude towards life, and to convert him from spiritual indifference to spiritual enthusiasm. The healing of the body was but a by-product and took place only after these inner processes had been successfully carried out. When the higher elements in a man's character got the better of his lower ones, the victory was followed by, and symbolized in, a return of health to the sick body. It was a visible sign of the reality of the invisible healing. Jesus could not have cured the physical sicknesses if the sufferers had not previously felt his greatness, repented of their former way of life, asked forgiveness and resolved to become righteous. The Gospels record the cases of those who were able to do this; they do not record the cases of the far larger number who could not and whose bodily maladies therefore remained uncured. Most readers erroneously believe that Jesus could heal any and every person. Nobody can do that because nobody can force faith, conversion, penitence, moral evolution, and spiritual aspiration into a stubborn man's heart. There is a further factor in Jesus' healings. They were often accompanied by the proclamation that the patient's sins were forgiven him. This means first, that the aforesaid prerequisite conditions had been established and second, that the man's Overself had intimated its gracious cancellation of the particular bad destiny which had expressed itself in the sickness. The forgiveness came through Jesus as a medium, it did not originate in him. Those who believe that Jesus personally could unburden all men's evil fate, err. He could do it only in those cases where a man's own higher self willed it. Jesus then became a medium for its grace.

§

The New Thought or Christian Science claims, where correct, are true only of the adept, for he alone has fully aligned himself with the Spirit.

§

Healing is but a mere incident in the work of a sage. Such a one will always keep as his foremost purpose the opening of the spiritual heart of man.

§

It is a great error for an ordinary person to sit down when confronted by practical problems and say, "God will take care of this for me." God may do so but it is just as likely that God will not do so. John Burroughs wrote the lines, "I sit serene, with folded hands and wait, My own, my own, shall come to me," as also found in the sayings of Lao Tzu: "He who takes a back seat shall be first. He who hides his own greatness shall be put in front," etc. These assertions are perfectly true—but only of the Adept. For him, he need only sit still and all things come to him; but for the others—the unrealized, the materialistic—they must strive, struggle, and suffer for everything they need.

§

Pain and suffering, sin and evil, disease and death, exist only in the world of thoughts, not in the world of pure Thought itself. They are not illusions, however, but they are transient. Whoever attains to pure Thought will also attain *in consciousness* to a life that is painless, sorrow-free, sinless, undecaying, and undying. Being above desires and fears, it is necessarily above the miseries caused by unsatisfied desires and realized fears. But at the same time he will also have an *accompanying* consciousness of life in the body, which must obey the laws of its own being, natural laws which set limitations and imperfections upon it. This much can be said to be the element of truth contained in some theoretical doctrines of Vedantic Advaita and Christian Science.

§

If he can apply this teaching *now*, if he can put his faith in and make his contact with the higher power from this very moment, if he can forget himself for an instant, he can receive healing instantaneously.

§

11

THE NEGATIVES: DARK SHADOW ON THE WORLD

Nature—Roots in ego—Presence in the world—
In thoughts, feelings, and violent passions—
Their visible and invisible harm

In every human difficulty there are two ways open to us. The common way is familiar enough: it consists in reacting egoistically and emotionally with self-centered complaint, irritability, fear, anger, despair, and so on. The uncommon way is taken by a spiritually minded few: it consists in making something good out of something bad, in reacting selflessly, calmly, constructively, and hopefully. This is the way of practical philosophy, this attempt to transform what outwardly seems so harmful into what inwardly at least must be markedly beneficent. It is a magical work. But it can only be done by deep thought, self-denial, and love. If the difficulty is regarded as both a chance to show what we can do to develop latent resources as well as a test of what we have already developed, it can be made to help us. Even if we do not succeed in changing an unfavourable environment for the better, such an approach would to some extent change ourselves for the better. We must accept, with all its tremendous implications for our past, present, and future, that we are ultimately responsible for the conditions which stamp our life. Such acceptance may help to shatter our egoism and that, even though it is painful, will be all to the good. Out of its challenge can come the most blessed change in ourselves.

§

The lower nature is incurably hostile to the higher one. It prefers its fleeting joys with their attendant miseries, its ugly sins with their painful consequences, because this spells life to it.

§

Whoever seeks to tread a path such as the one shown here will sooner or later find that these forces set themselves in opposition to his interior journey. His way will be blocked by external circumstances that entangle him in hopeless struggles or heart-breaking oppressions and enslavements, or by psychical attacks which seek to sweep him off his spiritual feet and destroy his higher aspirations. Persons in his immediate environment may be moved by these invisible forces to work against him, causing uprisings of hatred and misunderstanding; one-time friends may turn into treacherous enemies more virulent than the poison of a cobra. Public critics will appear and endeavour to nullify whatever good he is doing for humanity, or to prevent its continuance. The single aim and object of all these attempts will be to prevent his alignment with the Overself, to render mental quiet impossible, or to keep his heart and mind crushed down to earth and earthly things. He must needs suffer these things. Their power, scope, and duration may be diminished, however.

§

Evil arises only when an entity goes astray into the delusions of separateness and materialism, and thence into conflict with other entities. There is no ultimate and eternal principle of evil, but there are forces of evil, unseen entities who have gone so far astray and are so powerful in themselves that they work against goodness, truth, and justice. But by their very nature such entities are doomed to eventual destruction, and even their work of opposition is utilized for good in the end and becomes the resistance against which evolution tests its own achievements, the grindstone against which it sharpens man's intelligence, the mirror in which it shows him his flaws.

§

Pessimism is practical defeatism and psychological suicide. It is the child of despair and the parent of dissolution.

§

In a negative situation, where negative criticisms and negative emotions are rampant, other persons may try to involve him in it, or at least get him to support their attitude and endorse their criticism. But a feeling may come over him preventing him from doing so. If so, he should obey and remain silent. With time the rightness of this course will be confirmed.

§

Because of what he is and what he seeks to do, the quester has special trials, special experiences and temptations, apart from the ordinary ones which accompany all human activities.

§

Elaborate traps are set at intervals along his road, made up of a combination of his own weaknesses with persons or events related to them. He must be wary of relapsing into complacency, must be prepared for tests and temptations in a variety of forms.

§

The risk is greater because a human emissary of the adverse element in Nature will automatically appear at critical moments and consciously or unconsciously seek hypnotically or passively to lead him astray as he or she has gone astray. Our own world-wide experience, embracing the written reports and spoken confidences of thousands of individual cases of mystical, yogic, and occult seekers—both Oriental and Occidental—has gravely taught the need of this warning.

§

Whenever a strong impulse becomes uppermost and inclines him toward some deed or speech of a negative kind, he had better scrutinize its source or nature as quickly as he can.

§

What lies at the root of all these errors in conduct and defects in character? It is the failure to understand that he is more than his body. It is, in one word, materialism.

§

The things which hamper the student's progress are varied, and although they may bring despondency and discouragement, impatience and rebellion, they need not and should not be permitted to bring the loss of all hope. Difficulties there must be, but they need not make us cowards. The times of swift progress are generally followed by times of slow moving; success alternates with failure as day with night. He must go on with the faith and trust that obstacles are not for all time, that fluctuations on the path are inevitable, and that his own inner divine possibilities are the best guarantee of ultimate attainment. The trials of the path, as indeed the trials of life itself, are inescapable. He should endure the tribulations with the inner conviction that a brighter world awaits him; hope and faith will lead him to it.

§

Why does God allow the evil and suffering when the same result of spiritual advantage could be got in other ways? There are some questions to which there are no answers because God alone can answer them, and this is one. We can however find what *human* intuition, *human* mystical revelation, has to say about these things and accept such contributions at their own value.

§

The dark and destructive forces show themselves in Nature and life. To leave them out, unaccounted for and ignored, is to leave a weak place in oneself.

§

These sinister figures seek, and often get, key positions in politics, organized groups, etc., and from there manipulate the mass and use them as blind unwitting tools.

What may be true on the ultimate level—the non-existence of evil, the reality of the Good, the True, the Beautiful—becomes false on the level of duality. Here the twofold powers, the opposites, do exist, do hold the world in their sway. To deny relative evil here is to confuse different planes of being.

§

It is a man's own internal defects which often conspire against him and which show their faces in many of the external troubles that beset him. Yet it is hard for him to accept this truth because his whole life-habit is to look outwards, to construct defensive alibis rather than to engage in censorious self-inquisition. Sheikh al Khuttali, a Sufi adept, addressing a disciple who complained at his circumstances, said: "O my son, be assured that there is a cause for every decree of Providence. Whatever good or evil God creates, do not in any place or circumstance quarrel with his action or be aggrieved in thy heart." Therefore, the aspirant who is really earnest about the quest should develop the attitude that his personal misfortunes, troubles, and disappointments must be traced back to his own weaknesses, defects, faults, deficiencies, and indisciplines. Let him not blame them on other persons or on fate. In this way he will make the quickest progress whereas by self-defending, or self-justifying, or self-pitying apportionment of blame to causes outside himself, he will delay or prevent it. For the one means clinging to the ego, the other means giving it up. Nothing is to be gained by such flattering self-deception while much may be lost by it. He must bring himself to admit frankly that he himself is the primary cause of most of his ills, as well as the secondary cause of some of the ills of others. He must recognize that the emotions of resentment, anger, self-pity, or despondency are often engendered by a wounded ego. Instead of reviling fate at each unfortunate event, he should analyse his moral and mental make-up and look for the weaknesses which led to it. He will gain more in the end by mercilessly accusing his own stubbornness in pursuing wrong courses than by taking shelter in alibis that censure other people. Like a stone in a shoe which he stubbornly refuses to remove, the fault still remains in his character when he stubbornly insists on blaming things or condemning persons for its consequences. In this event the chance to eliminate it is lost, and the same dire consequences may repeat themselves in his life again.

The faith of the lower ego in itself and the strength with which it clings to its own standpoint are almost terrifying to contemplate. The aspirant is often unconscious of its selfishness. But if he can desert its standpoint, he shall then be in a position to perceive how large an element it has contributed in the making of his own troubles, how heavy is its responsibility for unpleasant events which he has hitherto ascribed to outside sources. He shall see that his miserable fate derives largely from his own miserable faults. He is naturally unwilling to open his eyes to his own deficiencies and faults, his little weaknesses and large maladjustments. So suffering comes to open his eyes for him, to shock and shame him into belated awareness and eventual amendment. But quite apart from its unfortunate results in personal fortunes, whenever the aspirant persists in taking the lower ego's side and justifying its action, he merely displays a stupid resolve to hinder his own spiritual advancement. Behind a self-deceiving facade of pretexts, excuses, alibis, and rationalizations, the ego is forever seeking to gratify its unworthy feelings or to defend them. On the same principle as the pseudo-patriotism which prompted the Italians to follow Mussolini blindly throughout his Ethiopian adventure to its final disaster, the principle of "My country! right or wrong," he follows the ego through all its operations just as blindly and as perversely, justifying its standpoints merely because they happen to be his own. But the higher Self accepts no rivals. The aspirant must choose between denying his ego's aggressiveness or asserting it. The distance to be mentally travelled between these two steps is so long and so painful that it is understandable why few will ever finish it. It is only the exceptional student who will frankly admit his faults and earnestly work to correct them. It is only he whose self-criticizing detachment can gain the upper hand, who can also gain philosophy's highest prize.

§

If the ego cannot trap him through his vices it will try to do so through his virtues. When he has made enough progress to warrant it, he will be led cunningly and insensibly into spiritual pride. Too quickly and too mistakenly he will believe himself to be set apart from other men by his attainments. When this belief is strong and sustained, that is, when his malady of conceit calls for a necessary cure, a pit will be dug unconsciously for him by other men and his own ego will lead him straight into it. Out of the suffering which will follow this downfall, he will have a chance to grow humbler.

§

So what are depressions and sadnesses but the ego pitying itself, shedding silent tears over itself, loving itself, looking at itself and enwrapped in itself? What is a happy calm but a killing of such egoism?

§

His failure follows inevitably from his attempt to serve two masters. The ego is strong and cunning and clamant. The Overself is silent and patient and remote. In every battle the dice are loaded in the ego's favour. In every battle high principle runs counter to innate prejudice.

§

The root of all the trouble is not man's wickedness or animality or cunning greedy mind. It is his very I-ness, for all those other evils grow out of it. It is his own ego. Here is the extraordinary and baffling self-contradiction of the human situation. It is man's individual existence which brings him suffering and yet it is this very existence which he holds as dear as life to him!

§

What are the blockages which prevent the soul's light, grace, peace, love, and healing from reaching us? There are many different kinds, but they are resolvable into the following: first, all negative; second, all egoistic; and third, all aggressive. By "aggressive" I mean that we are intruding our personality and imposing our ideas all the time. If we would stop this endless aggression and be inwardly still for a while, we would be able to hear and receive what the Soul has to say and to give us.

§

You must plant your feet firmly on one definite purpose. Opposition will whirl around you, but hold on. Perverted Man is full of prejudice, and ninety-nine out of every one hundred you meet will unconsciously or consciously attempt to deflect you from your divine purpose.

§

It is tantalizingly hard to effect the passage from the lower to higher state. For between them lies an intermediate zone of consciousness which possesses an ensnaring quality and in which the ego makes its last desperate effort to keep him captive. Hence this zone is the source of attractive psychic experiences, of spiritual self-aggrandizements, of so-called messianic personal claims and redemptive missions, of great truths cunningly coalesced into great deceptions.

§

The path is beset not only by the pitfalls arising out of one's own human failings, but at critical times by unconscious or conscious evil beings in human form who seek to destroy faith through falsehoods and to undermine reliance on true guidance through sidetracks and traps.

§

The storms of violent passion are to be resisted as the smoothness of inner peace is to be invited.

§

We may regret the existence of these faults in others, but we may not refuse to recognize them if practical dealings are involved.

§

If he finds himself brought by circumstances into the society of evil-minded people, the first step to self-protection should be to switch the mind instantly into remembrance of the witness-self and to keep it there throughout the period of contact. To turn inwards persistently when in the presence of such discordant persons is to nullify any harmful or disturbing effect they might otherwise have on our thoughts.

§

Until such time as each member of a community, nation, or society practises sufficient self-control to bring about his own inner peace, it is illusory to expect outer peace in the world. This is why history is a record of conflict.

§

There is no perpetual peace anywhere on this planet, only perpetual strife. But it is open to man to take the violence, the murder, and the war out of this strife. He may purge it of its savage beast qualities.

§

The malign powers of evil in the world, which have been so widely spread, so active and so violent in our own generation, are not to be ignored by dreaming optimism.

§

The world's evil and untruth are plainly there. The saint may not want to see them, because he does not want to think badly about other people; but the philosopher must distinguish them and harms no one by doing so, because he sees the Good and the True behind everything at the same time.

§

If he must hate something, let him hate hatred itself.

§

Yes, there is odious evil in the world—much of it petty but some of it quite monstrous. It takes its genesis in the thoughts of men.

§

The nihilistic nature of Existentialism is shown by its founder, Sartre, holding the opinion, according to Simone de Beauvoir, that if there was nothing to attack and destroy, the writing of books would not be worthwhile.

§

The Existentialists have given pessimism and nihilism a morbid prestige.

§

He should never allow the actions or words of ignorant men to arouse in him reactions of anger, envy, or resentment.

§

Throw out negative thoughts as they would hinder the uplift of your mind. Replace them by frequent and positive remembrance of the Overself.

§

What we see around us in the world today—poison in the air, water, soil, food, even in the stratosphere, and destroying the human body through disease—is but a reflected crystallization of poison in the human mind and heart. If the invisible evil were not present, the visible one would not have come into existence. Even those whose faith can not stretch so far, can trace the direct lines of connection by the use of reason alone.

§

What is the opposing quality to the violence of today? Not merely non-violence—a negative one—but gentleness—a positive one.

§

Mentalism says that most of one's misery is inflicted on oneself by accepting and holding negative thoughts. They cover and hide the still centre of one's being, which is infinite happiness.

§

Long ago Buddha said that if we make room in our minds for negative, bitter thoughts of complaint, outrage, or injury against those who mistreat us, we shall not be free and will remain unable to find peace.

§

Their faith in a higher purpose of life having failed, it is not long before the labour of correcting and purifying human nature will seem unnecessary.

§

The sinister spread of black magic, witchcraft, sexual perversion, and drug-addiction in our own time is menacing. Some of their votaries are consciously worshipping demonic powers, evil as such, others only because they have been misled into the belief that it is the Good.

§

We would not allow full freedom of movement to plague-carrying rats in our kitchens and homes. Yet we allow these human carriers of mental plague the freedom to print and publish, declaim, and propagate their poisonous suggestions and negative ideas, their pornography and violence, their hates and moral subversion, their evil.

§

The evil forces working through mediums are cunning enough not to show their true ultimate aims all at once. These become clear to the observer only by successive stages, only gradually. Whoever has critically studied the ways of evil spirits will know that they first lure their mediumistic victims or gullible public along the path of self-injury or even self-destruction by winning their confidence with a series of successful predictions or favourable interventions. When this confidence has been well established, these dark forces then reveal their real intent by persuading their victims, through gigantic lies or false predictions, to commit a final act in which everything is staked on a single throw. The unhappy dupes invariably lose this last throw and are then overwhelmed by shattering disaster. This occurred in Hitler's case with his sudden attack on Russia in 1941. He then stated his belief that Moscow would be reached within six to seven weeks. But his soldiers never reached Moscow. His invisible guides had indeed betrayed him. How true are Shakespeare's words from *Macbeth*, Act 1, Scene 3: "But 'tis strange:/ And oftentimes, to win us to our harm,/ The instruments of darkness tell us truths,/ Win us with honest trifles, to betray us/ In deepest consequence."

§

Do not gaze overlong upon that person, that thing, that place, whose history is evil, whose nature is evil, lest you imperil yourself, or your health, or your fortunes. Better, avoid them if you can.

§

As that esteemed Indian yogi and philosopher the late Sri Aurobindo more than once mentioned, those who are working for the survival of Truth in a truthless world thereby become targets for powerful forces of hatred wrath and falsehood. Whoever publicly bears a deeply spiritual message to humanity, has to suffer from evil's opposition.

§

When men who have spent their whole lives harbouring destructive ideas are given a constructive teaching, they are naturally impermeable and unreceptive to it. There are materialists who are impatient at hearing philosophic truths and even irritated by them. Such persons may even become quite violently abusive. This happens because they have completely lost their capacity to practise calm unprejudiced abstract thinking, and because they have crushed the feeling of veneration before something higher or nobler than themselves—whether it be a beautiful landscape or God.

§

12

REFLECTIONS

This I may say that my work throughout has always been based on first-hand knowledge of what I write about and not upon hearsay or tradition.

§

There are times—and they are the times when, looking back, I love my profession most—when writing becomes for me not a profession at all but either a form of religious worship or a form of metaphysical enlightenment. It is then, as the pen moves along silently, that I become aware of a shining presence which calls forth all my holy reverence or pushes open the mind's doors.

§

The Writer who sometimes sits behind the writer of these lines smiling at my puny attempts to translate the Untranslatable, once bade me put away for an indefinite period the thought of any future publications. I obeyed and there was a long silence in the outer world—so long that two obituary notices were printed by newspapers! I had enough leisure to discover the faultiness of the earlier work and felt acutely that the world was better off without my lucubrations. But a day came when I felt the presence of the Presence and I received clear guidance to take the pen again.

§

Writing, which is an exercise of the intellect to some, is an act of worship to me. I rise from my desk in the same mood as that in which I leave an hour of prayer in an old cathedral, or of meditation in a little wood.

§

Much that was pertinent to the Quest was left unmentioned in the earlier books, partly through reluctance to speak of certain matters, partly through the writer's own need of further personal development to attain irrefragable conclusions about other matters. The reluctance has now been overcome and the development has been achieved.

§

All the volumes that I have previously written belong to the formative stage. Only now, after thirty years unceasing travail and fearless exploration have I attained a satisfying fullness in my comprehension of this abstruse subject, a clear perspective of all its tangled ramifications and a joyous new revelation from a higher source hitherto known only obscurely and distantly. All my further writings will bear the impress of this change and will show by their character how imperfect are my earlier ones. Nevertheless, on certain principal matters, what I then wrote has all along remained and still remains my settled view and indeed has been thoroughly confirmed by time. Such, for instance, are (1) the soul's real existence, (2) the necessity for and the great benefits arising from meditation, (3) the supreme value of the spiritual quest, and (4) the view that loyalty to mysticism need not entail disloyalty to reason.

§

It is regrettable in those early books that I over-estimated the pace of progress and brought the goal noticeably nearer than it really is.

§

I have gathered my materials from the West as well as the East, from modern science as well as ancient metaphysics, from Christian mysticism as well as Hindu occultism. The narrowness which would set up any Indian yoga as being enough by itself is something which I reject. And there is no cult, organization, or group with which I associate myself or within whose limitations I would ask others to confine themselves.

§

The purpose of these pages is not to attack but to explain, to appeal, and to suggest. Their criticism is constructive and untouched by malice. It comes from a well-wisher and not from an opponent of religion: therefore it ought not to be resented.

§

It demanded no less than hundreds of interviews with different teachers and hermits, thousands of miles of travel to reach them, and at least a hundred thousand pages of the most abstruse reading in the world before I could bring my course of personal study in the hidden philosophy to a final close. Today I have not got the time to take others through such a long and arduous course and they have probably not got the patience to endure it.

§

My researches were made not only amongst modern books and ancient texts and living men. They were also made in the mysterious within-ness of my own consciousness.

§

The world-wide extent of my correspondence and travels; the extraordinary variety of Oriental and Occidental human contacts which has fallen to my lot; the narratives and information which have fallen from the lips of those who have sought me out for interviews and those whom I, too, have sought out for the same purpose; the knowledge which I have gleaned from ancient little-known texts and modern printed books in four continents; experiments made and observations recorded amongst mystics and devotees of the most varied types—from all these sources an immense amount of valuable mystical occult and metaphysical knowledge, theoretical and practical, has fallen into my hands. Had I known all this at the beginning of my own quest—now thirty years ago, I would have been saved much trouble, many errors and constant sufferings. However, others will profit by it for I intend to make the best fruit of my own experience available to genuine seekers.

§

I am a researcher, that is my special job. Then I go on to convert the results of my researches into notes and reports, into analyses and reflections. Later I draw upon this material for my published writings.

§

I lay no special claim to virtue and piety which most men do not possess. But I do lay claim to indefatigable research into mystical truth, theory, and practice.

§

P.B. as a private person does not count. There are hundreds of millions of such persons anyway. What is one man and his quest? P.B.'s personal experiences and views are not of any particular importance or special consequence. What happens to the individual man named P.B. is a matter of no account to anyone except himself. But what happens to the hundreds of thousands of spiritual seekers today who are following the same path that he pioneered, is a serious matter and calls for prolonged consideration. Surely the hundreds of thousands of Western seekers who stand behind him and whom indeed, in one sense, he represents, do count. P.B. as a symbol of the scattered group of Western truth-seekers who, by following his writings so increasingly and so eagerly, virtually follow him also, does count. He personifies their aspirations, their repulsion from materialism and attraction toward mysticism, their interest in Oriental wisdom and their shepherdless state. As a symbol of this Western movement of thought, he is vastly greater than himself. In his mind and person the historic need for a new grasp of the contemporary spiritual problem found a plain-speaking voice.

§

I am only a generator of ideas, not a disseminator of them. My work is to inspire and direct others in private, that they might serve humanity spiritually in public.

§

The fact that I have had practical experience of earning my livelihood as an editor has been made a subject of criticism. Were my critics not so narrow-minded they would have had the sense to see that exactly therein lies one of my merits. For this experience has purified me of the common mystical defects of writing whole pages that mean nothing, of recommending readers to attempt impossible tasks, of getting both thought and pen lost in the clouds to the neglect of the earth. It has taught me a robust realism and a healthy self-reliance—two qualities which are notoriously absent from the ordinary mystical make-up and for lack of which they commit many mistakes. My critics try to give the impression that earning my livelihood was a low act and that being a journalist was a kind of crime. These two facts are indeed held up against me as though they prove that I am both mercenary and materialistic, as though nobody with mystical aspirations would do the one or be the other. Such facts really pay me a compliment and do me no dishonour. But the blind unreflective followers of a dying tradition cannot be expected to perceive that. They cannot be expected to comprehend that I am endeavouring to bring mysticism into mundane life, to throw a bridge across the chasm which has so often separated them. And I know no better way than to have done so in my own personal life first before attempting to tell others how to do it.

§

Those who look in these pages for an exact presentation of the Oriental doctrines look in vain. Scholars, purists, and pundits had better beware of these pages. We do not write for them. For the teachings which we have drawn from the East have been used as a base upon which to build independently; but the responsibility for the superstructure rests solely with us, for it is a building intended for the Modern West. Nevertheless those who decry our writings cannot deny that they have contributed much towards the creation of a new interest in Oriental literature. They would do well also to place some of their censure upon destiny, which all along has used me as an agent at first unwitting but later clearly conscious.

§

They alone will comprehend the purport of this volume who can comprehend that it does not only seek to present the pabulum of an ancient system for modern consumption but that it has integrated its material with the wider knowledge that has come to mankind during the thousands of years which have passed since that system first appeared. Consequently we offer here not only a re-statement but also an entirely new and radically fresh world-view which could not have been reached historically earlier.

If we study the history of human culture we shall begin to discern signs of an orderly growth, a logical development of its body. Truth has had different meanings at different periods. This was inevitable because the human mind has been moving nearer and nearer to it, nearer and nearer to the grand ultimate goal. And when we watch the way knowledge has mounted up during the last three centuries we ought not to be surprised at the statement that the culmination of all this long historical process, the end of thousands of years of human search, is going to crystallize in the new East-West philosophy which it is the privilege of this century to formulate. Here alone can the relative interpretations of truth which have been discovered by former men, rise to the absolute wherein they merge and vanish. This means that although truth has always existed, its knowledge has only existed at different stages of development, that we are the fortunate inheritors of the results gathered by past thinkers, and still more that we are now called to complete the circle and formulate a finished system of philosophy which shall stand good for all time.

All the conflicting doctrines which have appeared in the past were not meaningless and not useless; they have played their part most usefully even where they seemed most contradictory. They were really in collaboration, not in opposition. We need not disdain to illustrate the highest abstract principles by the homeliest concrete anecdotes, and we may describe them as pieces in a jig-saw puzzle which can now be fitted together for now we have the master pattern which is the secret of the whole. Hence all that is vital and valuable in earlier knowledge is contained in the East-West philosophy; only their fallacies have been shed. A full view of the universe now replaces all the partial views which were alone available before and which embodied merely single phases of the discovery of Truth. Thus the analytic movement which uncovered the various pieces of this world puzzle must now yield to a synthetic process of putting them together in a final united pattern. Culture, on this view, is the timeless truth appearing in the world of time and therefore in successive but progressive periods. Only now has it been able to utter its latest word. Only now does philosophy attain its maturest completion. Only now are we able to reap the fruit of seven thousand years of historical philosophy. Only now have we achieved a world-system, a universal doctrine which belongs to no particular place but to the planet. Knowledge has grown by analysis but shall finish by synthesis.

§

Not one but several minds will be needed to labour at the metaphysical foundation of the twentieth-century structure of philosophy. I can claim the merit only of being among the earliest of these pioneers. There are others yet to appear who will unquestionably do better and more valuable work.

§

Others will take up this work where we leave it unfinished. If my effort can do nothing more at least it will make easier for those who are destined to follow after me a jungle-road which I had to travel under great difficulties. I have roughly cleared an area of human culture which my successors may cultivate and on which they may perhaps produce a perfect crop one day. I did what I could but the fullness of results will be theirs alone. The effects of my thinking will not fully declare themselves in our own day. It is not pride that makes me say that the volume which follows *The Hidden Teaching Beyond Yoga* is the first methodical embodiment in a modern language of this tradition as well as the first synthetic explanation of it in scientific terminology, for the book is called forth by its epoch and someone would sooner or later have written it. What is really interesting is not who writes it but the fact that it was written in our own time. For something there achieved marks a most important stage of human cultural history.

I have indeed undertaken what I believe to be a pioneer work. I cannot give my patronage to any particular system. I can bestow it only on Truth, which is unique and systemless. For enough of the sacred presence is at my side, enough of the disciplinary self-transformation has been achieved, and enough of the mental perception arrived at, to enable me to take up the external task of preparing others for illumination in their turn.

§

This synthesis has developed from the world-wide researches of this writer, plus the secret traditions of Oriental teachers, the personal experiences of Occidental adepts, and the needs of modern aspirants. It notes with approval the trend toward interest in yoga and mysticism, but with regret where so much of this interest is directed to antique or medieval types unsuited to those needs, which are based on professional business and occupational conditions unknown to such earlier types. Into this synthesis has gone the garnerings from great storehouses of the past, but added to them are the fresh creative findings of the present. Orient and Occident, ancient and modern, have joined together to produce this distinctive teaching. It is not enough to resuscitate the doctrines and methods of a bygone era; we must also evolve our own. And this can be done only out of firsthand experience of illumination under modern conditions.

§

I did not *seek* to become the formulator of such a unique and priceless message to mankind. Indeed knowing myself in weakness as well as strength, I naturally shrink from seeking such an immense responsibility, and would rather have helped and served a worthier man to formulate the message. This is not to say that I underrate its value, its dignity, its public prestige. But all my previous attempts to evade the task having ended in failure, I now positively and affirmatively—no longer reluctantly and hesitantly—step forward to its accomplishment. I do so moreover with tranquil joy, for I am utterly convinced in the deepest recess of my heart no less than in the logical thinking of my brain, that the teaching is so greatly needed in our time by those who have sought in vain for comprehensive elucidation of the problem of their existence, that I feel the help it will give them constitutes the best possible use of my energies, talents, and days in this incarnation.

§

Although I was already travelling the road to the self-discovery of these truths, it is true that an apparent fortuitous meeting with an extraordinary individual at Angkor saved me from some of the time and labour involved in this process. For he turned out to be an adept in the higher philosophy who had not only had a most unusual personal history but also a most unusual comprehension of the problems which were troubling me. He put me through strange initiatory experiences in a deserted temple and then, with a few brief explanations of the hidden teachings, placed the key to their solutions in my hands. But after all it was only a key to the door-chamber, and not the entire treasure itself. These I had to ferret out for myself. That is, to say, I was given the principle but had to work out the details, develop the applications, and trace out the ramifications for myself. I was provided with a foundation but had to erect the superstructure by my own efforts. And all this has been a task for many years, a task upon which I am still engaged.

§

Henceforth the background of this teaching will be, nay must be, a universal one. It shall resist those who would label it Eastern because they will not be able to deny its Western contents, form, and spirit. It shall resist those who would label it Western, because they too shall not be able to deny its Eastern roots and contents.

§

Let them remember that the Truth comes not from any person but from the Holy Spirit. It is from such a source that what is worthy in my writings has come; the errors however are mine. Let them therefore describe themselves as students of philosophy, not as followers of Brunton.

§

I try to practise the advice I give others and to live according to the teachings I write down. This does not mean that I always succeed in doing so. But the endeavour being there, the ideas they concern have been put through some testing in action: they are not left in the air as mere untried theories. Today, through a world-wide correspondence and formerly through numerous interviews I have uncovered in addition to them the experiences of people standing in every grade of development.

§

Once I took it upon myself to interpret Oriental mysticism to the West. Now after long experience and longer thought, I find it necessary to stand aside from all the dead and living sources of knowledge with which I had established contact, if I am not to misinterpret Oriental mysticism. I am compelled to walk in lonely isolation, even though I respect and honour not a few of those sources. What I learnt and assimilated from them stood finally before a bar of my own making. For I thought, felt, walked, worked, and lived in terms of a twentieth-century experience which, seek as I might, could not be found in its fullness among them. However satisfactory to others, their outlook was too restricted for me. Either they could not come down to the mental horizons of the people who surrounded me, or else they came down theoretically with their heads and not with their hearts. This does not mean that I question their immediate correctness; it means that I question their ultimate usefulness.

It would be as absurd to deduce that I am now inconsistently rejecting mysticism as it would be absurd to declare that I reject the first three letters of the alphabet, merely because I refuse to limit my writing to the combination of ABC alone. I am trying to say that the whole content of mysticism is not identifiable with what is ordinarily known as such; it exceeds the sphere of the latter to such an extent that I have preferred to return to the ancient custom and call it *philosophy*.

§

This book is but a mirror, in which I have shown the facts and events of a life devoted to the quest of Realization. Whether the conclusions it contains are to your taste or not, please deign to believe that as a record I have endeavoured to invest it with absolute verity.

§

It is not without much reluctance that I have ventured to betray aloud the intimate experiences received in secret and solitary communion with nature. I would fain have harboured them until this body was gone, when their fate would carry no concern for me. But the bidding of my spiritual Guides was such that these words have gone out into print.

§

Paul Brunton is trying to do something new. He went to India to learn from the most perceptive Indians, not to copy their followers. Yet the latter at times lack the wide tolerance of their teacher. Merely and politely to disagree with them is denounced as immense arrogance. "Who are you," these followers shout, "to dare to have an opinion contrary to the divine word of our Holy one?" Brunton has the highest regard affection and reverence for these Indian teachers, and especially for the ones who freely initiated him into their knowledge and inner circle. But this regard does not necessarily mean that he is obliged always to agree with them and always to think along with them. Indeed, they did not agree with each other. Those who might deem it ungracious of him to criticize their doctrines at certain points, should know that he speaks not only on his own personal behalf but also with certain sanctions—derived from the most ancient esoteric initiatory Oriental traditions—behind him. Paul Brunton also has something of his own to give. He cannot merely copy these others in living or echo them in writing. He too must be himself just as they were themselves. He may be their friend but he cannot be their follower. If it is for others to be that, he rejoices; but if he is to be true to the light which has come to him, he must shed it by himself however small it be in contrast to theirs. He may be but a candle to the suns of other guides, but to hide it because their light is greater would be to disobey his own inner voice. There was a time when this same voice bade him give forth the message of a few among those he had sought out and studied with. He gladly did so. But now its bidding is different. He has to speak the Word which he alone can speak, for every individual is unique. Every man is born to be himself, to undergo a set of experiences which in their entirety no one else has undergone. He alone of all the human race has just the mental and emotional psyche which he has.

§

If this book can only make the Overself seem as real to the imagination of others as it is to me in actuality, as living a presence to their faith as it is to my meditation, it may be of some service to them.

§

In this book I have considered myself to be a sensitive recording instrument, carefully and minutely registering the impressions received from these higher states of consciousness.

§

My work is a "prophetic" message to our times, a religious revelatory work. An academic seal would put it on an intellectual and consequently lower plane.

§

If I make a first formal appearance as a teacher, it is only in deference to the mission now imposed on me and the mandate now given me. I prefer anonymity for my work but fate has ignored my preference.

§

Have I not searched far and suffered much to prepare an easier path for you all, to cut through thick jungles a track which others could follow with less pain and less labour? Have I not gleaned sufficient knowledge at great cost to be worthy of a hearing? Have I not attained sufficient proficiency in yoga and philosophy to be worthy at least of a claim on truth-seekers' attention? Have I not toiled and over-toiled in the effort to share both the modicum of knowledge and the measure of proficiency with others to be worthy at least of their interest?

§

Now comes the crux of the whole matter. So far as I can follow the teachings of the ancient sages, the path which stretches before mankind appears to have four gates set at intervals along its course. The first is open to the great majority of mankind and might be named "religion, theology, and scholasticism." The second is open to a much smaller number of persons and could conveniently be named Mysticism. The third which is rarely opened (for it is heavy and hard to move) is "the philosophy of truth," whilst the final gate has been entered only by the supermen of our species; it may be titled "Realization." Few readers would care to wander with me into the wilderness whither it leads. I refuse to tarry in the limited phases of development and have gone forward in further quest of the sublime verity which is presented to us as life's goal by the sages. I value tolerance. Let others believe or follow what suits or pleases them most; I trust they will allow me the same freedom to continue my own quest.

§

It is precisely because we are entering an epoch when the common people are at last coming into their own and when the world's conscience about its duty toward the underprivileged has been tardily aroused, that I feel I am obeying a divine command when I write of sacred things in direct manner, of metaphysical themes in a plain manner, and of mystical experiences in a familiar manner. Spiritual snobs may call my treatment of these subjects, cheap, and my work, journalese, but its result—faintly indicated by the long record of help gratefully acknowledged—is their best answer.

§

I have written this book because in an age when the two opposed conceptions of man are throwing the world into strife and revolution and war, there is clear need for personal testimony from those who ***know*** the truth rather than those who believe in it.

§

To attempt this book will be an adventure for the Warriors of Light, but the wanderers of night will put it down with much celerity. For these pages are enchanted with a white magic which can inflict no greater injury on adversaries than to permit them to resist the principles contained therein.

§

To the outside observer, my declining years have been dead ones, apparently spent in inactivity and futility. But this is only one side of the picture. For they have also been spent in a hidden activity on a higher plane, as much for my own spiritual growth as for the world's peace.

§

I have attempted to think out anew, and on the basis of my own experience and not that of men who lived five thousand years ago, what should be the attitude of a normal modern man toward life. Such blessed independence may be scorned by some, but it is a birthright which I jealously guard.

§

I believe that there is a soul in man. This is a frank if commonplace avowal. Yet as I look again at these words, I find a false modesty in them. It is a poor tribute to truth to hesitate timidly in making the open declaration that I *know* there is a soul because I daily commune with it as a real, living presence.

§

Life remains what it is—deathless and unbound. We shall all meet again. Know what you are, and be free. The best counsel today is, keep calm, *aware*. Don't let the pressure of mental environment break into what you know and what is real and ultimately true. This is your magic talisman to safeguard you; cling to it. The last word is—Patience! The night is darkest before dawn. But dawn comes.

§

13

HUMAN EXPERIENCE

Situation—Events—Lessons—World crisis—
Reflections in old age—Reflections on youth

I cannot reiterate enough that the fortunes, events, and experiences of human existence are controlled by higher laws, that there is meaning and purpose in them, and that it is the business of human intelligence to seek out and learn the reasons for them.

§

Let us not betray the good that is in us by a cowardly submission to the bad that is in society.

§

The experiences which come to him and the circumstances in which he finds himself are not meaningless. They usually have a personal karmic lesson for him and should be studied much more than books. He must try to understand impersonally the inner significance behind these events. Their meaning can be ascertained by trying to see them impartially, by evaluating the forces which are involved in them, by profound reflection, and by prayer. Each man gets his special set of experiences, which no one else gets. Each life is individual and gets from the law of recompense those which it really needs, not those which someone else needs. The way in which he reacts to the varied pleasant and unpleasant situations which develop in everyday life will be a better index to the understanding he has gained than any mystical visions painted by the imagination.

§

I am not one of those who deplore the modern way of life, who regret its increasing Americanization because of its emphasis on mechanical gadgets and conveniences. These things are good. But I do deplore the lack of a sense of proportion in pursuing these things, the lack of measure when these constitute the sole purpose of living.

§

Hope is the scaffolding of life. But unless the hands go out in action we may stand upon it forever yet the building will never be erected. That is why we who seek for Truth must work interiorly and work intensely amid the common mortar and bricks of mundane existence. Our dreams of a diviner life are prophetic, but we turn them to realities only when we turn our hands to the tasks and disciplines presented by the world.

§

Every new circumstance or happening in his life has some message from the Infinite Mind for him or some lesson to convey to him or some test to strengthen him. It is for him to seek out this inner significance and to readjust his thinking and actions in accordance with it.

§

Where so many creatures are at early stages of descent into ego-experience and ego-development, it is foolish to expect them to respond to teachings suitable for advanced stages alone—where the need is for growing release from the ego. The first group naturally and inevitably has different, even opposing, outlooks, trends, ideas, beliefs, inclinations, and desires from those of the second one. It wants to fatten the ego, whereas the other wants to thin it down. To condemn it as wrongly directed is ignorant, impractical, and mistaken. If the history of mankind has teemed with war and bloodshed in the past, part of the cause can be found here. But that same history moves also in cycles. We stand today between two cycles, two eras, two cultures. The next one will not only be new; it will also be brighter and better in every way.

§

He is to meet each experience with his mind, remembering his relationship to the higher self and, consequently, the higher purpose of all experiences. He is never to forget the adventure in identity and consciousness that life is.

§

The student must place this seed-thought in his mind and hold to it throughout the day. He need not fear that he will lose anything material thereby. Let him remember the definite promise of the Overself speaking through Krishna in the *Bhagavad Gita*: "I look after the interests and safety of those who are perpetually engaged on My service, and whose thoughts are always about Me and Me alone." He will learn by direct experience the literal meaning of the term Providence—"that which provides."

§

There is only room in your mind for a single thought at a time. Take care, then, that it be a positive one.

§

Let others not mistakenly believe that he has adopted a non-cooperative attitude, has fled from reality, renounced a human existence in exchange for an illusory one in an imaginary world, or deserted the paths of sanity and reason. If he wants to live in comparatively outer peace with them, he must make certain outer concessions. It is better to behave as unprovokingly as possible, to hide his deeper thoughts behind a screen, and to avoid being labelled as a religious fanatic or intellectual faddist. It is especially unwise to uncover one's philosophical thoughts before everybody. He must try to adjust himself smoothly to his environment. This is a hard task, but he must not shirk it and must do all that can be done in the given circumstances. He must fulfil his reasonable obligations towards society, must co-operate in turning the great wheel of human activity, must contribute his share in achieving the general welfare; but he should reserve the right to do so in his own way and not according to society's dictation. And because he has outstripped those around him in important ways, because he is already thinking centuries ahead of them, it is unlikely that he will succeed wholly in fending off their criticisms or even in avoiding their hostility. For with all his endeavours to placate them and with all his sacrifices for the sake of harmony, human nature being what it is—a mixture of good and evil, of the materialistic and the holy—crises may sometimes arise when society will attack him. If the inner voice of conscience bids him do so, then he will perforce have to make a firm stand for principles. It is then that he must summon enough courage to do what is unorthodox or to say what is unpopular and display enough independence to disregard tradition or ignore opinion. Up to a certain point he may walk with the crowd, but beyond it his feet must not move a step. Here he must claim the privilege of self-determination, concerning which there can be no compromise; for here, at the sacred bidding of the Overself, he must begin to live his own life. Consequently, although he will always be a good citizen he may not always be a popular one.

§

Should anyone lazily, passively, quietly, and cowardly accept things as they are? Or should he challenge them, rebel against them and criticize them irreverently, even scornfully? Are they correct, those saints who declare—or even Stoic thinkers like Seneca who accept—all suffering and pain not only as God's will for us but also as our own will? Seneca says, "Take all things as if desired and asked for." (He referred to tribulations.) But *philosophy* teaches that if you accept life do not accept blindly. Seek the lesson, the instruction, the education, and karmic reason and cause behind it. Add knowledge to your faith.

§

Out of suffering may come the transmutation of values, even the transfiguration of character. But these developments are possible only if the man co-operates. If he does not, then the suffering is in vain, fruitless.

§

When a man is crushed to the ground, when his ego is deflated and he calls out in sheer desperation for guidance or for help, the answer may not come to him in the form that he wants or expects; it may come in the form of clues and hints at best, of suggestions. It is for him then to patiently take them up and follow them to where they lead. The suffering which has come to him is not meaningless. There is a sublime rationality behind it, even if it is only the specific effect of a cause which he set going in previous incarnations.

§

You may have lost your long-held fortune, your wife may have shamefully betrayed you, your enemies may have spread false accusations against you, while your private world may have tumbled to pieces over your head. Still there remains something you have not lost, someone who has not betrayed you, someone who believes only the best about you, and an inner world that ever remains steady and unperturbed. That thing and that being are none other than your own Overself, which you may find within you, which you may turn to when in anguish, and which will strengthen you to disregard the clamant whine of the personal distress. If you do not do this, there is nothing else you can do. Whither can you turn save to the inner divinity?

§

It is pardonable to wish a change of situation when it is grievous but it is better to enquire first what message the situation holds for us. Otherwise we may be attempting to elude the Overself's directive and thereby incurring the danger of an even greater disaster.

§

What matters is not only the quality of a man's consciousness but also the quality of his day-to-day living, not only the rare special mystical ecstasies that may grace his experience but also his relationship with the contemporary world and his attitude toward it. It is not enough to be a mystic: he cannot avoid the common road which all men must travel. In brief, can he be in the world but not of it? Can he sanctify the ordinary, the customary; those actions, this business, that very work for a livelihood; the contacts with family, friends, critics, and enemies? After all he is a ***human being*** with personal concerns; he cannot live for twenty-four hours a day in abstract ideas alone, or in religious withdrawnness: he has a body of flesh, a relevant duty or responsibility to perform in the world outside.

§

Philosophy is naturally best expounded out of gaiety of heart at the universe's wonderful meaning; but its lessons are best received, and its discipline best enforced, in the sadness of mind which comes to thought over the conditions of life today.

§

The kind of experience which man most dislikes to have is the very kind which forces him to seek out its cause, and thus begin unwittingly the search for life's meaning. The disappointments in his emotional life, the sufferings in his physical body, and the misfortunes in his personal fate ought to teach him to discriminate more carefully, to examine more deeply, and in the end to feel more sympathy with the sorrowing.

§

A single mistake in the rejection of an opportunity or in the choice of direction at a crossroad may lead to a quarter-lifetime's suffering. The student may quite easily discover by analysis the smaller lessons embodied in that suffering and yet may quite overlook the larger lessons, for he may fail to ascribe major blame to the early rejection or choice. He may still not realize how it all stems out of that primary root, how each error in conduct that naturally happens after it becomes a channel for a further one, and that in its turn for still another, so that the descent is eventually inevitable and its attendant sorrows become cumulative. Thus all traces back to the initial foundational error, which is the most important one because it is the choice of wrong direction, because such a wrong choice means that the more he travels through life, the more mistaken all his later conduct becomes.

§

Poverty is a stiff test of moral fibre.

§

The failures which everyone has left behind him—whether in career, relationship, or the quest itself—do not necessarily represent wasted effort. From each of them he can salvage the tuition for a fresh start, the caution for a wiser one, and more knowledge of himself.

§

It is not always possible to judge appearances. There are failures in life who are successes in character. There are successes in life who are failures in character.

§

He will learn to measure the worth of another man or of an experience by the resulting hindrance to, or stimulation of, his own growth into a diviner consciousness.

§

Beware of your thoughts, for when long sustained and strongly felt, they may be reflected in external situations or embodied in other humans brought into your life. But they cannot, of themselves and devoid of physical acts, make the whole pattern of your life—only the adept can do that. For other factors are also contributing, such as the will of God—that is, evolutionary necessity, or the World-Idea.

§

The experiences of life, ennobling some people but degrading others, can in the end affect our thoughts, desires, and feelings only as we let them. It is for us to say whether they shall call forth our divinity or our brutality. Our attitude of mind helps to determine our experience of the world.

§

If you live *inwardly* in love and harmony with yourself and with all others, if you persistently reject all contrary ideas and negative appearances, then this love and this harmony must manifest themselves *outwardly* in your environment.

§

When we are brought face to face with the consequences of our wrongdoing, we would like to avoid the suffering or at least to diminish it. It is impossible to say with any precision how far this can be done for it depends partly on Grace, but it also depends partly on ourselves. We can help to modify and sometimes even to eliminate those bad consequences if we set going certain counteracting influences. First, we must take to heart deeply the lessons of our wrong-doing. We should blame no one and nothing outside of ourselves, our own moral weaknesses and our own mental infirmities, and we should give ourselves no chance for self-deception. We should feel all the pangs of remorse and constant thoughts of repentance. Second, we must forgive others their sins against us if we would be forgiven ourselves. That is to say, we must have no bad feelings against anyone whatsoever or whomsoever. Third, we must think constantly and act accordingly along the line which points in an opposite direction to our wrong-doing. Fourth, we must pledge ourselves by a sacred vow *to try* never again to commit such wrong-doing. If we really mean that pledge, we will often bring it before the mind and memory and thus renew it and keep it fresh and alive. Both the thinking in the previous point and the pledging in this point must be as intense as possible. Fifth, if need be and if we wish to do so, we may pray to the Overself for the help of its Grace and pardon in this matter; but we should not resort to such prayer as a matter of course. It should be done only at the instigation of a profound inner prompting and under the pressure of a hard outer situation.

§

What happens to a man is important, but not quite so important as what he makes of it.

§

Why should we individually undergo every possible experience? Can we not, by creative imagination, intuitive feeling, and correct thinking save ourselves the need of passing through some experiences? This is so, but it is so only for those who have developed such faculties to a sufficient degree.

§

When painful experiences are undergone by mind on the lower levels of evolution, very little is learnt from those experiences—and that little slowly. When the same experiences are undergone by mind on the higher level, much is learnt from them—and learnt quickly. This is because in the one case there is no desire to learn the causes of that suffering, and no capacity to learn them even when the causes are evident; whereas in the other case, there is a keen desire to master the lessons and a prepared attitude wherewith to receive them. When, therefore, the really earnest disciple who has asked for a quickened advance on the Quest finds that all kinds of experiences begin to follow each other for a period, he should recognize that this is part of the answer to his call. He will be made to feel loss as well as gain, bliss as well as pain, success as well as failure, temptation as well as tribulation at different times and in different degrees. He needs both kinds of experience if his development is to be a balanced one. But because he is still human, he will learn more from his sufferings than from his pleasures. And because their memory will last longer, he will not pass through this period of quickened experiences and extreme vicissitudes without much complaint. Each of those experiences represents a chance for him, not only to conserve what he has already gained, but to pass to a farther point where he can gain something new.

§

We shall not indulge the vain hope of guiding all humanity out of the chaos in which it now finds itself, for humanity will refuse to follow the light which is itself guiding us. Deluded by its lower nature, blinded by its hollow traditions and hypocritical conventions, indifferent to the still small voice of truth merely because the voice of untruth blares more impressively through the thousand loudspeakers of vested interests, the human race will continue to flounder confusedly and to suffer needlessly. But here and there are individuals who will nevertheless welcome the light we bring. For their sake we must patiently hold the torch aloft.

§

A Prayer For The World:

In this time of confusion and anxiety, of strife and trouble, it is our holy duty to remember our dependence on Thee, O real Governor of the world!

We realize that the darkness in the world today has come because so many have forgotten their dependence on Thee.

Those whose positions of power or influence have placed them in the nations' councils need, in their grave responsibility, the help of Thy communion and the benefit of Thy guidance as never before, that they may not stray into error or weakness.

Therefore, we shall daily pray for them and for ourselves, in minutes of private worship or silent meditation that all may regain the feeling of Thy presence. We shall constantly confess our shortcomings and faults, but we promise to strive to better and ennoble our lives. We shall endeavour to cast out all evil thinking and materialistic belief.

Our need of Thy mercy and grace is vast. Show us the way to win them, O Infinite Father of all beings, Whose love is our last resource.

§

Powerful forces in the heaven worlds are gathering for a transmission and will enter our world at an appropriate time, which is fixed and measurable within this century. These forces will stimulate new thoughts and new feelings, new intuitions and new ideals of a religious, mystical, and philosophic kind in humanity. It will verily be the opening of a new epoch on earth, comparable to that which was opened 2000 years ago by the coming of Christ. The impulse will bring science into religion and religion into science: each will sustain the other and both, purified and vitalized, will guide humanity to a better and truer life. Insofar as science is an expression of man's desire to know, it is in perfect harmony with the highest spirituality. Only when it is unguided by his intuitive feelings, his heart, and put at the service of his animal nature alone, does it become anti-spiritual and bring him self-destruction as a punishment.

§

The time has come when education should re-educate itself, when medicine should give Nature's herbs their due and demand that all foods be rid of their added poisons, when the body-soul relationship should be correctly revealed by psychology and psychiatry, when for their health's sake and their soul's sake human beings should stop devouring corpses. The events and changes which have come on the world scene since the turn of the century stagger the mind, but those which will come before the end of it will be even more startling.

§

The thing that really matters in the life of a nation is the quality of its leaders, the character of those who guide its destinies. Young men may not realize that enthusiasm alone is not enough, that character always does and always will count, that he who fits himself for greatness will see whole kingdoms delivered into his hands. Inspiration brings fortune in its train and inspired teachers will always rise.

§

What does the future hold for mankind?—this is a question often asked and variously answered. One of the answers is given by Hinduism which says that the present period is the Kali Yuga—that is, the iron age—when life is at its darkest, man more corrupt, sinful, and wicked than ever, spirituality, religion, morals at their lowest ebb, sufferings, catastrophes, diseases at their highest tide. Moreover it says we are only at the first quarter of the iron age and we still have the other three quarters to go and that as we go farther into Kali Yuga the conditions will get worse and man more wicked. However Hinduism also says in its scripture the *Bhagavad Gita*, through the person (mythological though he may be) of Sri Krishna, that the Avatar—one who descends from a higher plane into human incarnation to bring in a new and better period—will come near or at the end of the iron age and use his power and knowledge to usher in the reign of goodness and righteousness, Truth, and above all Peace. Everywhere throughout the world today we see violence, agitation, and destruction, and this too, according to Hinduism, is to be expected in the Kali Yuga. Therefore attempts to end war are unlikely to meet with much success until the Avatar comes. If however we go not to Hinduism, but to the astrologers, and ask for their predictions, the story changes, brightens, and becomes full of hope. For they say we are entering the Aquarian age, the age which spreads knowledge, goodness, harmony, and peace. It might be asked, "What does philosophy say?" Its answer is that there is something of truth in both the Hindu and the astrological prognostications. First the evils of war, violence, destruction, and so on, will come to a climax with the materialization of nuclear war. Too much has been created on the mental plane and is being created not to find its way back to earth again in physical explosion. Only after a nuclear war with the major part of the human population wiped out will it be possible for a new start to be made, will mankind have learnt the lesson of substituting goodwill for ill will. Secondly, philosophy says that there are ages within ages—that is to say minor, lesser, and shorter periods within the great period—and we will after the nuclear war and after the chaos it brings enter one of these better periods.

§

If industrial civilization has enriched our outer life it has also impoverished the inner life. It need not have done so if we had brought about a proper equilibrium between the two and if we had done so under the light of the guiding principle of what we are here on earth for.

§

The composer of music or poetry, the thinker or sculptor who brings into the outer world what he has felt, glimpsed, thought in his own inner world, experiences a certain kind of satisfaction by that very act. The craftsman or the artisan who is able to make something by his own handiwork shares a measure of this satisfaction too. But the mass of workers packed away into a factory and occupied solely with machinery repeating the same movements dozens and dozens of times can hardly hope to get even an inkling of this satisfaction. If such monotonous work is essential, then let it be performed at intervals and let there be a rhythm of recuperation where the workers can return to themselves.

§

Those whose good fortune has given them enough to satisfy many desires ought not wait for old age to see how these satisfactions were passing and uncertain. They ought to do the heroic thing and detach themselves from the desire while there is still vigour in their feeling and their will.

§

For those without a higher viewpoint, the prospect of old age is a difficult one. The clever attractive modern cosmetics may take the years off a woman's appearance, but the years remain—oppressive and disturbing—within her consciousness. Early enthusiasm for living must, in the end, give way to a saddened recognition of our mortality. Reflection warns both woman and man of the frustrations awaiting human desire, but it also tells them of the compensations. These, however, must be earned. Foremost comes peace of mind.

§

Every man over a certain age is under sentence of death. Some men below that age are equally threatened. Should not both groups be sobered enough by such a remembrance to ask "Why am I here?"

§

Our elders are worthy of respect, but their counsel is worthy of heeding only if they are old in soul as well as body, only if they have extracted through many lifetimes all the wisdom possible from each one. Experience without reflection misses most of its value, reflection without depth misses much of its value, depth without impartiality may miss the chief point. For all our experience, our life in the body and world, is a device to bring out our soul.

§

It is not pleasant to reach old age. One tires easily—not only physically but also mentally—and one begins to weary of the routines of merely living, performing similar acts day after day. I speak of course of the average person, mass humanity—but one who has kept his mind alive, alert, eager to know, learn, and understand, who has developed his inmost resources cultural and spiritual, can never get bored.

§

Young immature people lack balance, knowledge, experience, and responsibility so that they are more easily rushed into courses of action dictated by frantic passion or frenzied emotion. But if they live long enough, life itself will impose its own disciplines upon them and compel them to accept adult responsibility and make the necessary growth which goes with it. Otherwise they may come to write their lives off as failures in the real sense, which includes the visible results in the world and the invisible moral and mental consequences in themselves. Until the balance within themselves is got right, they are liable to make decisions and commit actions which will later be regretted.

§

I am in much sympathy with rebellions against much academic education, with protests against its dryness, its narrow limitations, its rigidities, its stuffiness, and its pedantic quibbling. But unless these protests and rebellions are led by older persons with enough experience, maturity, judgement, and balance, they fall into the hands of communists, naïve liberals, and other politically minded destructive forces.

§

I was critical of the sadhus in India on certain points—never mind what they were. The differences got aired in several Indian newspapers at the time rather sensationally, and with much miscomprehension—even malice. But I also admired them on other points, some of which I find present today among those young drop-outs who have a religious turn of mind. They are in rebellion against a materialistic society and refuse to join it. They remind us that Jesus was a drop-out too. They try to live by working on self, supporting themselves co-operatively and not competitively, without ambitions, without insurance, with only a few possessions—by sincerity and not by appearance.

§

The idea of authority is hotly contested by the young, who fail to see that it is just as necessary as the idea of non-authority or freedom. This is true whether it is imposed on us by the higher laws governing existence or by other persons who are qualified to do so or even imposed by ourselves in the form of ideals and standards.

§

§

Where the physical body is cherished as the sole reality and made the sole basis for social and political reform, where hate-driven men advocate physical violence as the sole means of effecting progress, be sure of the presence of evil forces, dangers to society, ignorant opponents of truth, and enemies of the Light.

§

Although I deplore the condemnation of everything bygone, everything old, which is indulged in by so many of the young today, I agree with them that new times may bring new forms of inspiration and that the Truth, the Reality, does not necessarily have to be tied to tradition or look heavy with age or be stiff with the shapes given to it by our forefathers; it can be new, fresh, vivid, original. I include under this heading not only religious and metaphysical matters, but also artistic ones.

§

We live in an age when false statements are passed off as true ones and when deceptive values are passed off as real ones, when the dissemination of knowledge is getting more and more into the hands of those who are themselves too young to wisely instruct the young, too unbalanced to help the characters of the young, and too theoretical to be able to pass over really practical information which will help their students.

§

It is not enough for parents to protect a child—they should also encourage and stimulate it to awaken spiritually.

§

Of what use is an education if it does not teach the young how to use their minds so as to promote their own welfare, instead of their own harm? All ought to be made aware of the value and need of emotional and thought control, of discriminating between destructive or negative thoughts and constructive or positive ones.

§

Going to school is one thing, getting educated is another, although they coincide at times. Learning from a teacher is preparation. Learning from life in the world is observation. Learning from oneself is intuition.

§

It is his choice whether to accept the trammels of family life or the freedom of celibate life. Both conditions have their advantages and disadvantages, their compensations and difficulties. Each is a valid form of experience. But because most scriptures of most religions have been written by monks, their own status has been favoured and set higher. But it must be repeated: there is no one way which is the only way.

§

In one of his essays, Bacon delivers himself of the thought that the man who marries gives a hostage to fortune. This is so but it is part of the picture of the pairs of opposites which is universal throughout the world and inseparable from human existence. It is yin and yang—the duality of all manifested life. However there is an aspect of this topic which he might have included and that is that in marrying the man takes on another person's burdens in addition to his own. Yet this is equally true of all other forms of personal association with other human beings—of the hiring of assistants and the joining of an organization, of the making of friends and enjoyment of social contacts, of the working in a profession or the maintaining of a business. In all these activities a man takes on either a little or a large share of the problems of others.

§

It has been said in *The Quest of the Overself* that a married couple should grow together in companionly worship of the Light. If they do this they have found the basis of true marriage, successful marriage. Now in India a newly wedded couple are pointed out in the sky at night by a Brahmin priest, a star called "Vasishtarundhati." It is a pleasant little ceremony and supposed to be auspicious. For Vasishta was a great sage who lived thousands of years ago, Arundhati was his wife, and their marriage was a model of its kind in perfect conjugal happiness, wifely devotion, and mutual spiritual assistance. The ancient records link this star with this couple in their legend. Now the invention of the telescope has enabled us to discover that this star, which is the middle one in the tail of Ursa Major, or the Great Bear, is really a double star; that is, it consists of two separate stars situated so close to each other as to appear a unit to our naked eyes. Moreover, it is also a binary star; that is, the pair revolve around a common centre of gravity. Can we not see a wonderful inner significance in the old Indian custom? For the marital happiness of Vasishta and his wife was due to their having found a common centre of spiritual gravity!

§

14

THE ARTS IN CULTURE

Appreciation—Creativity—Genius
—Art experience and mysticism
—Reflections on pictures, sculpture, literature, poetry, music

Beauty is as much an aspect of Reality as truth. He who is insensitive to the one has not found the other.

§

We must call in the services of art to give religion its finest dress. Music must show its triumphs in the individual soul, architecture must create the proper atmosphere for communion, painting and sculpture must give visual assistance to the mind's upward ascension.

§

Through the practice of art a man may come closer to soul than through occultism.

§

Art can take the place of, and be a substitute for religion only when it is truly inspired.

§

A gracious and refined style of living might be disapproved by those of ascetic tendencies and even decried as materialistic. But aesthetic feeling can be quite compatible with spirituality.

§

When they fulfil their highest mission, painting and sculpture try to make visible, music tries to make audible, prose literature tries to make thinkable, poetic literature tries to make imaginable the invisible, inaudible, unthinkable, and unimaginable mystery of pure Spirit. Although it is true that they can never give shape to what is by its very nature the Shapeless, it is also true that they can hint, suggest, symbolize, and point to It.

§

Judge a work of art by analysing its effect. Does it leave you feeling better or worse, inspired or disturbed, calmed or restless, perceptive or dulled? For every opportunity to behold great paintings or listen to inspired music or read deeply discerning literature is itself a kind of Grace granted to us.

§

What Buddha taught about the transient, the changing, the elusive character of all human joy is plainly true: he went further and declared it unsatisfactory because of these reasons. Still further and on the same grounds, he rejected the attractions of the Beautiful Form. We are not to be ensnared by these perfections of form, that shapeliness of figure, that stateliness of architecture, and those symmetries of pattern such as engaged the ancient Greek artist. But the philosopher who cannot accept this further attitude is entitled to ask, "So long as we do not permit ourselves to be deceived into regarding them as the ultimate happiness, so long as we acknowledge their relativity and brevity, so what if they do pass, if they have their day? Why not enjoy them to the utmost while they are there? Why refuse an exquisite sight or an enchanting sound if, apart from the pleasure it affords, it might even be used as a stepping-stone to spiritual uplift?"

§

Art fulfils its highest purpose, acquires more valuable significance, when it becomes a vehicle for spiritual beauty.

§

It is true that men learn through disappointment and develop through suffering. But this need not cause us to forget that they also learn and develop through joy and beauty.

§

Such an inspired production gives out a form of energy which makes those who can receive it with enough sympathy feel and see what its creator felt and saw. There is an actual transmission.

§

A work of art which awakens in its beholder or hearer or reader a deep feeling of reverential worship or inner strength or mental tranquillity, thereby gives him a blessing. It enables him to share the artist's inspiration.

§

There is this quality about an inspired work, that you can come back to it again and again and discover something fresh or helpful or beautiful or benedictory.

§

Anyone who is susceptible to beauty in music or place has a spiritual path ready-made for him.

§

The inspired beauty to which a true artist introduces the world is an aspect of the same power to which a true priest introduces his flock.

§

The writer or artist or musician who is to stir up the intuitions in your mind must be the human receptacle of divine inspiration.

§

An art production whose form derives from spiritual tradition or symbolism, whose content derives from spiritual experience or understanding, is at least as worthy of veneration as a religious relic.

§

A simple environment, even an austere one, is understandable and acceptable in the case of those who have outwardly renounced the world, as well as of those who try to live in the world and yet be inwardly detached from it. But an ugly environment, even a drab one, is neither understandable nor acceptable in the case of those who profess to worship the Spirit. For its attributes are not only Goodness and Truth, among others, but also Beauty. To cultivate an indifferent attitude toward material possessions is one thing, but to show an insensitive one toward beautiful creations and to feel no repugnance toward ugly ones is not a spiritual approach; it is anti-spiritual.

§

It is a fact that beautiful surroundings create an atmosphere, benefit the emotional-mental state, and rest or stimulate a man according to their nature.

§

A philosophic temperament, well-developed and sufficiently rounded, has little taste for the ugly bareness propagated in the name of simple living, or for the dreary denial of the beautiful arts in the name of anti-sensuality.

§

Whether it be a piece of glued furniture or a constructed building, a piece of written prose or a flying machine, it should serve not the functional alone nor the beautiful alone, but a blend of both together.

§

The artist has two functions: to receive through inspiration and to give through technique.

§

The creative faculty should be cultivated and developed as both a great aid to, and expression of, spiritual growth.

§

If he succeeds in transmitting through the medium of his work something of the inspiration he receives, be he priest or artist, he is truly creative.

§

This is creative stillness; it is also magical, for it brings about the merging of yin and yang.

§

No artist really creates anything. All he can do is to try to communicate to others in turn what has been communicated to him.

§

What is the final call of true art? Not to the work which expresses it but to the spirit which inspires it, the divine source of which it reminds us.

§

If he composes, paints, sculpts, or writes as the light within shows him the thing or thought to be depicted—not as opinion, bias, or untruth urges him—he will be truly inspired.

§

The artist may work to earn his livelihood. But if he is also to consult his conscience, he must at the same time strive to become a servant of the Holy Spirit.

§

The artist who is infatuated with himself uses his production to flatter and hence strengthen his ego.

§

An artistic production that is really inspired must give joy to its creator at the time of creation equally as to its possessor, hearer, or beholder. If it does not, then it is not inspired.

§

The genius is both receptive and expressive. What he gets intuitively from within he gives out again in the forms of his art or skill.

§

He creates, not to express his small personality as so many others do, but to escape from it. For it is to the divine which transcends him, which is loftily impersonal, that he looks for inspiration.

§

Method and technique are necessary in themselves but incomplete; inspiration and intuition should shine behind them.

§

Although technical equipment is not all there is to the practice of art, it must be mastered. Without it, inspiration suffers from a faulty or deficient medium.

§

In matter and manner, in content and technique, in substance and style, the productions of the faultless artist who is also only technically competent will never equal those of the faultless artist who is also spiritually mature.

§

The philosophic search for enlightenment and the artist's search for perfection of work can meet and unite.

§

Art can be a path to spiritual enlightenment but not to complete and lasting enlightenment. It can be born out of, and can give birth itself to, only Glimpses. For art is a search for beauty, which by itself is not enough. Beauty must be supported by virtue and both require wisdom to guide them.

§

When a piece of deep music or a chapter of illumined writing puts him under a kind of spell towards the end, when the aesthetic joy or intellectual stimulus of one or the other gives him the sensation of being carried away, he ought to take full advantage of what has happened by putting aside the thought of the music or book and remembering that he is at the gate of the Overself.

§

Beauty is one side of reality which attracts our seeking and our love. But because it is so subtle and our perceptions are so gross, we find it first in the forms of art and Nature, only last in the pure immaterial being of the intangible reality.

§

The artist must raise the cup of his vision aloft to the gods in the high hope that they will pour into it the sweet mellow wine of inspiration. If his star of fair fortune favours him that day, then must he surrender his lips to the soft lure of the amber-coloured drink that sets care a-flying and restores to the tongue the forgotten language of the soul. For these sibylline inspirations of his come from a sky that is brighter than his own and he cannot control it.

§

The function of art is different from that of mysticism, but both converge in the same ultimate direction. Both are expressions of the human search for something higher than the ordinary.

§

The supremely gifted artist who works primarily out of pure love of his art—whether it be writing, painting, or music—rather than out of love of its rewards, sometimes approaches and arrives at this same concept through another channel. Such a genius unconsciously throws the plumbline of feeling into the deep mystery of his being. He is lifted beyond his ordinary self at his most inspired moments. He feels that he is floating in a deeper element. He receives intimations of the pure timeless reality of Mind whose beauty, he now discovers, his best works have vainly sought to adumbrate. The flash of insight is granted him, although if he is only an artist and not also a philosopher he may not know how to retain it.

§

The creative artist is taken out of himself for a time and is serenely elevated, just as the meditative mystic is. But the two states, although psychologically similar, are not spiritually similar. For the mystic enters his elevated state consciously and deliberately goes in quest of his inner being or soul. He uses it as a springboard to escape from the world of space time and change. The artist, however, uses it as a means of creating something *in* the world of space time and change. Hence although art approaches quite close to mysticism, it has not the same divine possibilities, for it lacks the higher values, the moral disciplines, and the super-sensuous aims of mysticism.

§

The artist uses a medium *outside* himself to effect his own personal approach to the ecstatic state of ideal beauty as well as to inspire the appreciators of his artistic production. The mystic uses no external medium whatever, but makes his approach to the source he finds *inside* himself. Although the mystic, if he be blessed with intellectual talents or artistic gifts, can project his ecstatic experience into an intellectual or artistic production when he chooses, he is not obliged to do so. He has this internal method of transmitting his experience to others through mental telepathy. Hence mysticism is on a higher level than art. Nevertheless, art, being much easier for most people to comprehend and appreciate, necessarily makes the wider appeal and reaches hundreds of thousands where mysticism reaches only a few.

§

The artist's productions may be most inspired; he may glorify art and put it on a pinnacle as the noblest and loftiest human activity when at its best. But it is still a manifestation of man's ego, the finest and final one. He must transcend it in the end. Like yoga, it prepares the way, is a step not a stop.

§

Whoever accepts the higher mission of art and comes nearer and nearer to it through his creative activity, will then go on from art to the Spirit deep within his own self.

§

A mind caught up with spiritually significant meanings, or attentively held by highly beautiful sounds, is a mind that one day will respond to Truth.

§

It is a rare moment when he looks upon Beauty itself rather than upon the forms of Beauty.

§

It is a common mistake among artists and writers to regard inflammation as inspiration, and to take inflamed feelings for inspired revealings.

§

The human being is played upon by various influences at various stages of his life in the body. We all know what climate and music will do to create different moods, but one factor often not understood or neglected is the influence of colour. It is always there in our surroundings, in a room, apartment, or house, in our clothing and in our furnishings. It can contribute towards health or take away from it; it can cheer or depress the emotions; it can invigorate or devitalize the body; it can give pleasure to the eyes or irritate them. Red, for instance, colour of the planet Mars and associated in astrology with war and anger, can be stimulating and life-giving if it is in its pure clear form. But in its undesirable darkish shades, it simply stimulates the lower desires, the animal feelings. However, it is a warm colour and for those who are old in years and in whom the circulation of blood is poor, the presence of pure red in the decorations and furnishings will help to keep them warmer. Orange will give the beneficial side of red and less of its negative side. Yellow is the colour of reason and helps to lift a man above his lower desires. In its pure golden sun-coloured phase, it is the colour of spiritual attainment, of the master who has achieved rulership over his emotions and body and passions. Green, which is Nature's colour, is restful, soothing, cheerful, and health-giving. The pure azure blue of Italian skies is associated by astrology with the planet Venus, the star of art, beauty, and sympathy verging almost on love. In its purest form it denotes devotional love, spiritual aspiration. It is not enough to know the meaning of colours; one must also know two other things about them: first, how to blend different colours and second, how to contrast them.

§

The notion that the effects of inspiration should not be handled by the labours of revision is a wrong one. This is so, first, because few artists ever achieve a total purity of inspiration—however ecstatic their creative experience may be—and second, because even if achieved it is still limited by the personal nature of the channel through which it flows. The writer who refuses to touch manuscripts again or to correct proofs displays vanity or ignorance or both.

§

I shall never forget the wonderful message which Ramana Maharshi sent me by the lips of an Indian friend (he never wrote letters). It was some years before his death and my friend was visiting the ashram preparatory to a visit to the West, whither he was being sent on a mission by his government. I had long been estranged from the ashram management, and there seemed no likelihood of my ever seeing the saint again. The visitor mentioned to the Maharishee that he intended to meet me: was there any communication of which he could be the bearer? "Yes," said the Maharishee, "When heart speaks to heart, what is there to say?" Now I don't know if he was aware of Beethoven's existence in the distant world of Western music, but I am certain he could not have known that the dedication to the *Missa Solemnis* was "May heart speak to heart." This is a work whose infrequent performance stirs me to depths when I hear it, so reverential, so supernal is it. Few know that Beethoven himself regarded the *Missa* as his greatest composition. It must surely be his most spiritual composition, a perfect expression of the link between man and God.

§

Of all the arts which minister to the enjoyment of man, music is the loftiest. It provides him with the satisfaction which brings him nearer to truth than any other art. Such is its mysterious power that it speaks a language which is universally acknowledged throughout the world and amongst every class of people; it stirs the primitive savage no less than the cultured man of the twentieth century. When we try to understand this peculiar power which resides in music, we find that it is the most transient of all the others. The sounds which delight our ears have appeared suddenly out of the absolute silence which envelops the world and they disappear almost instantaneously into that same silence. Music seems to carry with it something of the divine power which inheres in that great silence, so that it is really an ambassador sent by the Supreme Reality to remind wandering mortals of their real home. The aspirant for truth will therefore love and enjoy music, but he must take care that it is the right kind of music—the kind that will elevate and exalt his heart rather than degrade and jar it.

§

Art is not only here to embellish human existence. It is also here to express divine existence. In good concert music, especially, a man may find the most exalted refuge from the drab realism of his prosaic everyday life. For such music alone can express the ethereal feelings, the divine stirrings and echoes which have been suppressed by mundane extroversion. The third movement of Beethoven's Quartet in A minor, for instance, possesses a genuine mystical fervour. He may derive for a few minutes from hearing its long, slow strains a grave reverence, a timeless patience, a deep humility, an utter resignation and withdrawnness from the turmoil of the everyday world.

§

Music can express the mystical experience better than language; it can tell of its mystery, joy, sadness, and peace far better than words can utter. The fatigued intellect finds a tonic and the harassed emotions find comfort in music.

§

Music like any of the intellectual arts may help or hinder this Quest. When it is extremely sensual or disruptive or noisy, it is a hindrance and perhaps even a danger. When it is uplifting or inspiring or spiritually soothing, it is a help.

§

The spiritual author who conforms to his own teachings, who is as careful of his ethics, motives, actions, and thoughts as he is of his style, is a rare creature. There is not less posing to a public audience in the world of religio-mysticism than there is in the world of politics. The completely sincere may write down their experiences or their ideas for the benefit of others, but they are more likely to do so for posterity rather than for their own era. Their most inspired work is published after their death, not before it. The half-sincere and the completely insincere feel the need of playing out their roles during life, for the ego's vanity, ambition, or acquisitiveness must be gratified. The half-sincere seldom suspect their own motives; the insincere know their own too well.

§

The writer who engages the reader's mind and invites it to think renders an intellectual service. But the writer who incites it to intuit renders a spiritual one.

§

Wisdom is all the better when it is likewise witty. Raise a laugh while you lift a man. Mix some humour with your ink and you shall write all the better. Sound sense loses nothing of its soundness when it is poured into bright, good-humoured phrases. Truth is often cold-blooded and a bath in warm smiles makes it all the more attractive.

§

There are phrases in the New Testament which must impress the mind of every sensitive person. These phrases embody truths but they embody them in language which carries added authority derived from the style. I refer to the King James version, the translation into English made in the seventeenth century and today replaced by several modern versions in plain everyday twentieth-century English. It is true that in the modern ones the ordinary person gets a clearer notion of the meaning and, therefore, for him the modern translation is undoubtedly more useful. But I wrote of the sensitive person. For him not only is the meaning clear enough in the old version, but the style, with its beauty and authority, makes the statements even weightier.

§

Refined and gracious living is an expression of refined taste. It does not necessarily need great wealth to support it, for even within a modest income it can still be expressed in a modest way. A few plants, soft lights, fine porcelain, pleasantly patterned carpet, brightly coloured pictures, and a minimum of decorative furniture will give a man comfort and beauty.

§

A creative work of music, pictorial art, or literature which kindles an inspired mood in the audience, the beholder, or the reader has justified itself. It has made a contribution to humanity not less valuable on its own different plane as that which is made by the engineer or the builder.

§

Even the highest art is only a means to an end—it ought not to be made an end in itself. The inspired artist must in the end put aside his theme, his medium, his work and turn to the Divine alone, not to its expressions down here.

§

It is not only the workers in art who may get carried away by their concentration, but also the laymen who become the recipients of their productions and put themselves under their charm with a similar degree of concentration. In both cases—in the artist who creates and the layman who contemplates—there is an approach to the borderline of yoga. If it is pure beauty which calls forth their adoration and not some lesser thing, they may indeed cross this borderline and find themselves in a yogic state. What is said here of art is true also of the impulses derived from Nature. If man would only take such moods more seriously and rise to the highest level towards which the mood can carry them, they may well return to ordinary consciousness if not with a glimpse then with the next best thing to a glimpse.

§

15

THE ORIENT

Meetings with the Occident
—Oriental people, places, practices
—Sayings of philosophers—Schools of philosophy

The present day needs not only a synthesis of Oriental and Occidental ideas, but also a new creative universal outlook that will transcend both. A world civilization will one day come into being through inward propulsion and outward compulsion. And it will be integral; it will engage all sides of human development, not merely one side as hitherto.

§

Those Westerners who try to ape Indians—and not only Indians, but the ancient Indians at that—by adopting their dress, clothes, beliefs, and general way of life are putting themselves in a somewhat ridiculous position, if not a false one. We may give admiration and sympathy to Indian ideas and ideals up to a certain point, but we need not do it by throwing away completely all our Western heritage, which also has its substantial value. We need not let them prevent us from giving an adequate appreciation to the offerings of our own culture.

§

The Western peoples will never be converted wholesale to Hinduism or Buddhism as religions, nor will their intelligentsia take wholesale to Vedanta or Theosophy as philosophies. These forms are too alien and too exotic to affect the general mass. Historically, they have only succeeded in affecting scattered individuals. The West's spiritual revival must and can come only out of its own creative and native mind.

§

He would do well to give respect, veneration, and love to the Oriental Wisdom. For when the structures that we Westerners have put up are gone, its verities will still be there, unchanged and unchangeable.

§

Sir S. Radhakrishnan, Vice President of the Indian Republic and honoured expounder of Indian philosophy, has humbly said that "there is much we have to learn from the peoples of the West and there is also a little which the West may learn from us." My own travel and observation in both hemispheres lead to a less humble conclusion. What each has to learn from the other is about equal.

§

I have for some years kept myself apart from Indian spiritual movements of every kind and do not wish to get associated with them in any way. Consequently, I shall not resume my contact with any swami or yogi, for I wish to work in utter independence of them. My reasons are based on the illuminations which have come to me, on my understanding that the West must work out its own salvation, and on the narrow-minded intolerance of the Indian mentality towards any such creative endeavour on the West's part.

§

Professor T.M.P. Mahadevan, head of the department of philosophy at Madras University, recognized instantly and delightedly the symbol painted on several Greek ikons when I took him into the church belonging to an Orthodox monastery in Athens. It was, he exclaimed, "the gnana mudra," the gesture made by touching the tip of the forefinger with the thumb to form a circle. The inner meaning is that the ego (forefinger) is a continuation, a connection, or a unity with the Overself (the thumb). Only in appearance is it otherwise.

§

No one need find himself faced with the choice between Orient and Occident in his search for truth. It is a false choice—the real one is within himself.

§

Those in the West who saw that it could not proceed metaphysically to its farther possibilities out of its own resources, nor develop mystically, had to call in the aid of Oriental knowledge, experience, and teaching. This was a wise and broad-minded move. But this is not the same as deserting the Occidental heritage, from the early Greeks onward. Some do this and become fanatics.

§

Most either fall in love with the Oriental presentations and attitudes on spiritual matters or underestimate them. There ought to be room for a few who want to take an independent stand, who try to be impartial, and who ***know*** the subject.

§

Just as the Westerner is feeding and clothing his physical body, furnishing his home, conducting his business and operating his factories with stuffs from all parts of the world, thus enjoying a fuller larger life than his forebears ever did, so he ought to feed his mind on ideas from all worthy sources and build it up in a healthy way. He ought to keep open the willingness to recognize and receive spiritualizing impressions from outside. Their acceptance ought not to be allowed to imply the renunciation of what he has developed out of his own original resources. He need not give it up in order to take the other in. If any of these values is missing from a full culture, the latter is thereby and to that extent impoverished. Each has its distinctive offering to make. Let him accept it then. Let him assimilate all worthy elements but let him take care to do so from his own independent point of view. If he is to receive Asiatic ideas, let him receive them respectfully and appreciatively but let him not surrender completely and uncritically to them. Thus at the same time he will remain faithful to his own inner vocation and fulfil the purpose of this particular incarnation in the Western world.

§

Those who are so fascinated by the ancient tenets and methods that they surrender themselves wholly to them are living in the past and are wasting precious time relearning the past. They are ignoring the lessons of Western civilization. Why were they reborn in the West if not to learn new lessons? Let them absorb whatever is good and useful and true in the old teaching, but let them give it the new form required by our altered conditions of life. They must be flexible enough to adapt themselves to the demands made by the present. Those teachers who have not perceived this continue to teach the old methods alone. They are phonographically handing down that which they have received by tradition. If they had realized the inner spirit of their inheritance rather than its musty outer form, they would have become utterly free of the past. For then they would stand *alone* in the great Aloneness. And out of such a spirit they would instinctively give what is needed now, not what was needed in past centuries. We may welcome the knowledge and custom which have come down to us from those who have lived before but we must not become embalmed in them. Our times are not theirs, our world shows large differences from that in which they dwelt, and our needs are peculiarly our own. Nature will not permit us to revert in complete atavism even if we try, for disappointment calls us back in the end. Here is today's book of life, she says; read it and master the fresh lessons it offers you.

§

It is no longer enough to be merely Western in standpoint. But this is not to say that we must consequently swing to the opposite extreme and adopt an Indian one, as some of those who have been unable to satisfy their spiritual needs in Christianity aver. On the contrary, the truth is to be regarded from a universalist standpoint, for this is the only correct one. If it be sought as being merely Indian, its Occidental seekers will go astray. This is so not only because their needs and their situation are exceptional, but also because a dozen different traditional conceptions of truth now befog the Indian scene and bewilder the Indian seekers themselves.

§

Youngsters who take to the Indian religions with all the enthusiasm of converts, too often get a hazy understanding of the philosophy associated with them if, intellectually, there is any interest beyond the religious one itself. Nor is this surprising when swamis who collect Western disciples confuse religion with philosophy in a kind of mixed-up Irish stew.

§

We need to carry something of the Oriental brain under our Occidental skulls, to seek for a kind of synthesis between the seething activities of the West and the dusty quietism of the East, to accept and use the advantages of modern technical civilization whilst avoiding the evils that come with it. We need the dynamic power of the Occident but must mingle with it something of the introspective qualities of the Orient. Such a combination of ideals would lead to a full and truly human life. We must be pioneers of a new and wiser age which would bring together the best elements of Asian thought with Euro-American practicality in happy marriage. This would not only bring us contentment, not only restore inner peace and outer prosperity, but also put the larger nations on the path to true greatness.

§

The bane of Indian higher cultural life is the lack of independent ventures of the mind. For hundreds of years men have not had the courage to do more than write interpretations of other books, which themselves were written thousands of years ago and hence *before* human knowledge had advanced to the degree it did later. We find in Sanskrit few original works but any number of commentaries.

§

Freemasonry: The roots of Freemasonry have been attributed both by its own pioneers and by history to lie embedded in ancient Egypt. The cultural connection of ancient Egypt and ancient India is now slowly being established; the philosophic and religious indebtedness of the country of the Nile to the country of the Ganges is being uncovered by history and archaeology. This esoteric system admittedly once fulfilled a far loftier mission than it does today and was therefore worked in an atmosphere of greater secrecy. It was closely connected with religion, mysticism, ethics, and philosophy. Even today we find that it still possesses three progressive degrees of initiation, whose names are drawn from the act of building: the "Entered Apprentice," the "Craftsman," and the "Master Mason." The first degree represents spiritual faculties just dawning; the second degree represents those same faculties grown quite active; the third degree represents the quest and the ultimate discovery within himself of the true Self. If the earlier degrees teach him how to behave towards others, the last degree teaches him rightly how to behave towards himself. For here his search ends in undergoing the mystical death of the ego, which allows him to live in his own spiritual centre henceforth. Whoever fulfils the Masonic rule of being "of lawful age and well recommended" may then knock as "a poor blind candidate" at the door of the Master's chamber for admittance. The initiation of the novice into the first degree of Masonry is symbolically performed while he is half-clothed. He is then called an "Entered Apprentice." All men throughout the world who sincerely and seriously adopt religion because they apprehend a mystery to be concealed behind the universe, thereby unconsciously enter this degree. All religious men who live up to their ethical obligation and thus make themselves worthy are eventually passed into the second degree, that of "Fellow Craft." This symbolizes the stage of mysticism wherein the seeking mind passes half-way behind the symbol. It is the mystics who consecrate their quest to inner contemplation within themselves rather than in external churches or temples. They furnish from among their number the few who have discovered that service is the most powerful means of advancement and who are raised to the third degree of a fully-robed "Master Mason." He alone is given the clue whereby he may recover the "Lost Word" of the true Self, the ultimate Reality, a secret now vanished from the ken of the modern successors of Enoch and Hiram Abiff. And he alone dons blue robes as a token of his universal outlook—that same blue which is the colour of the cloudless overarching sky that covers all creatures on the planet.

Apart from its use of the solar symbol, in this highest grade, of the sun at noon as a sign that the Master will work for the enlightenment of all, you will find that Masonry has indicated its worship of Light by including the cock in its ceremonial rites. For this is the bird which rises with the sun; which, in fact, vigorously and loudly informs its little world that the dawn is at hand and that the benign rays will soon be shed upon it.

§

There was a sanity, a wholeness, about the goal of the best Greeks which we do not find easily elsewhere in the antique or Oriental world. They appreciated art created by man, beauty created by Nature, and reason applied by man. They developed the body's health, strength, shapely form; they disciplined it at certain periods for special purposes, but without falling into the fanaticism and extremism of those ascetic religions which abjure enjoyment merely because it is enjoyment.

§

In my Asian wanderings I noticed that the people of sun-scorched plains were the most fatalistic and those of the hills were least so. Where the one group surrendered easily to lethargy, the other used will and energy to shape circumstance.

§

We hear of lamas in Tibet who immure themselves in sealed rooms, with but a small hole in the wall to receive their morsel of food, so that in total darkness and in total inactivity they may better concentrate all their attention on their inner practices. We hear of monks in the Zendo halls of Japan who sit half round the clock while holding the mind persistently to their meditations. We hear of yogis in India who forsake wife and home, position and possessions, and withdraw to forest, cave, or ashram. We shrink with terror from such hard exercises and abnegations. How puny seems our own effort by contrast, how paltry our own self-denial!

§

The ancient Hellenic mind was sharpened by the study of mathematics. This enabled it to search for truth unclogged by superstition and unswayed by imagination. It helped too by nurturing the power of concentration. But it was still inferior to the far more valuable capacity of the Indian mind to still thought altogether.

§

In the personal presence of Gandhi, one felt that he was being used by some tremendous impersonal, almost cosmic power. But the feeling was noticeably different in kind from that one experienced with, say, Sri Aurobindo or Ramana Maharshi. It may be that in Gandhi's case the inspirer was the energy of Karma, shaper of India's destiny!

§

For the first couple of hundred years of its history, Buddhist piety honoured Gautama as an enlightened man but did not worship him as a God. For this reason it refrained from depicting him in statue or picture, but figured him symbolically only by the Bo-tree or the Truth-wheel. Muhammed was even more emphatic in demanding no higher recognition than as a Messenger, a Prophet, and strictly forbade the representation of his human form. To this day, in no mosque throughout the Islamic world can a single one be found. But, in striking contrast, every Buddhist temple throughout Asia has its Buddha statue. That which overcame the earlier repugnance was human emotional need to admire the superhuman attainment of Nirvana, the religious desire to worship godlike beings or pray to them for help, the feeling of devotion toward a higher power. And a great help was given to breaking the ban by the spread of the Greek empire in the lands between Persia and India, as well as in Northwest India itself. For this brought Greek ideas and influence, a less otherworldly, more rationally human attitude, expressed in the way the Greeks figured their own gods always in human forms. When their artistic skills were called upon to make the first stone statues of the founder of Buddhism, they represented him not as a half-starved lean ascetic, not as a bare-shouldered shaven-headed monk, not even as a spiritual-looking saint, but as a curly haired, beautifully featured, Apollo-headed prince. For it was Greek sculpture which first portrayed the naked human body with a beauty, a poise, and a refinement unmatched earlier and hardly surpassed even in our own time.

§

A remark once made by Ramana Maharshi reminded me of Tagore's extraordinary statement in his poem *Vairagya*. A pilgrim goes in quest of God after leaving home. The more he travels, the farther he goes from his house, the more he puts himself farther from the object of his pilgrimage. In the end, God cries, "Alas! Where is my worshipper going, forsaking me?"

§

Sir Francis Younghusband crossed the Gobi Desert on foot and explored it again on a later occasion. Mongolia, where it is positioned, as a Lamaistic Buddhist country, owed spiritual fealty to the Dalai Lama in Tibet. Sir Francis told me one day of a mysterious Mongolian whom he had met and who without uttering a single word aloud, purely by telepathic contact, had powerfully influenced his mind and given it a greatly broader spiritual outlook. Many years later I met this same adept, then an exile in Cambodia from his native land which had fallen to the Communist-atheist regime. Through the services of an educated Chinese disciple who was with him, we were able to converse about Buddhism and other matters. He gave out a teaching which formed the basis of mentalism and which was occasionally so subtle that it went above my head, but which I understood sufficiently to revolutionize my outlook. Some of its tenets were incorporated in the mentalism explained in my books *The Hidden Teaching Beyond Yoga* and *The Wisdom of the Overself*.

§

Ramana Maharshi: One night in the spring of 1950, at the very moment that a flaring starry body flashed across the sky and hovered over the Hill of the Holy Beacon, there passed out of his aged body the spirit of the dying Maharshi. He was the one Indian mystic who inspired me most, the one Indian sage whom I revered most, and his power was such that both Governor-General and ragged coolie sat together at his feet with the feeling that they were in a divine presence. Certain factors combined to keep us apart during the last ten years of his life, but the inner telepathic contact and close spiritual affinity between us remained—and remains—vivid and unbroken. Last year he sent me this final message through a visiting friend: "When heart speaks to heart, what is there to say?"

§

Pathos in Ananda Mayee's singing voice caused her hearers to weep. It was like listening to a divine angelic voice.

§

Except for our first meeting, tea seems to be associated with my contacts with Professor D.T. Suzuki. He invited me to help myself from the ever bubbling samovar of light-coloured weak-tasting green tea which was the national Japanese drink. This was at the Engakuji Monastery, Temple, and Academy in those far-off years before the war. This was the fitting place, the pertinent atmosphere, in which to talk quietly about Zen. Then we met again, about a decade later, after the war, at the Los Angeles Japanese Buddhist Temple where he was staying as a guest. He offered some little round rice-cakes this time to eat with the tea. I noticed that he now put a lump of sugar between his front teeth and held it there while he drank. The third time he asked me to tea was a couple of years later at Columbia University, where he again was a guest. There we had Western-style rolls as the accompaniment. After his secretary-assistant removed the trays, we went at great length and in much detail into a comparison of Indian yoga, philosophy, and texts with Zen Chinese and Japanese meditation methods, philosophy, and texts. I was amazed at his extraordinary erudition, for he not only knew exactly where the references supporting his statements could be found, but his ability to read Sanskrit and Chinese, along with his native Japanese and early acquired English, gave a width and authority which few other men possessed. His basic point was that whereas Zen sought and achieved direct penetration to reality, Indian yoga sought and achieved mental stillness—not necessarily the same and certainly inferior. We were unable to come to a full agreement, so we gradually drifted away from the matter and he talked confidentially with touching humbleness of his own spiritual status. "They consider me a master," he said finally, "but I consider myself a student." Then before leaving I suggested that we meditate together, communing in the silent way that was well-understood in both Japan and India. "But I only meditate in private, alone," he protested, "or in the assembly of a zendo (monastic hall for group meditation). Nobody has ever asked me to do this before." But in the end he yielded, and there we sat with the grey university walls of Columbia all around, the warm summer sunshine coming in through the windows.

§

Ananda Mayee: Instead of using the personal pronoun "I," she often used the phrase "this body." She was born in 1896 in a Brahmin family noted for its religious learning and piety. When nearly thirteen years old, she was married to another Brahmin. She developed a great liking for religious music, from which she passed to mantra yoga practice. "Everything becomes possible by the power of pure concentrated thought," she says. No guru initiated her. From her middle teens to her twenty-fifth year, she passed more and more time in reveries, abstractions, and long periods of silence, until even trance states were achieved. Often she passed into states in which tears of joy or of longing and aspiration would well up in her eyes while singing devotional songs. Those who heard her were thrilled by the emotion in her voice. Strange phenomena manifested when she was alone. Her neck would be turned by some force and remain twisted for some time. A brilliant light would shine all around her; or her body would automatically assume one of the yogic postures, and she would stay in it for hours, eyes open and unblinking, in a trance so deep that no one could awaken her. She had to be left to come out of it of her own accord. Her food intake is very small. I first met her in Rajpur, at the foot of the Himalayas. Her husband had become her first disciple; his relationship with her was then a brother-and-sister one. She gives no formal initiation to disciples and recommends everyone to take a few minutes every day out of their routine for meditation. Benares is her headquarters now, but she goes on tour for a few months every year so that others elsewhere may benefit by her heavenly singing.

§

In the Musée Guimet in Paris, we may see a couple of wonderful ancient statuettes that perfectly portray Buddha's wonderful half-smile of happy deliverance from this world of ignorance, illusion, error, sin, and suffering.

§

Those Indian religions which preach futility and enjoin renunciation are as much a product of their tropical enervating climate as the malarias and fevers and choleras which beset Indian bodies.

§

The story that Pythagoras was murdered because he refused to pass through a bean field (which was his only way of escape) owing to his aversion to beans is as untrue as so many other legends of antiquity. When there was trouble at Crotona and his work there became impossible, he simply removed in 515 B.C. to Metapontum, the capital city of a small state, and continued there until he died peacefully. His ban on beans in the diet of his followers applied to the large "fava" bean, as it is called in Italy where he then lived, or the "horse bean," as it is now called in some other European countries. This definitely contains a poisonous element, and I remember two cases of food poisoning in villagers who had eaten too largely of them during my sojourn in Greece.

§

In the blind adherence to superstitious beliefs which affects Westerners who try to turn themselves into Hindus, I am more anti-Hindu than most prejudiced sceptics; but in the deep acclaim for the wonderful truth-statements to be found in some ancient Indian texts, I am more pro-Hindu than the swami followers. This is because in both cases I write from inside knowledge and personal experience. My attitude is consequentially a semi-detached one.

§

It was a widely travelled, well-educated, but deeply spiritual Indian who said to me, because he was free from narrow religious sectarianism, that "India is a dying land." Once noted for its intense religious faith, the latter exists now more outwardly than inwardly and the depths of human search for the highest Truth are being covered up. This search is passing over to the Western countries.

§

Those who care for koans will wander about in circles and in the end come back with empty hands. They will have to start afresh on a new road having learnt that wisdom is not hidden in lunacy—except for minds already confused or distorted.

§

Why did Buddha not wait even a week after his enlightenment near Benares before going out to preach among the people? Why did he keep up this spreading of his message so incessantly for the remaining forty-five years of his life? Contrast this with the many Hindu sages and mystics, from his own time till this day, who sit and wait for would-be disciples to approach them. The answer lies only partly in the special mission and power with which he was invested by the World Mind.

§

The Oriental use of the term "wisdom" not only includes our Occidental notion of Solomonic judgement in dealing with a situation, but ranges far enough to include the capacity to understand the universe as it really is in depth, and not merely in terms of sensory experience.

§

Confucius lived 2500 years ago yet for 1500 years his wisdom was highly prized throughout China. He described a standard and ideal to be sought for human behaviour and human social intercourse. Character and conduct need to be disciplined and polished, he affirmed, and proper decorum must enter into one's relations with others. Proper respect must be shown to those entitled to it. The Chinese rightly considered him a sage who knew the ultimate significance of life, who was enlightened and understood the hidden meaning and the higher purpose of human existence. For these reasons I also advocate that this matter of refined behaviour be regarded in a totally new light as a form of spiritual expression and development.

§

To leave out of one's reckoning both the body and the world as non-existent is not an idea that has profited India in any way, if we look at her history. In the very act of denying them as illusions, the Indian has himself fallen into an illusion.

§

It is my well considered belief that Ananda Metteya was a Bodhisattva, come from a higher plane to penetrate those Western minds which could appreciate, and benefit by, Buddhism as meeting their intellectual and spiritual needs. He gave the hidden impetus, but others came later to do the outer work.

§

The tea ceremony was started in China 1000 years ago by Zen priests and spread into Japan a couple of centuries later. Whereas Chinese priests started it to ward off drowsiness in meditation, the Japanese laity made it popular. Slowly it changed until the sixteenth century, when the present rite was finalized by Zen priests. The greatest possible economy of movements is aimed at. The rite is an exercise in refinement, gracefulness, and calm. But surprising humility is also embodied in it in a way strangely reminiscent of the Egyptian Great Pyramid, for like the entrance to the King's Chamber, the entry to the Tea-Chamber is through an opening so small and so low in the wall that a visitor is forced to bend down and almost crawl through.

§

It could be said that to put fine points upon these three Sanskrit words which are used so loosely today might be helpful to students. First, the word "guru" applies to the man who opens the eyes of those who are spiritually blind. The title "swami" applies to the man who provides spiritual teaching for the ignorant. The term "acharya" applies to the man who provides the best example of spiritual conduct.

§

If we enquire why communism is now a sort of nemesis to the religion of Tibet and even begins to threaten India, we must remember that the villagers are ruled as much by superstition and fanaticism as by piety and wisdom. They are certainly not guided in their everyday living by the higher philosophic or mystic culture which mostly attracts the interest of foreigners to Buddhism and Hinduism.

§

The contrast between loquacious Americans of the cities and silent Arabs of the desert is unforgettable. The Bedouin can sit in a group and say nothing at all for hours! The desert's peace has entered into them to such an extent that the social duty of laryngeal activity is unknown among them, and regarded as unnecessary!

§

Whoever understands the workings of the Indian mind where it has not been changed by overmuch contact with Western men or modern thought, will understand its pessimistic trend. For it imperiously demands and strongly needs the consolation of a world-escaping religion. The undertones of Indian life are not happy; they speak of resignation and melancholy, of unalterable destiny and the insignificance of man.

§

Lu Hsiang-shan (1139–1193) originated a school of philosophy boldly developed from the Neo-Confucianist one of the Sung Dynasty (960–1280). His teaching, a Monistic Idealism, reached its culmination with Wang Yang-ming (1472–1529), who expounded and developed it.

Lu Hsiang-shan lectured for several years at Elephant Mountain in Kiangsi, so called himself "the old man of Elephant Mountain." He married at twenty-nine to a cultured woman. In the national examination for governmental posts, his paper stood out as distinctive among several thousand. He was given an official post in the Imperial Academy. His lectures were so eloquent as to attract large crowds. When the celebrated Chu Hsi asserted that width of knowledge should be considered the foundation of virtue, Lu replied that discovery of the Original Mind should precede it. When he became a magistrate, he proved himself to be as practical in worldly matters as he was penetrating in metaphysical ones. He rebuilt the crumbling city walls, eliminated official extravagance, reduced corruption, cut down crime, and quickened legal proceedings. Yet later he declined promotion, for, with all this activity, he continued to lecture whenever possible. He died peacefully after telling his family "I am going to die," and sitting in meditation for several hours. Some of his sayings and his few writings were collected together and it was this book that Wang Yang-ming republished in 1521, so highly did he esteem it.

One should cultivate the feeling of Reverence, taught Lu. He writes: "It is incorrect to explain that the Mind of man is equivalent to desire and the Mind of Spirit to Heavenly Law. How can man have two Minds? Mind and Law do not admit of dualism. . . . This Mind has no beginning or end; it permeates everywhere. Evil is an inescapable fact and a practical experience. A scholarly man must first make firm his will."

§

To think of Gautama the Buddha, the picture of his face appears as emanating pure intelligence tinted by compassion. To read his printed sayings is to feel that attention must move slowly, that the mind needs all its seriousness to absorb their meanings.

§

If I admire *Wang Yang-ming* so greatly it is because he combined in his person qualities and capacities which proved that it is possible to live the philosophic life to the full. He was in his fifty-seven years of life a successful military commander, an excellent magistrate, a talented poet, a discriminating analyst of religions, a cultivator of intuition, a practiser of meditation, and a teacher of philosophy. He not only brought together the best in Confucius' teaching, in Buddhism and Taoism, but made valuable contributions of his own to this synthesis. It is however needful to explain to Western students that Wang's teaching of the unity of Knowledge and Conduct does not refer to intellectual knowledge but to intuitive Knowledge. To this union or Mutuality of KNOWING and DOING he gave the name of "SINCERITY." The theory learnt from books or lectures does not of itself necessarily have power to move the will; but intuition developed in the course of time by practising mental quiet, emotional calm, and personal detachment has this power. What the Indian gurus called detachment is really the same as what the Chinese philosophers like Lao Tzu called "non-action," and this is the term Wang used. It does not mean doing nothing but keeping to a certain emotional dis-involvement while doing things, an attitude itself arising from, or helped by, the quiescence practice. Another definition of "Sincerity" is harmony with the Principle of the Universe.

§

There is this difference between the two largest and oldest Asiatic peoples. The mystics of India always sought an idealized human being as their master. When they found him, he was proclaimed God incarnate; everything he said or did, everything about him was considered perfect. Consequently they fell into self-deception and in their excess created an unhealthy relationship. The mystics of China were not such dreamers. They sought no impossible human perfection; they recognized necessary human limitations and inescapable human flaws.

§

The Vedantin needs Buddhism to complete and to equilibrate his outlook; the Buddhist needs Vedanta for the same purpose. Otherwise, there is a kind of one-sidedness in each one. A widening-out will improve their views and better the persons.

§

Tantra has been greatly misunderstood in the West by those who have seized upon the merely physical aspect of it alone. Its highest and primary reference is not to men and women in their sexual body relationships. The aim of the higher Tantra is to bring the personal self and the Overself together in harmony balance and union. Then only is the full human being likely to be developed. Then only are all the miseries and troubles so often associated with sexual ignorance and sexual indiscipline likely to be overcome.

§

The first doctrine presented by Hinduism is what the absolute Self, Brahman, *is*. The second doctrine is the identity of the absolute Self with Brahman. According to the second of these doctrines (whose profundity makes the services of an expounder and a commentator so useful), the inmost Being of man, Atman, is divine and perfect, as is the cosmic Being of the Lord, Ishvara. The third doctrine is that the universe is maya, an illusory thing that has no ultimate reality. The fourth doctrine is that history is not a meaningless scramble of happenings, but flows through karma—God's law—and through avatars—God's incarnations. The traditional mission of all the Shankaras has been to guard, protect, or preach the doctrines and beliefs, from the simple commandments for illiterate peasants, to the higher mystical experiences of the yogis and metaphysical teachings of Advaita.

§

The concept of nonduality given by the Advaitins seems impossible to grasp and to accept to the normal Western mind and quite rightly so. This impasse must exist unless and until the situation is clarified and the only way to do so lies through mentalism. The human mind normally functions in a dualistic manner—that is, it identifies itself as a subject with an object of its consciousness outside. This dualism penetrates the practices followed on the Quest and the knowledge gained as a consequence of them. It can not be got rid of until both subject and object are thrown into and unified by the pure consciousness—Mind—in which, from which, and by which all happens. In this connection a further point must be established. I have written admiringly of two great souls—Sri Ramana Maharshi and the Shankaracharya of Kanchi, the spiritual head of South India. Now both these are strict followers of the original, the first Shankaracharya, who lived more than a thousand years ago and they quote from his writings very frequently. Whoever studies those writings will discover that Adi Shankara, meaning the first Shankara, in his arguments against the Buddhists—especially those of the idealistic Yogacara and Vijnana schools—seems to reject idealism which is an incomplete form of mentalism. But let us not forget that Shankara was engaged in a campaign to reduce the power of Buddhism and increase the power of Hinduism. Let us not forget too that Buddha himself was not bound by any such bias; he was a free thinker and he did not hesitate to question the authority of the Vedas which Shankara followed and accepted. The Buddha rejected animal sacrifices and futile religious rituals, for instance. It is to Shankara's credit that he gave out the Advaitic teaching of nonduality—which is impossible for a Western mind in all its rationality to accept unless it falls into mysticism and yoga. Both the living Shankara and Ramana Maharshi were upholders of Hinduism. As I have said, the doctrine of nonduality is quite acceptable when presented with a mentalistic explanation or through a mystical experience but not otherwise.

§

ZEN BUDDHISM is a form of mysticism, perhaps one of its highest if most puzzling forms, and not a philosophy. Therefore it is incomplete, one-sided. The evidence for this is inherent in itself for it disdains metaphysics, study, reason, and stakes everything on a flash intuition got by meditation. There is here no such check on the correctness completeness and finality of such an intuition as is provided by philosophy. A further evidence lies in the history of its own founder. Bodhidharma admittedly travelled to China to give out his teaching yet, after his arrival, he contented himself with sitting in complete solitude for nine years at Sung-Shan, waiting for a prospective disciple to approach him. Had he been a sage, however, he would surely have filled those nine years with making his knowledge readily available to whoever was ready for it and if there existed no such elite, he would in that case have helped the masses with simpler if more indirect forms of truth.

§

The Muhammedan and Hindu authors of important spiritual works including scriptural works usually began with an invocation. This prefatory act was both part of putting themselves into the mood, the passive mood, of receiving inspiration from the Higher Power and part a reminder to the reader to approach his reading with sufficient reverence and seriousness.

§

Atman—one of the most important and basic doctrines in Sanskrit learning. To take Atman as self is to confirm and strengthen the very error which the doctrine of Atman seeks to refute! Such a procedure imbues the mind anew with the thought of "I." For in Atman there can be no such thing as a personal entity, no existence of an ego at all. Those who have studied both the Hindu *Upanishads* and the Buddhist *Abhidhamma* sufficiently and profoundly cannot fail to observe that Atman is merely the intellectual parallel and counterpart of Nirvana. And who has more strongly fought the belief in self than Buddha?

§

And yet, if everything is incessantly changing, still there is a certain continuity of substance or essence throughout these changes which prevents us from asserting that it has become a totally different thing; if every human being is not the same as he was some time ago, still we have also to admit, with Buddha, he is not another being. The alterations we witness occur in the realm of form, not of essence.

§

The Chinese temperament was too realistic to follow the Indian into a merely metaphysical view of life and too practical to run away with it into an escapist view. Indeed, the very name of the principal religion of China—Confucianism—is the Doctrine of the Mean, the Mean being the middle point between two extremes, the balance between two sides. Even the two most celebrated Chinese mystics exhibited their national tendencies in their writing and philosophically united the idea of real being with the idea of illusory being. Such were Lao Tzu and Chuang Tzu. Like the Indians, the Chinese were ready to find out what other-worldliness had to offer them; but unlike the Indians, they were not ready permanently to forsake the worldly life while doing so. Even the Buddhist school, which has lasted longest and remained strongest in China, is the one named "The Round Doctrine"—meaning that it is widely rounded to include both the spiritual and the material. This is the "Tendai" school.

§

16

THE SENSITIVES

Psychic and auric experiences—Intuitions
—Sects and cults

What they seldom see is that spiritual illumination and psychical error can and do exist in the same mind at the same time.

§

He will lose nothing and gain much if he tries to know scientifically why these experiences arise. And he will be a better mystic if he can relate them to the rest of life, if he can move forward to a fuller understanding of his place in the universal scheme, if he can reach an explicit and self-conscious comprehension of his own mysticism. If we grant that he can successfully attain his mystical goal without this definite knowledge, he cannot become an effective teacher and guide without it. So long as his interest is confined to himself this need not matter, but as soon as he seeks to serve mankind it does matter. For then only can he present the way and the goal in the detail and with the clarity that helps to convince others.

§

It is true that to analyse with scientific detachment these most intimate and precious experiences, visions, and messages could if imprudently done easily destroy their value or prevent their recurrence. Yet this is precisely what he has to do if he is to protect himself against illusions.

§

God will appear to us in Spirit alone, never in Space. To see him is to see the playing and posturing of our own mind.

§

The only elementals are vivified thought-forms. If they are evil and attack you, oppose them with thoughts of an opposite character. If your thoughts are strong enough and sustained enough, the elementals will eventually vanish.

§

If he can catch any of these psychic manifestations at the very moment when they begin, that is the best time to prevent their arisal altogether, for then they are at their weakest. That is the proper time to nip them in the bud.

§

If the voices which he hears are audible in the same way that one hears the voices of people through the ears, it is merely psychic and undesirable. If, however, it is a very strong mental impression and also very clear, then it is the mystic phenomenon known as the "Interior Word" which is on a truly spiritual plane and therefore is desirable.

§

H.P.B.'s *Voice of the Silence* tells of seven mystical sounds which are heard by the aspirant. The first is like the nightingale's voice, whereas the sixth is like a thunder-cloud. This passage has been much misunderstood both by novices and by unphilosophical mystics, whilst in India and Tibet whole systems of yoga have been built up on their supposed psychic existence. The sounds are not actually heard. The reference to them is merely metaphorical. It speaks rather of the silent intuitive feeling of the Overself's existence which becomes progressively stronger with time, until finally, in H.P.B.'s own eloquent words, "The seventh swallows all the other sounds. They die, and then are heard no more." This represents the stage where the voice of the ego is completely unified with the voice of the Overself, where occasional realization is converted into a constant one.

§

All occult experiences and spirit visions are mental, and not spiritual, in the sense that the mind has various latent powers which pertain to the ego, not Overself. The question which is real can be answered differently according to standpoint. He need not trouble about the occult side, which would be a degeneration for him. His chief aim must be to realize pure B-e-i-n-g, not to see or experience anything outside it. Only after this has been done is it safe or wise to concern himself with anything occult.

§

Tantrika Yoga: Its methods are physical, ceremonial, sensual, and dangerous; its aims are the arousal of sleeping occult strength. In its highest phase, where the motive is pure and egoless, it is an attempt to take the kingdom of heaven by violence. But few men have such an exalted motive, as few are pure enough to dabble in such dangerous practices. Consequently, it need hardly be said that in most cases this road easily leads straight down to the abyss of black magic. This indeed is what has happened in its own history in Bengal and Tibet.

§

A part of the illumination does not rise from within. It is implanted from without. It is not a contribution from divine wisdom, but a suggestion from human thought. It is really an activation by the soul's newly found power of ideas put into the mind previously by others. For example, many Indian yogis actually hear the word "aum" sounding through the mind in their deep and prolonged meditation. A few, belonging to a particular sect, hear the word "Radhasoami" in the same condition. Why is it that no Western mystic, uninitiated into Eastern Yoga, has ever recorded hearing either of these words? This phenomenon is really due in one group of cases to hypnotic suggestion by a guru, and in the other group to unconscious suggestion by a tradition. All that does not however negate its actuality and genuineness, nor detract from its value in first, strengthening the aspirant's religious faith, second, promoting his mystical endeavours, and third—which is most important of all—providing him with a diving board whence to plunge into the vast silence of the Void, where no words can be formulated and no sounds can be heard, because it is too deep for them or anything else. These, being the most advanced form of psychic phenomena, occur in the last stage of meditation and just before contemplation proper begins.

§

One fact about most mystical phenomena is that they are transient. Strains of heavenly music may be heard by the inner ear and intoxicate the heart with their unearthly beauty—but they will pass away. Clairvoyant visions of Christ-like beings or of other worlds may present themselves to the inner sight—but they will not remain. A mysterious force may enter the body and travel transformingly and enthrallingly through it from the soles of the feet to the crown of the head—but it will soon vanish. Only through the ultramystic fourfold path can an enduring result be achieved.

§

He must test these experiences not only by their internal evidences but also by their external results. Do they make him humbler or prouder? Do they improve the balance of his faculties or disturb it?

§

Philosophy rejects such psychic, occult, mediumistic, or trance experiences when imagination runs unbraked into them, or emotion heaves hysterically in them. It is then time to stop the dangerous tendency by applying a firm will and cold reason. Philosophy welcomes only a single mystic experience—that of the Void (Nirvikalpa Samadhi), where every separate form and individual consciousness vanishes, whereas all other mystic experiences retain them. This is the difference.

§

Students must guard against faulty technique. They misuse meditation when they force it to serve their fantasies and errors, ascetic phobias and religious fanaticisms. Then they become bogged in their own conceptions or in idealized projections of their own selves. It is easy to mistake the voice of the ego for the voice of the Overself. And it is not hard for the meditators to see things in their imagination which have no reality corresponding to them or to cook a deceptive mixture of fact and imagination.

The sceptic's doubts—whether in this condition one acquires spiritual affinity with the Divine or merely creates a hallucination—are not infrequently justified. Much that passes for mystical experience is mere hallucination. Even where there is genuine mystical experience, it is often mixed with hallucinatory experience at the same time. The subconscious mind easily formulates prepossessions, preconceived notions, externally received suggestions, and so on, into visual or auditory experiences which emphatically confirm the ideas or beliefs with which the meditator originally started. Instead of liberating him from errors and delusions, mysticism thus practised may only cause him to sink deeper and firmer into them. For he will convert what formerly he held on mere faith to what he now holds as assured mystical realization. In the course of an extensive experience, we have found that meditation, unchecked by reason and unbalanced by activity, has not infrequently produced monomaniacs. A "pure" experience is rare and belongs to a highly advanced stage. Only where there has been the proper preparation, self-purification, and mental discipline can a genuinely pure experience arise.

If these twisted truths and disguised emotions are such common fruit of mystical orchards, may it not be because they are inescapable corollaries of mystical attitudes? With a higher criterion, could they even come into existence?

§

It was our own widening experience and personal disillusionments that forced us to examine not only the profits of yoga and the successes of its followers, but also the deficiencies of yoga and the failures of its followers. Thus in this reconsideration there developed an attempt at a more scientific approach to the subject. And such were the practical observations which arose out of these experiences and out of the analysis of these failures, that they compelled us and must one day compel other seekers also to look for a corrective for the maladies which have affected the body of mysticism, as well as to discover a purgative for the primitive errors which have secured lodgement under its name.

§

How simple is the path itself, how complex is the pseudo-path offered by occultism and exaggerated asceticism. "All that God asks of them," writes Thomas Merton, "is to be quiet and keep themselves at peace, attentive to the secret work that He is beginning in their souls."

§

There are fourteen signs of the mediumistic condition. The medium suffers from: (1) loss of memory, (2) inability to keep mind on conversation, (3) frequent mental introversion, (4) decreasing power of prolonged concentration, study, thought, analysis, and intellectual work, (5) increasing emotionality, (6) weakened willpower, (7) greater sensitivity to trifles, with nervous irritability and silly vanity resulting therefrom, (8) more suspicions of others in his environment, (9) more self-centered and egotistic, (10) frequent glassy stare of the eyes, (11) increased sexual passion, (12) appearance of hysteria or uncontrollable temper where previously absent, (13) disappearance of moral courage, (14) the feeling at times that some unseen entity takes possession of him.

§

It is only after the mystic has felt human desires and known human joys, come up against intellectual limitations, suffered worldly disappointments, that he can evaluate. If he has not had sufficient experience of common life, he may not adequately assess the values indicated by mystical intuitions nor properly understand the meaning of his mystical experiences themselves. Thus, what he gets out of both depends to some extent on what he brings to them. If he brings too little or too lopsided a contribution, then his higher self will gradually lead him to seek development along the lines of deficiency. And to compel him to make the diversion when he fails to respond to the inner leading, it will throw the terrible gloom of the dark night over him for a time.

§

The intrusion of the thinking intellect or the egoistic emotion into the intuitive experience presents a danger for all mystics. And it is a danger that constantly remains for the more advanced as for the mere neophyte, although in a different way. It is the source of flattering illusions which offer themselves as authentic infallible intuitions. It crowns commonplace ideas which happen to enter the mind with a regality that does not belong to them. The prudent mystic must be on his guard against and watch out for this peril. He must resist its appeals to vanity, its destruction of truth.

§

Make it a definite rule in every single instance to check your intuitions by the light of reason.

§

Even where sensitivity of telepathic reception has been developed, the ego still cunningly interferes with accurate reception. It will take the current of inspiration from the master and, by adding what was never contained in it, give a highly personal, vanity-flattering colour to it. It will take the message of guidance from the higher self and, by twisting it to conform to the shape of personal desire, render it misleading. It will take a psychical or intuitive reading of a situation and, in its eager seeking of wish-fulfilment, confuse the reading and delude itself. It may even, by introducing very strong emotional complexes, create absolutely false suggestions and suppose them to be emanating from the master or the higher self.

§

No matter how he try, the mystic will not be able to express his inspiration on a higher intellectual level than the one on which he habitually finds himself. This has been plain enough in the past when over-ambitious attempts have brought ridicule to an otherwise inspired message. This is why the best prophet to reach the educated classes is an educated man who possesses the proper mental equipment to do it, and why uneducated masses are best reached by one of themselves. What is communicated—and even the very language in which this is done—always indicates on what levels of human intellect, character, and experience the mystic dwells, as it also indicates what level of mystical consciousness he has succeeded in touching.

§

Revelations come from the Overself; messages are transmitted to us and they are true enough in their beginning. But personal desires seize on them instantly, change and fashion them to suit the ego.

§

We should distinguish the theories and doctrines woven round the mystic's experience from the significant features of the experience itself. And those features are: the awareness of another and deeper life, a sacred presence within the heart, the certitude of having found the Real, the gladness and freshness which follow the sense of this discovery.

§

If the personality has been unevenly developed, if its forces have not been properly harmonized with each other and defects remain in thinking, feeling, and willing, then at the threshold of illumination these defects will become magnified and overstimulated by the upwelling soul power and lead to adverse psychical results.

§

All occult and psychic powers are either extensions of man's human capacity or of his animal senses. They are still semi-materialistic, because connected with his ego or his body. All truly spiritual powers are on a far higher and quite different plane. They belong to his divine self.

§

The mystic seeks to stifle all thinking activity by a deliberate effort of willpower and thus arrive at a sense of oneness with the inner being which lies behind it. When his practice of the exercise draws to a successful end, the object upon which he concentrates vanishes from his field of focus but attention remains firmly fixed and does not wander to anything else. The consequence is that his consciousness is centered and this is true whether he feels it to be withdrawn into a pin-point within his head, as results from the commoner methods, or bathed in a blissful spot within his heart, as results from other ones.

§

He cannot obtain from ordinary mystical experience alone, precise information upon such matters as the universe's evolution, God's nature, or the history of man. This is because it really does lack an intellectual content. The only reliable increment of knowledge he can obtain from it is an answer to the question "What am I?"—an affirmation of the existence of man as divine soul apart from his existence as body. Apart from that his inner experience only improves the quality and increases the intensity of his life, does not constitute a way to new knowledge about what extends beyond it.

§

There are likely to be many who will reject these criticisms and revaluations of yoga because they emanate from one who is a Westerner and who is therefore supposed not to know what he is talking about in such an exotic matter. Let us therefore learn what some competent Indian authorities themselves say. His late Highness, The Maharaja of Baroda, who was famous for his frequent association and patronage of the most learned Indian pundits, scholars, philosophers, and yogis, said in his inaugural address to the Third Indian Philosophical Congress held in Bombay in 1927: "The Yoga system in its essence is a series of practical means to be adopted as a preliminary to the attainment of the highest knowledge. . . . what the yoga system may have to teach us as to the preparation for the attainment of true philosophic insight needs to be disassociated from the fantastic and the magical." And at the same Congress, the general president, Sir S. Radhakrishnan, did not hesitate to declare that "the Indian tradition gives the *first place* to the pursuit of philosophy."

§

We do not need to seek our vindication in the witness of contemporary conditions and inside ashrams; it exists in the writings of mystics themselves and as far back as the Middle Ages. Suso, Tauler, Guyon, Saint Teresa, Saint John of the Cross, Ramakrishna, and others have all had occasion to observe the same sad consequences which we also have observed, and they have passed caustic comments upon their fellow aspirants in their own writings. One of the most illustrious and advanced of medieval mystics, John Ruysbroeck, vigorously criticized his fellow mystics for defects he had observed among them. He denounced those who mistook mere laziness for meditative sanctity, as well as those who take every impulse to be a divine one. (See E. Underhill's *Mysticism*, page 335, for a quote from Mme. Guyon criticizing visionary experiences of mysticism.) The Spanish Saint John of the Cross wrote: "It is very foolish, when spiritual sweetness and delight fail, to imagine that God has failed us also; *and to imagine that because we have such sweetness we have God also.*"

Four centuries ago another Spanish mystic perceived the subtle selfishness which underlay this attitude. He was Saint Pedro de Alcantara, who wrote that such devotees of spiritual joy "are much rather loving themselves than God." Even many a genuine mystic of high achievement is not altogether exempt from this charge of spiritual selfishness. His ineffable ecstasies deceive him by their very sweetness into barring himself from concern with the woes of the outside world. This often arises quite innocently because the sense of joy which follows success in meditation is easily misinterpreted to mean the end of the quest. It may indeed be the end of most mystical quests, but it is only the beginning of the ultimate one! Only a few of the wisest and most advanced mystics have placed it where it rightly belongs. The danger was so clearly seen by Buddha that he specifically warned his disciples not to stop at any of the four degrees of rapt meditation, where, he said, they might easily be deceived into thinking that the goal had been attained. It was seen too by Sri Ramakrishna, the renowned Bengali yogi. He once disclosed to a disciple: "Mystic ecstasy is not final." He severely chided his famous pupil, the monk Swami Vivekananda, when the latter replied to a question about his ideal in life with the words: "To remain absorbed in meditative trance." His master exclaimed, "Can you be so small-minded as that? Go beyond trance; it is a trifling thing for you."

§

The mystic is on a loftier plane than the occultist and psychic. The various systems of occultism, theosophy, and psychism are all objective to the true Self of man, and hence distract him from the straight and narrow path. Yet they are useful and necessary for those egoistic and over-intellectualized natures who cannot aspire to the rarefied reaches of the real Truth. Everything—including the fascinating systems of knowledge and practice that comprise ancient and modern occult teachings—which distracts man from becoming the truly spiritual, distracts him from the real path. Only when all objective things and thoughts have disappeared into the subject, the self or the seer, can man achieve his highest purpose. All other activities simply cause him to stray from the highest truth. So I have abandoned the study and practice of occultism. I have given it up unwillingly, for the power it promises is not to be despised. Yet I recognize that my past is strewn with errors and mistakes. I imagined that a great personal experience of the psychic and mysterious side of Nature would bring me nearer Truth. As a fact, it has taken me farther from it. Once I enjoyed frequent glimpses of a great bliss and intense state of samadhi; then I was unfortunate enough to come into contact with theosophists and others of that ilk who subtly supplanted my real inward happiness with intellectual systems and theories upon which I was thenceforward to ponder. Alas! I was too young and too green to know what was happening. The bliss went before long; the samadhis stopped, and I was cast upon the shore of the Finite, an unhappy and problem-puzzled bit of human wreckage! No promise of wonderful initiations at some future time will lure me to trust my life into the care of a so-called guru who is either unable to or unwilling to give me a glimpse of the God-consciousness he claims to possess. I am not inclined to follow a trail which may land me somewhere out in the middle of the desert, bereft of reason, hope, and fortune.

§

If a man spends a total of six hours a day in meditation practices, as some I have known have done, but is unable to perceive the truth about the character of other men with whom he is brought into contact, then it is absurd to believe that he is able to perceive the truth about the immeasurably more remote, more intangible and ineffable Transcendental Reality.

§

He will be all the better and not worse if he brings to his mystical path a scientific method of approach, a large historical acquaintance with the comparative mysticisms of many countries, a scientific knowledge of psychology, and a practical experience of the world. He will be all the better and not worse if he learns in advance, and in theory, what every step of the way into the holy of holies will be like.

§

If there were nothing other than our ideas of things, and if it were impossible to cross their boundaries, all that we could discover would never be anything more than an exploration from our own imaginings and conceptions. Then, everything holy and divine would be robbed of its value and meaning. But mystical experience intrudes here to show us a world beyond thoughts, a reality beyond ideas.

§

The more I travel the world of living men and study the recorded experiences of dead ones, the more I am convinced that mystical powers, religious devotion, intellectual capacity, and ascetic hardihood do not possess anything like the value of noble character. I no longer admire a man because he has spent twenty years in the practice of yoga or the study of metaphysics; I admire him because he has brought compassion, tolerance, rectitude, and dependability into his conduct.

§

If those who have hitherto given their faith and thought to the ordinary presentations of yoga will now give further faith and more thought to the higher teaching here offered, they need lose nothing of their earlier understanding but will rather amplify it. Nor is anyone being called upon to renounce meditation; those who criticize me for this are as mistaken as they are unjust. What is really being asked for is the purging of meditation, the putting aside as of secondary and temporary interest those phases of yoga experience which are not fundamental and universal. But meditation itself should and must continue, for without it the Ultimate can never be realized. Only let it be directed rightly. Hence the inferior yogas are not for a moment to be despised, but it should be recognized that they are only relative methods useful at a particular stage only. Thus they will take their place as fit means leading towards the ultramystic practices and not be confounded with them.

§

The quietistic condition got by ordinary yoga is got by withdrawing from the five senses. But the hidden prenatal thought tendencies which are the secret origin of these senses still remain, and the yogi has not withdrawn from them because his attention has been directed to vacating the *body*. Thus the trance-condition he attains is only a temporary, *external* inactivity of the senses. Their *internal* roots still abide within him as mental energies which have evolved since time immemorial. Without adequate insight into the true nature of sense operations, which are fundamentally exteriorizations of interior mental ones, the yogi has only deceived himself when he thinks he has conquered them.

§

So long as the mystic is unable to function fully in his intellect, why should he expect to function clearly in what is beyond intellect?

§

However essential this seeking of the spiritual self must obviously be, however splendid the attainment of such a peace-filled, desire-free state must and will always seem, it cannot in itself constitute an adequate goal. Two important elements are lacking in it. The first is knowledge and the second is compassion. The first would show precisely what is the place of such an attainment in the full pattern of human existence; the second would bring it into active relation with the rest of social existence. Whilst these are lacking, this state can only partially understand itself and only negatively affect others. It keeps its own peace by ignoring the world's suffering.

§

The mystic who overbalances himself with ephemeral ecstasies pays for them by deep moods of depression. This is worth noting, but it is not all. If there is not a rationally thought-out metaphysical foundation to give constant and steady support to his intuitions of truth, he may find these intuitions telling him one thing this year and the opposite next year. But this foundation must be a scientific and not merely a speculative metaphysics, which means that it must itself be irrefragable, gathering its facts not with the critical intellect alone, but also with the spontaneous intuition and above all with the insight. Such a system exists only in the metaphysics of truth.

§

When the whole world lies stretched out before them, how dare they go on ignoring it, or else dismissing it as a device of Satan to entrap and ensnare them! We must enquire into the world which the senses contact no less than into the self which is viewing that world. How can the ascetic obtain the knowledge of the All when he gives up such a huge portion of it? Giving up the world does not lead to Reality, but it leads to peace of mind. Men who lack intelligence, who possess little brains, must take to mysticism and yoga, but only the mature and developed mind can enter the quest of enquiry into Truth. This means therefore that pupils are generally not initiated into this enquiry by gurus prematurely. They must first have developed their egos and their minds to a high degree, and only after that should they be taught to renounce what has been fostered with so much pain. This is evolution: although Truth is ideally attainable here and now, technically it is attainable only at the end of the pageant of evolution, when the whole being of man has been highly developed and is ripe to receive the greatest of all gifts.

§

There are three major and progressive goals open to the mystic. The first is to become conscious of the fringe or aura of his divine soul, the Overself. Most mystics, elated by the emotional thrill of its discovery, stop here. The second is to penetrate to its serene centre and pass during trance into the undifferentiated void of its non-sensed, non-thinged essence. The more intelligent and superior mystics, who are naturally much fewer in number than the first kind, are not satisfied until they reach this attainment. It is upon this world-vanishing experience that most Indian yogic metaphysicians base their theory that the universe is an illusion. To the ordinary yogi, this is the summit of achievement and represents for him the goal of human existence. But the trance itself is only temporary. How can a mental self-abstraction, however prolonged, a merely temporary condition, be a final goal for mankind? This is the problem which indeed was stated in *The Hidden Teaching Beyond Yoga*. All such theories merely show that such mystics have their limitations, however admirable may be their capacity to enter into and sustain the trance state. The third goal is to bring the true self, the essential emptiness and the universal manifestation, into a harmonious, unified experience during full normal wakefulness. This last is philosophical mysticism. Being a complex and complete attainment, it naturally calls for a complex and complete effort. Careful analytical and historical study of mystical practices and mystical biographies will show that it is these three different goals which have always been pursued or achieved, no matter to what external religion, country, or race individual mystics may themselves have belonged. Thus the ordinary mystic's account of the Overself is true but incomplete, his experience of it authentic but insufficient. He has yet to undergo the whole, the complete experience which mysticism can yield. But then, if he does so, if he refuses to remain satisfied with an incomplete and imperfect attainment, he will no longer remain a mystic. He will become a philosopher.

§

The successful mystic certainly comes into contact with his real "I." But if this contact is dependent upon meditational trance, it is necessarily an intermittent one. He cannot obtain a permanent contact unless he proceeds further and widens his aspiration to achieve contact with the universal "I." There is therefore a difference between the interior "I" and the universal "I," but it is a difference only of degree, not of kind, for the latter includes the former.

§

The mystical ideal of finding his relationship to the spiritual self must be broadened out to include the metaphysical ideal of finding his relationship to the universe.

§

At a time like the present when the world is passing through a critical phase of wholesale reconstruction, every opponent of reason and proponent of superstition is rendering a serious disservice to mankind.

§

It would be a grave mistake to believe that the following of ascetic regimes and the stilling of wandering thoughts *causes* the higher consciousness to supervene. What they really do is to *permit* it to supervene. Desires and distraction are hindrances to its attainment and they merely remove the hindrances. This makes possible the recognition of what we really are beneath them. If however we do nothing more than this, which is called yoga, we get only an inferior attainment, often only a temporary one. For unless we also engage in the rooting out of the ego, which is called philosophy, we do not get the final and superior transcendental state.

§

From the point of view of yoga practice, the yogi gradually succeeds in bringing his field of awareness to a single centre, which is at first located in the head and later in the heart. This achievement is so unusual that he experiences great peace and exaltation as a result—something utterly different from his normal condition. For him this is the soul, the kingdom of heaven, the Overself. *But from the point of view of the philosophy of Truth*, any physical localization of the Overself is impossible, because space itself is entirely within the mind, and the mind is therefore beyond any limits of here and there, and the Overself and Pure Mind (unindividualized) holds all bodies within it without being touched by them.

§

We personally believe that Gandhi is as self-realized a mystic as his contemporaries like Ramana Maharishi, Aurobindo, and Ramdas. His whole life and thought, his writing and speech, his deeds and service proclaim it. He himself has declared that he feels "the indefinable mysterious power that pervades everything" and that he is "surer of His existence than of the fact that you and I are sitting in this room." Then why is it that Gandhi's view of the world war was so widely different from Sri Aurobindo's, if both are divinely inspired men? The answer is that in Gandhi we find a perfect illustration of the defects of ordinary mysticism, of the insufficiency of its spiritual self-realization, and of the need for philosophical mysticism. There is no need to doubt, as so many doubt, that he is a genuine saint turned to genuine service of humanity. But he has carried into that service the unbalance, the fanaticism, and the impracticality which mark so many saints throughout history. This conclusion may be unpalatable to some, but it is unavoidable. Perfect mystics are not the same as perfect beings. They are liable to error.

§

Edgar Cayce was not a mystic, he was a psychic. Although he brought much knowledge of a curious or interesting kind from his psychic experiences, it would be an error to regard them all as reliable, for most psychics can be misled.

§

Mystical experience does not yield a cosmogony, hence does not tell us something new about the universe or about God's relation to the universe, even though it does tell us something gloriously new about ourselves—that is, about man. In such experience, it is not the universe that reveals the inner mysteries of its own nature, but man.

§

An important query now arises, although hardly a mystic ever conceives the challenge of its existence and consequently ever seeks its answer. We have to enquire about what really happens during the highest effort of the meditator, when thought is so overcome that it appears as if about to lapse. Will he enter a higher dimension of existence as he believes? Will the self-revelation of the hidden reality really occur? Is this thrilling ecstasy or this stilled peace, which has begun to supervene, the peculiar sign of a revolutionary shifting of spiritual gravity from mortal concerns to eternal life, from mere appearance to basic reality? Many mystics think that the mere elimination of thoughts during self-absorption is a sufficient achievement. The world is then forgotten and with it all the personal cares. This state really arises from the extreme diminution of the working and tempo of thought, with the consequent diminution of attention to the man's own personality, to its varied cares and affairs, as well as to the external world with its insistent claims and constant demands. Thus it is simply one of exquisite relief from human burdens (whether of pain or pleasure, for here there is no distinction between both), from attention to the external world, and from the strain of supporting a continuous series of thoughts. The result is a delightful lightness and soothing peace. But the feeling of peace is alone no guarantee of the attainment of true realization. Peace is admittedly one of its signs. But there are different grades of peace, ranging from the negative stillness of the tomb to the positive mind-mastery of the sage. The arrestation of thoughts touches the fringe of the transcendental state, but not more than the fringe. When I wrote in *The Hidden Teaching Beyond Yoga* (page 309, British edition) that the mystic only penetrates to the illusion of reality, I referred to visions of forms and ecstasies of emotion. If however the mystic does achieve a visionless serene unexcited beness, then it is the Overself, for he touches the Void wherein is no form and no thoughts; then he does touch reality. I admit this. But this task is still incomplete, because this experience which occurs in trance is transient; hence the need of gaining metaphysical insight also for permanency.

§

The developed mystic needs but neglects the undeveloped thinker within himself, just as the thinker needs but neglects the mystic. It is not enough to arrive at truth through mystical feelings; we must also arrive at it through metaphysical thinking. The liability to strive for unrealizable ends, as well as the tendency to mistake in his hurry mere reflection of reality for the Real itself, will then be eliminated. Truth can never suffer from the proper activity of human reason and experiment, but only from their improper or unbalanced activity. The moment the mystic seeks to convey his experience to others, when his trance, ecstasy, or inspiration is over, that moment he has to begin to analyse it. If he lacks the proper intellectual equipment to do this with scientific objectivity and precision, he will convey it faultily, insufficiently, and to some extent ineffectively. This is most often the case, unfortunately, because the distaste for intellectual activity is one of the customary reasons why a number of men have taken to mysticism. Without such equipment, the aspirant will be unable to extract the precise significance of his own mystical experiences, as he will be unable to check the correctness of his opinions upon them; whereas with it in his possession, he will be able to examine any such experience and any such opinion by the light of a systematic, thoroughly tested world view. The vagueness of his concepts, the looseness of his thinking, the confusion of his facts, and the partisan character of his conception of life all combine to render the average mystic's understanding of the truth about his own inner experience often unsatisfactory and his evaluation of other men's vaunted occult claims often untenable. We must distinguish between ebullient emotion and deep love. Those whose aspirations are still in the region of the first may sneer at any other spiritual path than the devotional one, yet if an aspirant is really devoted to the Divine, as he says, he ought not to object to learning all he can about his beloved, which is to say that he ought not to be averse to study of the metaphysics of truth, however difficult and strange it is likely to be.

§

Beware of cults and their exaggerated claims. The IS is not an ISM.

§

All religious occupations lend themselves to hypocrisy, and this is no exception. The twentieth-century mystics are often pious impostors, playing upon the credulity of their ignorant following. There exists among them a solid, saving remnant of noble men who are making arduous and genuine efforts to attain the superhuman wisdom which mysticism promises to devotees.

§

The great error of all these worldly-happiness Spiritual teachings like New Thought, Unity, Christian Science, and especially Dr. Peale's "Power of Positive Thinking" is that they have no place for pain, sorrow, adversity, and misfortune in their idea of God's world. They are utterly ignorant of the tremendous truth, voiced by *every* great prophet, that by divine decree the human lot mixes good and bad fortune, health, events, situations, and conditions; that suffering has been incorporated into the scheme of things to prevent man from becoming fully satisfied with a sensual existence. They demand only the pleasant side of experience. If this demand were granted, they would be deprived of the chance to learn all those valuable and necessary lessons which the unpleasant side affords and thus deprived of the chance ever to attain a full knowledge of spiritual truth. It is the ego which is the real source of such a limited teaching. Its desire to indulge itself rather than surrender itself is at the bottom of the appeal which these cults have for their unwary followers. These cults keep the aspirant tied captive within his personal ego, limit him to its desires. Of course, the ego in this case is disguised under a mask of spirituality.

§

Since all things have come out of the primal Source, all that I really need can directly come out of it to me if I put myself in perfect harmony with the Source and stay therein. This is the truth behind the fallacy of these cults. For to put myself into such harmony, it is not enough to pronounce the words, or to hold the thought, or to visualize the things themselves. More than this must be done—no less a thing than all that labour of overcoming the ego which is comprised in the Quest. How many of the followers of the cults have even understood that, and all its implications in connection with their desires? How many of them have tried to overcome the ego? If they have not succeeded in understanding and complying with the divine law governing this matter, why should the divine power be at their beck and call to bring what they want? If they have not sought and largely attained that mastery of the animal propensities and that deep concentration in the centre of consciousness which the Quest seeks, is it not impertinent to expect to reach that power with their voice?

§

17

THE RELIGIOUS URGE

Origin — Recognition — Manifestations — Traditional and less known religions — Connection with philosophy

We need religion, yes assuredly, but we need it freed from superstition.

§

A quester necessarily becomes a pilgrim seeking his destination in a Holy City. He may be a metaphysician or mystic, a profound thinker or connoisseur of Orientalisms, but he may not leave out the simple humble reverences of religious feeling.

§

He only has the fullest right to talk of God who *knows* God, not his idea, fancy, belief, or imagination about God. He only should write of the soul, its power, peace, and wisdom, who lives in it every moment of every day. But since such men are all too rare and hard to find, mankind has had to accept substitutes for them. These substitutes are frail and fallible mortals, clutching at shadows. This is why religionists disagree, quarrel, fight, and persecute both inside and outside their own groups.

§

It is unjust to deny the truths of religion in efforts to show up its superstitions or to decry its services and contributions to human welfare in order to point at its persecutions.

§

The public demonstration of one's religion in church or temple does not appeal to all temperaments. Some can find holiest feelings only in private. Those in the first group should not attempt to impose their will on the others. Those in the second group should not despise the followers of conventional communion. More understanding between the two may be hard to arrive at, but more tolerance would be a sign that the personal religious feeling is authentic.

§

The sceptic, the anthropologist, and the philosopher of Bertrand Russell's type say that religion arose because primitive man was terrified by the destructive powers of Nature and endeavoured to propitiate them or their personifications by worship and prayer. They say further that civilized man, having achieved some measure of control over natural forces, feels far less in need of religious practices. This is an erroneous view. Religions were instituted by sages who saw their need as a preparatory means of educating men's minds for the higher truths of science and philosophy.

§

Its originator left some power behind which was partly responsible for its wide and deep spread. This is the vivifying principle behind the spread of every historic religion, a principle whose results make us exclaim with Origen, "It is a work greater than any work of man." We should regard the great originators, the great religious saviours of the human race like Jesus and Buddha, as divinely used instruments. The individual centre of power which each left behind on our planet extended for long beyond his bodily death, continued to respond helpfully to those who trusted it, but then gradually waned and will eventually terminate after a historic period has ended. No organized religion ever endures in its original form for more than a limited period. All the great religions of the earliest antiquity have perished. The originators were admittedly not ordinary men. They belonged to higher planes of thought and being. They came from spheres of consciousness superior to that of average humanity. This was highly exceptional, but it does not turn them into gods. Nor does it justify us today in living in the past and leaning on what is vanishing. For despite all lapses and regressions, humanity is now coming of intellectual age. This is one reason why it must now furnish its own teachers, must recognize and appreciate its own wise men. For in the coming age, no further descents of these superior beings like the two just named may be expected. There will be no other Messiahs than those we can evolve from amongst ourselves.

§

The general line of inner development for the human race is in the first stage right action, which includes duty, service, responsibility. In the second stage religious devotion appears. This engenders worship of the higher power, moral improvement, holy communion. The third stage is mystical and involves practice of meditation to get a more intimate communion. The fourth stage is the awakening of need to understand truth and know reality. Its completed product is the sage, who includes in himself the civilized man, the religionist, the mystic, and the philosopher.

§

The dangers and downfall of every religion begin when its symbols are taken as substitutes for its realities, and when attendance at its public services replaces efforts at individual development.

§

Each person has some kind of faith; this includes the person whose faith reposes in scepticism.

§

It is right and proper that a building put to a sacred use should be reserved for it and kept apart from profane activities.

§

The exhibition of relics, the erection of shrines, or the creation of memorials, statues, paintings, and sects to record the name of a saint or prophet or holy man is useful to impress their attainments upon the minds of others living long after he has gone, and perhaps to inspire them to do something for themselves in the same direction.

§

In some rose-stained-glass-windowed church one may sense the strong atmosphere of true devotion so acutely that one instinctively falls on bended knee in humble prayer and in remembrance that self is nought, God is all.

§

God is Mind and they that would worship it in truth must worship it mentally. The ostentatious ceremonies set up by paid professionals enable men and women to obtain pleasing emotional effects but they do not enable them to worship God. A building becomes a sacred temple when it ceases to hear phonographic mumblings and when it ceases to witness theatrical mimicries, and when it provides a fitting place where its visitors can engage in undisturbed silent and inward-turned communion with their own deeper Mind.

§

Men who imagine that if they take part in the ritual of a cult they have done their religious duty are dangerously self-illusioned. By attaching such a narrow meaning to such a noble word, they degrade religion. We have progressed in religion to the extent that whereas ancient man sacrificed the animal *outside* him upon the altar of God-worship, modern man understands that he has to sacrifice the animal *inside* him. The external forms of religion are not its final forms. Jesus ordered one convert to worship "in spirit and in truth," that is, *internally*. The two phases of worship—external and internal—are not on the same level; one is a higher development of the other.

§

The controversy between those who believe ritual to be indispensable and those who believe it to be irrelevant nearly always ignores four truths which, understood, dismiss the controversy itself—as ordinarily carried on—as futile. The first is that any means that adapts the truth to the limitation of intelligence which is present in the masses is useful *to those masses*. The artistic symbolism of ritual is such a means. The second is that the idolatry which the puritan objects to in ritual, reappears in his own use of mental images and limiting attributes, or anthropomorphic terms in thought, speech, and literature about God. The third truth is that the puritan's means is obviously adapted to a higher grade of intellect than the ritualist's and that one day the physical worship will have to give way through evolution to metaphysical worship. The fourth truth is that since each means helps different groups of men, its advocates should not attempt to impose it on a group to whom it is unsuited and consequently unhelpful. The diverse levels of human minds must be recognized. If it is wrong for the ritualist to interfere with the non-ritualist who has outgrown this level, the latter needs to be tolerant of the former who has something more to exploit in the lower level.

§

The degradation, falsification, commercialization, and exploitation which men, making use of institutional religion, have made of a prophet's mission, speaks clearly of what these men themselves are made. The fact is that they are not fit to be trusted with the power which institutionalism gives them. Religion is safer and healthier and will make more genuine progress if left free and unorganized, to be the spontaneous expression of inspired individuals. It is a personal and private matter and always degenerates into hypocrisy when turned into a public matter. The fact is, you cannot successfully organize spirituality. It is an independent personal thing, a private discovery and not a mass emotion.

§

It is right that the principal cathedrals, temples, and mosques of religion should be built on a majestic plan to impress those who go there to worship and to express the faith of those who put the buildings up. Such structures are not only symbolic of the importance of religious faith, but also conducive to the humility with which worship should be conducted.

§

Many people have so meditated upon their concept of God that they have become one with the concept and not one with God, as they vainly delude themselves. The concept is not reality.

§

No church can keep its primitive spirituality unless it keeps its political independence. And this in turn it cannot have if it accepts a preferred position above other churches as a state establishment. It was not the leader of Russian atheism but the leader of the Russian Orthodox Church itself, the late Patriarch Segius, Metropolitan of Moscow, who admitted that the disestablishment of the State Church in his country by the Bolsheviks was really "a return to apostolic times when the Church and its servants did not deem their office a profession intended to earn their living." Such were his own words.

§

Those who think that because a statement appears in sacred scripture such appearance terminates all further controversy upon a question are deluding themselves. They base their unqualified assent upon the undeniable fact that the ancient sages knew what they were talking about, but they ignore the other fact that some of their followers did not. They do not know that the scriptural texts have been peppered with later interpolations or debased with superstitious additions and are consequently not always reliable. But even if they were, still, the human mind must keep itself unfettered if it would achieve truth.

§

When religion identifies itself with an ecclesiastical organization and forgets itself as an individual experience, it becomes its own enemy. History proves again and again that institutionalism enters only to corrupt the purity of a religion.

§

It is something in history to ponder over that in the Alban hills, a few kilometres from Rome, there was once a Temple of Orpheus where, 3000 years ago, the Orphic mysteries were celebrated, where Orphic religion prevailed with its tenets of rebirth, fleshless diet, the quest, and inner reality. It is arguable whether the two other religions which followed it in that area have brought a better message.

§

If the credo of a religion insists on keeping these allegorical, symbolical, or child-directed early myths even in an age like our own when knowledge, education, scientific discovery, and observed facts require higher mental satisfaction, the masses will consider themselves deceived and back away from their faith in the truly authentic beliefs; whereas if the religious authority has the courage to revalue its credo, explaining why it does so, it can continue to hold them.

§

It must be said, and said quite plainly, that the Western and Near Eastern worlds would have had a better history, and Christianity would have had a stronger foundation because truer, if Saint Paul had never been converted but had remained a Jew. For the vision on the road to Damascus, although a genuine one, was totally misinterpreted. It was a command (to stop persecuting Christians) of a solely personal nature; but he went much farther and not only began the construction of a new world-religion but shifted its emphasis from where Jesus had put it (the kingdom of heaven within men) to Jesus himself, from faith in the Christ-consciousness to faith in a crucified corpse.

§

Was not the most important council of all the Council of Nicaea, which finally settled Christian doctrines for a thousand years, but which foolishly dropped the tenet of metempsychosis as heresy after it had survived the first five centuries of *anno domino*; was not this great gathering composed of men who mostly could neither write nor read, who were stern extreme ascetics, fanatical in character and behaviour, narrow, intolerant?

§

James, the brother of Jesus and an Apostle, was a vegetarian. But the theologians and historians ignore this fact which was testified to by the Judeo-Christian Hegesippus, who lived in the century following and had contact with the Palestinian circles of the Apostolic time. Moreover Hegesippus asserts that James had been brought up in this way since childhood. Does this imply that the family circle was vegetarian?

§

Intolerant religious organizations which would allow no other voice, however harmless, to speak than one which echoes their own must in the end fall victim to their own intolerance; for as men through their education and contact with more developed persons come to perceive the Truth, their hostility and enmity to those religions are inevitably aroused. They will then either fall into agnosticism or into sheer atheism, or they will find their way to other and truer expressions of what religion should be if it is to fulfil its highest mission. Therefore, it is not the work of a philosopher to reverse, correct, or otherwise disturb other people's religious beliefs. If the latter are faulty and if the organization propagating them is intolerant, he may be sure that given enough time others will arise to do this negative and destructive work; and this saves him the trouble of these unpleasant tasks. His own work is a positive one.

§

It is a tragedy of all history that the names of Men like Jesus, who came only to do good, are invariably exploited by those who fail to catch their spirit and do more harm than good. Formal entry into any religious organization relates a man only to that organization, not at all to the Prophet whose name it claims. No religious institution in history has remained utterly true to the Prophet whose name it takes, whose word it preaches, whose ethic it inculcates. A religious prophet is mocked, not honoured, when men mouth his name and avoid his example. No church is a mystical body of any prophet. All churches are, after all, only human societies, and suffer from the weaknesses and selfishnesses, the errors and mistakes, inseparable from such societies. It is an historical fact that where religious influence upon society has bred the evils of fanaticism, narrow-mindedness, intolerance, superstition, and backwardness, their presence may be traced back to the professional members and monkish institutions of that religion. Priestcraft, as I have seen it in certain Oriental and Occidental lands, is often ignorant and generally arrogant. Throughout the world you may divide clergymen and priests into two categories—those who are merely the holders of jobs and those who are truly ministers of religion.

§

What other way have undeveloped masses to enter into some kind of communion with God except the way of a church established by other men and of doctrines promulgated by other men, when the masses have not the necessary capacity for either an intellectual or a mystical communion? But when the established religious institution becomes a barrier to further inner growth of the masses and when the doctrines block the path for a more reasonable or more felt understanding of the Higher Power, then it is time for a revision of both things.

§

Until about the turn of the previous century, the truth about religion was never published frankly and plainly. This was because those who wrote about it were either one-sidedly biased in its favour and so refused to see the undesirable aspects, or else they were hostile in their personal standpoint which stopped them from mentioning the deeper merits. Those who really knew what religion was in theory and practice, what were its goods and bads, kept silent. This was because they did not wish to disturb the established faith of the simple masses or else because the latter, being uneducated, were unprepared to receive subtleties which required sufficient mental development to comprehend.

§

Religion was devised to assist the masses. Mysticism was designed to assist the individual. When religion has led a man to the threshold of deeper truths behind its own, its task is done. Its real value is attained in mysticism. Henceforth, the practice of mystical exercises can alone assure his further spiritual progress. For mysticism does not rest upon the shifting sands of faith or the uncertain gravel of argument, but upon the solid rock of experience. The first great move forward in his spiritual life occurs when he moves from religion to mysticism, when he no longer has to go into some stone building or to some paid mediator to feel reverential towards God, but into himself. Mysticism is for the man who is not in a hurry, who is willing to work persistently and to wait patiently for consciousness of his divine soul. The others who have not the time for this and who therefore resort to religion must live by faith, not by consciousness. The man who wishes to rise from sincere faith and traditional belief in the soul to practical demonstration and personal experience of it must rise from religion to mysticism. Mysticism seeks to establish direct contact with the divine soul, without the mediation of any man and without the use of any external instrument. Hence it must seek inward and nowhere else. Hence, too, the ordinary forms and methods of religion are not necessary to it and must be dropped. When the mystic finds the divine presence enlightening and strengthening him from within, he cannot be blamed for placing little value upon sacramental ceremonies which claim to achieve this from without. Nor is he censurable if he comes to regard church attendance as unnecessary and sacramental salvation as illusory. If a man can find within himself the divine presence, divine inspiration, and divine guidance, what need has he of church organization? It can be useful only to one who lacks them.

§

If the transition from religion to mysticism is to be conveniently made, it must be gradually made. But this can be done only if the teachers of religion themselves approve and promote the transition. But if they do not, if they want to keep religion imprisoned in ecclesiastic jail-irons, if they persist in a patriarchal attitude which indiscriminately regards every member of their flock as an intellectual infant who never grows up, the transition will happen all the same. Only it will then happen abruptly and after religion itself has been discarded either for cynical atheism or for bewildered apathy.

§

A man may be holy without being wise, but he cannot be wise without being holy. That is why philosophy is necessary, why religion and mysticism are not enough, although excellent as far as they go.

§

Whoever limits himself in his search, faith, and acquaintance to a single book—the Bible—limits the truth he finds. Such is the position of those sects with narrow outlooks like the Lutheran Church, the Calvinists, the Jehovah Witnesses and several other churches. They silently proclaim their own lack of culture when the bibles, texts, hagiographs, and recorded wisdom of all lands, all historic centuries, and all languages are today available or translated or excerpted.

§

He will become truly religious if he ceases to remain sectarian and begins to take the whole world-wide study of religious manifestations for his province.

§

The old theology invested God with the quality of man. It belittled the Infinite power and imputed petty motives to the motiveless. Such a theology really worshipped its own thought of God, not God in reality, its own cruel and pitiful concept of the Inconceivable. Can we wonder that it provoked atheism and led to agnosticism when the human race began to outgrow its intellectual childhood? However fitted to that early stage of our growth, such an idea is unfitted to this mid-twentieth century of our history. We must and can face the truth that God is not a glorified man showing wilful characteristics but a Principle of Being, of Life, and of Consciousness which ever was and therefore ever shall be. There is only one Principle like that, unique, alone, the origin of all things. The imagination cannot picture it, but the intuition can receive some hint of its solitary grandeur. Such a hint it may receive through its worship of its own source, the Overself which links man with this ineffable power, the Divine Spirit within him which is his innermost Self. The personal concept of Deity was intended to satisfy the race's childhood, not to enlighten the race's adulthood. The time has come to do away with such a false concept and to accept the purity of this philosophic truth.

§

The philosophical teaching is that the return of every prophet is an inward event and not a physical one. The common people, with their more materialist and less subtle apprehension, expect to see his body again. The initiates expect only to find his mental presence in themselves.

§

Because philosophy includes and extends religion, it necessarily supports it. But it does not support the erroneous dogmas and misguided practices which are cloaked under religion's mantle, nor the human exploitations which are found in its history.

§

Real religion is as universal as the wind. Cut and dried religions are mere local limitations; they were originally put up as temporary trellis-work for the young souls of man to climb and grow upward, but they have become imprisoning hatches and sometimes instruments of torture. Let us look only for that which is *salient* in a religion, and we shall find ourselves set free from its lassoing limitations. We shall not arrive at its meaning by muddled talk in its favour any more than by muddled talk in its despite, for the powers of calm judgement and reasoned reflection are then stupefied. The philosophical student's attitude is simply this, that he can *begin* no discussion with acceptance of the existence of any dogma; such acceptance is only proper as the *culmination* of a discussion. He must question and cross-question every inherited belief, every acquired doctrine until he can elicit what we really know out of the mass of pseudo-knowledge, until he becomes conscious of the ignorance which is so often veiled by the mask of supposed knowledge. Through such agitated unsettlement and such sharp doubt alone can we win our way to rocklike certitude ultimately.

§

In religion, metaphysical *principles* become symbolized by mythological *persons*. Thus Adi Buddha, the primeval Force, becomes the first historic Buddha, while Christos, the Higher Self, becomes the man Jesus. Thus the universal gets shrunken into the local.

§

If we gaze into the soul of modern man as it has been during the present century, we shall discern therein a state of long-drawn crisis. For two opposed and conflicting world-views have been taught him during his youth: the one religious and the other scientific and both accusing each other of being untrue. The emotional consequences of this have manifested themselves in instability, immorality, cynicism, hypocrisy, and despair. The mental consequences have manifested themselves in frustration, uncertainty, and bewilderment. So long as these two forces cannot come to terms with each other within him, so long will they exhaust and not nourish him. Such a widespread and deep crisis, such a fateful and difficult situation cannot be left unresolved for long. It is driving men to sink in bewilderment and despair, where they fail to comprehend and master it, or to rise in clarity and strength where they do. It is inevitable that man should try to unify his thoughts into a coherent system and his experiences into a coherent pattern. All traditional concepts of religion will have to be reshaped to conform to this new knowledge. If, for example, his religion tells him that the world was created five thousand years ago whereas his science tells him that it was created very much more than five million years ago, a nervous tension is set up within him which harms his mental sight and hurts his physical health. Only when he can find a satisfactory synthesis which consolidates the claims of reason and feeling without sacrificing either can he find healing of his trouble. And such a synthesis exists only in philosophy.

§

The enlightened philosopher has no conflict with religion so long as it retains its ethical force. When a religion is crumbling, when men reject its moral restraining power, when they refuse to accept its historical incidents and irrational dogmas as being vital to living, when in consequence they are becoming brutalized and uncontrolled, as our own epoch has painfully seen, then this religion is losing its raison d'etre and the people among whom it held sway are in need of help. The mass of the common people now in the West mentally dwell outside any church, and are consequently outside its disciplinary moral influence. They cannot be left to perish unguided when religion becomes just a means of duping simple minds in the interests of ruling or wealthy classes, and is no longer an ethical force. This puts the whole of society in danger, and such a religion will inevitably fall, bringing down society with itself in the crash as it did in France and later in Russia. When the old faith fails then the new is needed. Thinking men refuse to bind their reason to the incredible articles of a dogmatic creed. They refuse to swear belief in queer concepts which they find impossible to reconcile with the rest of human life and certainly with modern knowledge. The philosopher finds that religion looms against a much larger background; it is the mere shadow cast by philosophy, but for the masses the shadow suffices.

§

18

THE REVERENTIAL LIFE

Prayer—Devotion—Worship—Humility—
Surrender —Grace: real and imagined

A worldly refusal to honour the sacred is as unbalanced as a monastic refusal to honour the secular. In a balance of both duties, in a commonsense union of their ordained roles in a man's life lies the way for present-day man. Each age has its own emphasis; ours should be equilibrium.

§

We do not feel the need of hallowing our days. That is our great loss.

§

Metaphysical study will not weaken reverence but will rather put it on firmer ground. Metaphysical understanding will not weaken devotion but will rather more firmly establish it. What it will weaken, however, is the attachment to transient forms of reverence; what it will destroy is the error of giving devotion exclusively to the individual and refusing to include the Universal.

§

When devotion worship and reverence are fortified by knowledge, they can one day reach a stage where notably less is desired or demanded and peace then naturally arises. Nor is a measure of peace the only gain. Virtue later follows after it, quietly and effortlessly growing.

§

The sceptic who deems all prayer vain and useless, who regards the reasons for it as foolish, is too often justified. But when he ceases to search farther for the reasons behind prayer, he becomes unjustified. For if he did search, he might discover that true prayer is often answered because it is nothing less than making a connection—however loose, ill-fitting, and intermittent it be—with the life-force within the universe.

§

There is no one so sinful or so degraded in character that he is denied this blessed privilege of a contrite yearning for communion with his own divine source. Even the failure to have ever prayed before, even a past life of shame and error, does not cancel but, on the contrary, merely enhances this right. This granted, it will be found that there are many different forms of such communion, different ways of such prayer.

§

He should not hesitate to pray humbly, kneeling in the secrecy of his private room, to the Overself. First his prayer should acknowledge the sins of his more distant past having led to sufferings in the later past or his immediate present, and he should accept this as just punishment without any rebellious feeling. Then he may throw himself on the Grace as being the only deliverance left outside his own proper and requisite efforts to amend the causes. Finally let him remember the living master to whom he has given allegiance and draw strength from the memory.

§

There are those who object to the introduction of prayer into the philosophic life. In a world governed by the law of cause and effect, of what avail is this whining petition for unearned boons, they ask? Is it not unreasonable to expect them? Would it not be unfair to others to grant them?

These objections are valid ones. But the subject is covered with clouds. To dispel two or three of them, it is worth noting two or three facts. The first is that whether a prayer is addressed to the Primordial Being, to the Overself, or to a spiritual leader, it is still addressed to a higher power, and it is therefore an abasement of the ego before that power. When we remember the smug self-complacency of man, and the need of disturbing it if he is to listen to a truer Voice than his own, what can be wrong with such self-humbling? He will not be exempted by his petitioning from the sway of the law of cause and effect. If he seems to get an answer to his prayer we may be sure it will be for reasons that are valid in themselves, even if he is ignorant of those reasons. But how many prayers get answered? Everyone knows how slight the proportion is.

The man who is earnestly seeking to advance spiritually will usually be ashamed to carry any worldly desire into his sacred prayer. He will be working hard upon himself to improve, purify, and correct himself, so he need have no hesitation to engage in prayer—for the right things. He will pray for better understanding of the higher laws, clearer sight as to what his individual spiritual obligation consists in, more and warmer love for the Overself.

§

Pray by listening inwardly for intuitive feeling, light, strength, not by memorized form or pauperized begging.

§

The devotee who is mainly trying to draw God's attention to himself is still ego-centered.

§

It is strange that most just persons usually acknowledge having no right to get something for nothing, yet in the matter of prayer they feel no shame in requesting liberation from their particular weaknesses or habitual sins. Are they entitled to ask—often in a mechanical, importunate, or whining manner—for a result for which other persons work all-too-hard? Is it not effrontery to ask for divine intervention which should favour them while the others toil earnestly at reshaping themselves?

How then should a man pray? Should he beg for the virtues to be given to him gratis and unearned for which other men have to strive and labour? Is it not more just to them and better in the end for himself if, instead of demanding something for nothing, he prays thus: "I turn to you, O Master, for inspiration to rise above and excel myself, but I create that inspiration by my own will. I kneel before you for guidance in the problems and decisions of life, but I receive that guidance by taking you as an example of moral perfection to be followed and copied. I call upon you for help in my weakness and difficulty, my darkness and tribulation, but I produce and shape that help by trying to absorb it telepathically from your inner being." This is a different kind of prayer from the whining petitions often passing under that name, and whereas they seldom show direct, traceable results, this always shows them.

§

To enter this stillness is the best way to pray.

§

It is not to be, as it is with so many unenlightened religionists, nothing more than a request to be given something for nothing, a petition for unearned and undeserved personal benefit. It is to be first, a confession of the ego's difficulty or even failure to find its own way correctly through the dark forest of life; second, a confession of the ego's weakness or even helplessness in coping with the moral and mental obstacles in its path; third, an asking for help in the *ego's own strivings* after self-enlightenment and self-betterment; fourth, a resolve to struggle to the end to forsake the lower desires and overcome the lower emotions which raise dust-storms between the aspirant and his higher self; and fifth, a deliberate self-humbling of the ego in the admission that its need of a higher power is imperative.

§

At no level of his spiritual development need a man leave off the custom of prayer. The religious devotee, the mystical meditator, the metaphysical thinker, and the integrated philosopher alike need its fruits.

§

Self-purification is the best prayer, self-correction is the most effectual one.

§

It seems to be a law of the inner life that we have to ask for the inner help that is needed long long before it begins to manifest.

§

Both prayer and receptivity are needed. First we pray fervently and feelingly to the Overself to draw us closer to it, then we lapse into emotional quietness and patiently wait to let the inner self unfold to us. There is no need to discard prayer because we take up meditation. The one makes a fit prelude to the other. The real need is to purify prayer and uplift its objectives.

§

Meditation in a solitary place remote from the world may help others who are still in the world, but only under certain conditions. It must, for example, be deliberately directed towards named individuals. If it floats away into the general atmosphere without any thought of others, it is only a self-absorption, barren to others if profitable to oneself. It can be turned toward the spiritual assistance of anyone the practiser loves or wishes to befriend. But it should not be so turned prematurely. Before he can render real service, he must first acquire the power to do so. Before he can fruitfully pray for persons, he must first be able to draw strength from that which is above all persons. The capacity to serve must first be got before the attempt to serve is made. Therefore he should resist the temptation to plunge straightway into prayer or meditation on behalf of others. Instead he should wait until his worship or communion attains its highest level of being. Then—and then only—should he begin to draw from it the power and help and light to be directed altruistically towards others. Once he has developed the capacity to enter easily into the deeply absorbed state, he may then use it to help others also. Let him take the names and images of these people with him after he has passed into the state and let him hold them there for a while in the divine atmosphere.

§

The love which he is to bring as sacrificial offering to the Overself must take precedence of all other loves. It must penetrate the heart's core to a depth where the best of them fails to reach.

§

Love is both sunshine for the seed and fruit from the tree. It is a part of the way to self-realization and also a result of reaching the goal itself.

§

Since true philosophy is also a way of life, and since no such way can become effectual unless the feelings are involved, it includes and cultivates the most refined and most devotional feelings possible to man.

§

Remember that no enterprise or move should be left to depend on the ego's own limited resources. The humble invocation of help from the Higher Self expands those resources and has a protective value. At the beginning of every day, of every enterprise, of every journey, and of every important piece of work, remember the Overself, and remembering, be obedient to its laws. Seek its inspiration, its power. To make it your silent partner is to double your effectiveness.

§

He should not fall into the error of believing that the transition to philosophical study has exempted him from the duty of mystical practice or that the transition to the latter has exempted him from the need of religious devotion. We do not drop what belongs to a lower stage but keep and preserve it in the higher one. Aspiration is a vital need. He should become as a child at the feet of his divine Soul, humbly begging for its grace, guidance, and enlightenment. If his ego is strong, prayer will weaken it. Let him do this every day, not mechanically but sincerely and feelingly until the tears come to his eyes. The quest is an integral one and includes prayer alongside of all the other elements.

§

The way to be admitted to the Overself's presence can be summed up in a single phrase: *love it*. Not by breathing in very hard nor by blowing out very slow, not by standing on the head nor by contorting like a frog can admission be gained. Not even by long study of things divine nor by acute analysis of them. But let the love come first, let it inspire the breathing, blowing, standing, or contorting, let it draw to the study and drive to the thinking, and then these methods will become really fruitful.

§

Thanks for Thy presence and existence here and now.

Praise for making life on earth more bearable and more endurable when it becomes oppressive.

§

God needs no worship, no praise, no thanksgiving. It is man himself who needs the benefit to be derived from these activities.

§

He who sits with humbled, bowed head and folded, clasped, or knees-rested hands, with mind and heart in awed reverence, in sincere, worshipful, and rapt absorption which is aware of nothing else than the divine presence—he is praying, is meditating, is worshipping, is in heaven already.

§

In the adoration of his higher self he reaches the apex of existence. It proves that he has found out the secret of his own personality and solved the mystery of his relation to God.

§

Look how the smaller birds greet the sun, with so much merry chirruping and so much outpouring of song! It is their way of expressing worship for the only Light they can know, an outer one. But man can also know the inner Sun, the Light of the Overself. How much more reason has he to chirp and sing than the little birds! Yet how few men feel gratitude for such privilege.

§

The humility needed must be immensely deeper than what ordinarily passes for it. He must begin with the axiom that the ego is *ceaselessly* deceiving him, misleading him, ruling him. He must be prepared to find its sway just as powerful amid his spiritual interests as his worldly ones. He must realize that he has been going from illusion to illusion even when he seemed to progress.

§

The higher he climbs, the humbler he becomes. Only he will not make an exhibition of his humility to the world, for it is not needed there and might even harm him and others. He will be humble deep down in his heart where it is needed, in that sacred place where he faces the Overself.

§

Within his heart, he may call or keep nothing as his own, not even his spirituality. If he really does not want to cling to the ego, he must cling to nothing else. He is to have no sense of inner greatness, no distinct feeling of having attained some high degree of holiness.

§

But selflessness does not mean the surrender of one's own ego to someone else's ego. Renouncing the personal will does not mean becoming the creature of another person's will. Humility does not mean becoming the helpless victim of other people's wrong-doing. The only surrender that we are entitled to make is surrender to the Higher Power.

§

The unfulfilled future is not to be made an object of anxious thought or joyous planning. The fact that he has taken the tremendous step of offering his life in surrender to the Overself precludes it. He must now and henceforth let that future take care of itself, and await the higher will as it comes to him bit by bit. This is not to be confounded with the idle drifting, the apathetic inertia of shiftless, weak people who lack the qualities, the strength, and the ambition to cope with life successfully. The two attitudes are in opposition.

The true aspirant who has made a positive turning-over of his personal and worldly life to the care of the impersonal and higher power in whose existence he fully believes, has done so out of intelligent purpose, self-denying strength of will, and correct appraisal of what constitutes happiness. What this intuitive guidance of taking or rejecting from the circumstances themselves means in lifting loads of anxiety from his mind only the actual experience can tell. It will mean also journeying through life by single degrees, not trying to carry the future in addition to the present. It will be like crossing a river on a series of stepping-stones, being content to reach one at a time in safety and to think of the others only when they are progressively reached, and not before. It will mean freedom from false anticipations and useless planning, from vainly trying to force a path different from that ordained by God. It will mean freedom from the torment of not knowing what to do, for every needed decision, every needed choice, will become plain and obvious to the mind just as the time for it nears. For the intuition will have its chance at last to supplant the ego in such matters. He will no longer be at the mercy of the latter's bad qualities and foolish conceit.

§

There are great dangers in falling into a supine attitude of *supposed* submission of our will, an attitude into which so many mystics and religionists often fall. There is a profound difference between the pseudo-surrendered life and the genuine surrendered life. It is easy enough to misinterpret the saying "Thy will be done." Jesus, by his own example, gave this phrase a firm and positive meaning. Hence this is better understood as meaning "Thy will be done *by me.*" A wide experience has revealed how many are those who have degenerated into a degrading fatalism under the illusion that they were thereby co-operating with the will of God; how many are those who have through their own stupidity, negligence, weakness, and wrong-doing made no effort to remedy the consequences of their own acts and thus had to bear the suffering involved to the full; how many are those who have failed to seize the opportunity presented by these sufferings to recognize that they arose out of their own defects or faults and to examine themselves in time to become aware of them and thus avoid making the same mistake twice. The importance of heeding this counsel is immense. For example, many an aspirant has felt that fate has compelled him to work at useless tasks amid uncongenial surroundings, but when his philosophic understanding matures, he begins to see what was before invisible—the inner karmic significance of these tasks, the ultimate educative or punitive meaning of those environments. Once this is done he may rightly, and should for his own self-respect, set to work to free himself from them. Every time he patiently crushes a wrong or foolish thought, he adds to his inner strength. Every time he bravely faces up to a misfortune with calm impersonal appraisal of its lesson, he adds to his inner wisdom. The man who has thus wisely and self-critically surrendered himself may then go forward with a sense of outward security and inward assurance, hopeful and unafraid, because he is now aware of the benign protection of his Overself. If he has taken the trouble to understand intelligently the educative or punitive lessons they hold for him, he may then—and only then—conquer the evils of life, if at the same time of their onset, he turns inward at once and persistently realizes that the divinity within offers him refuge and harmony. This twofold process is always needful and the failures of Christian Science are partially the consequence of its failure to comprehend this.

§

He who surrenders his future to the Higher Power surrenders along with it the anxieties and cares which might otherwise have infested the thought of his future. This is a pleasant result, but it can only be got by surrendering at the same time the pleasureable anticipations and neatly made plans which might also have accompanied this thought. "Everything has to be paid for" is a saying which holds as true in the realm of the inner life as it does in the marketplace. The surrender of his life to the Higher Power involves the surrender of his ego. This is an almost impossible achievement if thought of in terms of a complete and instant act, but not if thought of in terms of a partial and gradual one. There are parts of the ego, such as the passions for instance, which he may attempt to deny even before he has succeeded in denying the ego itself. Anyway, he has to make clear to himself the fact that glib talk of surrender to God is cancelled if he does not at the same time attempt to surrender the obstructions to it.

§

To surrender a problem to the Overself is to cease worrying about it. If the worry still remains, its presence is proof that the surrender has not really been made.

§

The indispensable prerequisite to mystical illumination is self-surrender. No man can receive it without paying this price. Any man in any degree of development may pay it—he has to turn around, change his attitude, and accept the Christ, the higher self, as his sovereign. But once this happens and the Grace of illumination descends, it can affect the self only as it finds the self. An unbalanced ego will not suddenly become balanced. An unintellectual one will not suddenly become learned. His imperfections remain though the light shines through them.

§

He is to sacrifice all the lower emotions on the altar of this quest. He is to place upon it anger, greed, lust, and aggressive egoism as and when each situation arises when one or another of them shows its ugly self. All are to be burnt up steadily, if little by little, at such opportunities. This is the first meaning of surrender to the higher self.

§

The intuitive sensitivity of the artist and the discriminating intellect of a scientist are needed to keep that delicate balance which knows when to assume responsibility for one's own decision, action, and life and when to shift this responsibility to a higher power. The novice's statement that he commits his life into God's hands is not enough, for obviously if he continues to repeat the same foolish judgements and the same guilty conduct as before this commitment, his life still remains in the personal ego's hands. If his commitment is to be effective, it must be accompanied by the duty of self-improvement. Surrender to a higher power does not relieve him of this duty; on the contrary, it compels him more than ever before to its carrying out. The shifting of personal responsibility is achieved only when the awakening of consciousness to the higher self is itself achieved. The mere desire and consequent say-so of the aspirant does not and cannot become factual until then. He may seek to relieve himself of the pressure of obligation and the irritation of obstacles by this device, but the relief will be merely fictional and not factual.

§

When a man feels the authentic urge to walk a certain way, but cannot see how it will be possible either because of outer circumstances or of inner emotions, let him trust and obey it. For if he does so, the Grace of the Overself will manipulate these circumstances or alter his feelings accordingly. But it will do this so as to lead to his further growth and real need, not for satisfaction of his personal desires or his supposed wants. Let him accept its leading, not the ego's blindness.

§

The rejection of the idea of Grace is based on a misconception of what it is, and especially on the belief that it is an arbitrary capricious gift derived from favouritism. It is, of course, nothing of the kind, but rather the coming into play of a higher law. Grace is simply the transforming power of the Overself which is ever-present but which is ordinarily and lawfully unable to act in a man until he clears away the obstacles to this activity. If its appearance is considered unpredictable, that is because the karmic evil tendencies which hinder this appearance vary considerably from one person to another in strength, volume, and length of life. When the karma which generated them becomes weak enough, they can no longer impede its action.

§

There are three types of Grace: firstly, that which has the appearance of Grace but which actually descends out of past good karma and is entirely self-earned; secondly, that which a Master gives to disciples or aspirants when the proper external and internal circumstances exist—this is in the nature of a temporary glimpse only but is useful because it gives a glimpse of the goal, a sense of the right direction, and inspiring encouragement to continue on the Quest; thirdly, when a man attains the fullest degree of realization, he is enabled in some cases to modify overhanging negative karma or in others to negate it because he has mastered the particular lessons that needed to be learned. This is particularly evident when the Hand of God removes obstructions in the path of his work. The philosophic conception of Grace shows it to be just and reasonable. It is indeed quite different from the orthodox religious belief about it, a belief which regards it as an arbitrary intervention by the Higher Power for the benefit of its human favourites.

§

He may know that the work of Grace has begun when he feels an active drawing from within which wakes him from sleep and which recurs in the day, urging him to practise his devotions, his recollections, his prayers, or his meditations. It leads him from his surface consciousness to his inner being, a movement which slowly goes back in ever-deepening exploration and discovery of himself.

§

It seems as if grace visits us at moments of its own choosing. That is the truth, but not the only truth. For study, practice of exercises, training, self-discipline, prayer, aspiration, and meditation also form a total effort which must attract grace as its reward eventually.

§

If the existence of grace is granted, the question of its means of transmission arises. Since it is a radiation issuing from the Overself, it can be directly bestowed. But if there are internal blockages, as in most cases there are, and insufficient force on the man's part to break through them, then it cannot be directly received. Some thing or person outside him will have then to be used as means of indirect transmission.

§

No Maharishee, no Aurobindo, no Saint Francis can save you. It is the Holy Spirit which saves man by its Grace. The ministrations of these men may kindle faith and quiet the mind, may help you to prepare the right conditions and offer a focus for your concentration, but they offer no guarantee of salvation. It is highly important not to forget this, not to deify man and neglect the true God who must come to you directly and act upon you directly.

§

Two things are required of a man before Grace will manifest itself in him. One is the capacity to receive it. The other is the co-operation with it. For the first, he must humble the ego; for the second, he must purify it.

§

The closer he comes to the Overself, the more actively is the Grace able to operate on him. The reason for this lies in the very nature of Grace since it is nothing other than a benign force emanating from the Overself. It is always there but is prevented by the dominance of the animal nature and the ego from entering his awareness. When this dominance is sufficiently broken down, the Grace comes into play more and more frequently, both through Glimpses and otherwise.

§

The real bar to the entry of grace is simply the preoccupation of his thoughts with himself. For then the Overself must leave him to his cares.

§

By grace I mean the manifestation of God's friendliness.

§

If you seek to invoke the divine grace to meet a genuine and desperate physical need or human result, seek first to find the sacred presence within yourself and only after you have found it, or at least only after you have attained the deepest point of contemplation possible to you, should you name the thing or result sought. For then you will not only be guided whether it be right to continue the request or not, but you will also put yourself in the most favourable position for securing grace.

§

No one but a man's own Being gives him grace. From the moment when he lays his head prostrate before It, and returns again and again to that posture, mentally always and physically if urged, grace is invoked.

§

In the early stages of spiritual progress, Grace may show itself in the bestowal of ecstatic emotions. This encourages him to pursue the Quest and to know that he is so far pursuing it rightly. But the purpose gained, the blissful states will eventually pass away, as they must. He will then falsely imagine that he has lost Grace, that he has left undone something he should have done or done something he should not have done. The true fact is that it is Grace itself which has brought this loss about, as constituting his next stage of progress, even though it affords no pleasure to his conscious mind, but only pain. His belief that he has lost the direct contact with the higher power which he formerly enjoyed is wrong: his actual contact was only an indirect one, for his emotions were then occupied with themselves and with their pleasure in the experience. He is being separated from them so that he may be emptied of every desire and utterly humbled in his ego, and thus made ready for the time when joy, once regained, will never leave him again. For he is now on the threshold of the soul's dark night. In that state there is also a work being done for him by Grace, but it is deep in the subconscious mind far beyond his sight and beyond his control.

§

When the Quest becomes the most important activity in a man's life, even more important than his worldly welfare, then is Grace likely to become a reality rather than a theory in his life too.

§

If there is any law connected with grace, it is that as we give love to the Overself so do we get grace from it. But that love must be so intense, so great, that we willingly sacrifice time and thought to it in a measure which shows how much it means to us. In short, we must give more in order to receive more. And love is the best thing we can give.

§

19

THE REIGN OF RELATIVITY

Consciousness is relative—Dream, sleep, wakefulness—
Time as past, present, future—Space—
Twofold standpoint—Void as metaphysical fact

Here is the essence of both the Theory of Relativity and philosophy's development of it. Two men standing on two different planets moving at different speeds and at disproportionately different distances from the same object at the same instant of time, will differently perceive this object and differently estimate both its character and the measure of the forces working upon it. How can it be said that one of these results is wrong and the other right? Both are correct, for both must be what they are from their respective standpoints. But the same object and the same forces cannot at one and the same time possess contradictory measurements and properties. Therefore these men are not really dealing with *it* but with *their own* observations of it. On the other hand, two entirely different objects may produce two entirely similar sets of sense-impressions, as in the case of the meteor called shooting-star and a genuine star. Hence the things and forces in the world are not really the world-in-itself but what we individually see and experience as the world. All that we really know of them in the end is the picture which forms itself out of our sense-impressions, and this picture alone has genuine existence. Anything beyond it has only a supposed existence. But these impressions when thoroughly analysed are found to be only forms which the mind has unconsciously made for itself, just as a dreamer unconsciously makes his dream world for himself. The world of man's experience is always entirely relative to the individual man himself. All that he sees and smells lies wholly within his consciousness and not outside it.

§

As we try to think away all the objects which space contains, we must not forget to think away the *light* with which we unconsciously fill all space. We shall find if we succeed in this admittedly difficult exercise, that space itself will then disappear. Thus the common belief in space as a kind of vast vessel containing everything, as depending on being determined by the distances between two or more objects and the relative positions occupied by these objects, is hardly a correct one. Both "inside" and "outside" are merely relative terms. All this again is because, as mentalism declares, space is really the idea which we subconsciously impose on. Hence, when for a few brief moments the mind transcends its creations and returns to itself in mystical abstraction, we lose the feeling of the "outsideness" of things and the world fades into being our own unreal dream. This happens because, as mentalism has already taught us, space is needed by the mind to contain its images, to measure its forms, and therefore mind accordingly makes it. Now the same considerations apply to time, for if we think away all the objects which have their life in the past present or future, there will be no time left to flow onwards. There will be no independent thing called time. Nevertheless, the mind is not left in a wholly negative state after this is done. Whatever we may possibly experience or know in the external world must necessarily be experienced or known under the forms of space and time; to be at all, they have to be as they are. But these forms are variable and changeable, relative and dependent. Therefore these events or things are not themselves eternal and enduring realities. Space and time are ways in which we experience existence; they are not things in themselves.

§

The relativity theory brings space and time together as having no existence independent of each other. Mentalism explains why this is so. They are both inherent in one and the same thing—imagination; they are two ways in which the creative aspect of mind functions simultaneously.

§

The most valuable metaphysical fruit of the quantum theory is its finding that the processes of the universe which occur in space and time, emanate from what is fundamentally not in space and time.

§

The time-space-causality reference is an essential part of human nature, a governing law of human thinking. These three hold good solely within such thinking and can have no possible or proper application outside it. Man does not consciously or arbitrarily impose them upon his thought; it is beyond his individual power to reject them.

§

Such is this relativity of all things to their knower that because the world we experience is *our* mental world, we never see the world as it really is in itself or as a being who was observing it from outside would observe it. The consequence is that we never see the world without unconsciously seeing the world mixed up with the self. The "I" plus something other than the "I" constitute our field of consciousness. We never know the world-in-itself but only the world-in-a-state-of-interaction-with-the-self. We never know the self-in-itself but only the self-in-a-condition-of-interaction-with-the world. Such are the actual and compulsory conditions of the so-called experience of the world and our so-called experience of the self.

§

Can the observer who sees, the knower who knows be himself made an object to be perceived? No! says the intellectual; Yes! says the mystic philosopher.

§

There are different strata of the finite mind. He learns to see how the self is caught and works in them in order to go beyond them and become aware of That which is infinite Mind.

§

Notes on Causality/Non-causality:

All our thinking is shaped into the mold of causality and this not by our own choice but by Nature's.

Nothing can enter experience which is not thrown by the mind into a causal form. The mind being capable only of experiencing in this way is incapable of grasping the essentially real in experience.

All that we know of Nature is our mental experience of it; and all that we know of causality in Nature is likewise only the way in which that mental experience arranges itself.

The causal habit, like that of time and space, is one of the cardinal habits of thinking and one of the fixed forms of awareness. It is our lack of comprehension of the way in which the mind works, the relation between consciousness, ego, and mind, which makes it inevitable for us to fall victim to these three great illusions of the race.

The bias towards belief in causality is so universally ingrained in mankind that religious teachers had to explain the world in causal terms first. But the Vedantists used such causal explanations as steps to mount up towards non-causality. They taught that the world is a creation and its creator the pure spirit Brahman, and then led the pupil to enquire into the nature of Brahman, gradually showing him that Brahman is one, indivisible and partless. Such a partless being cannot change or produce change, therefore there can be no creation, that is, the truth of non-causality. In this way the pupil was led from religion to philosophy.

Creation as an act is different from creation as a fact. Advaita challenges the reality of the first but admits the second in the sense that it does not deny the existence of the world. But the question "How did God create the world?" does not admit of a simple accurate answer. In the first place it is oversimple and therefore inadequate; secondly it is mis-stated and omits at least two other questions the answers to which are prerequisite to an answer to the question in its present form. The infinite principle of Mind does not will or create the Universe, but within its seeming darkness there arises a point of light which becomes the centre of a potential universe. A first beginning of the Universe has never happened, because the Universe is a manifestation of Mind, the reality which, existing in timeless duration as it does, has never had a beginning itself.

Causality functions in the ordinary world. To doubt that would be to doubt all human experience. But when we enquire into its ultimate abstraction we find causality contradicts itself, it is relative and an appearance. At the same time we see that the causal thought-form must be added to the percepts of space and time to bring experience into ordered relationship during the manifestation of the universe, and lapse when the mind sinks again into consciousness.

Even so supreme a teacher as the Buddha had to confess, "Unknowable is the beginning of beings."

What it is in Mind that impels it to make these myriad appearances as ideas we do not and cannot know. The question itself is based on belief in causation, which is another idea, and is therefore invalid because it is without meaning to Mind.

One valid application of the tenet of non-causality is this—when water is converted into steam we cannot say steam is a new creation, for it is still nothing but water albeit its expression has changed.

The world being but an expression of the Overself is not a new creation, for fundamentally no new thing has come into being. The world is but a changed expression of Overself, and as cause implies effect, that is, duality, and as there is no duality, so there is no causal relation behind the universe. From the empiric standpoint—that is, disregarding fundamentals and looking at secondary elements only—within the universe causality clearly reigns. V.S.L.'s application of non-causality to the interrelations within the world is illegitimate.

If causality were not a practical working truth we should plant grass seed in the hope of getting grapefruit.

We must get our minds quite clear about this position. It is all a matter of standpoint. From a practical standpoint the world is composed of many entities affecting and inter-reacting with each other in a causal manner. From the ultimate standpoint the world is Mind-essence, and this being the only existence cannot change its nature and come into a second birth; it cannot fall into the duality of cause and effect. But the Mind's finite productions, ideas, can do so.

Therefore it is admitted that causality fully reigns in the realm of ordinary experience. But when we seek to understand Mind in itself we seek to transcend ordinary experience. Mind in itself is not subject to causality.

The question of causality depends, like the question of the universe, on the particular point of view which we take up. It is real when considered as pertaining to two things, just as a dream table and chairs are real when considered by the dreamer himself. It is fictitious when we look not at the multiplicity of things but at the essence wherefrom they are derived, just as the dream table and chairs are fictitious when looked at from the broader point of view of the man who has awakened with the dawn.

Whereas experience presupposes the relation of causality, reality itself stands out of all relations. Causality is a condition of knowing and thus confines us to the familiar world. The category of causality is inapplicable to Brahman.

If there is one rigid law in nature it would seem to be none other than the law of causality, for how can the chain of causation ever be broken?

The reticence of the Buddha in discussing problems concerning the First Cause is made explicable by his knowledge of non-causality.

Sub-atomic science—indeterminacy, Heisenberg's Quantum Theory; Super-atomic science—Einstein's relativity; milliards of galaxies which made the universe.

Sub-atomic physics reveals that the ultramicroscopic electrons and protons are disobedient to the law which science took as the best established of all laws—that of cause and effect. This revealment may even bring the theoretical search for reality into a cul-de-sac. What was once a philosophical tenet may become a scientific one too. What was once the consequence of man's keenest reflection may become the consequence of his ascertainment of facts.

Scholars often use the words cause and effect with less warrant than truth demands. The phrase is profusely sprinkled over lecture and book until we accept their statement as unquestioningly as we accept today's sunrise. But it behooves the few who would root up the reason for all things to look a little closer into this usage. When we do this, those smooth and finished doctrines which have held us captive so long may be compelled to open their doors and set us free. We may discover, as did David Hume, that whether in the behaviour of matter or of mind, much that we accept as causal is nothing of the kind, it is merely consecutive.

Hume said that a thing or self was only a bundle of relations, being nothing in itself.

It is very easy to fall into what may be called the fallacy of the single cause, as when Hitler—conveniently overlooking himself and those like him—asserted that the Jews were the cause of Germany's worst troubles. The truth is that most problems are many sided, and behind the simplest effects there lie usually a combination of causes.

Causality is a misapprehension from the philosophical standpoint, but quite correct from the physical and practical.

In the last reckoning life is really a process whereby the individual becomes conscious of his own true identity. The spiritual nature of man does not exist potentially, but actually. The discovery of his own identity is simply man's destruction of the hypnotic illusions of Ego, Time, Space, Matter, and Cause—his moment of release from untruth.

The Overself is not subject to causality, but the ideas which appear to arise in it are. This is where students become confused.

We must not ascribe activity to the Overself. This does not mean that it is wrapped in everlasting slumber. The possibility of all activity is derived from it. It is the life behind the Cosmic Mind's own life.

§

Living in time and space as we do, we perforce live always in the fragmentary and imperfect, never in the whole, the perfect. Only if, at rare moments, we are granted a mystical experience and transcend the time-space world, do we know the beauty and sublimity of being liberated from a mere segment of experience into the wholeness of Life itself.

§

The first and root error which has vitiated the philosophy of the West is its assumption that the world of waking life is the only real world.

§

In unwittingly setting up waking consciousness as the sole arbiter of all his knowledge, Western man limits that knowledge unnecessarily. And in regarding other forms of consciousness as mere copies or aberrations of waking consciousness, or else denying their existence altogether, he bars himself from the supreme insight and the highest felicity open to him. Unless he brings the dream and the deep sleep states also into his reckoning, he will continue to be deceived by the Unreal and to mistake the shadow for the substance.

§

As human life extends as an indivisible whole through all three states and is never limited to any one of them alone, it is unscientific and unphilosophic arbitrarily to select the waking condition and ignore the facts of the other two. All the data obtainable ought to be secured, and then integrated into a synthetic system by apprehending them simultaneously in their entirety. The synthesis of all life's states can alone produce sufficient data upon which to grasp the true nature of the world. Only a superior mind, free from vulgar prejudice against sleep and dream, will realize the immense importance of such co-ordination.

§

A comparison of the waking with the dream state yields two striking similarities. Firstly, neither in one state nor the other do we make our planetary environment, or the other persons who figure in it, or cause all its happenings. We are born into our waking world—it is there ready-made. We find ourselves abruptly in our dream world. The other persons just happen to be in both worlds with us. We do not deliberately prefabricate most of the everyday happenings in the waking world and we do not do this with the dream happenings either. Secondly, in neither world can we predict exactly how we shall behave, react, or feel in all their situations. This is all intended to say that our waking life is really a kind of sleep, from which we need to wake up; that just as the dreamer only awakens when his fatigue exhausts itself or when someone else arouses him, so we, too, only awaken from life's illusions when we are exhausted with all the many different kinds of experience we get from many different incarnations or when a teacher appears to reveal the truth to us. Further, what we have done or desired in former incarnations predetermines a large part of the picture of our present one. Yet, the connection between this cause and this effect is unseen by us until someone else, a master of insight, shows it to us. Until then we are like sleeping dreamers.

§

Just as the spiritual ignorance of man reveals itself during his slumbers by his total lack of knowledge that the dream-experience is only a series of ideas, so the evil character of man reveals itself during his slumbers by the rule it imposes—unrepressed by legal sanctions or social codes—upon his dreams. This is one of the elements of truth in Freud's otherwise grossly materialistic teaching. The dream is partially a self-revelation. Hence it is the teaching of the mystical order of Turkish Sufis that the progress of a disciple is partially to be measured by his teacher by the progressive purification attained in the character of his dream life.

§

Unreflective life is often impatient with such enquiries into the relative value of the waking state, for to them its superior reality in contrast with dream is completely beyond all question. They denounce the sleep enquiry as being altogether too flimsy a premise on which to build great conclusions. Yet when we remember that all living creatures from ant to man are plunged into intermittent sleep for substantial portions of their whole lives, how can we hope to grasp the meaning of their existence and the meaning of the universe of which they are parts, without examining the full meaning and proper value of sleep-states? Whatever we learn from a single state alone may always be liable to contradiction by the facts of another state. Therefore unless we co-ordinate and evaluate the truth of the waking state with the truth of the sleep state we cannot hope to arrive at ultimate truth in its fullness. But when we venture to make such a co-ordination we shall discover that in sleep there lies the master-key of life and death!

§

Dreams occur for several different reasons. And two parts of one and the same dream occur for two different reasons. It is unscientific to say—as the materialistic medicos, the psychoanalysts, and the fortune-tellers stubbornly say—that dreams are determined by a single particular cause. And it is just as unscientific to say that dreams have only one function to perform. Therefore the student must move warily when trying to understand dream processes or to interpret individual dream happenings. It is quite true to assert, for example, that some dreams or some parts of a dream represent unconscious desires or repressed emotions, but it is equally true to assert that most dreams don't represent them at all. It is fallacious to make the dream a metaphor pointing to future events. More often, it is an Irish stew cooked up out of past ones. For most dreams merely reveal what happens when the image-making faculty breaks loose from the general mental equipment and works out a series of self-deceptive illusions based on real material picked up during the previous day's experiences.

§

Consider the fact that our individual lives are totally suspended during sleep, that the waves of personal consciousness then merge utterly in the ocean. How clearly this shows the Divine to be also the Infinite and Universal, our lack of true spirituality, and our possession at best of its pale reflection! For where else could we go to sleep except in this Infinite and Universal Mind? Yet we know it not! To get rid of such ignorance, to attain transcendental insight into the fourth state of being, is the most wonderful of all the tasks which this philosophy sets before us.

§

In sleep the non-existence of things is ***not*** known to you; therefore sleep is a state of ignorance, not of Gnanam, for the Gnani knows everything to be Brahman. The nonduality of sleep is not the nonduality of Gnanam. Brahman is not known in deep sleep but is known in Gnanam.

§

In our view, even deep sleep unconsciousness is a form of this "consciousness" which transcends all the states we ordinarily know—waking, dream, and deep sleep—yet includes them when they merge back into it. Such a "consciousness" is unthinkable, unimaginable, but it is the true objective awareness. It is also the *I* you are seeking so much. But to reach it, then you have to let go of the I which you know so well.

§

Once he has attained the philosophic realization of the Overself, he goes nightly to sleep *in it*, if the sleep is dreamless and deep, or inserts it into his dreams if it is not. Either way he does not withdraw from it.

§

The transcendental being is not an unconscious one. The absolute consciousness could not be other than self-conscious in its own impersonal way. Hence the fourth state is not the same as deep sleep.

§

A subtle, careful analysis of the three states of consciousness will show the logical need of a fourth, which is their hidden basis.

§

The space in which the process of thinking takes place, is time. It could not exist without the dimension of time. If thought is ever transcended, time is transcended along with it. Such an achievement throws the mind into the pure present, the eternal now, "the presence of God" of all mystics.

§

Do not confuse infinite time, which is duration, with timelessness, which is eternity. The first is just the lengthening of the ego's past, present and future; the second is their dissolution in ecstatic smiling ego-free being.

§

Eternity contains, undivided, the past present and future. How it can do so is a mystery which human perception and human understanding may not ordinarily grasp. The unaided intellect is powerless to solve it. But there is, potentially, a fourth-dimensional intuitive faculty which can succeed where the others fail.

§

The real heaven is a state of delightful rest which the finite human mind cannot correctly imagine and usually misconceives as a state of perpetual idleness for the ego.

§

Is it not a strange thing that after a night's dreaming sleep when we may become some other person, some other character during our dreams, we yet wake up with the old identity that we had before the dream? And is it not equally strange that after a night's sweet, deep, dreamless slumber when we actually forget utterly that same previous identity, we are able to pick it up once more on awakening? What is the explanation of these strange facts? It is that we have never left our true selfhood, whether in dreams or deep slumber, never been other than we really were in essence, and that the only change that has taken place has been a change of the *state* of our consciousness, not of the consciousness itself.

§

That there is an insight where all times lie side by side—the past, the present, the future—the twentieth century B.C. and the twentieth century A.D., may seem impossible to the ordinary mind.

§

It is in the fullness of the eternal present, the eternal now, that a man can really live happily. For by seeking That which makes him conscious of the present moment, by remembering it as being the essence of his fleeting experience, he completes that experience and fulfils its lofty purpose.

§

The fourth dimension is in everything existing in the three-dimensional space and at the same time exists in its own dimension. *Now* in the fourth is the same as *here* in the third dimensional world.

§

Materialism is compelled to hold that there is only one uniform time. Mentalism holds that there are different kinds of time, not only for different kinds of beings but even for one and the same being.

§

In contemplating deeply Nature's beauty around one, as some of us have done, it is possible to slip into a stillness where we realize that there never was a past but always the *NOW*—the ever-present timeless Consciousness—all peace, all harmony; that there is no past—just the eternal. Where are the shadows of negativity then? They are non-existent! This can happen if we forget the self, with its narrowed viewpoint, and surrender to the impersonal. In that brief experience there is no conflict to trouble the mind.

§

It is our innate inertia which keeps us set in habitual outlooks and thus keeps us victims of our own past experience. We copy again every day what we did before, what we thought and felt before. We live in both the conscious and the subconscious memories, desires, fears which time has accumulated for us, and that the ego has created to bind us to itself. We are ruled by compulsions, fixations, and neuroses—some of them not even known—that freeze us, preventing further real advancement. We rarely enter the day to gain really fresh experience, think really new thoughts, or assume really different attitudes. We are prisoners of time. This is because we are so ego-bound. The compulsion which makes us conform ourselves to dead yesterday's ideas and practices, concepts and habits, is an unreal one, an illusory one. In letting ourselves become victims of the past by letting it swallow up the present, we lose the tremendous meaning and tremendous opportunity which the present contains. Whereas the Overself speaks to us from tomorrow's intuitive understanding, the ego speaks to us through memory. Its past enslaves us, preventing a new and higher way of viewing life from being born.

But it is possible to arouse ourselves and to begin viewing life as it unfolds in the Eternal Present, the Now, with wholly fresh eyes. Every morning is like a new reincarnation into this world. It is a fresh chance to be ourselves, not merely echoes of our own past ideological fixations. Let us take it then for what it is and live each moment anew.

When a master mystic like Jesus tells men to refrain from being anxious about the morrow and to let today's evil be sufficient for today, He speaks out of his own consciousness of living in this Eternal Now. Consequently, he spoke not of periods involving twelve or twenty-four hours, but of pinpoints of a moment. He told them to live timelessly, to let the dead past bury itself. He is indeed a Christian, a Christ-self man, who lives cleanly and completely in the present—free, uncontrolled, and unconditioned by what he was, believed, or desired yesterday.

§

The mystery of the atom has resolved itself into the mystery of light, which is now the greatest mystery of physics. Einstein demonstrated the dependence of time upon the position and speed of motion of an observer. He showed, too, the amazing consequence of placing the latter in a stream of light wherein if he moved with the same velocity as light, the observer would then possess no sense of the passage of time. If this happened, what sort of a sense would he possess? Einstein could not tell us, but the mystic who has conquered mind can. He will possess the sense of eternity. He will live in the eternal, in the Kingdom of Heaven.

§

During the night when Gautama entered Buddhahood and the great revelation of the Good Law was made to him, he discovered that existence was from moment to moment, discontinuous. The Hindu sages deny this and assert it is *continuous* in the Self. The pity of it is that both are right. For what happens in every interval between two moments? We then live solely and exclusively in the Self, the Absolute, delivered from Relativity and Finitude.

Many "still" photographs make up a cinema film. The break between every pair of pictures is not reported to the conscious mind because fast movement outruns attention. The symbolism is interesting: see *The Wisdom of the Overself*, Chapter 14, seventh meditation, for a more detailed explanation. Whoever attempts this exercise should practise it with the eyes only slightly open.

Then why did not the Buddha finish his announcement and give the entire truth? For the same reason he carefully kept quiet on several other points which could disturb men dependent on religion—on its representatives and rites, its customs and dogmas, and especially its past—to the point of enslavement. He likened the human predicament to being in a burning house and directed attention to the urgent need, which was to get out *now* and thus get saved. Here is a key word: the Present, manipulated rightly, can open the practitioner's mind. Then the Timeless itself may take him out of time (he, the personal self, cannot do it), out of the now into the Eternal NOW. If it is no easily successful way there is always the long detour of other ways found by men.

§

The feeling until now was one of living *in* time. Imperceptibly or suddenly this goes and he finds himself in a timeless condition, with the tick-tock of thoughts following one another absolutely stilled. It is temporary but it is also glorious.

§

The immediate present is not the eternal NOW.

§

Psychologically the void trance is deeper than the world-knowing insight, but metaphysically it is not. For in both cases one and the same Reality is seen.

§

What is the practical value of the teaching about time? The full answer to this question would embrace many fields, but here is one of the most important. Philosophy teaches its student to apply the double point of view to the outward happenings of his life as it does to the inward contents of his sense-experience. From the ordinary point of view, the nature of an event determines whether it is a good or evil one; from the philosophic point of view, the way he thinks about the event will determine whether it is good or evil for him. He should always put the two points of view together and never separate them, always balance the short-range one by the long-range one.

The higher point of view enables him to escape some of the suffering which the lower one would impose upon him. An event which to the worldly man seems staggeringly important and evil from the point of view of the moment, becomes smaller and smaller as the years recede and, consequently, less and less hurtful. Twenty years later it will have lost some of its power to shake him; fifty years later it will have lost still more—indeed, it may have lost so much as to cause him no further pain; one incarnation later it will not trouble him at all. When the student adopts the long-range point of view he achieves the same result in advance and by anticipation of time. It is said that time heals all sorrows; if we seek the reason why, we shall find it is because it insensibly gives a more philosophic point of view to the sorrowful. The taste of water in a jar will be strongly sweetened by a cupful of sugar; the taste of water in a bucket will be moderately sweetened by it; the taste of water in a bathtub will be only slightly sweetened by it; and water in a lake will be apparently quite unmodified by it at all. In exactly the same way, the stream of happenings which makes up time for human consciousness gradually dilutes the suffering which each individual event may bring us.

The student is not content, however, to wait for such a slow process in order to reduce his suffering. By bringing the philosophic attitude to bear upon each event, as and when it occurs, he immediately reduces his suffering and fortifies his peace. Every calamity which is seen from this standpoint becomes a means whereby he may ascend, if he will, to a higher level of understanding, a purer form of being. What he thinks about it and what he learns from it will be its real legacy to him. In his first fresh anguish the unawakened man may deny this; in the mental captivity which gives reality to the Present and drops it from the Past, he may see no meaning and no use in the calamity; but either by time or by philosophy he will one day be placed at the point of view where the significance of suffering will be revealed to him and where the necessity of suffering will be understood by him. This, indeed, is one of the great paradoxes of the human development: that suffering leads him step by step from the false self to the acceptance of the true self, and that the true self leads him step by step back to the acceptance of suffering.

If the worldly man agitatedly sees the event against the background of a moment, if the philosophic student calmly sees it against the background of an entire lifetime, the sage, while fully aware of both these points of view, offsets them altogether by adding a third one which does not depend on any dimension of time at all. From this third point of view, he sees both the event itself and the ego to whom it happens as illusory. He feels the sense of time and the sense of personality as unreal. Deep within his mind he holds unshakeably to the timeless character of true being, to the eternal life of the kingdom of heaven. In this mysterious state time cannot heal, for there are no wounds present whereof to be healed. So soon as we can take the reality out of time, so soon can we take the sting out of suffering. For the false self lives like a slave, bound to every passing sensation, whereas the true self lives in the timeless peace of the kingdom of heaven. As soon as we put ourselves into harmony with the true self, we put ourselves into harmony with the whole universe; we put ourselves beyond the reach of calamity. It may still happen, but it does not happen to nor is it felt by our real self. There is a sense of absolute security, a feeling that no harm can come to us. The philosophic student discovers the mission of time; it heals sorrows and, under karma or through evolution, cures evils. The sage solves the mystery of timelessness, which redeems man.

§

Philosophy would not be worthwhile if it did not take the view that for the practical purposes of life, it must turn around and adopt a non-metaphysical approach. Thus a twofold attitude is the only complete and therefore correct one which it may approve. We have the right and bear the duty to ask ourselves in what way is a teaching related to everyday living; in what way is it connected with the world we know? If both relation and connection are absent, it is fair to say that the teaching is inadequate and lacks the necessary balance of interests.

§

Whatever the universe be in human experience, it is, in important ways, like a dream. That is, we must grant existence to a dream world as an indubitable fact because it is a perceived and experienced world; but at the same time we must refuse its form ultimate existence, and hence enduring reality, because it is neither perceived nor experienced after we awake from sleep. This twofold character of the dream world also belongs to the familiar and so-called real universe. It is plain, yet paradoxical at the same time. For this reason, ancient Tibetan philosophers declared the world to be both existent and non-existent. To the unenquiring mind it vividly is what it seems to be, but to the awakened insight of the sage its form presents itself like a more enduring version of the transient form of a dream world. Both forms are thought-constructions. Both have Mind as their underlying "substance." Therefore Mind is their reality. Apart from Mind the world could not even exist just as apart from the dreamer his dream could not exist.

§

Life is changing dream-stuff to the thinker but it nevertheless is spun out of immutable reality.

§

Metaphysically, every thing and every thought contains in itself the form of its opposite. We must try not to be attached to one opposite and not to be repelled by the other in a *personal* way. This does not mean that we may ignore them—indeed we cannot do so, for practical life requires that we attempt at least to negotiate them—but that we deal with them in an equable and impersonal way. Thus we keep free of the bonds of possessiveness. If we try to cling to one of the opposites alone whilst rejecting the other, we are doomed to frustration. To accept what is inherent in the nature of things is therefore a wise act. If, through being personally hurt by it, we are unwilling to do so, if we rebel against it, then we shall succeed only in hurting ourselves all the more. To run away from one of the opposites and to run after the other is an unwise act. We must find a balance between them; we must walk between the two extremes; we must ascend the terrace above the standpoint which affirms and above that which negates: for the entire truth is never caught by either and is often missed by both. For the way in which our consciousness works shuts us up, as it were, in a prison house of relativistic experiences which are the seeming real but never the actually real. To accept both and yet to transcend both, is to become a philosopher. To transcend the opposites we have to cease thinking about what effect they will have upon us personally. We have to drop the endless "I" reference which blinds us to the truth about them. We must refuse to set up our personal preferences as absolute standards, our relative standpoints as eternal ones. To do this is to cease worrying over events on the one hand, to cease grabbing at things on the other. It is indeed to rise to an impersonal point of view and enter into harmony with what Nature is seeking to do in us and in our environment. We have to find a new and higher set of values. For so long as we cling to a personal standpoint we are enslaved by time and emotion, whereas so soon as we drop it for the philosophic one, we are liberated into a serene timeless life.

§

Once the double viewpoint is understood and set up as the necessary starting point, the timed measure and the timeless order fall into his scheme of things. Practical experience carries him through the ordinary existence, and divine experience—the eternal Now—is not displaced by it. Success in living the philosophic life and maturing the mentality it requires makes this possible.

§

There is only one real presence, the divine Presence. This is the final truth we all have to learn, and to experience. When this happens we see the world as it is in appearance, just as other persons do, but we also intuit it at the same time as it is in essence and feel it held in that Presence.

§

The apparent void out of which the universe seems to have been made, created, born, or evolved, is really the essence, the being, the life-power of God.

§

The momentary pause in every heartbeat is a link with the still centre of the Overself. Where the rhythm of activity comes to an end—be it a man's heart or an entire planet—its infinite and eternal cause is there. All this vast universal activity is but a function of the silent, still Void.

§

The One behind the Many is not to be mistaken for the figure one which is followed by two, three, and so on. It is on the contrary the mysterious Nought out of which all the units which make up multiple figures themselves arise. If we do not call it the Nought it is only because this might be mistaken as utter Nihilism. Were this so then existence would be meaningless and metaphysics absurd. The true ineffable Nought, like the superphysical One, is rather the reality of all realities. From it there stream forth all things and all creatures; to it they shall all return eventually. This void is the impenetrable background of all that is, was, or shall be; unique, mysterious, and imperishable. He who can gaze into its mysterious Nothingness and see that the pure Divine Being is forever there, sees indeed.

§

The Void is the state of Mind in repose, and the appearance-world is its (in)activity. At a certain stage of their studies, the seeker and the student have to discriminate between both in order to progress; but further progress will bring them to understand that there is no *essential* difference between the two states and that Mind is the same in both.

§

20

WHAT IS PHILOSOPHY?

Definition—Completeness—Balance—
Fulfilment in man

People sometimes ask me to what religion I belong or to what school of yoga I adhere. If I answer them, which is not often, I tell them: "To none and to all!" If such a paradox annoys them, I try to soften their wrath by adding that I am a student of philosophy. During my journeys to the heavenly realm of infinite eternal and absolute existence, I did not once discover any labels marked Christian, Hindu, Catholic, Protestant, Zen, Shin, Platonist, Hegelian, and so on, any more than I discovered labels marked Englishman, American, or Hottentot. All such ascriptions would contradict the very nature of the ascriptionless existence. All sectarian differences are merely intellectual ones. They have no place in that level which is deeper than intellectual function. They divide men into hostile groups only because they are pseudo-spiritual. He who has tasted of the pure Spirit's own freedom will be unwilling to submit himself to the restrictions of cult and creed. Therefore I could not conscientiously affix a label to my own outlook or to the teaching about this existence which I have embraced. In my secret heart I separate myself from nobody, just as this teaching itself excludes no other in its perfect comprehension. Because I had to call it by some name as soon as I began to write about it, I called it philosophy because this is too wide and too general a name to become the property of any single sect. In doing so I merely returned to its ancient and noble meaning among the Greeks who, in the Eleusinian Mysteries, designated the spiritual truth learnt at initiation into them as "philosophy" and the initiate himself as "philosopher" or lover of wisdom.

Now genuine wisdom, being in its highest phase the fruit of a transcendental insight, is sublimely dateless and unchangeable. Yet its mode of expression is necessarily dated and may therefore change. Perhaps this pioneering attempt to fill the term "philosophy" with a content which combines ancient tradition with modern innovation will help the few who are sick of intellectual intolerances that masquerade as spiritual insight. Perhaps it may free such broader souls from the need of adopting a separative standpoint with all the frictions, prejudices, egotisms, and hatreds which go with it, and afford them an intellectual basis for practising a profound compassion for all alike. It is as natural for those reared on limited conceptions of life to limit their faith and loyalty to a particular group or a particular area of this planet as it is natural for those reared on philosophic truth to widen their vision and service into world-comprehension and world-fellowship. The philosopher's larger and nobler vision refuses to establish a separate group consciousness for himself and for those who think as he does. Hence he refuses to establish a new cult, a new association, or a new label. To him the oneness of mankind is a fact and not a fable. He is always conscious of the fact that he is a citizen of the world-community. While acknowledging the place and need of lesser loyalties for unphilosophical persons, he cannot outrage truth by confining his own self solely to such loyalties.

Why this eagerness to separate ourselves from the rest of mankind and collect into a sect, to wear a new label that proclaims difference and division? The more we believe in the oneness of life, the less we ought to herd ourselves behind barriers. To add a new cult to the existing list is to multiply the causes of human division and thence of human strife. Let those of us who can do so be done with this seeking of ever-new disunity, this fostering of ever-fresh prejudices, and let those who cannot do so keep it at least as an ideal—however remote and however far-off its attainment may seem—for after all it is ultimate direction and not immediate position that matters most. The democratic abolishment of class status and exclusive groups, which will be a distinctive feature of the coming age, should also show itself in the circles of mystical and philosophic students. If they have any superiority over others, let them display it by a superiority of conduct grounded in a diviner consciousness. Nevertheless, with all the best will in the world to refrain from starting a new group, the distinctive character of their conduct and the unique character of their outlook will, of themselves, mark out the followers of such teaching. Therefore whatever metaphysical unity with others may be perceived and whatever inward willingness to identify interests with them may be felt, some kind of practical indication of its goal and outward particularization of its path will necessarily and inescapably arise of their own accord. And I do not know of any better or broader name with which to mark those who pursue this quest than to say that they are students of philosophy.

§

It may be asked why I insist on using the word "philosophy" as a self-sufficient name without prefixing it by some descriptive term or person's name when it has held different meanings in different centuries, or been associated with different points of view ranging from the most materialistic to the most spiritualist. The question is well asked, although the answer may not be quite satisfactory. I do so because I want to restore this word to its ancient dignity. I want it used for the highest kind of insight into the Truth of things, which means into the Truth of the unique Reality. I want the philosopher to be equated with the sage, the man who not only knows this Truth, has this insight, and experiences this Reality in meditation, but also, although in a modified form, in action amid the world's turmoil.

§

The practice of philosophy is an essential part of it and not only consists in applying its principles and its wisdom to everyday active living, but also in realizing the divine presence deep, deep within the heart where it abides in tremendous stillness.

§

The Advaitin who declares that as such he has no point of view, has already adopted one by calling himself an Advaitin and by rejecting every other point of view as being dualistic. A human philosophy is neither dualistic alone nor nondualistic alone. It perceives the connection between the dream and the dreamer, the Real and the unreal, the consciousness and the thought. It accepts Advaita, but refuses to stop with it; it accepts duality, but refuses to remain limited to it; therefore it alone is free from a dogmatic point of view. But in attempting to bring into harmony that which forever is and that which is bound by time and space, it becomes a truly human philosophy of Truth.

§

Two things have to be learned in this quest. The first is the art of mind-stilling, of emptying consciousness of every thought and form whatsoever. This is mysticism or Yoga. The disciple's ascent should not stop at the contemplation of anything that has shape or history, name or habitation, however powerfully helpful this may have formerly been to the ascent itself. Only in the mysterious void of Pure Spirit, in the undifferentiated Mind, lies his last goal as a mystic. The second is to grasp the essential nature of the ego and of the universe and to obtain direct perception that both are nothing but a series of ideas which unfold themselves within our minds. This is the metaphysics of Truth. The combination of these two activities brings about the realization of his true Being as the ever beautiful and eternally beneficent Overself. This is philosophy.

§

Viewed from the standpoint of the house in which we all have to live —that is, the body—Advaita Vedanta seems to deal only in ultimate abstractions—however admirable and lofty its outlook. The body is there and its actuality and factuality must be noted and, more, accepted. This is why I do not give any other label to the ideas put into my later books than the generic name philosophy. I do not call it Indian philosophy since there are ideas in the books which do not belong to India at all. I do not identify it with any particular land, race, religion, or teacher from the ancient past or the modern present. Philosophy can not be limited only to abstract ideas. It includes those ideas but it also includes other things. Its original Greek meaning "love of wisdom" concerns the whole of man, and not only his abstract thoughts, intellect, feelings, body, or relation to the world around him. It concerns his entire life: his contacts with other people, the morality which guides him in dealing with them, and finally his attitude towards himself. Philosophy must be universal in its scope; therefore, it may embrace ideas which originate not only in India or in America or in Europe, but in every other country and in every other period of civilization. Not all ideas are philosophical, but only those which are true, useful, in harmony with the World-Idea, and able to survive the test of practice and applicability.

§

Truth will not insult intelligence, although it soars beyond intellect. Let the religionists talk nonsense, as they do at times; but holiness is not incompatible with the use of brains, the acquisition of knowledge, and the rational faculties.

§

To view the inferior mystical experiences or the ratiocinative metaphysical findings otherwise than as passing phases, to set them up as finally representative of reality in the one case or of truth in the other, is to place them on a level to which they do not properly belong. Those who fall into the second error do so because they ascribe excessive importance to the thinking faculty. The mystic is too attached to one faculty, as the metaphysician is to the other, and neither can conduct a human being beyond the bounds of his enchained ego to that region where Being alone reigns. It is not that the mystic does not enter into contact with the Overself. He does. But his experience of the Overself is limited to glimpses which are partial, because he finds the Overself only within himself, not in the world outside. It is temporary because he has to take it when it comes at its own sweet will or when he can find it in meditation. It is a glimpse because it tells him about his own "I" but not about the "Not-I." On the other hand, the sage finds reality in the world without as his own self, at all times and not at special occasions, and wholly rather than in glimpses. The mystic's light comes in glimpses, but the sage's is perennial. Whereas the first is like a flickering unsteady and uneven flame, the second is like a lamp that never goes out. Whereas the mystic comes into awareness of the Overself through feeling alone, the sage comes into it through knowledge plus feeling. Hence, the superiority of his realization.

The average mystic is devoid of sufficient critical sense. He delights in preventing his intellect from being active in such a definite direction. He has yet to learn that philosophical discipline has a steadying influence on the vagaries of mystical emotion, opinion, fancy, and experience. He refuses to judge the goal he has set up as to whether it be indeed man's ultimate goal. Consequently he is unable to apply correct standards whereby his own achievements or his own aspirations may be measured. Having shut himself up in a little heaven of his own, he does not attempt to distinguish it from other heavens or to discover if it be heaven indeed. He clings as stubbornly to his self-righteousness as does the religionist whom he criticizes for clinging to his dogma. He does not comprehend that he has transferred to himself that narrowness of outlook which he condemns in the materialistic. His position would be preposterous were it not so perilous.

Mysticism must not rest so smugly satisfied with its own obscurity that it refuses even to make the effort to come out into the light of critical self-examination, clear self-determination, and rational self-understanding. To complain helplessly that it cannot explain itself, to sit admiringly before its own self-proclaimed impalpability, or to stand aristocratically in the rarefied air of its own indefinability—as it usually does—is to fall into a kind of subtle quackery. Magnificent eulogy is no substitute for needed explanation.

§

We do not claim that an entirely new teaching has been given to the world. But we do claim that a teaching and a praxis which we found in a primitive antique form have been brought up-to-date and given a scientific modern expression, that some parts of it which were formerly half-hidden and others wholly so, have been completely revealed and made accessible to everyone who cares for such things.

§

This is a pioneer work, this making of a fresh synthesis which draws from, but does not solely depend upon, the knowledge of colleagues scattered in different continents as well as the initiations of masters belonging to the most different traditions.

§

There is a kind of understanding combined with feeling which is not a common one here in the West, indeed uncommon enough to seem more discoverable and less puzzling in the Asiatic regions. It is puzzling for four reasons. One is that it cannot be attributed to the intellect alone, nor to the emotional nature alone. Another is that it provides an experience so difficult to describe that it is preferable not to discuss it at all. A third is that although the most reverent it is not allied to religion. A fourth point is that it is outside any precise labelling as for instance a metaphysics or cult which could really belong to it. Yet it is neither anything new or old. It is nameless. But because there is only one way to deal with it honestly—the way of utter silence, speechless when in contact with other humans, perfectly still when in the secrecy of a closed room—we may renew the Pythagorean appellation of "philosophy" for it is truly the love of wisdom-knowledge.

§

Such a revolutionary acquisition as insight must necessarily prove to be in a man's life can only be developed by overcoming all the tremendous force of habitual wrong thinking, by neutralizing all the tremendous weight of habitual wrong feeling, and by counteracting all the tremendous strength of habitual wrong-doing. In short, the familiar personal "I" must have the ground cut from under its feet. This is done by the threefold discipline. The combined threefold technique consists of metaphysical reflection, mystical meditation, and constant remembrance in the midst of disinterested active service. The full use and balanced exercise of every function is needful. Although these three elements have here been isolated one by one for the purpose of clearer intellectual study, it must be remembered that in actual life the student should not attempt to isolate them. Such a division is an artificial one. He who takes for his province this whole business of truth-seeking and gains this rounded all-comprehensive view will no longer be so one-sided as to set up a particular path as being the only way to salvation. On the contrary, he will see that salvation is an integral matter. It can no more be attained by mere meditation alone, for example, than by mere impersonal activity alone; it can no more be reached by evading the lessons of everyday external living than by evading the suppression of such externality which meditation requires. Whereas metaphysics seeks to lift us up to the superphysical idea by thinking, whereas meditation seeks to lift us up by intuition, whereas ethics seeks to raise us to it by practical goodness, art seeks to do the same by feeling and appreciating beauty. Philosophy in its wonderful breadth and balance embraces and synthesizes all four and finally adds their coping stone, insight.

§

Philosophy must critically absorb the categories of metaphysics, mysticism, and practicality. For it understands that in the quest of truth the co-operation of all three will not only be helpful and profitable to each other but is also necessary to itself. For only after such absorption, only after it has travelled through them all can it attain what is beyond them all. The decisive point of this quest is reached after the co-operation between all three activities attains such a pitch that they become fused into a single all-comprehensive one which itself differs from them in character and qualities. For the whole truth which is then revealed is not merely a composite one. It not only absorbs them all but transcends them all. When water is born out of the union of oxygen and hydrogen, we may neither say that it is the same as the simple sum-total of both nor that it is entirely different from both. It is a fluid and therefore possesses properties which they as gases do not at all possess. We may only say that it includes and yet transcends them. When philosophic insight is born out of the union of intellectual reasoning, mystical feeling, and altruistic doing, we may neither say that it is only the totalization of these three things nor that it is utterly remote from them. It comprehends them all and yet itself extends far beyond them into a higher order of being. It is not only that the philosopher synthesizes these triple functions, that in one and the same instant his intellect understands the world, his heart feels a tender sympathy towards it, and his will is moved to action for the triumph of good, but also that he is continuously conscious of that infinite reality which, in its purity, no thinking, no emotion, and no action can ever touch.

§

The hidden teaching starts and finishes with experience. Every man must begin his mental life as a seeker by noting the fact that he is conscious of an external environment. He will proceed in time to discover that it is an ordered one, that Nature is the manifestation of an orderly Mind. He discovers in the end that consciousness of this Mind becomes the profoundest fact of his internal experience.

§

Truth existed before the churches began to spire their way upwards into the sky, and it will continue to exist after the last academy of philosophy has been battered down. Nothing can still the primal need of it in man. Priesthoods can be exterminated until not one vestige is left in the land; mystic hermitages can be broken until they are but dust; philosophical books can be burnt out of existence by culture-hating tyrants, yet this subterranean sense in man which demands the understanding of its own existence will one day rise again with an urgent claim and create a new expression of itself.

§

Those who would assign philosophy the role of a leisurely pastime for a few people who have nothing better to do, are greatly mistaken. Philosophy, correctly understood, involves living as well as being. Its value is not merely intellectual, not merely to stimulate thought, but also to guide action. Its ideas and ideals are not left suspended in mid-air, as it were, unable to come down to earth in practical and practicable forms. It can be put to the test in daily living. It can be applied to all personal and social problems without exception. It shows us how to achieve a balanced existence in an unbalanced society. It is truth made workable. The study of and practice of philosophy are particularly valuable to men and women who follow certain professions, such as physicians, lawyers, and teachers, or who hold a certain social status, such as business executives, political administrators, and leaders of organizations. Those who have been placed by character or destiny or by both where their authority touches the lives of numerous others, or where their influence affects the minds of many more, who occupy positions of responsibility or superior status, will find in its principles that which will enable them to direct others wisely and in a manner conducive to the ultimate happiness of all. In the end it can only justify its name if it dynamically inspires its votaries to a wise altruistic and untiring activity, both in self-development and social development.

§

We may begin by asking what this philosophy offers us. It offers those who pursue it to the end a deep understanding of the world and a satisfying explanation of the significance of human experience. It offers them the power to penetrate appearances and to discover the genuinely real from the mere appearance of reality; it offers satisfaction of that desire which everyone, everywhere, holds somewhere in his heart—the desire to be free.

§

It is the joyous duty of philosophy to bring into systematic harmony the various views which mankind has held and will ever hold, however conflicting they seem on the surface, by assigning the different types to their proper level and by providing a total view of the possible heights and depths of human thought. Thus and thus alone the most opposite tendencies of belief and the most striking contrasts of outlook are brought within a single scheme. All become aspects, more or less limited, only. None ever achieves metaphysical finality and need never again be mistaken for the whole truth. All become clear as organic phases of mankind's mental development. Philosophy alone can bring logically opposite doctrines into harmonious relation with each other by assigning them to their proper places under a single sheltering canopy. Thus out of the medley of voices within us philosophy creates a melody.

§

The quest has three aspects: metaphysical, meditational, and morally active. It is the metaphysician's business to think this thing called life through to its farthest end. It is the mystic's business to intuit the peaceful desireless state of thoughtlessness. But this quest cannot be conducted in compartments; rather must it be conducted as we have to live, that is, integrally. Hence it is the philosopher's business to bring the metaphysician's bloodless conclusions and the mystic's serene intuition into intimate relation with practical human obligations and flesh-and-blood activities. Both ancient mystical-metaphysical wisdom and modern scientific practicality form the two halves of a complete and comprehensive human culture. Both are required by a man who wants to be fully educated; one without the help of the other will be lame. This may well be why wise Emerson confessed, "I have not yet seen a man!" Consequently, he who has passed through all the different disciplines will be a valuable member of society. For meditation will have calmed his temperament and disciplined his character; the metaphysics of truth will have sharpened his intelligence, protected him against error, and balanced his outlook; the philosophic ethos will have purified his motives and promoted his altruism, whilst the philosophic insight will have made him forever aware that he is an inhabitant of the country of the Overself. He will have touched life at its principal points yet will have permitted himself to be cramped and confined by none.

§

Philosophy takes its votaries on a holy pilgrimage from ordinary life in the physical senses through mystical life in the sense-freed spirit to a divinized life back in the same senses.

§

The sincere, who are honestly desirous of discovering Truth at whatever cost, will be helped within their limitations; the insincere, who seek to support their petty prejudices rather than to follow Truth, will have their hearts read and their hollowness exposed.

§

Is there a universal truth? Is there a doctrine which does not depend on individual opinion or the peculiarities of a particular age or the level of culture of a particular land? Is there a teaching which appeals to universal experience and not to private prejudice? We reply that there is, but it has been buried underneath much metaphysical lumber, much ancient lore, and much Oriental superstition. Our work has been to rescue this doctrine from the dead past for the benefit of the living present. In these pages we explode false counterfeits and expound the genuine doctrine.

§

We may generally distinguish three different views of the world. The first is that which comes easily and naturally and it depends on five-sense experience alone. It may be called materialism, and may take various shapes. The second is religious in its elementary state, depending on faith, and mystical in its higher stage, depending on intuition and transcendental experience. The third is scientific in its elementary state, depending on concrete reason, and metaphysical in its higher state, depending on abstract reason. Although these are the views generally held amongst men, they do not exhaust the possibilities of human intelligence. There is a fourth possible view which declares that none of the others can stand alone and that if we cling to any one of them alone to the detriment of the others we merely limit the truth. This view is the philosophic. It declares that truth may be arrived at by combining all the other views which yield only partial truths into the balanced unity of whole truth, and unfolding the faculty of insight which penetrates into hidden reality.

§

There are three things man needs to know to make him a spiritually educated man: the truth about himself, his world, and his God. The mystic who thinks it is enough to know the first alone and to leave out the last two, is satisfied to be half-educated.

§

The first step is to discover that there is a Presence, a Power, a Life, a Mind, Being, unique, not made or begot, without shape, unseen and unheard, everywhere and always the same. The second step is to discover its relationship to the universe and to oneself.

§

It is not enough to attain knowledge of the soul; any mystic may do that. It is necessary to attain *clear* knowledge. Only the philosophic mystic may do that. This emphasis on clarity is important. It implies a removal of all the obstructions in feeling, the complexes in mind, and obfuscations in ego which prevent it. When this is done, the aspirant beholds truth as it really is.

§

In the first stage of progress we learn to stand aside from the world and to still our thoughts about it. This is the mystical stage. Next, we recognize the world as being but a series of ideas within the mind; this is the mentalist-metaphysical stage. Finally, we return to the world's activity without reacting mentally to its suggestions, working disinterestedly, and knowing always that all is One. This is the philosophical stage.

§

The faith in and the practice of reverential worship into which he was initiated by religion must not be dropped. It is required by philosophy also. Only, he is to correct, purify, and refine it. He is to worship the divine presence in his heart, not some distant remote being, and he is to do so more by an act of concentrated thought and unwavering feeling than by resort to external indirect and physical methods. With the philosopher, as with the devotee, the habit of prayer is a daily one. But whereas he prays with light and heat, the other prays with heat alone. The heart finds in such worship a means of pouring out its deepest feelings of devotion, reverence, humility, and communion before its divine source. Thus we see that philosophy does not annul religious worship, but purifies and preserves what is best in it. It does annul the superstitions, exploitations, and futilities connected with conventional religious worship. In the end philosophy brings the seeker back to religion but not to *a* religion: to the reverence for a supreme power which he had discarded when he discarded the superstitions which had entwined themselves around it. Philosophy is naturally religious and inevitably mystical. Hence it keeps intact and does not break to pieces that which it receives from religion and yoga. It will, of course, receive only their sound fruits, not their bad ones. Philosophic endeavour does not, for instance, disdain religious worship and humble prayer merely because its higher elements transcend them. They are indeed part of such endeavour. But they are not, as with religionists, the whole of it. The mystic must not give up being religious merely because he has become a mystic. In the same way, the philosopher must not give up being both mystical and religious merely because he has become a philosopher. It is vitally important to know this. Philosophy does not supersede religion but keeps it and enlarges it.

§

Science suppresses the subject of experience and studies the object. Mysticism suppresses the object of experience and studies the subject. Philosophy suppresses nothing, studies both subject and object; indeed it embraces the study of all experience.

§

Although philosophy propounds statements of universal laws and eternal truths, nevertheless each man draws from its study highly personal application and gains from its practices markedly individual fulfilment. Although it is the only Idea which can ever bring men together in harmony and unity, nevertheless it becomes unique for every fresh adherent. And although it transcends all limitations imposed by intellect emotion form and egoism, nevertheless it inspires the poet, teaches the thinker, gives vistas to the artist, guides the executive, and solaces the labourer.

§

Philosophy is faced with the problem of educating each individual seeker who aspires to understand it. There is no such thing as mass education in philosophy.

§

The theory of philosophy is suited and available to everyone who has the intelligence to grasp it, the faith to accept it, the intuition to recognize its supreme pre-eminence. The practice of philosophy is more restricted, being for those who have been sufficiently prepared by previous inner growth and outer experience to be willing to impose its higher ethical standards, mental training, and emotional discipline upon themselves. To come unprepared for the individual effort demanded, unfit for the intellectual and meditational exertions needed, unready for the teacher or the teaching, is to find bewilderment and to leave disappointed. A premature attempt to enter the school of philosophy will meet with the painful revelation of the dismaying shortcomings within oneself, which must be remedied before the attempt can be successful.

§

It is the business of philosophy to cast out error and establish truth. This takes it away from the popular conceptions of religion. Philosophy by its very nature must be unpopular; hence it does not ordinarily go out of its way to spread its ideas in the world. Only at special periods, like our own, when history and evolution have prepared enough individuals to make a modest audience, does philosophy promulgate such of its tenets as are best suited to the mind of that period.

§

Such a teaching cannot indulge in propagandist methods or militant sectarianism. It must live quietly and offer itself only to those who are intellectually prepared and emotionally willing to receive it.

§

The spiritual seekers who followed René Guénon and the poets who followed T.S. Eliot fell into the same trap as their leaders. For in protesting, and rightly, against the anarchy of undisciplined and unlimited freedom, both Guénon and Eliot retreated backwards into formal tradition and fixed myth. Both had served their historic purpose and were being left behind. Both men were brilliant intellectuals and naturally attracted a corresponding type of reader. Their influence is understandable. But it is not on the coming wave of the Aquarian Age. New forms will be needed to satisfy the new knowledge, the new outlook, the new feelings. The classical may be respected, even admired; but the creative will be followed.

§

The esoteric meaning of the star is "Philosophic Man," that is, one who has travelled the complete fivefold path and brought its results into proper balance. This path consists of religious veneration, mystical meditation, rational reflection, moral re-education, and altruistic service. The esoteric meaning of the circle, when situated within the very centre of the star, is the Divine Overself-atom within the human heart.

§

Whatever were the motives which dictated the exclusive reservation of ultimate wisdom in former centuries and the extraordinary precautions which were taken to keep it from the larger world, we must now reckon on the dominant fact that humanity lives today in a cultural environment which has changed tremendously. The old ideas have lost their weight among educated folk—except for individuals here and there—and this general decay has passed by reflex action among the masses, albeit to a lesser extent. Whether in religion or science, politics or society, economics or ethics, the story of prodigious storm which has shaken the thoughts of men to their foundations is the same. The time indeed is transitional. In this momentous period when the ethical fate of mankind is at stake because the religious sanctions of morality have broken down, it is essential that something should arise to take their place. This is the supreme and significant fact which has forced the hands of those who hold this wisdom in their possession, which has compelled them to begin this historically unique disclosure of it, and which illustrates the saying that the night is darkest just before dawn. This is the dangerous situation which broke down an age-old policy and necessitated a new one whose sublime consequences to future generations we can now but dimly envisage.

§

The goal of self-elimination which is held up before us refers only to the animal and lower human selves. It certainly does not refer to the annihilation of all self-consciousness. The higher individuality always remains. But it is so different from the lower one that it does not make much sense to discuss it in human language. Hence, those who have adequately understood it write or talk little about its higher mysteries. If the end of all existence were only a merger at best or annihilation at worst, it would be a senseless and sorry scheme of things. It would be unworthy of the divine intelligence and discreditable to the divine goodness. The consciousness stripped of thought, which looks less attractive to you than the hazards of life down here, is really a tremendous enlargement of what thought itself tries to do. Spiritual advance is really from a Less to a More. There is nothing to fear in it and nothing to lose by it—except by the standards and values of the ignorant.

§

It is perhaps the amplitude and symmetry of the philosophic approach which make it so completely satisfying. For this is the only approach which honours reason and appreciates beauty, cultivates intuition and respects mystical experience, fosters reverence and teaches true prayer, enjoins action and promotes morality. It is the spiritual life fully grown.

§

Not to escape life, but to articulate it, is philosophy's practical goal. Not to take the aspirant out of circulation, but to give him something worth doing is philosophy's sensible ideal.

§

The philosophic student will not make the mistake of using the quest as an excuse for inefficiency when attending to duties. There is nothing spiritual in being a muddler. The performance of worldly duties in a dreamy, casual, uninterested, and slovenly manner is often self-excused by the mystically minded because they feel superior to such duties. This arises out of the false opposition which they set up between Matter and Spirit. Such an attitude is not the philosophical one. The mystic is supposed to be apathetic in worldly matters, if he is to be a good mystic. The philosophical student, on the contrary, keeps what is most worthwhile in mysticism and yet manages to keep alert in worldly matters too. If he has understood the teaching and trained himself aright, his practical work will be better done and not worse because he has taken to this quest. He knows it is perfectly possible to balance mystical tendencies with a robust efficiency. He will put as much thought and heart into his work as it demands.

§

It is not enough to negate thinking; this may yield a mental blank without content. We have also to transcend it. The first is the way of ordinary yoga; the second is the way of philosophic yoga. In the second way, therefore, we seek strenuously to carry thought to its most abstract and rarefied point, to a critical culminating whereby its whole character changes and it merges of its own accord in the higher source whence it arises. If successful, this produces a pleasant, sometimes ecstatic state—but the ecstasy is not our aim as with ordinary mysticism. With us the reflection must keep loyally to a loftier aim, that of dissolving the ego in its divine source. The metaphysical thinking must work its way, first upwards to a more and more abstract concept and second inwards to a more and more complete absorption from the external world. The consequence is that when illumination results, whether it comes in the form of a mystical trance, ecstasy, or intuition, its character will be unquestionably different and immeasurably superior to that which comes from the mere sterilization of the thinking process which is the method of ordinary yoga.

§

The activity of analytic thinking has been banned in most mystical schools. They regard it as an obstacle to the attainment of spiritual consciousness. And ordinarily it is indeed so. For until the intellect can lie perfectly still, such consciousness cannot make itself apparent. The difficulty of making intellect quite passive is however an enormous one. Consequently different concentration techniques have been devised to overcome it. Nearly all of them involve the banishment of thinking and the cessation of reasoning. The philosophical school uses any or all of them where advisable but it also uses a technique peculiarly its own. It makes use of abstract concepts which are concerned with the nature of the mind itself and which are furnished by seers who have developed a deep insight into such nature. It permits the student to work out these concepts in a rational way but leading to subtler and subtler moods until they automatically vanish and thinking ceases as the transcendental state is induced to come of itself. This method is particularly suited either to those who have already got over the elementary difficulties of concentration or to those who regard reasoning power as an asset to be conserved rather than rejected. The conventional mystic, being the victim of external suggestion, will cling to the traditional view of his own school, which usually sees no good at all in reasoned thinking, and aver that spiritual attainment through such a path is psychologically impossible. Never having been instructed in it and never having tried it, he is not really in a position to judge.

§

Continued and constant pondering over the ideas presented herein is itself a part of the yoga of philosophical discernment. Such reflection will as naturally lead the student towards realization of his goal as will the companion and equally necessary activity of suppressing all ideas altogether in mental quiet. This is because these ideas are not mere speculations but are themselves the outcome of a translation from inner experience. While such ideas as are here presented grow under the water of their reflection and the sunshine of their love into fruitful branches of thought, they gradually begin to foster intuition.

§

The logical movement of intellect must come to a dead stop before the threshold of reality. But we are not to bring about this pause deliberately or in response to the bidding of some man or some doctrine. It must come of its own accord as the final maturation of long and precise reasoning and as the culmination of the intellectual and personal *discovery* that the apprehension of mind as essence will come only when we let go of the idea-forms it takes and direct our attention to it.

§

The use of metaphysical thinking as part of the philosophic system is a feature which few yogis of the ordinary type are likely to appreciate. This is both understandable and pardonable. They are thoroughly imbued with the futility of a merely rational and intellectual approach to reality, a futility which has also been felt and expressed in these pages. So far there is agreement with them. But when they proceed to deduce that the only way left is to crush reason and stop the working of intellect altogether, our paths diverge. For what metaphysics admittedly cannot accomplish by itself may be accomplished by a combination of metaphysics and mysticism far better than by mysticism alone. The metaphysics of truth, which is here meant, however, must never be confused with the many historical speculative systems which exist.

§

This is the paradox that *both* the capacity to think deeply and the capacity to withdraw from thinking are needed to attain this goal.

§

We cannot afford to dispense with mysticism merely because we take to philosophy. Both are essential to this quest and both are vital in their respective places. The mystic's power to concentrate attention is needed throughout the study of philosophy. The philosopher's power to reason sharply is needed to give mystical reverie a content of world-understanding. And in the more advanced stages, when thinking has done its work and intellect has come to rest, we cease to be a philosopher and dwell self-absorbed in mystic trance, having taken with us the world-idea without which it would be empty. We can only afford to dispense with both mysticism and philosophy when we have perfectly done the work of both and when, amid the daily life of constant activity, we can keep unbroken the profound insight and selfless attitude which time and practice have now made natural.

§

The mistake of the mystics is to negate reasoning *prematurely*. Only after reasoning has completed its own task to the uttermost will it be psychologically right and philosophically fruitful to still it in the mystic silence.

§

The highest contribution which mysticism can make is to afford its votaries glimpses of that grand substratum of the universe which we may call the Overself. These glimpses reveal It in the pure unmanifest non-physical essence that It ultimately is. They detach It from the things, creatures, and thoughts which make up this world of ours, and show It as It is in the beginning, before the world-dream made its appearance. Thus mysticism at its farthest stretch, which is Nirvikalpa samadhi, enables man to bring about the temporary disappearance of the world-dream and come into comprehension of the Mind within which, and from which, the dream emerges. The mystic in very truth conducts the funeral service of the physical world as he has hitherto known it, which includes his own ego. But this is as far as mysticism can take him. It is an illuminative and rare experience, but it is not the end. For the next task which he must undertake if he is to advance is to relate his experience of this world as real with his experience of the Overself as real. And this he can do only by studying the world's own nature, laying bare its mentalistic character and thus bringing it within the same circle as its source, the Mind. If he succeeds in doing this and in establishing this relation correctly, he will have finished his apprenticeship, ascended to the ultimate truth and become a philosopher. Thenceforward he will not deny the world but accept it.

The metaphysician may also perform this task and obtain an intellectual understanding of himself, the world, and the Overself. And he has this advantage over the mystic, that his understanding becomes permanent whereas the mystic's rapt absorption must pass. But if he has not passed through the mystical exercises, it will remain as incomplete as a nut without a kernel. For these exercises, when led to their logical and successful issue in Nirvikalpa samadhi, provide the vivifying principle of experience which alone can make metaphysical tenets real.

From all this we may perceive why it is quite correct for the mystic to look undistractedly within for his goal, why he must shut out the distractions and attractions of earthly life in order to penetrate the sacred precinct, and why solitude, asceticism, meditation, trance, and emotion play the most important roles in his particular experience. What he is doing is right and proper at his stage but is not right and proper as the last stage. For in the end he must turn metaphysician, just as the metaphysician must turn mystic and just as both must turn philosopher—who is alone capable of infusing the thoughts of metaphysics and the feelings of mysticism into the actions of everyday practical life.

§

The crucial point of our criticism must not be missed. Our words are directed against the belief which equates the criterion of truth with the unchecked and unpurified feeling of it—however mystical it be. We do not demand that feeling itself shall be ignored, or that its contribution—which is most important—toward truth shall be despised. Our criticism is not directed against emotion, but against that unbalanced attitude which sets up emotion almost as a religion in itself. We ask only that the reaction of personal feeling shall not be set up as the *sole* and sufficient standard of what is or is not reality and truth. When we speak of the unsatisfactory validity of feeling as providing sufficient proof by itself of having experienced the Overself, we mean primarily, of course, the kind of passionate feeling which throws the mystic into transports of joy, and secondarily, any strong emotion which sweeps him off his feet into refusal to analyse his experience coldly and scientifically. Three points may be here noted. First, mere feeling alone may easily be egoistic and distort the truth or be inflamed and exaggerate it or put forward a wanted fancy in place of an unwanted fact. Second, there is here no means of attaining certainty. Its validity, being only personal, is only as acceptable as are the offerings of poets and artists who can talk in terms of psychological, but not metaphysical, reality. For instance, the mystic may gaze at and see what he *thinks* to be reality, but some one else may not think it to be so. Third, the path of the philosophical objection to appraising feeling *alone* as a criterion of truth and of our insistence on checking its intimations with critical reasoning may be put in the briefest way by an analogy. We *feel* that the earth is stable and motionless, but we *know* that it traces a curve of movement in space. We *feel* that it is fixed in the firmament, but we *know* that the whole heliocentric system has its own motion in space. The reader should ponder upon the implications of these facts. Are not the annals of mysticism stained by many instances of megalomaniacs who falsely set themselves up as messiahs merely because they *felt* that God had commissioned them to do so? This is why the philosopher is concerned not only with the emotional effects of inner experience, as is the mystic, but also with the *truth* about these effects.

§

The philosopher is satisfied with a noble peace and does not run after mystical ecstasies. Whereas other paths often depend upon an emotionalism that perishes with the disappearance of the primal momentum that inspired it, or which dissolves with the dissolution of the first enthusiastic ecstasies themselves, here there is a deeper and more dependable process. What must be emphasized is that most mystical aspirants have an initial or occasional ecstasy, and they are so stirred by the event that they naturally want to enjoy it permanently. This is because they live under the common error that a successful and perfect mystic is one who has succeeded in stabilizing ecstasy. That the mystic is content to rest on the level of feeling alone, without making his feeling self-reflective as well, partly accounts for such an error. It also arises because of incompetent teachers or shallow teaching, leading them to strive to perform what is impracticable and to yearn to attain what is impossible. Our warning is that this is not possible, and that however long a mystic may enjoy these "spiritual sweets," they will assuredly come to an end one day. The stern logic of facts calls for stress on this point. Too often he believes that this is the goal, and that he has nothing more about which to trouble himself. Indeed, he would regard any further exertions as a sacrilegious denial of the peace, as a degrading descent from the exaltation of this divine union. He longs for nothing more than the good fortune of being undisturbed by the world and of being able to spend the rest of his life in solitary devotion to his inward ecstasy. For the philosophic mystic, however, this is not the terminus but only the starting point of a further path. What philosophy says is that this is only a preliminary mystical state, however remarkable and blissful it be. There is a more matured state—that of gnosis—beyond it. If the student experiences paroxysms of ecstasy at a certain stage of his inner course, he may enjoy them for a time, but let him not look forward to enjoying them for all time. The true goal lies beyond them, and he should not forget that all-important fact. He will not find final salvation in the mystical experience of ecstasy, but he will find an excellent and essential step towards salvation therein. He who would regard rapturous mystical emotion as being the same as absolute transcendental insight is mistaken. Such a mistake is pardonable. So abrupt and striking is the contrast with his ordinary state that he concludes that this condition of hyper-emotional bliss is the condition in which he is able to experience reality. He surrenders himself to the bliss, the emotional joy which he experiences, well satisfied that he has found God or his soul. But his excited feelings about reality are not the same as the serene experience of reality itself. This is what a mystic finds difficult to comprehend. Yet, until he does comprehend it, he will not make any genuine progress beyond this stage.

§

What science calls the "critical temperature," that is, the temperature when a substance shares both the liquid and gaseous states, is symbolic of what philosophical mysticism calls the "philosophic experience," that is, when a man's consciousness shares both the external world of the five senses and the internal world of the empty soul. The ordinary mystic or yogi is unable to hold the two states simultaneously and, quite often, even unwilling to do so, because of the false opposition he has been taught to set up between them.

§

There is a fundamental difference between mystical escapism and mystical altruism. In the first case, the man is interested only in gaining his own self-realization and will be content to let his endeavours stop there. In the second case, he has the same aim but also the keen aspiration to make his achievement, when it materializes, available for the service of mankind. And because such a profound aspiration cannot be banished into cold-storage to await this materialization, he will even sacrifice part of his time, money, and energy to doing what little he can to enlighten others intellectually during the interval. Even if this meant doing nothing more than making philosophical knowledge more easily accessible to ordinary men than it has been in the past, this would be enough. But he can do much more than that. Both types recognize the indispensable need of deliberately withdrawing from society and isolating themselves from its activities to obtain the solitude necessary to achieve intensity of concentration, to practise meditative reflection upon life, and to study mystical and philosophical books. But whereas the first would make the withdrawal a permanent, lifelong one, the second would make it only a temporary and occasional one. And by "temporary," we mean any period from a single day to several years. The first is a resident of the ivory tower of escapism, the second merely its visitor. The first can find happiness only in his solitariness and must draw himself out of humanity's disturbing life to attain it. The second seeks a happiness that will hold firm in all places and makes retirement from that life only a means to this end. Each is entitled to travel his own path. But at such a time as the present, when the whole world is being convulsed and the human soul agitated as never before, we personally believe that it is better to follow the less selfish and more compassionate one.

§

Life is not a matter of meditation methods exclusively. Their study and practice is necessary, but let them be put in their proper place. Both mystical union and metaphysical understanding are necessary steps on this quest, because it is only from them that the student can mount to the still higher grade of universal being represented by the sage. For we not only need psychological exercises to train the inner being, but also psychological exercises to train the point of view. But the student must not stay in mysticism as he must not stay in metaphysics. In both cases he should take all that they have to give him but struggle through and come out on the other side. For the mysticism of emotion is not the shrine where Isis dwells but only the vestibule to the shrine, and the metaphysician who can only see in reason the supreme faculty of man has not reflected enough. Let him go farther and he shall find that its own supreme achievement is to point beyond itself to that principle or Mind whence it takes its rise. Mysticism needs the check of philosophic discipline. Metaphysics needs the vivification of mystical meditation. Both must bear the fruit in inspired action or they are but half-born. In no other way than through acts can they rise to the lofty status of facts.

The realization of what man is here for is the realization of a fused and unified life wherein all the elements of action, feeling, and thought are vigorously present. It is not, contrary to the belief of mystics, a condition of profound entrancement alone, nor, contrary to the reasonings of metaphysicians, a condition of intellectual clarity alone, and, still less, contrary to the opinions of theologians, a condition of complete faith in God alone. We are here to live, which means to think, feel, and act also. We have not only to curb thought in meditation, but also to whip it in reflection. We have not only to control emotion in self-discipline, but also to release it in laughter, relaxation, affection, and pleasure. We have not only to perceive the transiency and illusion of material existence, but also to work, serve, strive, and move strenuously, and thus justify physical existence. We have to learn that when we look at what we really are we stand alone in the awed solitude of the Overself, but when we look at where we now are we see not isolated individuals but members of a thronging human community. The hallmark of a living man, therefore, ought to be an integral and inseparable activity of heart, head, and hand itself occurring within the mysterious stillness and silence of its inspirer, the Overself.

The mistake of the lower mystic is when he would set up a final goal in meditation itself, when he would stop at the "letting-go" of the external world which is quite properly an essential process of mysticism, and when he would let his reasoning faculty fall into a permanent stupor merely because it is right to do so during the moments of mental quiet. When, however, he learns to understand that the antinomy of meditation and action belongs only to an intermediate stage of this quest, when he comes later to the comprehension that detachment from the world is only to be sought to enable him to move with perfect freedom amid the things of the world and not to flee them, and when he perceives at long last that the reason itself is God-given to safeguard his journey and later to bring his realization into self-consciousness—then he shall have travelled from the second to the third degree in this freemasonry of ultimate wisdom. For that which had earlier hindered his advance now helps it; such is the paradox which he must unravel if he would elevate himself from the satisfactions of mysticism to the perceptions of philosophy. If his meditations once estranged him from the world, now they bring him closer to it! If formerly he could find God only within himself, now he can find nothing else that is not God! He has advanced from the chrysalis-state of X to the butterfly state of Y.

If there be any worth in this teaching, such lies in its equal appeal to experience and to reason. For that inward beatitude which it finally brings is superior to any other that mundane man has felt and, bereft of all violent emotion itself though it be, paradoxically casts all violent emotions of joy in the shade. When we comprehend that this teaching establishes as fact what the subtlest reasoning points to in theory, reveals in man's own life the presence of that Overself which reflection discovers as from a remote distance, we know that here at long last is something fit for a modern man. The agitations of the heart and the troublings of the head take their dying breaths.

§

The principle of balance is one of the most important of philosophic principles.

§

The basis of the universe is its equilibrium. Only so can the planets revolve in harmony and without collision. The man who would likewise put himself in tune with Nature, God, must establish equilibrium as the basis of his own nature.

§

The required condition of balance as the price of illumination refers also to correcting the lopsidedness of letting the conscious ego direct the whole man while resisting the superconscious spiritual forces. In other words, balance is demanded between the intellect which seeks deliberate control of the psyche and the intuition which must be invited by passivity and allowed to manifest in spontaneity. When a man has trained himself to turn equally from the desire to possess to the aspiration to being possessed, when he can pass from the solely personal attitude to the one beyond it, when the will to manage his being and his life for himself and by himself is compensated by the willingness to let himself and his life be quiescent, then his being and his life are worked upon by higher forces. This also is the kind of balance and completeness which the philosophic discipline must lead to so that the philosophic illumination may give him his second birth.

§

But it is of the highest importance to note that the principle of balance cannot be properly established in any man until each of the elements within him has been developed into its completeness. The failure to do so produces the type of man who knows truth intellectually, talks it fluently, and does the wrong in spite of it. A balance of immature and half-developed faculties is transitory by its very nature and never wholly satisfactory, whereas a balance of fully matured ones is necessarily durable and always perfectly gratifying.

§

Those who talk or write truth, but do not live it because they cannot, have glimpsed its meaning but not realized its power. They have not the dynamic balance which follows when the will is raised to the level of the intellect and the feelings. It is this balance which spontaneously ignites mystic forces within us, and produces the state called "born again." This is the second birth, which takes place in our consciousness as our first took place in our flesh.

§

It is most important to get rid of an unbalanced condition. Most people are in such a condition although few know it. For example, intellectuality without spirituality is human paralysis. Spirituality without intellectuality is mental paralysis. No man should submit to such suicidal conditions. All men should seek and achieve integrality. To be wrapped up in a single side of life or to be overactive in a single direction ends by making a man mildly insane in the true and not technical sense of this word. The remedy is to tone down here and build up there, to cultivate the neglected sides, and especially to cultivate the opposite side. Admittedly, it is extremely difficult for most of us, circumstanced as we usually are, to achieve a perfect development and equal balance of all the sides. But this is no excuse for accepting conditions completely as they are and making no effort at all to remedy them. The difficulty for many aspirants in attaining such an admirably balanced character lies in their tendency to be obsessed by a particular technique which they followed in former births but which cannot by itself meet the very different conditions of today. We must counterbalance the habit of living only in a part of our being. When we have become harmoniously balanced in the philosophic sense, heart and head will work together to answer the same question, the unhurrying sense of eternity and the pressing urge of the hour will combine to make decisions as wise as they are practical, and the transcendental intuitions will suggest or confirm the workings of reason. In this completed integral life, thought and action, devotion and knowledge do not wrestle against each other but become one. Such is the triune quest of intelligence, aspiration, and action.

§

This perfect harmony between the various elements of his personality is not to be achieved with some in the state of half-development and others of full development. All are to be brought up to the same high level.

§

Even our understanding of balance has to be corrected. It is not, for philosophic purposes, the mean point between two extremes but the compensatory union of two qualities or elements that need one another.

§

The danger of a lopsided character is seen when humility reverence and piety are largely absent whilst criticism logicality and realism are largely present. The intellect then becomes imperiously proud, arrogantly self-assured, and harshly intolerant. The consequence is that its power to glean subtler truths rather than merely external data is largely lost.

§

The balance needed by faith is understanding; by peacefulness, energy; by intuition, reason; by feeling, intellect; by aspiration, humility; and by zeal, discretion.

§

Inner balance is not established by setting two polar opposites against each other, as miserliness against extravagance, but by combining two necessary qualities together such as bravery with caution.

§

Manifested life remains no less real because we belittle it with the harsh cognomen of "illusion." Our active existence requires no apology on its behalf to the one-eyed philosophers who accuse Westerners of being entrapped by "Maya."

§

Neither the Buddhistic emphasis on suffering nor the hedonistic emphasis on joy are proper to a truly philosophical outlook. Both have to be understood and accepted, since life compels us to experience both.

§

A well-balanced person is not necessarily one who takes the measured midpoint between two extremes but one who *lets* himself be taken over by the inner calm. The needed adjustment is then made by itself. Although this avoids his falling into lopsided acts or exaggerated views, a merely moderate character is not the best result. More important is the *surrender* to the higher power which is implicit in the whole process of becoming truly balanced.

§

It is good for an ascetic or monk to sit idle and inactive whilst he contemplates the futility of a life devoted solely to earthly strivings, but it is bad for him to spend the whole of a valuable incarnation in such idleness and in such contemplation. For then he is fastening his attention on a single aspect of existence and losing sight of all others. It is good for a metaphysician to occupy himself with noting the logical contradictions involved in the world's existence and in the reason's own discoveries, but bad for him to waste a whole incarnation in fastening his attention on a single aspect. It is good for the worldling to accumulate money and enjoy the good things it can buy, marry a wife and adorn his home with comforts, but it is bad for him to waste his valuable incarnation without a higher purpose and a loftier goal. Nor is this all. Mysticism, metaphysics, and worldliness are useless unless they succeed in affording a man a basis of altruistic ethics for everyday living. The average mystic does not see that his lapse into loss of interest in the world around him, his indifference to positive and practical service of mankind, in short his whole other-worldliness, is not a virtue as he believes, but a defect. Hermits who withdraw from the troubled world to practise the simplicity, monks who retreat from the active world to muse over the evanescence of things, defeatists who flee from their failure in life, marriage, or business to the lethargy which they believe to be peace, thereby evidence that they have not understood the higher purpose of incarnation. It is to afford them the opportunity to realize in waking consciousness their innermost nature. This cannot be done by turning their face from the experiences of human existence, but by boldly confronting them and mastering them. Nor can it be done by retreating into the joys of meditation. The passionate ecstasies of lower mysticism, like the intellectual discoveries of lower metaphysics, yield only the illusion of penetrating into reality. For the world, as well as the "I," must be brought into the circle of meditation if the whole truth is to be gained. The one-sided, monkish doctrine which indicts the world's forms with transiency and illusiveness must be met and balanced by the philosophic doctrine which reveals the world's essence as eternal and real. There will then be no excuse for lethargy, defeatism, or escapism. A metaphysical outlook often lacks the spark of vitality; a mystical outlook often lacks the solidity of reasoned thought; and both often lack the urge to definite action. The practical failures of metaphysics are traceable to the fact that it does not involve the exercise of the will as much as it involves the exercise of the intellect. The intellectual failures of metaphysics are due to the fact that the men who taught it in the past knew nothing of science and those who teach it in the present know nothing of higher mystical meditation, whilst both have usually had little experience of the hard facts of life outside their sheltered circle. The failures of mysticism are due to the same causes, as well as others we have often pointed out. Finally, the failure of metaphysicians to produce practical fruit is partly due to the fact that they perceive *ideas* of truth and not truth itself, as the failure of mystics is partly due to the fact that they experience *feelings* of reality and not reality itself. The successes and services of the sage on the contrary are due to the fact that he perceives truth and experiences reality and not merely thoughts or feelings about them.

§

It is not only balance inside the ego itself that is to be sought, not only between reason and emotion, thought and action, but also and much more important, outside the ego: between it and the Overself.

§

From all these studies, meditations, and actions the student will little by little emerge an inwardly changed man. He comes to the habitual contemplation of his co-partnership with the universe as a whole, to the recognition that personal isolation is illusory, and thus takes the firm steps on the ultimate path towards becoming a true philosopher. The realization of the hidden unity of his own life with the life of the whole world manifests finally in infinite compassion for all living things. Thus he learns to subdue the personal will to the cosmic one, narrow selfish affection to the wide-spreading desire for the common welfare. Compassion comes to full blossom in his heart like a lotus flower in the sunshine. From this lofty standpoint, he no longer regards mankind as being those whom he unselfishly serves but rather as being those who give him the opportunity to serve. He will suddenly or slowly experience an emotional exaltation culminating in an utter change of heart. Its course will be marked by a profound reorientation of feeling toward his fellow creatures. The fundamental egoism which in open or masked forms has hitherto motivated him will be abandoned: the noble altruism which has hitherto seemed an impracticable and impossible ideal, will become practicable and possible. For a profound sympathy to all other beings will dwell in his heart. Never again will it be possible for him wilfully to injure another; but on the contrary the welfare of the All will become his concern. In Jesus' words he is "born again." He will find his highest happiness, after seeking reality and truth, in seeking the welfare of all other beings alongside of his own. The practical consequence of this is that he will be inevitably led to incessant effort for their service and enlightenment. He will not merely echo the divine will but will allow it actively to work within him. And with the thought comes the power to do so, the grace of the Overself to help him to achieve quickly what the Underself cannot achieve. In the service of others he can partially forget his loss of trance-joy and know that the liberated self which he had experienced in interior meditation must be equated by the expanded self in altruistic action.

§

In observation a scientist, at heart a religious devotee, in thought a metaphysician, in secret a mystic, and in public an efficient honourable useful citizen—this is the kind of man philosophy produces.

§

He who has sufficiently purified his character, controlled his senses, developed his reason, and unfolded his intuition is always ready to meet what comes and to meet it aright. He need not fear the future. Time is on his side. For he has stopped adding bad karma to his account and every fresh year adds good karma instead. And even where he must still bear the workings of the old adverse karma, he will still remain serene because he understands with Epictetus that "There is only one thing for which God has sent me into the world, and that is to perfect my nature in all sorts of virtue or strength; and there is nothing that I cannot use for that purpose." He knows that each experience which comes to him is what he most needs at the time, even though it be what he likes least. He needs it because it is in part nothing else than his own past thinking, feeling, and doing come back to confront him to enable him to see and study their results in a plain, concrete, unmistakable form. He makes use of every situation to help his ultimate aims, even though it may hinder his immediate ones. Such serenity in the face of adversity must not be mistaken for supine fatalism or a lethargic acceptance of every untoward event as God's will. For although he will seek to understand why it has happened to him and master the lesson behind it, he will also seek to master the event itself and not be content to endure it helplessly. Thus, when all happenings become serviceable to him and when he knows that his own reaction to them will be dictated by wisdom and virtue, the future can no more frighten him than the present can intimidate him. He cannot go amiss whatever happens. For he knows too whether it be a defeat or a sorrow in the world's eyes, whether it be a triumph or a joy, the experience will leave him better, wiser, and stronger than it found him, more prepared for the next one to come. The philosophic student knows that he is here to face, understand, and master precisely those events, conditions, and situations which others wish to flee and evade, that to make a detour around life's obstacles and to escape meeting its problems is, in the end, unprofitable. He knows that his wisdom must arise out of the fullness and not out of the poverty of experience and that it is no use non-cooperatively shirking the world's struggle, for it is largely through such struggle that he can bring forth his own latent resources. Philosophy does not refuse to face life, however tragic or however frightful it may be, and uses such experiences to profit its own higher purpose.

§

When a certain balance of forces is achieved, something happens that can only be properly called "the birth of insight."

§

He who knows and feels the divine power in his inmost being will be set free in the most literal sense of the word from anxieties and cares. He who has not yet arrived at this stage but is on the way to it can approach the same desirable result by the intensity of his faith in that being. But such a one must really have the faith and not merely say so. The proof that he possesses it would lie in the measure with which he refuses to accept negative thoughts, fearful thoughts, despondent thoughts. In the measure that he does not fail in his faith and hence in his thinking, in that measure, the higher power will not fail to support him in his hour of need. This is why Jesus told his disciples, "Take no anxious thought for the morrow." In the case of the adept, having given up the ego, there is no one left to take care of him, so the higher Self does so for him. In the case of the believer, although he has not yet given up the ego, nevertheless, he is trying to do so, and his unfaltering trust in the higher Self is rewarded proportionately in the same way. In both cases the biblical phrase, "The Lord will provide," is not merely a pious hope but a practical fact.

§

The free soul has brought his thought and actions into perfect harmony with Nature's morality. He lives not merely for himself alone, but for himself as a part of the whole scheme. Consequently, he does not injure others but only benefits them. He does not neglect his own benefit, however, but makes the two work together. His activities are devoted to fulfilling the duties and responsibilities set for him by his best wisdom, by his higher self.

The world is necessarily affected by his presence and activities, and affected beneficially. First, the mere knowledge that such a man exists helps others to continue with their efforts at self-improvement, for they know then that the spiritual quest is not a vain dream but a practicable affair. Second, he influences those he meets to live better lives—whether they be few or many, influential or obscure. Third, he leaves behind a concentration of spiritual forces which works on for a long time, through other persons, after he leaves this world. Fourth, if he is a sage and balanced, he will always do something of a practical nature for the uplift of humanity instead of merely squatting in an ashram.

§

A mystic experience is simply something which comes and goes, whereas philosophic insight, once established in a man, can not possibly leave him. He understands the Truth and can not lose this understanding any more than an adult can lose his adulthood and become an infant.

§

"Intuition" had come to lose its pristine value for me. I cast about for a better one and found it in "insight." This term I assigned to the highest knowing-faculty of sages and was thus able to treat the term "intuition" as something inferior which was sometimes amazingly correct but not infrequently hopelessly wrong in its guidance, reports, or premonition. I further endeavoured to state what the old Asiatic sages had long ago stated, that it was possible to unfold a faculty of direct insight into the nature of the Overself, into the supreme reality of the universe, that this was the highest kind of intuition possible to man, and that it did not concern itself with lesser revelations, such as giving the name of a horse likely to win tomorrow's race, a revelation which the kind of intuition we hear so much about is sometimes able to do.

§

Insight is a function of the entire psyche and not of any single part of it.

§

This is the true insight, the permanent illumination that neither comes nor goes but always *is*. While being serious, where the event or situation requires it, he will not be solemn. For behind this seriousness there is detachment. He cannot take the world of Appearances as being Reality's final form. If he is a sharer in this world's experiences, he is also a witness and especially a witness of his own ego—its acts and desires, its thoughts and speech. And because he sees its littleness, he keeps his sense of humour about all things concerning it, a touch of lightness, a basic humility. Others may believe that he stands in the Great Light, but he himself has no particular or ponderous self-importance.

§

He who possesses insight does not have to use arguments and reach conclusions. The truth is there, self-evident, inside himself as himself, for his inner being has become one with it.

§

Whenever I have used the term "the centre of his being," I have referred to a state of meditation, to an experience which is felt at a certain stage. Because the very art of meditation is a drawing inwards and the finer, the more delicate, the subtler this indrawing becomes, the closer it is to this central point of consciousness. But from the point of view of philosophy, meditation and its experiences are not the ultimate goal—although they may help in preparing one for that goal. In that goal there is no kind of centre to be felt nor any circumference either—one is without being localized anywhere with reference to the body, one is both in the body and in the Overself. There is then no contradiction between the two.

§

Philosophy seeks not only to know what is best in life but also to love it. It wants to feel as well as think. The truth, being above the common forms of these functions, can be grasped only by a higher function that includes, fuses, and transcends them at one and the same time—insight. In human life at its present stage of development, the nearest activity to this one is the activity of intuition. From its uncommon and infrequent visitations, we may gather some faint echo of what this wonderful insight is.

§

Attention is forever being caught by some thought or some thing, by some feeling or some experience. In the case of the ordinary man, consciousness is lost in the attention; but in the case of the philosophic man there is a background which evaluates the attention and controls it.

§

Insight is the flower of reason and not its negation.

§

The ever changing world-movement is suspended and transcended in the mystical trance so that the mystic may perceive its hidden changeless ground in the One Mind, whereas in the ultramystic insight its activity is restored. For such insight easily penetrates it, and always sees this ground without need to abolish the appearance. Consequently the philosopher is aware that everyday activity is as much and as needful a field for him as mystical passivity. Such expression, however, cannot be less than what he is within himself through the possession of insight. Just as any man cannot express himself as an ant, do what he may, simply because his human consciousness is too large to be narrowed down to such a little field, so the philosopher cannot separate his ultramystic insight from his moment-to-moment activity. In this sense he has no option but to follow and practise the gospel of inspired action.

§

To arrive at great certitude is to arrive at great strength. Truth not only clears the head but also arms the will. It is not only a light to our feet but is itself a force in the blood.

§

The mystic will not care and may not be able to do so but the philosopher has to learn the art of combining his inward recognition of the Void with his outward activity amongst things without feeling the slightest conflict between both. Such an art is admittedly difficult but it can be learnt with time and patience and comprehension. Thus he will feel inward unity everywhere in this world of wonderful variety, just as he will experience all the countless mutations of experience as being present in the very midst of this unity.

§

Where we speak either metaphysically or meditationally of the experience of pure consciousness, we mean consciousness uncoloured by the ego.

§

The mastery of philosophy will produce a supreme self-confidence within him throughout his dealings with life. The man who knows nothing of philosophy will declare that it has nothing to do with practical affairs and that it will not help you to rise in your chosen career, for instance. He is wrong. Philosophy gives its votary a thoroughly scientific and practical outlook whilst it enables him to solve his problems unemotionally and by the clear light of reason. He will, however, be under certain ethical limitations from which other men are exempt, for he takes the game of living as a sacred trust and not as a means for personal aggrandizement at the expense of others.

§

It may be said that the world's supreme need is exactly what the illumined man has found, therefore his duty is to give it to the world. This is true, but it is equally true that the world is not ready for it any more than he himself was ready for it before he underwent a long course of purification, discipline, and training. Accepting these realities of the situation, he feels no urge to spread his ideas, no impulse to organize a following. However that does not mean that he does nothing at all; it only means that he will help in the ways he deems to be most effective even if they are the least publicized and the least apparent. He is not deaf to the call of duty but he gives it a wider interpretation than those who are ignorant of the state and powers which he enjoys.

§

Whoever attains this, the topmost peak of the philosophic life, will naturally possess the capacity—rather the genius—to help the internal evolutionary advance of mankind. Indeed, it will be the principal and secret business of his life, whatever his external and conventional business may be. Those who stood closest to Jesus were asked to preach the gospel. Clearly therefore he conceived the spreading of truth to be their primary task. That other tasks, such as feeding and clothing the poor, had their own particular importance too, was acknowledged in his injunction to *other* persons. But that such tasks were secondary ones is clear inference from his instructions to the apostles. And in this critical passage of humanity from a used-out standpoint to a newer one which confronts it today, such a service is more than important. In his own humbler way and in a quiet unobtrusive manner, remembering always that people will find the best account of his beliefs in his deeds, even the neophyte who has still to climb the foothills of philosophy can and must communicate so much of this knowledge as he finds men may be ready for, but not an iota more. His task is not, like that of the apostles, to convert them but to help them. He may be only a firefly with little light to shed but he should desert the esotericism of former centuries and try to enlighten others because he must understand the unique character of this century and see the dangerous gaping abyss which surrounds its civilization. Moreover he may take refuge in the words of *Tripura*, an archaic Sanskrit text, which, if its archaic idiom be translated into modern accents, says: "An intense student may be endowed with the slenderest of good qualities, but if he can readily understand the truth—however theoretically—and expound it to others, this act of exposition will help him to become himself imbued with these ideas and his own mind will soak in their truth. This in the end will lead him to actualize the Divinity within himself."

§

When he first attains to this clear vision, he sees not only that which brings him great joy but also that which brings him great sorrow. He sees men bewildered by life, pained by life, blinded by life. He sees them wandering into wrong paths because there is no one to lead them into right ones. He sees them praying for light but surrounded by darkness. In that hour he makes a decision which will fundamentally affect the whole of his life. Henceforth he will intercede for these others, devote himself to their spiritual service.

§

After the desire for the fullest overshadowing by the Overself, which must always be primal, his second desire is to spread out the peace, understanding, and compassion which now burn like a flame within him, to propagate an inward state rather than an intellectual dogma, to bless and enlighten those who seek their divine parent.

§

The man who lives in the physical senses alone reaches and affects those other men only whom he can come into contact with physically. He is entirely limited by time and space. The man who lives in the developed intellect or feelings also reaches and affects those other men who can respond to his written or printed ideas or his artistic inspirations. He is limited only partially by time and space. But the man who lives in the godlike Overself within him is freed from time and space and uplifts all those who can respond intuitively, even though they may never know him physically. For in the spiritual world he cannot hide his light.

§

The philosopher accepts his predestined isolation not only because that is the way his position has to be, but also because his physical presence arouses negative feelings in the hearts of ordinary people as it arouses positive ones in the hearts of certain seekers. The negatives may range all the way from puzzlement, bewilderment, and suspicion to fear, opposition, and downright enmity. The positives may range from instinctive attraction to a readiness to lay down life in his defense or service. All these feelings arise instantly, irrationally, and instinctively. And they are unconnected with whether or not he reveals his true personal identity. This is because they are the consequence of a psychical impingement of his aura upon theirs. The contact is unseen and unapparent in the physical world, but it is very real in the mental-emotional world. It is truly a psychical experience for both: clear and precise and correctly understood by him, vague and disturbing and utterly misunderstood by ordinary people as well as pseudo-questers. It is both a psychical and a mystical experience for those genuine questers with whom he has some inward affinity, a glad recognition of a long-lost, much revered Elder Brother. Unfortunately, despite the generous compassion and enormous goodwill which he bears in his heart for all alike, it is the unpleasant contacts which make up the larger number whenever the philosopher descends into the world. Let him not be blamed if he prefers solitude to society. For there is nothing he can do about it. People are what they are. Most times when he tries to make himself agreeable to them, as though they both belonged to the same spiritual level, he fails. He learns somewhat wearily to accept his isolation and their limitation as inevitable and, at the present stage of human evolution, unalterable. He learns, too, that it is futile to desire these things to be otherwise.

§

The peace to which he has become heir is not self-absorbed rest from old activities that he deserts, but a divine awareness that subsists beneath new ones that he accepts.

§

21

MENTALISM

Mind and the five senses—World as mental experience — Mentalism is key to spiritual world

The materialist's mistake primarily consists in this, that his mind considers its impressions and sensations—entirely dependent as they are on its own presence—as external realities, whilst dismissing its own independent reality as a fiction.

§

"Recent scientific theory calls attention not to the uniformity but to the indeterminacy of nature which, by transferring probability from human thought to objective reality, suggests that matter is mind externalized." —*Times Literary Supplement*, May 12, 1945

§

The mysterious power of the mind, which makes us feel the world to be outside of and separate from ourselves, disappears during certain ultramystical experience.

§

If Matter has any existence at all, it is as the externalizing power of the mind.

§

Matter cannot be honestly denied by the ordinary man since it is fully real to his senses. Its reality but not its appearance can be denied by the scientist, since it is a compound of invisible and intangible forces to his intellect.

§

The spirit of true Science must be ours, too. We can accept nothing as true which is dubious as undemonstrable. The modern world, and especially the Western world, can sympathize with a teaching only if it will stand the double test of reason and experience.

§

When a mystical seer proclaimed on the basis of his own insight that the reality of the universe was not matter but mind, educated people could afford to disregard his proclamations. But when leading scientists themselves proclaimed it on the basis of verifiable facts and rational reflections, they could not help giving their confidence to it. Consequently, those who have seriously absorbed the latest knowledge have been falling away from intellectual materialism. It is indeed only the uneducated, the half-educated, the pseudo-educated, and the word-educated who today believe in this miserable doctrine.

§

Mentalism, the teaching that this is a mental universe, is too hard to believe for the ordinary man yet too hard to disbelieve for the illumined man. This is because to the first it is only a theory, but to the second it is a personal experience. The ordinary man's consciousness is kept captive by his senses, each of which reports a world of matter outside him. The illumined man's consciousness is free to be itself, to report its own reality and to reveal the senses and their world to be mere ideation.

§

Since the world is never found to be apart from our own minds, we are forced to relate it to them. And since it is equally obvious that the surface part of them does not deliberately bring it into existence we are further forced to deduce, first, that the deeper and unconscious part must do so and, second, that this second part must be cosmic in nature and hold all other individual minds rooted in its depths. This deduction, arrived at by reason, is confirmed by experience but not by ordinary experience. It is confirmed by sinking a shaft down through the mind in mystical meditation and arriving at our secondary cosmic self.

§

We do not intend to deal here with some supernatural "spirit" which does not explain the world but only mystifies us, which is beyond all ordinary experience and whose existence cannot be irrefutably proved. We do not need to go beyond Mind—which explains the world as a form of consciousness, which is everyone's familiar experience at every moment of the day or night, and whose existence is unquestionably self-evident, for it makes us aware of every other kind of existence.

§

Mentalism does not deny the existence of the natural universe. It denies the materialistic view of that universe. It refuses to attribute to matter a creative power to be found only in life, an intelligent consciousness to be found only in mind.

§

We do not bring out the old arguments for the acceptance of an inner Reality to persuade anyone to drop his faith in the reality of the world without.

§

Only a highly educated mind can appreciate *intellectually* the truth which lies in mentalism, as only a highly intuitive one can *feel* its truth.

§

The ignorance which accepts matter as a reality rather than as an idea can be overcome only by a course of emotional purification, mystical contemplation, and metaphysical reflection.

§

The practical message of mentalism is not only to warn us of the creative value of our thought but also to bid us seek out the *source* of thought. For there lies our real home, and there we must learn to dwell habitually.

§

Psychology, like all the sciences, has to turn itself into philosophy the moment it puts to itself such a radical question as "what is mind?"

§

What is Mind? It is that in us which thinks, which is aware, and which knows.

§

Mind is the power to be conscious, to think, and to imagine. It is not the fleshly brain.

§

If we want to think correctly of the form and dimensions of mind, we must try to think of it as unbounded space. Thus it is everywhere.

§

Mind must precede any thought, any knowing. It must be there to make any thinking possible at all.

§

Only when an object is registered in consciousness is it really seen at all. Not even all the physical details of vision constitute the real experience of seeing it, for the *awareness* of it is not a physical experience at all.

§

The deceptions bred by an unreflective attitude towards the reports of sense and an unintuitive one towards the feeling of personality, enter so deeply into his mental principle because of their growing prevalence during a large number of births that they become almost an integral part of it. The melancholy consequences of this disposition are an inability to believe in mentalism and an incapacity to progress in mysticism.

§

The statement that we can know only our own sensations and that we do not experience the world directly constitutes the very beginning of the doctrine of mentalism.

§

The mind interprets its own experience in a particular way because, owing to its structure, it could not do so in another way. But these limitations are not eternal and absolute. When, as in dream, yoga, death, or hallucination, they are abruptly loosened, then experience is interpreted in a new and different way.

§

It is because men are deceived by their senses into accepting materialism that they are deceived by their ego into committing sin. Mentalism is not only an intellectual doctrine but also an ethical one.

§

It is only after several years of constant reflection upon this topic, helped by occasional mystical glimpses or experiences, that anyone can dissolve such troubling questions about the truth of mentalism.

§

He will come to see by experience, as science is coming to see by experiment, that this vast universe is real in its present form to his bodily senses only. As soon as his mind is freed from them, it takes on quite a different form, the old form having no further existence at all. He is then compelled to correct his false belief in the world's reality. If there were nothing more than the five senses, then this correction would make the universe an illusion. But the presence of mind in him makes it an idea.

§

Sankara's Snake-Rope illusion is out of date. Science provides better illustration based on facts of *continuous experience* instead of exceptional or occasional ones. Indians ignore the fact that a thousand years have travelled on and away since Sankara's time. Human intelligence has probed and discovered much. Modern evidence for mentalism is more solid today. The tremendous advance of knowledge since his time has shown that the substance of which this universe is made turns out to be no substance at all.

§

The totality of the immeasurably rich nature of the universe never reaches the human senses. This is not their fault. They cannot help but receive nothing more than a limited selection from it. There are numerous vibrations beyond their range and also beneath it. And yet we have the temerity to assert that the world of our experience, the only one we know, is the real world and that all others are illusory!

§

There are sixty-four different points of the compass. Therefore, it is possible for sixty-four men to take up all these different positions and look at an object. Each will see a different appearance of it. Thus there will be sixty-four different appearances. Yet all the men will glibly talk, when questioned, of having seen the same object when they have done nothing of the kind. And if any one of them asserts that he has studied only the appearance of the real thing and the whole thing, he is obviously talking nonsense. Yet this is what most of us do when we say we have seen the world that surrounds us—this and nothing less. It is completely impossible through the instrumentality of the senses to see the whole of any object, let alone the whole of the world. They can only view aspects. But what cannot be done by the senses can be done by the mind, which can form an idea of the whole of anything. Therefore it is only through reflection—that is, through philosophy—that we can ever get at a grasp of the whole of life and the universe.

§

But all this does not mean that philosophy asks us to mistrust the witness of our senses. That is correct enough for all ordinary, practical uses. But it does ask us to search more deeply into the significance of all sense-experience.

§

No discoveries made in a physiological laboratory can ever annul the primary doctrine of mentalism. The mechanism of the brain provides the condition for the manifestation of intellectual processes but does not provide the first originating impulse of these processes. The distinction between mind and its mechanism, between the mentalness of experience and the materiality of the content of that experience, needs much pondering.

§

It is not the five senses which know the world outside, since they are only instruments which the mind uses. It is not even the intellect, since that merely reproduces the image formed out of the total sense reports. They are not capable of functioning by themselves. It is the principle of Consciousness which is behind both, and for which they are simply agents, that really makes awareness of the world at all possible. It is like the sun, which lights up the existence of all things.

§

The distinction which is often made (especially by the school of Faculty-Psychology) between sensation and idea or between sense-data and thought was once believed to be an actuality, but it is now believed to be only a convenience for intellectual analysis. A compromise view now regards our experience of the world as being a compound of the two, but a compound which is never split up into separate elements. This view represents a big step towards the mentalist position but is still only a step. And this position is that there is only a single activity, a single experience—thought. The idea *is* the sensation, the sensation *is* the idea. The sense datum which our present day psychologists find as an element of experience, is really their *interpretation* of experience. Hence it is nothing else than a thought. And that which it unconsciously professes to interpret is likewise a thought!

§

It is not possible to explain intellectually how sensations of the physical world are converted into ideas, how the leap-over from nervous vibrations into consciousness occurs, and how a neurosis becomes a psychosis. No one has ever explained this, nor will any scientist ever succeed in doing so. Truth alone can dispose of this poser by pointing out that sensations never really occur, but that the Self merely projects ideas of them; just as a man sees a mirage and mistakes it for real water merely by his mental projection, so people regard the world as real when they are merely transferring their own mental ideas to the world.

§

It is natural for the materialist to ask how any sense can function without a sense organ. It is natural for the mentalist to point to the experience of dreams for the answer. All the senses are functioning during the dream but they do so without the apparatus of sense organs. This fact alone indicates in the clearest possible manner to anyone sufficiently perceptive to understand the indication that it is the mind and the mind alone which is the real agent in all the senses' experience. When, because of distracted attention, our mind is not aware of a thing which stands before our eyes, that particular thing temporarily ceases to exist for us. This means, if it means anything at all, that the thing receives its existence partly at the very least from us. It does not stand alone. Sense-experience actually takes place in consciousness itself: the five senses do not create but limit, canalize, and externalize this experience. We receive the various sensations of hardness, colour, shape, and so on, but they are not received from outside the mind. They are all received from within our consciousness. This is because they are received from the World-Mind's master image *within* us. The objects which cause those sensations truly exist, but they exist within this image—which itself exists within our field of consciousness. The things of experience are not different from the acts of knowing them. Hence the world exists in our thoughts of it.

§

It is not possible for sincere, scrupulous thinking to admit, and never possible to prove, the existence of a world outside of, and separate from, its consciousness. The faith by which we all conventionally grant such existence is mere superstition.

§

The object which the senses directly establish contact with is regarded as one thing; the mental impression they have when thinking of that object is regarded as another and totally different thing. This is a very simple and apparently very obvious view of the matter. To the ordinary mind, by which I mean the metaphysically unreflective mind, the statement is unarguable and its implied division of Nature into mental and material, uncontestable. But if you analyse the way you perceive objects, you will find that both the perceiver and the perceived are inseparable in the act of perception. You cannot show a duality of idea and thing but only a unity of them.

§

A curious example, but one helpful to the enquirer, exists in the case of bodily pain. It is utterly impossible for us to imagine pain in the abstract—existing without any mind to be conscious of it. The word becomes quite meaningless if we try to separate it from someone or something to perceive or feel it. Its very existence depends entirely on being thought of, on being related to a conscious percipient. The sensation of being felt, this alone gives reality to pain. This fact refers equally to past or present pain. It should be easy to apply this analogy to the case of mere ideas, for the latter—like pain—can never come into existence without something, some mind, to think of them. Consciousness, on the part of someone or something, alone makes them real and factual.

§

The world must be present in my mind or it is not present at all to me. Only as an idea does it truly exist for me.

§

The world is never really given to us by experience nor actually known by the mind. What is given is idea, what is known is idea, to be transcended only when profound analysis transforms the Idea into the Reality.

§

Mentalism teaches that it is our thought activity which brings the whole world into our consciousness, and that when this thought activity comes to an end, the world also comes to an end, *for us*. It teaches that there is no other object than the thought itself.

§

The mind deals directly with its objects and not through the intermediary working of ideas for the ideas are its only objects.

§

We have to overcome the habitual custom of thinking that the "I" is one thing and that its experience in a world totally outside it is another. Both are mental.

§

Mind is governed by its own laws and conjures up its own creations. The universe, at any particular moment of its history, is formed by the action and reaction of these creations.

§

It is not because a thing is existent that you think it but because you think it, even if involuntarily, that it is existent. And this thought of it is a part of your own consciousness, not outside you.

§

Mental activity need not be conscious.

§

It is absurd even to suggest that there is an external world wholly outside of one's consciousness and wholly independent of it. One knows only certain changes of mental awareness, never of externals. The mind can only know its changes of individual consciousness. All its observations, each of its inferences, everything it knows—these lie enclosed within that consciousness and are never beyond it.

One's knowledge of anything whatsoever is simply one's *thought* of it. This is not to be confused with one's *right* thought of it. It is a conscious mental state, and even other persons are but appearances within this state, creatures in the cosmic dream. To follow this line of reflection to its inevitable end demands courage and candour of the highest kind, for it demands as ultimate conclusion the principle that knowledge being but ideas in the mind, the whole universe is nothing but an immense idea within one's own mind. For the very nature of knowledge is thus *internal*, and hence the individual mind cannot know any reality external to itself. It believes that it observes a world without when it only observes its own mental pictures of that world.

§

Is there some precise universal criterion of truth which will be applicable at all times and under all circumstances, in short, something unchanging and therefore supreme? For scientists know that the great principles which formed landmarks in the history of science were really successive stages on the route towards the precise truth. Science changes, its doctrines change, and its earlier approximations are replaced from time to time by more accurate points. We cannot hope to find an ultimate truth nowadays, when science itself is so rapidly on the march. There remains, however, one unfailing all-embracing fact which will forever remain true and which cannot possibly change. Indeed, every advance in experiment and theory made by enterprising scientists will only help to verify this grand discovery. What is it? It is that the whole world which every department of science is busily engaged in examining is nothing but an idea in the human mind. Physics, chemistry, geology, astronomy, biology, and all the other sciences without a single exception are concerned solely with what is ultimately a thought or series of thoughts passing through human consciousness. Here, therefore, we possess a universal law which embraces the entire field in which science is operating. This is an ultimate truth which will stand immortal, when every other hypothesis formulated by science has perished through advancing knowledge.

§

A popular misconception of mentalism must be cleared. When we say that the world does not exist *for man* apart from his own mind, this is not to say that man is the sole world-creator. If that were so, he could easily play the magician and reshape a hampering environment in a day. No! —what mentalism really teaches is that man's mind perceives, by participating in it, the world-image which the World-Mind creates and holds. Man alone is not responsible for this image, which could not possibly exist if it did not exist also in the World-Mind's consciousness.

§

We do *not* dream the waking world as we dream during sleep. For the latter is spun out of the individual mind alone, whereas the former is spun out of the cosmic mind and presented to the individual mind. However, ultimately, and on realization, both minds are found to be one and the same, just as a sun ray is found to be the same as the sun ultimately. The difference which exists is fleeting and really illusory but so long as there is bodily experience it is observable. It is correct to note that the present birth-dream is caused by past tendencies; we are hypnotized by the past and our work is to dehypnotize ourselves, that is, to create new thought-habits until the flash comes of itself. But the flash itself comes during a kind of trance state, which may last for a moment or longer. It comes during the higher meditation of supramysticism.

§

The World-Mind is not a magnified man and the world-image is not "pushed" into our consciousness by its personal and persistent effort. The mere presence of this image in it is sufficient to produce a reflected image in all other minds although they will absorb only so much as their particular plane of space-time perception can absorb.

§

The individual mind presents the world-image to itself through and in its own consciousness. If this were all the truth then it would be quite proper to call the experience a private one. But because the individual mind is rooted in and inseparable from the universal mind, it is only a part of the truth. Man's world-thought is held within and enclosed by God's thought.

§

The precise shape which the idea will take when it reaches consciousness will depend on the general tendencies of the person.

§

Our idea of the external world is caused partly by the energies of our own mind and partly by the energies of the World-Mind. It is *not* caused by a separate material thing acting on our sense organs.

§

It is a generative idea. Here is a whole philosophy congealed into a single phrase: the world is an idea.

§

In one of those apocryphical books which was rejected by those men who formed the canonical collection called the New Testament—a rejection in which they were sometimes wrong, and certainly in this instance—there occurred a saying of Jesus which runs, "When the outside becomes the inside, then the kingdom of heaven is come." Can we expand this mystical phrase into non-mystical language? Yes, here it is: "When the outside world is known and felt to be what it really is—an idea—it becomes a part of the inside world of thought and feeling. When its joys and griefs are known to be nothing more than states of mind, and when all thoughts and feelings and desires are brought from the false ego into the true Self at their centre, they automatically dissolve—and the kingdom of heaven is come."

§

Think of yourself as the individual and you are sure to die; think of yourself as the universal and you enter deathlessness, for the universal is always and eternally there. We know no beginning and no ending to the cosmic process. Its being IS: we can say no more. Be that rather than this—that which is as infinite and homeless as space, that which is timeless and unbroken. Take the whole of life as your own being. Do not divorce, do not separate yourself from it. It is the hardest of tasks for it demands that we see our own relative insignificance amid this infinite and vast process. The change that is needed is entirely a mental one. Change your outlook and with it "heaven will be added unto you."

§

Our own mind is a human analogue of the Universal Mind. Thus in its character and working, Nature provides an easy lesson in divine metaphysics. If we wish to obtain some slight hint as to the nature of the highest kind of mental existence, that is, of God, we must examine the nature of our own individual mind, limited and imperfect though it be. Now philosophy is not afraid to admit pantheism but does not limit itself to pantheism. It also affirms transcendentalism but does not stop with it. It declares that the Unique Reality could never become transformed into the cosmos in the sense of losing its own uniqueness. But at the same time it declares that the cosmos is nevertheless one with and not apart from the Reality. The easiest way to grasp this is to symbolize the cosmos as human thoughts and the Reality as human mind. Our thoughts are nothing other than a form of mind, yet our mind loses nothing of itself when thoughts arise. The World-Mind is immanent in but not confined by the universe in the same way that a man's mind may be said to be immanent in but not confined by his thoughts. Furthermore, not only may we find it helpful in the effort to understand the relation which the cosmos bears to the World-Mind, to compare it with the relation which a thought bears to its thinker or his speech to a speaker, but when we consider how our own mind is able to generate thoughts of the most multivaried kind, we need not be surprised that the Universal Mind is able to generate the inexhaustibly varied host of thought-forms which constitute the cosmos.

§

Whoever can understand that substance is inseparable from life and that life is inseparable from mind, whoever can intellectually perceive that the whole universe itself is nothing less than Mind in its different phases, has found the theoretical basis for an appreciation of the wonderful possibilities which dwell behind human experience. The mind's powers can indeed be extended far beyond their present puny evolutionary range. He who reflects constantly upon the true and immaterial nature of Mind and upon its magically creative powers tends to develop these powers. When he becomes capable of successful and ego-free concentration, these powers of mind and will come to him spontaneously. It is natural that when his will becomes self-abnegated, his emotion purified, his thought concentrated, and his knowledge perfected that higher mental or so-called occult powers arise of their own accord. It is equally natural that he should remain silent about them, even if only because they do not really belong to the named personality which others see. They belong to the Overself.

§

To arrive at the understanding that the universe is non-material and is *mental*, is to be liberated from materialism. It produces a sensation like that felt by a prisoner who has spent half a lifetime cooped up in a dark and dingy fetid dungeon and who is suddenly liberated, set free, put out of doors in the bright sunshine and fresh clean air. For to be a materialist means to be one imprisoned in the false belief that the matter-world is the real world; to become spiritual is to perceive that all objects are mental ones; the revelation of the mental nature of the universe is so stupendous that it actually sets mind and feeling free from their materialistic prison and brings the whole inner being into the dazzling sunshine of truth, the fresh atmosphere of Reality. All those who believe in the materiality of the material world and not in its mental nature, are really materialists—even if they call themselves religious, Christians, spiritualists, occultists, or Anthroposophists. The only way to escape materialism is not to become a follower of any psychic cult or religious faith, but to enquire with the mind into the truth of matter and to be rewarded at length by the abiding perception of its mental Nature. All other methods are futile, or at best are but preparatory and preliminary steps.

§

Because mentalism is to become a vivid fact for him and not remain a mere theory, the advanced disciple will have to convert his joys and agonies into real-seeming dream-stuff. And he will have to achieve this conversion by the power of his own hard will and his own keen understanding. The higher self may help him do this, for he may find that some of the deepest sorrows which befall him are of a special kind. They may be extremely subtle or strikingly paradoxical or tremendous in vicissitudes. For instance, he may be estranged in the most poignant way from those dearest to him, from the master he reveres, the friends he needs, the woman he loves. He may be permitted to meet them *in the flesh* only briefly and only rarely, so that he will seek compensation by learning the art of meeting them often and long *in thought*. If these inner experiences can utterly absorb his imaginative attention, they will come to seem as actual as outer ones. If the capacity to introspect be united with the capacity to visualize in this intense way, the result will be astonishingly effectual. Thus he comes in time to see the Mental as Real. Thus he lifts himself from a lower point of view to a higher one. Thus he thoroughly overcomes the extroverted materialism of ordinary human perception.

§

Telepathy is possible not because thought can travel in space but because space is actually in thought.

§

The human body is a part of consciousness, indeed a major part, but consciousness itself is only a part of a larger and deeper consciousness of which we are normally unaware. Yet it is in this mysterious region that the creative origin of the body-idea lies. If the ordinary "I" cannot make the body keep well by merely holding the thought, this is because the creative power lies in an "I" which transcends it. The ego which identifies itself with the body thereby stultifies its latent powers. But as soon as it begins to identify itself with pure Mind, certain powers may begin to unfold. Many cases of mystic phenomena, such as the stigmata of Catholic saints, confirm this.

§

It is one and the same Reality which *appears* in different ways to beings on different planes of perception. If it is true that they are dealing only with Appearance because they are perceiving only its forms, it is equally true that, as soon as they discover what it is that projects these forms, they will discover that life is a harmonious whole and that there is no fundamental conflict between the so-called worldly life and the so-called spiritual life.

§

Every kind of experience, whether it be wakeful, dream, hypnotic, or hallucinatory is utterly and vividly real to the ego at the time its perceptions are operating on that particular level. Why then, amidst such bewildering relativity, do we talk of divine experience as being the ultimate reality? We speak this way because it is concerned with what bestows the sense of reality to all the other forms of experience. And that is nothing else than the central core of pure Mind within us, the unique mysterious source of *all* possible kinds of our consciousness. This, if we can find it, is what philosophy calls the truly real world.

§

The way out is constantly to remember to think and to affirm that the world and all one sees and experiences in it has no other substance than Mind and gets its brief appearance of reality from Mind. When this is thoroughly understood and applied its truth will one day stay permanently with him.

§

The mental character of the world of our experience, once accepted, changes our religious, metaphysical, scientific, moral, and practical attitudes. Much in it does not need much thought for us to realize how grave is the importance of this fact, how momentous the results to which it leads!

§

Reality is inaccessible to thought so long as we regard the latter as separate from it. The moment this illusion is dropped, the truth is revealed.

§

If he does not wish to trouble his head, he can comfortably accept the appearances of things; but then he will be living only in the comfort of illusion. If however he wants to ferret out what is *real* in existence he must put himself to some trouble. He must persevere, read and re-read these pages until the meaning of it all dawns suddenly upon him, as it will if he does. It is perfectly natural for man to regard as the highest reality the experiences which impress themselves most forcibly upon him, which are those gained externally through his physical senses, and to regard as but half-real the experiences which impress themselves least forcibly upon him, which are those created internally by his own thoughts and fancies. But if he can be brought, as a true metaphysics can bring him, to arrive intellectually at the discernment that when he believes he is seeing and experiencing matter he is only seeing and experiencing thought, and that the entire cosmos is an image co-jointly held in the cosmic and individual minds, he will not unconsciously set up all those artificial resistances to the mystical intuitions and ultramystical illuminations which wait in the future for him.

§

The mental images which make up the universe of our experience repeat themselves innumerable times in a single minute. They give an impression of continuity and permanency and stability only because of this, in the same way that a cinema picture does. If we could efface them and yet keep our consciousness undiminished, we would know for the first time their source, the reality behind their appearances. That is, we would know Mind-in-itself. Such effacement is effected by yoga. Here then is the importance of the connection between mentalism and mysticism.

§

Whoever understands that every object and every person he sees around him is separate only in appearance, and appears so only through the unexamined working of his mind, is becoming ripe for realization. But very few are those who have come to such advanced understanding.

§

When we come at last to perceive that all this vast universe is a thought-form and when we can feel our own source to be the single and supreme principle in and through which it arises, then our knowledge has become final and perfect.

§

22

INSPIRATION AND THE OVERSELF

Intuition the beginning—Inspiration the completion —Its presence—Glimpses

The concept of the Overself is foundational. It provides meaning for life.

§

Here is the focal point of all spiritual searching, here man meets God.

§

The Overself is not merely a mental concept for all men but also a driving force for some men, not merely a pious pleasant feeling for those who believe in it but also a continuing vital experience for those who have lifted the ego's heavy door-bar.

§

When man shall discover the hidden power within himself which enables him to be conscious and to think, he will discover the holy spirit, the ray of Infinite Mind lighting his little finite mind.

§

The Overself is the point where the One Mind is received into consciousness. It is the "I" freed from narrowness, thoughts, flesh, passion, and emotion—that is, from the personal ego.

§

No one can explain what the Overself is, for it is the origin, the mysterious source, of the explaining mind, and beyond all its capacities. But what can be explained are the effects of standing consciously in its presence, the conditions under which it manifests, the ways in which it appears in human life and experience, the paths which lead to its realization.

§

The fact that we know our bodies is a guarantee that we can know our souls. For the knowing principle in us is derived from the soul itself. We have only to search our own minds deeply enough and ardently enough to discover it.

§

When you begin to seek the Knower, who is within you, and to sever yourself from the seen, which is both without and within you, you begin to pass from illusion to reality.

§

The mind's chief distinguishing power is *to know*—whether the object known is the world around or the ideas within. When this is turned in still deeper upon itself, subject and object are one, the thought-making activity comes to rest, and the "I" mystery is solved. Man discovers his real self, or being—his soul.

§

That point where man meets the Infinite is the Overself, where he, the finite, responds to what is absolute, ineffable and inexhaustible Being, where he reacts to That which transcends his own existence—this is the Personal God he experiences and comes into relation with. In this sense his belief in such a God is justifiable.

§

Because of the paradoxically dual nature which the Overself possesses, it is very difficult to make clear the concept of the Overself. Human beings are rooted in the ultimate mind through the Overself, which therefore partakes on the one hand of a relationship with a vibratory world and on the other of an existence which is above all relations. A difficulty is probably due to the vagueness or confusion about which standpoint it is to be regarded from. If it is thought of as the human soul, then the vibratory movement is connected with it. If it is thought of as transcending the very notion of humanity, and therefore in its undifferentiated character, the vibratory movement must disappear.

§

Overself is the inner or true self of man, reflecting the divine being and attributes. The Overself is an emanation from the ultimate reality but is neither a division nor a detached fragment of it. It is a ray shining forth but not the sun itself.

§

The Overself is utterly above all personality yet is not bereft of a kind of individuality.

§

It is that part of man which is fundamental, real, undying, and truly *knowing*.

§

It is a state of pure intelligence but without the working of the intellectual and ideational process. Its product may be named intuition. There are no automatically conceived ideas present in it, no habitually followed ways of thinking. It is pure, clear, stillness.

§

It is true that the nature of God is inscrutable and that the laws of God are inexorable. But it is also true that the God-linked soul of man is accessible and its intuitions available.

§

What we are ordinarily conscious of are the thoughts and feelings of the ego, but there is much more in us than that. There is the true self, of which the ego is only a miserable caricature. If we could penetrate to this, the fundamental element of our selfhood, we would never again be satisfied with a wholly egoistic life—the call of the Quest would come again and again in our ears. And indeed it is through such rare glimpses, such exalted moments, when they become conscious of a presence, higher and more blessed than their ordinary state, that men are drawn to the Quest in the effort to recapture those moments and those moods. The recapturing is done, not by taking possession of something but by allowing oneself to be possessed, not by a positive and affirmative movement of the will, but by a yielding to, and acceptance of, the gentlest and most delicate thing in man's psyche—the intuition.

§

Knowledge of the facts concerning man and his nature, his general destiny and spiritual evolution, can be gained by the intuition; but information concerning the details of his personal history must be gleaned, if at all, by the psychical faculty.

§

Whereas we can reach the intellect only through thinking, we can reach the spirit only through intuition. The practice of meditation is simply the deepening, broadening, and strengthening of intuition. A mystical experience is simply a prolonged intuition.

§

The intuition appears indirectly in aesthetic ecstasy and intellectual creativity, in the pricking of conscience, in the longing for relief from anxieties, or peace of mind. It appears directly only in mystical realization.

§

Intuition tells us *what* to do. Reason tells us *how* to do it. Intuition points direction and gives destination. Reason shows a map of the way there.

§

There is no single pattern that an intuitively guided life must follow. Sometimes he will see in a flash of insight both course and destination, but at other times he will see only the next step ahead and will have to keep an open mind both as to the second step and as to the final destination.

§

Intuitive guidance comes not necessarily when we seek it, but when the occasion calls for it. It does not usually come until it is actually needed. The intellect, as part of the ego, will often seek it in advance of the occasion because it may be driven by anxiety, fear, desire, or anticipation. Such premature seeking is fruitless.

§

The intuition comes from, and leads to, the Overself.

§

It is the strength or feebleness of our intuition which determines the grade of our spiritual evolution. What begins as a gentle surrender to intuition for a few minutes, one day resolves into a complete surrender of the ego to the Overself for all time.

§

The intuitive faculty can be deliberately cultivated and consciously trained.

§

The secret is to stop, on the instant, whatever he is doing just then, or even whatever he is saying, and reorient all his attention to the incoming intuition. The incompleted act, the broken sentence, should be deserted, for this is an exercise in evaluation.

§

Wrong personal intention may be negated by right intuitive guidance, but it is not easy to recognize the latter as such. The difference between a mere impulse and a real intuition may often be detected in two ways: first, by waiting a few days, as the subconscious mind has then a chance to offer help in deciding the matter; second, by noting the kind of emotion which accompanies the message. If the emotion is of the lower kind, such as anger, indignation, greed, or lust, it is most likely an impulse. If of the higher kind, such as unselfishness or forgiveness, it is most likely an intuition.

§

When one has reviewed a problem from all its angles, and has done this not only with the keenest powers of the mind but also with the finest qualities of the heart, it should be turned over at the end to the Overself and dismissed. The technique of doing so is simple. It consists of being still. In the moment of letting the problem fall away, one triumphs over the ego. This is a form of meditation. In the earlier stage it is an acknowledgment of helplessness and weakness in handling the problem, of personal limitations, followed by a surrender of it (and of oneself) to the Overself in the last resort. One can do no more. Further thought would be futile. At this point Grace may enter and do what the ego cannot do. It may present guidance either then, or at some later date, in the form of a self-evident idea.

§

So subtle is the oncoming and so mysterious is the working of the true intuition, so open and blatant is the fantasy that is false intuition, that the first test of authenticity is indicated here.

§

You may recognize the voice of wisdom when having to make a decision by the fact that it proceeds out of deep inner calm, out of utter tranquillity, whereas impulse is frequently born in exaggerated enthusiasm or undue excitement.

§

A compelling inner conviction or intuition need not necessarily collide with cold reason. But as an assumed intuition which may be merely a bit of wishful thinking or emotional bias, it is always needful to check or confirm or discipline it by reasoning. The two can work together, even whilst recognizing and accepting each other's peculiar characteristics and different methods of approach. Hence all intuitively formed projects and plans should be examined under this duplex light. The contribution of fact by reason should be candidly and calmly brought up against the contribution of inward rightness made by "intuition." We must not hesitate to scrap intuitively formed plans if they prove unworkable or unreasonable.

§

The promptings that come from this inner being are so faintly heard at first, however strong on their own plane, that we tend to disregard them as trivial. This is the tragedy of man. The voices that so often mislead him into pain-bringing courses—his passion, his ego, and blind intellect—are loud and clamant. The whisper that guides him aright and to God is timid and soft.

§

The commonest error is to try to produce and manufacture intuition. That can't be done. It is something which comes to you. Hence don't expect it to appear when concentrating on a problem, but if at all *after* you've dismissed the problem. Even then it is a matter of grace—it may or may not come.

§

How can he tell if inner guidance is truly intuitive or merely pseudo-intuitive? One of the ways is to consider whether it tends to the benefit of all concerned in a situation, the others as well as oneself. The word "benefit" here must be understood in a large way, must include the spiritual result along with the material one. If the guidance does not yield this result, it may be ego-prompted and will then hold the possibility of error.

§

An intuitive feeling is one untainted by the ego's wishes, uncoloured by its aversions.

§

Let no one imagine that contact with the Overself is a kind of dreamy reverie or pleasant, fanciful state. It is a vital relationship with a current of peace, power, and goodwill flowing endlessly from the invisible centre to the visible self.

§

To the extent that a man is conscious of the presence of the Overself, he becomes inspired. To the extent that he is also talented in any of the arts, his work also becomes inspired.

§

His activity as a merely selfish person comes to an end; his activity as a divinely inspired one begins. It is a transformation from "works of the flesh" to "fruits of the spirit" in the Bible's phrase.

§

When the ego is displaced and the Overself is using him, there will be no need and no freedom to choose between two alternatives in regard to actions. Only a single course will present itself, directly and unwaveringly, as the right one.

§

To gain such an inspiration in all its untarnished purity, his egoism must be totally lost and absorbed in the experience.

§

Inspired action becomes possible when, to speak in spatial metaphors, every deed receives its necessary and temporary attention within the foreground of the mind whilst the Overself holds the permanent attention of the man within the background of his mind.

§

Those critics who assert that we have lost our mystical values because we teach that mystical contemplation is not an end in itself but rather a means to action, have not understood our teaching. The kind of action we refer to is not the ordinary one. It is something higher than that, wiser than that, nobler than that. It is everyday human life divinized and made expressive of a sublime FACT. We have indeed often used the phrase "inspired action" to distinguish it from the blind and egotistic kind. He who practises it does not thereby desert the contemplative path. This inner life is kept deep full and rich, but it is not kept refrigerated and isolated. He reflects it deliberately into the outer life to satisfy a twofold purpose. First, to be on the earth, so far as he can, what he is in heaven. Second, to work actively for the liberation of others. This cannot be achieved by inertia and indifference—which are virtues to the mystic but defects to the philosopher.

§

There are men who may be high in talent but low in character. Notice that I use the word talent. I can not believe that it is possible to possess true inspiration and yet deny it or fail to express it in one's conduct.

§

To the man who has come along the path of loving devotion to God and finally gained the reward of frequent, joyous, ardent, inward communion with God, equally as to the man who has practised the way of mystical self-recollection and attained frequent awareness of the Overself's presence, an unexpected and unpalatable change may happen little by little or suddenly. God will seem to withdraw from the devotee, the Overself from the mystic. The blisses will fade and end. Although this experience will have none of the terror or isolation and misery of the "dark night" it will be comparable to that unforgettable time. And although it will seem like a withdrawal of Grace, the hidden truth is that it is actually a farther and deeper bestowal of Grace. For the man is being led to the next stage—which is to round out, balance, and complete his development. This he will be taught to do by first, acquiring cosmological knowledge, and later, attaining ontological wisdom. That is, he will learn something about the World-Idea and then, this gained, pass upward to learning the nature of that Reality in whose light even the universe is illusion. Thus from study of the operations of the Power behind the World-Idea he passes on to pondering on the Power itself. This last involves the highest degree of concentration and is indeed the mysterious little practised Yoga of the Uncontradictable. When successfully followed it brings about the attainment of Insight, the final discovery that there is no other being than THAT, no second entity.

§

Although we are divided in awareness from the higher power, we are not divided in fact from it. The divine being is immanent in each one of us. This is why there is always some good in the worst of us.

§

If a man asks why he can find no trace of God's presence in himself, I answer that he is full of evidence, not merely traces. God is present in him as consciousness, the state of being aware; as thought, the capacity to think; as activity, the power to move; and as stillness, the condition of ego, emotion, intellect, and body which finally and clearly reveals what these other things simply point to. "Be still, and know that I am God" is a statement of being whose truth can be tested by experiment and whose value can be demonstrated by experience.

§

Even while working in an office or factory or field, a man is not prevented from continuing his search for the inner mind. The notion that this quest requires aloofness from the commonplace utilitarian world is one which philosophy does not accept. Distraction and action are not so mutually inclusive as we may think. The student may train himself to maintain calm and serene poise even in the midst of strenuous activity, just as he also avails himself of the latest discoveries of scientific technique and yet keeps his mind capable of browsing through the oldest books of the Asiatic sages. He can discipline himself to returning from meditation to the turmoil, go anywhere, do anything, if truth is carried in the mind and poise in the heart. He may learn to live in reality at all times. The sense of its presence will need no constant renewal, no frequent slipping into trance, no intermittent escape from the world, if he follows the philosophic threefold path.

§

The question whether someone is a mystic or yogi can be answered easily enough once we understand what is his state of consciousness and what the mystical condition really is. All the annals of the vanished past and all the experiences of the living present inform us that whoever enters into it feels his natural egotism subside, his fierce passions assuaged, his restless thoughts stilled, his troubled emotions pacified, his habitual world-view spiritualized, and his whole person caught up into a beatific supernal power. Did he ever have this kind of consciousness? His words and deeds, his personal presence and psychological self-betrayal should proclaim with a united voice what he is. No man who habitually enters such a blessed state could ever bring himself to hate or injure a fellow human being.

§

If he feels this presence, and can do his work without deserting it, then his is a sacred function, no matter whether it be an artist's or an artisan's.

§

Although it is true that the Overself is the real guardian angel of every human being, we should not be so foolish as to suppose its immediate intervention in every trivial affair. On the contrary, its care is general rather than particular, in the determination of long-term phases rather than day-by-day events. Its intervention, if that does occur, will be occasioned by or will precipitate a crisis.

§

If we are to think correctly, we cannot stop with thinking of the Overself as being only within us. After this idea has become firmly established for its metaphysical and devotional value, we must complete the concept by thinking of the Overself as being also without us. If in the first concept it occupies a point in space, in the second one it is beyond all considerations of place.

§

When we realize that the intellect can put forth as many arguments against this theme as for it, we realize that there is in the end only one perfect proof of the Overself's existence. The Overself must prove itself. This can come about faintly through the intuition or fully through the mystical experience.

§

It would be unreasonable to expect anyone to give up his worldly attachments until he sees something more worthwhile. Consequently his soul gives him a foretaste, as it were, through these ecstatic moments and brief enlightenments, of its own higher values.

§

The point which has to be made is that these glimpses are *not* supernatural superhuman and solely religious experiences. When scientific psychology has advanced to the point where it really understands the human being in all his height and depth, and not merely his surface, it will see this.

§

Although he is normally quite unconscious of this connection with the Overself, once at least in a lifetime there is a flash which *visits* him and breaks the unconsciousness. He has a glimpse of his highest possibility. But the clearness and intensity of this glimpse depend upon his receptivity. They may amount to little or much.

§

Many people without pretensions to mystical knowledge or belief have had this experience, this glimpse of timeless loveliness, through Nature, art, music, or even for no apparent reason at all.

§

Without learning, studying, or practising yoga, Heisenberg, famed nuclear physicist, formulator of the Law of Indeterminacy, unwittingly entered what is a high goal to yogis, Nirvikalpa Samadhi. This happened at times at the end of the deepest abstract thinking about his subject. Thoughts themselves ceased to be active. He found himself in the Stillness of the Void. He knew then, and knows today, his spiritual being.

§

Those who have followed the Quest in previous lives will generally receive a glimpse at least twice during the present one. They will receive it in early life during their teens or around the threshold of adult life. This will inspire them to seek anew. They will receive it again in late life during the closing years of the reincarnation. This will be bestowed as a Grace of the Overself. Those aspirants who bemoan the loss of their early glimpse should remind themselves, in hours of depression, that it will recur before they leave the body. In addition to those glimpses which attend the opening and closing years of a lifetime, a number of others may be had during the intervening period as a direct consequence and reward of the efforts, disciplines, aspirations, and self-denials practised in that time.

§

What are the signs whereby he shall know that this is an authentic glimpse of reality? First, it is and shall remain ever present. There is no future in it and no past. Second, the pure spiritual experience comes without excitement, is reported without exaggeration, and needs no external authority to authenticate it.

§

Every man who passes through this experience and holds its memory, verifies for himself that there is an Infinite Life-Power pervading the entire universe—also that it is ever present, perfectly wise, and all-knowing. Its point of contact with him is his Overself.

§

Yes it is a wonderful feeling, this which accompanies a glimpse of the higher self; but when it is also merged with a knowing, a positive perception beyond the need of discussion, interpretation, formulation, or judgement, it gives the philosophical seeker a certitude which is like a benediction.

§

In that sudden moment of spiritual awareness, or that longer period of spiritual ecstasy, he identifies himself no more with the projection from Mind but with pure Mind itself. In that severance from its projection, the shadow becomes the sun.

§

In this mysterious moment the two are one. He no longer abides with the mere images of reality. He is now in the authentic world of reality itself.

§

I remember the first time I had this astonishing experience. I was fond of disappearing from London whenever the weather allowed and wandering alongside the river Thames in its more picturesque country parts. If the day was sunny I would stretch my feet out, lie down in the grass, pull out my notebook and pen from my pocket—knowing that thoughts would eventually arise that would have for me an instructive or even revelatory nature, apart from those ordinary ones which were merely expressive. One day, while I was waiting for these thoughts to arise, I lost the feeling that I was there at all. I seemed to dissolve and vanish from that place, but not from consciousness. Something was there, a presence, certainly not me, but I was fully aware of it. It seemed to be something of the highest importance, the only thing that mattered. After a few minutes I came back, discovered myself in time and space again; but a great peace had touched me and a very benevolent feeling was still with me. I looked at the trees, the shrubs, the flowers, and the grass and felt a tremendous sympathy with them and then when I thought of other persons a tremendous benevolence towards them.

§

Glimpses vary much in their nature. Some are soft, mild and delicate, quiet and restrained; others are ecstatic, rapturous, and excited. All give some sort of uplift, exaltation, enlightenment, or revelation and also to varying degrees.

§

The glimpse gives him a journey to a land flowing not with milk and honey, but with goodness and beauty, with peace and wisdom. It is the best moment of his life.

§

When a man's consciousness is turned upside-down by a glimpse, when what he thought most substantial is revealed as least so, when his values are reversed and the Good takes on a new definition, he writes that day down as his spiritual birthday.

§

A glimpse may exalt the man and give him inspiration, but above everything else it attests for him the fact that he is fundamentally Spirit. This is the commonest kind of Glimpse but there is another kind which, in addition to doing these things, opens mysterious doors and provides inlooks to the working of secret laws and occult processes in Nature, the world and the life of man. This kind of glimpse may fitly be termed "a revelation."

§

The glimpse does not necessarily have to come to you during meditation, even though the work in meditation helps to bring about its occurrence. It may come at any time.

§

The sudden but gentle drawing away from outer activity to the inner one, "the melting away in the heart," as Oriental mystics call it, felt actually inside the middle-chest region, may make itself felt occasionally, or, in an advanced or regular meditator, every day. In the last case it will tend to appear at around the same hour each time. This is a call which ought to be treated properly with all the reverence it deserves. But before it can be honoured it must be recognized. Its marks of identification must be studied in books, learned from experience, gleaned from the statements of other persons, or obtained from a personal teacher. When it comes, the man should heed the signal, drop whatever he is doing, and obey the unuttered command to turn inwards, to practise remembrance, or to enter meditation.

§

The significant points in this matter are three: first, it is a call to be recognized and understood; second, it is a command from the highest authority to be obeyed instantly, as disregard brings its own punishment, which is that the call may not come again; third, it is an offer of grace. If the call is heeded and its meaning known or intuited, the aspirant should first of all arrest his movements and remain utterly frozen, as if posing for a portrait painter. Let the mind be blank, held as empty of thoughts as possible. After a while, when adjusted to this sudden suspension of activity, he may with extreme slowness and with utmost gentleness assume a bodily posture where he will be more relaxed and more comfortable, or perhaps even a formal meditation posture. He may then shut his eyes or let them stay in a steady gaze as if he were transfixed, or he may alternate with both according to the urge from within. If everything else is dropped and all these conditions are fulfilled, then a successful meditation bringing on a spiritual glimpse is sure to follow.

§

The holy feelings generated by the Glimpse ought to be protected against the world's disintegrating power and shielded against your own tendency to dissipate them by hasty violent movements or needless irrelevant chatter.

§

The concentration upon the glimpse must be full, complete, and sustained. If, for only a single moment, he allows his attention to be diverted toward some outer thing or person, or to be divided with some inner idea, the glimpse may instantly disappear.

§

The Glimpse will be at its best when his ego is not present to interfere with it. Such interference can not only come from its misinterpretations and distortions, against which philosophy so constantly warns its disciples, but also from the self-consciousness which wants him to notice how the experience is happening, to analyse what effect it is having, and to observe the reactions of other people to it. All these may be done but not then, not at the same time as the glimpse itself. Instead, they may be studied afterwards, when his consciousness has resumed its ordinary state. During the glimpse, he must let himself be completely surrendered to it.

§

During such unforgettable moments the Soul will speak plainly, if silently, to him. It may tell him about his true relationship to the universe and to his fellow creatures. It will certainly tell him about Itself. It may separate him from his body and let him gaze down upon it as from a height, long enough to permit him to comprehend that the flesh is quite the poorest and least significant part of him. And perhaps best of all it will certainly fill him with the assurance that after his return to the world of lonely struggle and quick forgetfulness, It will still remain beside and behind him.

§

It is a state of exquisite tenderness, of love welling up from an inner centre and radiating outward in all directions. If other human beings or animal creatures come within his contact at the time, they become recipients of this love without exception. For then no enemies are recognized, none are disliked, and it is not possible to regard anyone as repulsive.

§

We cannot see the Truth and still be what we were before we saw it. That is why Truth comes in glimpses, for we cannot sustain staying away from ourselves too long, that is to say, from our egos.

§

There are three stages in each glimpse. The initial one brings a soft feeling of its gentle approach. The second carries the man to its peak of upliftment, enlightenment, and peace. The final one draws him down again into a fading glow which occupies the mind's background and later survives only in memory.

§

A passing sign of progress in arousing latent forces and a physical indication that he is on the eve of noteworthy mystical experience may be a sudden unexpected vibratory movement in the region of the abdomen, in the solar plexus. It usually comes when he has been relaxed for a short time from the daily cares, or after retiring to bed for the night. The diaphragmatic muscle will appear to tremble violently and something will seem to surge to and fro like a snake behind the solar plexus. This bodily agitation will soon subside and be followed by a pleasant calm and out of this calm there will presently arise a sense of unusual power, of heightened control over the animal nature and human self. With this there may also come a clear intuition about some truth needed at the time and a revelatory expansion of consciousness into supersensual reality.

§

The glimpse also does in part for a man what initiation did in some ancient mystical institutions. It sets him on the road of a new life, a life more earnestly and more consciously devoted to the quest of the Overself. It silently bids him dedicate, or rededicate anew, the remainder of his life on earth to this undertaking. It is a baptism with inner light more far-reaching than the baptism with physical water.

§

The insight, once caught, and however briefly, will leave behind a calm discontent with the triviality of ordinary life, a lucid recognition of its pathetic futility and emptiness, as well as a calm dissatisfaction with the man himself.

§

Once he has attained this inner realization, the student should cling persistently to it, for the world's multifarious forces will come to hear of it and seek to drag him away.

§

If he is tempted by these sudden glimpses to enquire whether there is a method or technique whereby they may be repeated at will, he will find that there is and that it is called meditation. If he wishes to go farther and enquire whether his whole life could continuously enjoy them all the time, the answer is that it could and that to bring it about he needs to follow a way of life called The Quest.

§

In spite of itself the ego is drawn more and more to the spiritual grandeur revealed by these glimpses. Its ties to selfishness, animality, and materiality are loosened. Finally it comes to see that it is standing in its own way and light and then lets itself be effaced.

§

Another purpose of these glimpses is to show him how ignorant of truth he really is, and, having so shown, to stimulate his effort to get rid of this ignorance. For they will light up the fanciful or opinionative nature of so much that he hitherto took to be true.

§

It is important to remember that such experiences may be expected only rarely in most cases, perhaps once or twice in a lifetime, if the person is not consciously on the quest. It is natural to hope that it will be repeated. The first glimpse is given to show the way, to throw light on the path ahead, to give direction and goal to the person. But if the glimpse is only temporary and rare, the metaphysical understanding to be derived from it is the permanent benefit. So seek to get and clarify the understanding.

§

That glimpse is his initiation into the spiritual life and therefore into the sacrificial life. It is but the first step in a long process wherein he will have to part with his lower tendencies, give up his ignoble passions, surrender his baser inclinations, and renounce egoistic views.

§

Under the emotional thrill of a religious conversion, many people have thought themselves saved and have believed they live in Christ. Yet how many of them have later fallen away! They thought the conversion was enough to bring about a permanent result, whereas it was only the first step toward such a result in reality. The same situation holds with those who have undergone the emotional thrill of a mystical experience. The illumination they have achieved is not the end of the road for them but the beginning. It gives them a picture of the goal and a glimpse of the course to it. It gives them right direction and an inspirational impetus to move towards it. But still it is only the first step, not the last one. They should beware of the personal ego's vanity which would tell them otherwise, or of its deceitfulness, which would tell it to others.

§

If illumination does not become permanent, if it does not stay with its host, that is because it does not find a proper place within him for such abiding stay. His heart is still too impure, his character still too imperfect for the consciousness of the Overself to associate constantly with him.

§

Islamic mystics called Sufis differentiate between glimpses, which they call "states," and permanent advances on the path, which they call "stations." The former are described as being not only temporary but also fragmentary, while the latter are described as bearing results which cannot be lost. There are three main stations along the path. The first is annihilation of the ego; the second is rebirth in the Overself; and the third is fully grown union with the Overself. The Sufis assert that this final state can never be reached without the Grace of the Higher Power and that it is complete, lasting, and unchangeable.

§

It must be remembered that the glimpse is not the goal of life. It is a happening, something which begins and ends, but something which is of immense value in contributing to the philosophic life, its day-to-day consciousness, its ordinary stabilized nature. Philosophic life is established continuously and permanently in the divine presence; the glimpse comes and goes within that presence. The glimpse is exceptional and exciting; but *sahaja*, the established state, is ordinary, normal, every day. The glimpse tends to withdraw us from activity, even if only for a few moments, whereas *sahaja* does not have to stop its outward activity.

§

He must finish what he has started. He must go on until the peace, the understanding, the strength, and the benevolence of these rare uplifted moods have become a continuous presence within him.

§

It is possible for a man who knows of the Quest only through emotional faith or intellectual conviction to turn aside from it for the remainder of his incarnation, but it is not possible for a man who has enjoyed this Glimpse to do so. He may try—and some do—but each day of such alienation will be a haunted day. The ghost will not leave him alone until he returns.

§

Where the Greek Orthodox Church regards the Light experience as the highest point reachable by man, the Indian Philosophic Teaching regards it as the last stage before the highest. For anything which is "seen" implies the existence of a "seer" as separate from it. This is not less so even in the case of the Holy Light. Not seeing but be-ing is the final experience according to this Teaching. "You have to go beyond seeing and find out who is the 'I' who experiences this light," said Ramana Maharshi to a disciple.

§

Seeing the Light in front of him is one state; being merged into it is another, and superior.

§

What, it has been asked, if I get no glimpses? What can I do to break this barren monotonous dreary and sterile spiritual desert of my existence? The answer is if you cannot meditate successfully go to nature, where she is quiet or beautiful; go to art where it is majestic, exalting; go to hear some great soul speak, whether in private talk or public address; go to literature, find a great inspired book written by someone who has had the glimpses.

§

If the glimpse slips away from the great calm, where does it go? Into the ever-active outward-turned thinking movement.

§

23

ADVANCED CONTEMPLATION

Ant's long path—Bird's direct path—
Exercises for practice—Contemplative stillness—
"Why Buddha smiled"—Heavenly Way exercise—
Serpent's Path exercise—Void as contemplative experience

He should remember that there are two approaches to the Quest and both have to be used. There is the Long Path of self-improvement, self-purification, and self-effort; and there is the Short Path of forgetting the self entirely and directing his mind towards the Goal, towards the One Real Life, by constant remembrance of it and by practising self-identification with it. If he uses the first approach, he can progress to a certain point. But by bringing in the second approach, the Higher Power is brought in too and comes to his help with Grace.

§

The Short Path advocates who decry the need of the Long Path altogether because, being divine in essence, we have only to realize what we already are, are misled by their own half-truth. What we actually find in the human situation is that we are only potentially divine. The work of drawing out and developing this potential still needs to be done. This takes time, discipline, and training, just as the work of converting a seed into a tree takes time.

§

The limitation of the Long Path is that it is concerned only with thinning down, weakening, and reducing the ego's strength. It is not concerned with totally deflating the ego. Since this can be done only by studying the ego's nature metaphysically, seeing its falsity, and recognizing its illusoriness, which is not even done by the Short Path, then all the endeavours of the Short Path to practise self-identification with the Overself are merely using imagination and suggestion to create a new mental state that, while imitating the Overself's state, does not actually transcend the ego-mind but exists within it still. So a third phase becomes necessary, the phase of getting rid of the ego altogether; this can be done only by the final dissolving operation of Grace, which the man has to request and to which he has to give his consent. To summarize the entire process, the Long Path leads to the Short Path, and the Short Path leads to the Grace of an unbroken egoless consciousness.

§

Those who depend solely on the Short Path without being totally ready for it take too much for granted and make too much of a demand. This is arrogance. Instead of opening the door, such an attitude can only close it tighter. Those who depend solely on the Long Path take too much on their shoulders and burden themselves with a purificatory work which not even an entire lifetime can bring to an end. This is futility. It causes them to evolve at a slower rate. The wiser and philosophic procedure is to couple together the work on both paths in a regularly alternating rhythm, so that during the course of a year two totally different kinds of results begin to appear in the character and the behaviour, in the consciousness and the understanding. After all, we see this cycle everywhere in Nature, and in every other activity she compels us to conform to it. We see the alternation of sleep with waking, work with rest, and day with night.

§

The Long Path is taught to beginners and others in the earlier and middle stages of the quest. This is because they are ready for the idea of self-improvement and not for the higher one of the unreality of the self. So the latter is taught on the Short Path, where attention is turned away from the little self and from the idea of perfecting it, to the essence, the real being.

§

What is the key to the Short Path? It is threefold. First, stop searching for the Overself since it follows you wherever you go. Second, believe in its Presence, with and within you. Third, keep on trying to understand its truth until you can abandon further thoughts about it. You cannot acquire what is already here. So drop the ego's false idea and affirm the real one.

§

This is the concept which governs the Short Path: that he is in the Stillness of central being all the time whether he knows it or not, that he has never left and can never leave it. And this is so, even in a life passed in failure and despair.

§

The Long Path devotee is concerned with learning how to concentrate his thoughts in the practice of meditation, and later even with meditation itself, to some degree, so far as it is an activity among ideas and images. The Short Path devotee is not. He is concerned with direct union with the object of all these efforts, that is, with the Overself. So he substitutes contemplation for meditation, the picture-free, idea-free purity of the mind's original state for the image- and thought-filled density of its ordinary state.

§

Continuous remembrance of the Stillness, accompanied by automatic entry into it, is the sum and substance of the Short Path, the key practice to success. At all times, under all circumstances, this is to be done. That is to say, it really belongs to and is part of the daily and ordinary routine existence. Consequently, whenever it is forgotten, the practitioner must note his failure and make instant correction. The inner work is kept up until it goes on by itself.

§

The Short Path is, in essence, the ceaseless practice of remembering to stay in the Stillness, for this is what he really is in his innermost being and where he meets the World-Mind.

§

The Short Path uses (a) *thinking*: metaphysical study of the Nature of Reality; (b) *practice*: constant remembrance of Reality during everyday life in the world; (c) *meditation*: surrender to the thought of Reality in stillness. You will observe that in all these three activities *there is no reference to the personal ego*. There is no thinking of, remembering, or meditating upon oneself, as there is with the Long Path.

§

A part of the Short Path work is intellectual study of the metaphysics of Truth. This is needful to expose the ego's own illusoriness, as a preliminary to transcending it, and to discriminate its ideas, however spiritual, from reality.

§

The essence of the matter is that he should be constantly attentive to the intuitive feeling in the heart and not let himself be diverted from it by selfishness, emotion, cunning, or passion.

§

It is quite true, as the extremist advocates of the Short Path, like Zen, say, that this is all that is really needed, that no meditation (in the ordinary sense), no discipline, no moral striving, and no study are required to gain enlightenment. We are now as divine as we ever shall be. There is nothing to be added to us; no evolution or development of our real self is possible. But what these advocates overlook is that, in the absence of the labours listed, the Short Path can succeed only if certain essential conditions are available. First, a teaching master must be found. It will not be enough to find an illumined man. We will feel peace and uplift in his presence, but these will fade away after leaving his presence. Such a man will be a phenomenon to admire and an inspiration to remember, not a guide to instruct, to warn, and to lead from step to step. Second, we must be able to live continuously with the teaching master until we have finished the course and reached the goal. Few aspirants have the freedom to fulfil the second condition, for circumstances are hard to control, and fewer still have the good fortune to fulfil the first one, for a competent, willing, and suitably circumstanced teaching master is a rarity. These are two of the reasons why philosophy asserts that a combination of both the Long and Short Paths is the only practical means for a modern Western aspirant to adopt. If, lured by the promise of sudden attainment or easy travelling, he neglects the Long Path, the passage of time will bring him to self-deception or frustration or disappointment or moral decline. For his negative characteristics will rise and overpower him, the lack of preparation and development will prevent him from realizing in experience the high-level teachings he is trying to make his own, while the impossibility of balancing himself under such circumstances will upset or rob him of whatever gains he may still make.

§

It is said by the advocates of the Short method that the power of the Spirit can remove our faults instantaneously and even implant in us the opposite virtues. That this has happened in some cases is made clear by the study of the spiritual biography of certain persons. But those cases are relatively few and those persons relatively advanced. This miraculous transformation, this full forgiveness of sins, does not happen to most people or to ordinary unadvanced people. A world-wide observation of them shows that such people have to elevate themselves by their own efforts first. When they embrace the Short method without this balancing work done by themselves upon themselves, they are likely to fall into the danger of refusing to see their faults and weaknesses which are their worst enemies, as well as the danger of losing the consciousness of sin. Those who fail to save themselves from these perils become victims of spiritual pride and lose that inner humility which is the essential price of being taken over by the Overself.

§

The Long Path is devoted to clearing away the obstructions in man's nature and to attacking the errors in his character. The Short Path is devoted to affirmatives, to the God-power as essence and in manifestation. It is mystical. It shows how the individual can come into harmonious relation with the Overself and the World-Idea. The first path shows seekers how to think rightly; the second gives power to those thoughts.

§

The Long Path is more easily practised while engaged in the world, the Short Path while in retreat from it. The experiences which the vicissitudes of worldly life bring him also develop him, provided he is a Quester. But the lofty themes of his meditations on the Short Path require solitary places and unhurried leisurely periods.

§

On the Long Path he trains himself to detect and reject the lower impulses, egoisms, and desires. On the Short Path he trains himself to be open to the higher impulses or intuitions and to absorb them.

§

It is as sure as the sun's rising that if the mass of people are taught that good is no better than evil, both being merely relative, or no more valuable than evil, both being concerned with the illusory ego, they will fall into immorality, wickedness, and disaster. To teach them the Short Path before they have acquired sufficient disciplinary habits from the Long one will only degrade them.

§

Those who take to the Short Path have to encounter the risk of self-deception, of falling victims to the belief in their own imaginary spiritual attainments.

§

The danger in both cases is in limiting one's efforts to the single path. It may invite disaster to give up trying to improve character just because one has taken to the Short Path. Yet it may invite frustration to limit one's efforts to such improvement. The wise balance which philosophy suggests is not to stop with either the Short or the Long Path but to use both together.

§

It might be said with some truth that the various Long Path processes are based upon the use of willpower whereas the Short Path ones are based upon auto-suggestion. The former employ the conscious mind in directed effort, whereas the latter implant ideas in the subconscious mind while it is in a relaxed state.

§

In the first and second stages of the Short Path, his aim is to set himself free from the egoism in which his consciousness is confined.

§

Wherever one is, whatever the place, or whoever the persons, one should think oneself to be in the divine presence.

§

The man on the Short Path moves forward directly to fulfil his objective. Instead of working by slow degrees toward the control of thoughts, he seeks to recollect the fact that the sacred Overself is present in his mind at this very moment, that It lives within him right now, and not only as a goal to be attained in some distant future. The more he understands this fact and holds attention to it, the more he finds himself able to feel the great calm which follows its realization, the more his thoughts automatically become still in consequence.

§

It is objected, why search at all if one really is the Overself? Yes, there comes a time when the deliberate purposeful search for the Overself has to be abandoned for this reason. Paradoxically, it is given up many times, whenever he has a Glimpse, for at such moments he knows that he always was, is, and will be the Real, that there is nothing new to be gained or searched for. Who should search for what? But the fact remains that past tendencies of thought rise up after every Glimpse and overpower the mind, causing it to lose this insight and putting it back on the quest again. While this happens he must continue the search, with this difference, that he no longer searches blindly, as in earlier days, believing that he is an ego trying to transform itself into the Overself, trying to reach a new attainment in time by evolutionary stages. No! through the understanding of the Short Path he searches knowingly, not wanting another experience since both wanting and experiencing put him out of the essential Self. He thinks and acts as if he is that Self, which puts him back into It. It is a liberation from time-bound thinking, a realization of timeless fact.

§

Why should the Short Path be a better means of getting Grace than the Long one? There is not only the reason that it is not occupied with the ego but also that it continually keeps up remembrance of the Overself. It does this with a heart that gives, and is open to receive, love. It thinks of the Overself throughout the day. Thus, it not only comes closer to the source from which Grace is being perpetually radiated, but it also is repeatedly inviting Grace with each loving remembrance.

§

It could well be said that the essence of the Short Path is remembering who he is, what he is, and then attending to this memory as often as possible.

§

One of the most valuable forms of yoga is the yoga of constant remembrance. Its subject may be a mystical experience, intuition, or idea. In essence it is really an endeavour to insert the transcendental atmosphere into the mundane life.

§

We keep nearly all our attention all the day on ourselves and only a slight part of it on the Overself. It is needful to change this situation if we want a higher state of consciousness. This is why the exercises in remembrance are much more valuable than their simplicity suggests.

§

The method of this exercise is to maintain uninterruptedly and unbrokenly the remembrance of the soul's nearness, the soul's reality, the soul's transcendence. The goal of this exercise is to become wholly possessed by the soul itself.

§

Concentrate on reliving in intense memorized detail former moments of egoless illumination.

§

He is wrong to object that you can't hold two different thoughts at the same time and that hence you can't remember God and attend to worldly details simultaneously. You can. God is *not* a thought, but an awareness on a higher level. Mind does not hold God. Certainly, mind can't have two objects of thought, for they are in duality, but they can be held by God's presence. Only here is the union of subject and object possible. All other thoughts are in duality.

§

If meditation may have unfortunate results when its concentrative power is applied negatively or selfishly, contemplation—its higher phase—may have similar results when its passive condition is entered without previous purification or preparation. Michael de Molinos knew this well and therefore put a warning in the preface of his book *The Spiritual Guide* which treats with the authority of an expert the subject of contemplation. "The doctrine of this book," he announced, "instructs not all sorts of persons, but those only who keep the senses and passions well mortified, who have already advanced and made progress in Prayer."

§

This constant remembrance of the higher self becomes in time like a kind of holy communion.

§

The practice of extending love towards all living creatures brings on ecstatic states of cosmic joy.

§

These exercises are for those who are not mere beginners in yoga. Such are necessarily few. The different yogas are successive and do not oppose each other. The elementary systems prepare the student to practise the more advanced ones. Anybody who tries to jump all at once to the philosophic yoga without some preliminary ripening may succeed if he has the innate capacity to do so but is more likely to fail altogether through his very unfamiliarity with the subject. Hence these ultramystic exercises yield their full fruit only if the student has come prepared either with previous meditational experience or with mentalist metaphysical understanding—or better still with both. Anyone who starts them, because of their apparent simplicity, without such preparation must not blame the exercises if he fails to obtain results. They are primarily intended for the use of advanced students of metaphysics on the one hand or of advanced practitioners of meditation on the other. This is because the first class will understand correctly the nature of the Mind-in-itself which they should strive to attain thereby, whilst the second class will have had sufficient self-training not to set up artificial barriers to the influx when it begins.

§

Although the writer regards it as unnecessary and inadvisable to disclose in a work of popular instruction those further secrets of a more advanced practice which act as short cuts to attainment for those who are ready to receive them, suffice to say that whoever will take up this path and go through the disciplinary practices here given faithfully and willingly until he is sufficiently advanced to profit by the further initiation of those secrets, may rest assured that at the right time he will be led to someone or else someone will be led to him and the requisite initiation will then be given him. Such is the wonderful working of the universal soul which broods over this earth of ours and over all mankind. No one is too insignificant to escape its notice just as no one is deprived of the illumination which is his due; but everything in nature is graduated, so the hands of the planetary clock must go round and the right hour be struck ere the aspirant makes the personal contact which in nine cases out of ten is the preliminary to entry into a higher realization of these spiritual truths.

§

Being based on the mentalist principles of the hidden teaching, they were traditionally regarded as being beyond yoga. Hence these exercises have been handed down by word of mouth only for thousands of years and, in their totality, have not, so far as our knowledge extends, been published before, whether in any ancient Oriental language like Sanskrit or in any modern language like English. They are not yoga exercises in the technical sense of that term and they cannot be practised by anyone who has never before practised yoga.

§

There is a single basic principle which runs like a thread through all these higher contemplation exercises. It is this: if we can desert the thoughts of particular things, the images of particular objects raised by the senses in the field of consciousness, and if we can do this with complete and intelligent understanding of what we are doing and why we are doing it, then such desertion will be followed by the appearance of its own accord of the element of pure undifferentiated Thought itself; the latter will be identified as our innermost self.

§

The student must for minutes deliberately recall himself from the external multitude of things to their single mental ground in himself. He must remind himself that although he sees everything as an objective picture, this picture is inseparable from his own mind. He has to transcend the world-idea within himself not by trying to blot it out but by thoroughly comprehending its mentalist character. He must temporarily become an onlooker, detached in spirit but just as capable in action.

§

Although the aspirant has now awakened to his witness-self, found his "soul," and thus lifted himself far above the mass of mankind, he has not yet accomplished the full task set him by life. A further effort still awaits his hand. He has yet to realize that the witness-self is only a *part* of the All-self. So his next task is to discover that he is not merely the witness of the rest of existence but essentially of one stuff with it. He has, in short, by further meditations to realize his oneness with the entire universe in its real being. He must meditate on his witness-self as being in its essence the infinite All. Thus the ultramystic exercises are graded into two stages, the second being more advanced than the first. The banishment of thoughts reveals the inner self whereas the reinstatement of thoughts without losing the newly gained consciousness reveals the All-inclusive universal self. The second feat is the harder.

§

We are meditating on something which will not arise and disappear, as ideas do and as material forms do, on something which is not ephemeral. Because that which vanishes contradicts its own arisal, we seek for that which does not contradict itself. Hence this kind of meditation which brings contemplation into action, sleep into wakefulness, has been called by the ancients, "The Yoga of the Uncontradictable."

§

It is not the *objects* of conscious attention which are to be allowed to trap the mind forever and divert the man from his higher duty. It is the *consciousness* itself which ought to engage his interest and hold his deepest concentration.

§

The adverse force present in his ego will continually try to draw him away from positive concentration on pure being into negative consideration of lower topics. Each time he must become aware of what is happening, of the change in trend, and resist it at once. Out of this wearying conflict will eventually be born fresh inner strength if he succeeds, but only more mental weakness if he fails. For meditation is potently creative.

§

When we comprehend that the pure essence of mind is reality, then we can also comprehend the rationale of the higher yoga which would settle attention in pure thought itself rather than in finite thoughts. When this is done the mind becomes vacant, still, and utterly undisturbed. This grand calm of nonduality comes to the philosophic yogi alone and is not to be confused with the lower-mystical experience of emotional ecstasy, clairvoyant vision, and inner voice. For in the latter the ego is present as its enjoyer, whereas in the former it is absent because the philosophic discipline has led to its denial. The lower type of mystic must make a special effort to gain his ecstatic experience, but the higher type finds it arises spontaneously without personal effort at all. The first is in the realm of duality, whilst the second has realized nonduality.

§

There is, in this third stage, a condition that never fails to arouse the greatest wonder when initiation into it begins. In certain ways it corresponds to, and mentally parallels, the condition of the embryo in a mother's womb. Therefore, it is called by mystics who have experienced it "the second birth." The mind is drawn so deeply into itself and becomes so engrossed in itself that the outer world vanishes utterly. The sensation of being enclosed all round by a greater presence, at once protective and benevolent, is strong. There is a feeling of being completely at rest in this soothing presence. The breathing becomes very quiet and hardly perceptible. One is aware also that nourishment is being mysteriously and rhythmically drawn from the universal Life-force. Of course, there is no intellectual activity, no thinking, and no need of it. Instead, there is a k-n-o-w-i-n-g. There are no desires, no wishes, no wants. A happy peacefulness, almost verging on bliss, as human love might be without its passions and pettinesses, holds one in magical thrall. In its freedom from mental working and perturbation, from passional movement and emotional agitation, the condition bears something of infantile innocence. Hence Jesus' saying: "Except ye become as little children ye shall in no wise enter the Kingdom of Heaven." But essentially it is a return to a spiritual womb, to being born again into a new world of being where at the beginning he is personally as helpless, as weak, and as dependent as the physical embryo itself.

§

Do not carry your own troubles or your temptations or other people's troubles and situations straight into your meditation. There is a proper time and place for their consideration under a mystical light or for their presentation to a mystical power. But that time and place is not at the *beginning* of the meditation period. It is rather towards the end. All meditations conducted on the philosophic ideal should end with the thoughts of others, with remembrance of their spiritual need, and with a sending-out of the light and grace received to bless individuals who need such help. At the beginning your aim should be to forget your lower self, to rise above it. Only after you have felt the divine visitation, only towards the end of your practice period should your aim be to bring the higher self to the help of the lower one, or your help and blessing to other embodied selves. If, however, you attempt this prematurely, if you are not willing to relinquish the personal life even for a few minutes, then you will get nothing but your own thought back for your pains.

§

The inner movement is like no other which he has experienced for it must guide itself, must move forward searchingly into darkness without knowing where it will arrive. He must take some chances here, yet he need not be afraid. They will be reasonable and safe chances if he abides by the advice given in these pages.

§

Only in perfect stillness of the mind, when all discursive and invading thoughts are expelled, can the true purity be attained and the ego expelled with them.

§

If he wishes to enter the stage of contemplation, he must let go of every thought as it rises, however high or holy it seems, for it is sure to bring associated thoughts in its train. However interesting or attractive these bypaths may be at other times, they are now just that—bypaths. He must rigidly seek the Void.

§

Contemplation is attained when your thinking about a spiritual truth or about the spiritual goal suddenly ceases of itself. The mind then enters into a perfectly still and rapt condition.

§

The resultant condition is no negative state. Those who imagine that the apparent blankness which ensues is similar to the blankness of the spiritualistic medium do not understand the process. The true mystic and the hapless medium are poles apart. The first is supremely positive; the second is supinely negative. Into the stilled consciousness of the first ultimately steps the glorious divinity that is our True Self, the world-embracing shining One; into the blanked-out consciousness of the second steps some insignificant person, as stupid or as sensible as he was on earth, but barely more; or worse, there comes one of those dark and malignant entities who prey upon human souls, who will drag the unfortunate medium into depths of falsehood and vice, or obsess her to the point of suicide.

§

It is not a dreamy or drowsy state. He is more lucidly and vitally conscious than ever before.

§

In the third stage, contemplation, the mind ceases to think and simply, without words, worships loves and adores the Divine.

§

It is not just ceasing to think although it prerequires that, but something more: it is also a positive alertness to the Divine Presence.

§

This last stage, contemplation, is neither deep reflective thinking nor self-hypnotic trance. It is intense awareness, without the intrusion of the little ego or the large world.

§

The principle behind it is that once this contact with the Overself has been established during the third stage, it is only necessary first, to prolong, and second, to repeat the contact for spiritual evolution to be assured.

§

Every state other than this perfect stillness is a manifestation of the ego, even if it be an inner mystical "experience." To be in the Overself one must be out of the ego, and consequently out of the ego's experience, thoughts, fancies, or images. All these may have their fit place and use at other times but not when the consciousness is to be raised completely to the Overself.

§

Follow this invisible thread of tender holy feeling, keep attention close to it, do not let other things distract or bring you away from it. For at its end is entry into Awareness.

§

The traditional Buddhist belief that all happiness must in the end change into unhappiness is not a cheerful one. It need never be taken too literally as being universally true, nor by itself alone, for there are counterweighting truths. When Buddha brought to an end the meditation which culminated in final enlightenment, dawn was just breaking.

The last star which vanished with the night and first one which he saw as he raised his head was Venus. What was his inner state, then? Did it synchronize with the reputed planetary influence of Venus—joyous and happy felicity—or with the gloomy view of life which tradition later associated with Buddhism? Who has had a glimpse of those higher states, felt their serenity, and can doubt it was the first? The Overself is not subjected to suffering. But this is not to say that it is bubbling with happiness. It is rather like an immensely deep ocean, perfectly tranquil below the surface. That tranquillity is its ever-present condition and is a true joyousness which ordinary people rarely know. This is what Buddha felt. This is what he called NIRVĀNA.

§

If we did not know that behind it there was Nirvana, we might regard the slight pleasant smile of Gautama as ambiguous. But we know that not only was he happy to have escaped from the trap of ephemeral human affairs; he was happy because he had entered an entirely new depth and dimension of consciousness.

§

I have often been asked what I thought was the secret of Buddha's smile. It is—it can only be—that he smiled at himself for searching all those years for what he already possessed.

§

On this Short Path he searches into the meaning of Being, of being himself and of being-in-itself, until he finds its finality. Until this search is completed, he accepts the truth, passed down to him by the Enlightened Ones, that in his inmost essence he is Reality. This leads to the logical consequence that he should disregard personal feelings which continue from past tendencies, habits, attitudes, and think and act as if he were himself an enlightened one! For now he knows by evidence, study, and reflection that the Overself is behind, and is the very source of, his ego, just as he knows by the experience of feeling during his brief Glimpses. Bringing this strong conviction into thought and act and attitude is the "Heavenly Way" exercise, a principal one on the Short Path.

§

He pretends to be what he aims to become: thinks, speaks, acts, behaves as a master of emotion, desire, ego because he would be one. But he should play this game for, and to, himself alone, not to enlarge himself in others' eyes, lest he sow the seed of a great vanity.

§

The "As-If" exercise is not merely pretense or make-believe. It requires penetrative study and sufficient understanding of the high character and spiritual consciousness in the part to be played, the role to be enacted, the auto-suggestion to be realized.

§

We must move from consciousness to its hidden reality, the mind-essence which is alone true consciousness because it shines by its own and not by a borrowed light. When we cease to consider Mind as this or that particular mind but as all-Mind; when we cease to consider Thought as this thought or that but as the common power which makes thinking possible; and when we cease to consider this or that idea as such but as pure Idea, we apprehend the absolute existence through profound insight. Insight, at this stage, has no particular object to be conscious of. In this sense it is a Void. When the personal mind is stripped of its memories and anticipations, when all sense-impressions and thoughts entirely drop away from it, then it enters the realm of empty unnameable Nothingness. It is really a kind of self-contemplation. But this self is not finite and individual, it is cosmic and infinite.

§

During the gap—infinitesimal though it be—between two thoughts, the ego vanishes. Hence it may truly be said that with each thought it reincarnates anew. There is no real need to wait for the series of long-lived births to be passed through before liberation can be achieved. The series of momentary births also offers this opportunity provided a man knows how to use it.

§

Now an extraordinary and helpful fact is that by making Mind the object of our attention, not only does the serenity which is its nature begin to well up of its own accord but its steady unchanging character itself helps spontaneously to repel all disturbing thoughts.

§

All that he knows and experiences are things in this world of the five senses. The Overself is not within their sphere of operation and therefore not to be known and experienced in the same way. This is why the first real entry into it must necessarily be an entry into no-thing-ness. The mystical phenomena and mystical raptures happen merely on the journey to this void.

§

When he attains the state of void, all thoughts cease for then pure Thought thinks itself alone.

§

What we call here the Void, following the Mongolian-Tibetan tradition, is not dissimilar from what Spanish Saint John of the Cross called "complete detachment and emptiness of spirit." It is a casting-out of all impressions from the mind, an elimination of every remembered or imagined experience from it, a turning-away from every idea even psychically referable to the five senses and the ego; finally, even a loss of personal identity.

§

God as MIND fills that void. In being deprived first of his ego and then of his ecstatic emotional union with the Overself, the mystic who is thereby inwardly reduced to a state of nothingness, comes as near to God's *state* as he can. However this does not mean that he comes to God's consciousness.

§

If the consciousness has not previously been prepared, by competent instruction or intuitive understanding, to receive this experience, then the passage out of the body will begin with a delightful sense of dawning liberation but end with a frightful sense of dangerous catastrophe. Both knowledge and courage are needed here, otherwise there will be resistance to the process followed by an abrupt breaking away from it altogether.

§

We may now perceive a further reason why all great teachers have enjoined self-denial. For at this crucial point of perfected concentration, when the senses are still and the world without remote, the mystic must renounce his thoughts in favour of Thought. He can do this only by a final act of surrender whereby his whole sense of personality—all that makes up what he believed to be "I"—is let go as the last of his thoughts to vanish into a Void. He must make the abrupt leap into self-identification with the wide pure impersonal thought-less Thought. He must give up the last of all thoughts—which is the "I" thought—and accept in return whatever may come to him out of the great Unknown. A fear rises up and overcomes him for a time that with this leap he may so endanger his own existence as to plunge into utter annihilation. This naturally makes him cling all the more to his sense of personality. Shall we wonder then, that every student shrinks at this order?

§

Students draw back affrighted at the concept of a great void which leaves them nothing, human or divine, to which they may cling. How much the more will they draw back, not from a mere concept, but from an actual experience through which they must personally pass! Yet this is an event, albeit not the final one on the ultimate ultramystic path, which they can neither avoid nor evade. It is a trial which must be endured, although to the student who has resigned himself to acceptance of the truth whatever face it bears—who has consequently comprehended already the intellectual emptiness of both Matter and Personality—this experience will not assume the form of a trial but rather of an adventure. After such a rare realization, he will emerge a different man. Henceforth he will know that nothing that has shape, nobody who bears a form, no voice save that which is soundless can ever help him again. He will know that his whole trust, his whole hope, and his whole heart are now and forevermore to be surrendered unconditionally to this Void which mysteriously will no longer be a Void for him. For it is God.

§

We must withdraw every thing and thought from the mind except this single thought of trying to achieve the absence of what is not the Absolute. This is called Gnana Yoga: "Neti, Neti" (It is not this), as Sankara called it. And he must go on with this negative elimination until he reaches the stage where a great Void envelops him. If he can succeed in holding resolutely to this Void in sustained concentration—and he will discover it is one of the hardest things in the world to do so—he will abruptly find that it is not a mere mental abstraction but something real, not a dream but the most concrete thing in his experience. Then and then only can he declare positively, "It is *This*." For he has found the Overself.

§

It comes as a state of intense bliss, and then you are your personal self no longer. The world is blotted out; Being alone exists. That Being has neither shape nor form. It is shall we say coexistent with space . . . in it you seem to fulfil the highest purpose of our Being. It is not the Ultimate, but for the sake of your meditation practice you nevertheless may regard it as the Ultimate. You will come back after a while. You cannot stay in it for long. You will come back and when you come back you will come back to the intellect; then you will begin to think very, very slowly at first, and each thought will be full of tremendous meaning, tremendous vitality, tremendous beauty and reality. You will be alive and inspired and you will know that you have had a transcendent experience. You will feel a great joy, and then for some time you may have to live on the memory of this glorious experience. Such experiences do not come often, but they will provide a memory that will act as a positive inspiration to you from time to time.

§

In this experience he finds himself in sheer nothingness. There is not even the comfort of having a personal identity. Yet it is a paradoxical experience for despite the total nothingness, he is neither asleep nor dead nor unconscious. Something *is*, but *what* it is, or how, or anything else about it, stays an unravelled mystery.

§

When all thoughts are extinguished; when even the thought of the quest itself vanishes; when even the final thought of seeking to control thoughts also subsides, then the great battle with the ego can take place. But the last scene of this invisible drama is always played by the Overself. For only when its Grace shoots forth and strikes down this final thought, does success come.

§

Everything that intrudes upon the mental stillness in this highly critical stage must be rejected, no matter how virtuous or how "spiritual" a face it puts on. Only by the lapse of all thought, by the loss of all thinking capacity can he maintain this rigid stillness as it should be maintained. It is here alone that the last great battle will be fought and that the first great fulfilment will be achieved. That battle will be the one which will give the final deathblow to the ego; that fulfilment will be the union with his Overself after the ego's death. Both the battle and the fulfilment must take place within the stillness; they must not be a merely intellectual matter of thought alone nor a merely emotional matter of feeling alone. Here in the stillness both thought and emotion must die and the ego will then lose their powerful support. Therefore here alone is it possible to tackle the ego with any possibility of victory.

§

He separates the thought of his own existence from all other thoughts, then attacks and annuls it by the most penetrating insight he has ever shown.

§

The root-thought which underlies the ego that has to be slain is not that it is separate from all other creatures but that it is separate from the one infinite life-power.

§

He who passes through these deeper phases of the Void can never again call anything or anyone his own. He becomes secretly and spiritually deprived of all personal possessions. This is because he has thoroughly realized the complete immateriality, spacelessness, timelessness, and formlessness of the Real—a realization which consequently leaves him nothing to take hold of, either within the world or within his personality. Not only does the possessive sense fall away from his attitude towards physical things but also towards intellectual ones.

§

In that sacred moment when an awed silence grips the soul, we are undone. The small and narrow bricks with which we have built our house of personal life collapse and tumble to the ground. The things we worked and hungered for slip into the limbo of undesired and undesirable relics. The world of achievement, flickering with the activities of ambition, pales away into the pettiness of a third-rate play.

§

24

THE PEACE WITHIN YOU

Be calm—Practise detachment—Seek the deeper Stillness

The Overself remains always the same and never changes in any way. It is the hunger for this quality, thought of as "peace of mind," which drives men to seek the Overself amid the vicissitudes of health or fortune which they experience.

§

Young souls look for happiness, older ones for peace, calm, and equilibrium.

§

The importance of cultivating calmness is well known in India. The Brahmin youth at puberty when initiated into his caste status and given the sacred thread is taught to make the first sought-for attribute calmness. Why is this? Because it helps a man to achieve self-control and because without it he becomes filled with tensions. These tensions come from the ego and prevent him from responding to intuitive feelings and intuitive ideas. For the student of philosophy it is of course absolutely essential to achieve a composed and relaxed inner habit.

§

It is far subtler than the first ecstasies of a newly made mystic, much more refined than the personal joys of a religious saint. It is deeper, quieter, more relaxed yet, withal exquisite—this peace.

§

To be at peace means to be empty of all desires—a state the ordinary man often ridicules as inhuman or dismisses as impossible. The spiritual seeker goes farther and understands better, so he desires to be without desire—but only to a limited extent. Moreover, some of his desires may be hidden from consciousness. Only the sage, by which I do not mean the saint, is completely free from desires because the empty void thus created is completely filled by the Overself.

§

There is a materialistic serenity and a spiritual serenity. The first comes from the possession of money, property, position, or affection. The other comes from no outward possessions but from inward ones. The first can be shattered at a single blow; the other soon recovers.

§

No pleasure which is brief, sensual, and fugitive is worth exchanging for equanimity and peace, not even if it is multiplied a thousand times during a lifetime's course.

§

To attain knowledge of Brahman, the mind must be held in the prerequisite state of being calm, tranquil, and in equilibrium—not carried away by attachment to anything. *After* this is established, and only then, can you begin enquiry with any hope of success. Unless the mind is balanced you cannot get Brahman.

§

When the I is no longer felt then all the problems and burdens associated with it are also no longer felt. This is the state of inner calm which philosophy seeks to bring about in a man.

§

Holding on to the future in anxiety and apprehension must be abandoned. It must be committed to the higher power completely and faithfully. Calmness comes easily to the man who really trusts the higher power. This is unarguable.

§

After he has learnt to practise inner stillness during the set daily period, he must learn how to carry it into his ordinary activities.

§

Does the phrase "peace of mind" suggest that he will not suffer in a suffering world? This can hardly be true, or even possible. As actual experience, it means that his thoughts are brought under sufficient control to enable him to repel disturbance and to retain sensitivity. The sacred stillness behind them becomes the centre.

§

Do not confuse inner detachment with callous indifference. Do not search after impossible results. A worthy goal for human beings cannot be devoid of human feelings, however elevated they may be: it cannot be a glacial one.

§

Being detached from the world, which philosophy practises, is not the same as being indifferent to the world, which mysticism preaches.

§

This is what he has to learn—and it can be learnt only by personal practice, not from any book—how to keep in beautiful equipoise receptivity to his sacred Centre and efficiency in attending to the world's demands. This is answering Jesus' call to be in the world but not of it. This is the union of busy actuality with central tranquillity.

§

In deepest contemplation, the Nirvikalpa Samadhi of the Indian yogis, both egolessness and blissful peace can be experienced. But it is a temporary state; return to the world must follow, so the quest is not finished. The next step or stage is *application*, putting into the active everyday life this egoless detachment and this satisfying calmness.

§

It is not that he has no likes and dislikes—he is still human enough for them—but that he knows that they are secondary to a true and just view, and that his inner calm must not be disturbed by them.

§

The Buddha tried to teach men to look only on the decay and death and suffering inherent in existence on this physical plane. This is as unfair and as extreme—if isolated—as the teaching of modern American cults which look only on the growth and life and joy which are also inherent here.

§

After the brief hour of peace come the long months of storm: its purity is then contested by opposition, its light by the world's darkness. It is through the varying episodes of experience that he must struggle back to the peace and purity which he saw in vision and felt in meditation. True, he had found them even then but they were still only latent and undeveloped.

§

He becomes not only a spectator of others, but also of himself. If such detachment is seldom seen, it may be because it is seldom sought.

§

Try to do your new duties with inner calmness and outer efficiency. But whatever you are doing, try to keep ever in the background of consciousness the remembrance of the Overself; it will be both a form of yoga and a protective influence.

§

He can find the Overself even if he is caught up in the work of earning a livelihood. But his participation in the world's activity and pleasure will have to be a limited one. Not other men's voices but his own inner voice should say how far he should go along with the world.

§

In the foreground of his thought he deals with practical affairs in a practical way; in the background he remembers always that they are only transitory manifestations of an Element beyond all transitoriness, an Element to which he gives his deepest self. But only when his power of yogic concentration is complete and his knowledge of philosophic truth mature, does the possibility of achieving such harmony arrive—not before.

§

To be detached from the world does not mean to be uninterested in the world.

§

To turn one's mind instantly towards the divinity within, when in the presence of discordant people, is to silence harsh thoughts and to banish hurtful feelings. This frequent turning inward is necessary not only for spiritual growth, but for self-protection. Everything and everyone around us plays a potent influence upon our minds, and this is the best means of detaching oneself from this ceaseless flow of suggestions.

§

Do not be anxious about making provision for the future, if you are in a state of surrender to the Overself; but if you are not, then indeed you need to be anxious. The first relies on a superior power, the second on an inferior. If you will trust the Overself today, it will provide for you tomorrow. If you repose trust in the Overself, it will never let you down and you may go forward in surety. It is indeed the "Father who gives us each day our daily bread."

§

We think that this or that will bring us to the great happiness. But the fortunate few know that in meditation the mind is at its most blissful when it is most empty.

§

Joy and sorrow are, after all, only states of mind. He who gets his mind under control, keeping it unshakeably serene, will not let these usurpers gain entry. They do not come from the best part of himself. They come from the ego. How many persons could learn from him to give up their unhappiness if they learnt that most of their sorrows are mental states, the false ego pitying itself?

§

He may become detached without becoming dehumanized. He may live inwardly apart from the rest of the world without lessening his goodwill and good feeling for others.

§

Those activities which belong to a human existence in the world may still go on, and need not be renounced, although they may be modified or altered in certain ways as intuition directs. His business, professional, family, and social interests need not be given up. His appreciations or creations of art need not be abandoned. His intellectual and cultural life can remain. It is only demanded of him that none of these should be a self-sufficient thing, existing in total disregard of the Whole, of the ultimate and higher purpose which is behind reincarnation.

§

Where others get caught in the whirlpool and spend themselves, their energies, and their years in the piling-up of earthly possessions or the exhausting of earthly pleasures, he says to his instincts: "Thus far, and no farther." For him there is satisfaction in a restrained enjoyment of this world, with enough time and thought and strength for study of the great gospels and the practice of going into the Silence.

§

We must use the material things, yes, and not abandon them; but we must do so without attachment. We may love the good things of life like other men, but we ought not to be in bondage to this love. We should be ready to abandon them at a moment's notice, if need be. It is not things that bind us, not marriage, wealth, or home, but our *craving* for marriage, wealth, or home. And what is such craving in the end but a line of thinking, a series of mental images?

§

He becomes detached when he frees himself from the universally prevalent tendency to connect every experience with the personal ego. Detachment takes him out of himself and saves him from getting emotionally involved in his environment.

§

If he is to keep his inner peace he must always keep the innermost part of himself aloof and deny the world any intimacy with it.

§

The complete happiness which people look forward to as the objective of their life on earth can never be attained. For it is mostly based on things and persons, on what is outside the seeker, and on what is perishing. The happiness which they can truly attain is not of this kind, although it may include and does not exclude this kind. It is mostly based on thoughts and feelings, on what is inside the seeker, and on what is abiding.

The disciple's serenity must remain unbroken whether he succeeds in any enterprise or not, and whether he is able to do so soon or late. For it must not depend on these outward things; it must depend on inward realization of truth. He should do all that is humanly possible to succeed. But, this done, he should follow the *Gita* counsel and leave the results in the hands of God or fate. Thus, whatever the results may be, whether they are favourable or not, he can then accept them and keep his peace of mind.

Even if he is doubtful about a favourable result, he must resign himself to the situation as being truly the Overself's will for him just now. By this acceptance, the sting is removed, and patient resignation to the divine will is practised. He will then have no feeling of frustration but will retain his inner peace unshattered. He should remember, too, that he is not alone. He is under divine protection, for if he is a true disciple he has surrendered himself to his higher self. Therefore let him cast out all worry in connection with the matter, placing it in higher hands and leaving the issues to It. Let him refuse to accept the depression and anxiety. They belong to the ego which he has given up. They have no place in the quest's life of faith, trust, and obedience. Let him resort to prayer to express this humble resignation and trust in superior guidance, this belief in the Overself's manipulation of the results of this matter for what will be really the best in the end.

Fate provides him with difficulties from which it is often not possible to escape. But what *must* be borne may be borne in either of two ways. He may adjust his thinking so that the lessons of the experience are well learnt. Or he may drop it, for he need not carry the burden of anxiety, and remember the story of the man in the railway carriage who kept his trunk on his shoulders instead of putting it down and letting the train carry it. So let him put his "trunk" of trouble down and let the Overself carry it.

§

No other person can bring us happiness if he or she does not possess it in himself or in herself. The romantic urge to seek in a second individual that which neither of the two has, can never find successful fulfilment.

§

The attitude of Emerson, which induced him to call himself "a professor of the science of Joy," is more attractive than that of Schopenhauer, who taught the futility of life, proclaimed the vanity of existence, and spread the mood of despair. Emerson declined to accept the massive Oriental doctrine of melancholy resignation along with the Oriental gems of wisdom which he treasured. "This world belongs to the cheerful!" he said.

§

Pleasure is satisfaction derived from the things and persons outside us. Happiness is satisfaction derived from the core of deepest being inside us. Because we get our pleasures through the five senses, they are more exciting and are sharper, more vivid, than the diffused self-induced thoughts and feelings which bring us happiness. In short, pleasure is of the body whereas something quite immaterial and impalpable is the source of our happiness. This is not to say that all pleasures are to be ascetically rejected, but that whereas we are helplessly dependent for them on some object or some person, we are dependent only on ourselves for happiness.

§

From the moment that a man begins to look less to his changeful outer possessions and more to his controllable internal ones, he begins to gain the chance for real happiness. When this truth breaks upon the intelligence, he learns to keep his final reserves hidden in his heart. Then whatever happens, whatever course fortune takes, no one and nothing can take it from him. So long as he can carry the knowledge of truth in his head and the peace of God in his heart, he can carry the best of all his possessions with him wherever he may go. Not having lodged his possessions—whether material things or human affections, capitalized wealth or social honours—in his heart but having kept them outside it where they belong, he can remain calm and unmoved when Fortune's caprice disturbs or even destroys them. He has learnt to keep within his heart only inalienable possessions like wisdom and virtue, only what renders him serenely independent of her revolutions.

He who depends on externals plays dice with his happiness. He who depends on his own Overself attains unfailing serenity.

§

"Sadness does not befit a sage" is the reminder of an ancient Confucian text. "He is a man inwardly free of sorrow and care. He should be like the sun at midday—illuminating and gladdening everyone. This is not given to every human—only one whose will is directed to 'The Great' is able to do it. For the attribute of 'The Great' is joyousness."

§

It is not that the years pass by unregarded, nor that he is dead to human feelings, but that at this centre of his being to which he now has access, there is utter calm, a high indifference to agitations which compels him to treat them with serene dignity. He is a dweller in two worlds more or less at the same time.

§

Gautama's assertion that "life is suffering" may be matched with Socrates' assertion that "life is terrible." But both Indian and Greek sage referred solely to life in the ego. Is it quite fair to stress the misery of human existence without pointing to its mystery? For that is just as much there even if attention is seldom turned toward it. Man, in order to complete and fulfil himself, will and must rise to life in the Overself with the ego put into place, belittled and broken.

§

There is a silence born of ignorance and another born of knowledge—mystical knowledge. The right interpretation comes only through the intuitive faculty—not through the intellect.

§

This stillness is the godlike part of every human being. In failing to look for it, he fails to make the most of his possibilities. If, looking, he misses it on the way this happens because it is a vacuity: there is simply nothing there! That means no things, not even mental things, that is, thoughts.

§

The spirit (Brahman) is NOT the stillness, but is found by humans who are in the precondition of stillness. The latter is *their* human reaction to Brahman's presence coming into their field of awareness.

§

The Stillness is both an Understanding, an Insight of the mind, and an Experience of the being. The whole movement or vibration comes to a stop.

§

It is not easy to translate this sacred silence into comprehensible meaning, to describe a content where there is no form, to ascend from a region as deep as Atlantis is sunk today and speak openly in familiar, intelligible language; but I must try.

§

As his centre moves to a profounder depth of being, peace of mind becomes increasingly a constant companion. This in turn influences the way in which he handles his share of the world's activities. Impatience and stupidity recede, wrath at malignity is disciplined; discouragement under adversity is controlled and stress under pressures relaxed.

§

Truth lies hidden in silence. Reveal it—and falsehood will creep in, withering the golden image. Communication by speech or paper was not necessary.

§

Whatever the trouble be which distresses any man—be it physical or mental, personal or public, worldly or spiritual—there is one sure refuge to which he can always turn and return. If he has learnt the art of being still, he can carry his trouble to the mind's outer threshold and leave it there, passing himself into its innermost recess of utter serenity and carefree tranquillity. This is not a cowardly escapism or a foolish self-deception, although with the unphilosophical mystic it could be and often is. For when he emerges from the inner silence and picks up his trouble again, he will pick up also the strength to endure it bravely and the wisdom to deal with it rightly. This will always be the case if his approach is through *philosophical* mysticism, which makes inspired action and not inspired dreaming its goal. Furthermore, his contact with the inner Mind will set mysterious forces working on his behalf to solve the problem quite independently of his conscious effort and knowledge.

§

Truth may be written or spoken, preached or printed, but its most lasting expression and communication is transmitted through the deepest silence to the deepest nature in man.

§

The reason why this silent, inward, and pictureless initiation in the stillness is so much more powerful *ultimately*, is that it reaches the man himself, whereas all other kinds reach only his instruments or vehicles or bodies.

§

When the personal ego's thoughts and desires are stripped off, we behold ourselves as we were in the first state and as we shall be in the final one. We are then the Overself alone, in its Godlike solitude and stillness.

§

When he temporarily achieves this lofty condition, he ceases to think, for his mind becomes inarticulate with heavenly peace.

§

However dark or blundering the past, however miserable the tangle one has made of one's life, this unutterable peace blots it all out. Within that seraphic embrace error cannot be known, misery cannot be felt, sin cannot be remembered. A great cleansing comes over the heart and mind.

§

To complain that you get no answer, no result from going into the silence indicates two things: first, that you do not go far enough into it to reach the intuitive level; second, that you do not wait long enough for it to affect you.

§

The effort should be to find inward stillness through a loving search within the heart's depths for what may be called "the soul," what I have called "the Overself." This is not the soul thought of by a judge when he passes the sentence of death and asks the Lord to have mercy on the condemned man's soul. It is the Holy Ghost of Christian faith, the diviner part of man which dwells in eternity. The nearer we get to it in our striving, the greater will be the mental peace we shall feel. It can be found and felt even whilst thoughts continue to move through the mind, although they will necessarily be thoughts of a most elevated nature for the baser ones could not obtain entry during this mood.

§

The attention must be concentrated at this stage solely on the hidden soul. No other aim and even no symbol of It may now be held. When he has become so profoundly absorbed in this contemplation that his whole being, his whole psyche of thought, feeling, will, and intuition are mingled and blent in it, there may come suddenly and unexpectedly a displacement of awareness. He actually *passes out* of what he has hitherto known as himself into a new dimension and becomes a different being. When first experienced and unknown, there is the fear that this is death itself. It is indeed what is termed in mystical traditions of the West as "dying to oneself" and of the East as "passing away from oneself." But when one has repeated periodically and grown familiar with this experience, there is not only no fear but the experience is eagerly sought and welcomed. There I dissolved myself in the lake of the Water of Life.

§

In this deep stillness wherein every trace of the personal self dissolves, there is the true crucifixion of the ego. This is the real meaning of the crucifixion, as it was undergone in the ancient Mystery Temple initiations and as it was undergone by Jesus. The death implied is mental, not physical.

§

He who attains this beautiful serenity is absolved from the misery of frustrated desires, is healed of the wounds of bitter memories, is liberated from the burden of earthly struggles. He has created a secret, invulnerable centre within himself, a garden of the spirit which neither the world's hurts nor the world's joys can touch. He has found a transcendental singleness of mind.

§

Only he is able to think his *own* thought, uninfluenced by others, who has trained himself to enter the Stillness, where alone he is able to transcend all thought.

§

A man may fall into the sin of vanity because of the facility with which he is able to work up the devotional feelings or excite the spiritually rapturous ones. But those who enter into the Void because they are able to enter into the innermost part of themselves, cannot fall into this sin. They are detached not only from the emotions but also from themselves. This is why they live in so great and so constant a peace.

§

The truth which leads a man to liberation from all illusions and enslavements is perceived in the innermost depths of his being, where he is shut off from all other men. The man who has attained to its knowledge finds himself in an exalted solitude. He is not likely to find his way out of it to the extent, and for the purpose, of enlightening his fellow men who are accustomed to, and quite at home in, their darkness unless some other propulsive force of compassion arises within him and causes him to do so.

§

If he has succeeded in holding his mind somewhat still and empty, his next step is to find his centre.

§

It is not enough to achieve peace of mind. He must penetrate the Real still farther and achieve joy of heart.

§

If you investigate the matter deeply enough and widely enough, you will find that happiness eludes nearly all men despite the fact that they are forever seeking it. The fortunate and successful few are those who have stopped seeking with the ego alone and allow the search to be directed inwardly by the higher self. They alone can find a happiness unblemished by defects or deficiencies, a Supreme Good which is not a further source of pain and sorrow but an endless source of satisfaction and peace.

§

If the mind can reach a state where it is free from its own ideas, projections, and wishes, it can reach true happiness.

§

That beautiful state wherein the mind recognizes itself for *what it is*, wherein all activity is stilled except that of awareness alone, and even then it is an awareness without an object—this is the heart of the experience.

§

This is that ultimate solitude to which all human beings are destined.

§

25

WORLD-MIND IN INDIVIDUAL MIND

Their meeting and interchange —Enlightenment which stays—Saints and sages

The soul in man, the Overself, is linked with, or rooted in, the soul in the universe, the World-Mind.

§

The teaching of a higher individuality needs to be correctly understood. It is not that a separate one exists for each physical body. The consciousness which normally identifies itself with the body—that is, the ego—when looking upward in highest devotion or inward in deepest meditation, comes to the point of contact with universal being, World-Mind. This point is its own higher self, the divine deputy within its own being. But if devotion or meditation are carried still further, to the very utmost possible stretch of consciousness, the point itself merges into its source. At this moment the man is his source. But—"Man shall not see My face and live!" He returns eventually to earth-consciousness, where he must follow out its requirements. Yet the knowledge of what he is *in essence* remains. The presence of the deputy is always there meanwhile, always felt. It may fittingly be called his higher individuality.

§

Union with the Overself is not the ultimate end but a penultimate one. What we look up to as the Overself looks up in its own turn to another and higher entity.

§

The gap between the finite human mind and the infinite World-Mind is absolute. A union between them is not possible unless the first merges and disappears into the second.

§

If the claim of complete merger is valid, if the individual self really disappears in the attainment of Divine Consciousness, of whom then was this same self aware in the experience of attainment? No—it is only the lower personal self that is transcended; the higher spiritual individuality is not.

§

The unit of mind is differentiated out and undergoes its long evolution through numerous changes of state, not to merge so utterly in its source again as to be virtually annihilated, but to be consciously harmonized with that source whilst yet retaining its individuality.

§

The danger of men's deifying themselves afflicts the mystic path. This mind-madness must first be frankly admitted as a danger, for then only can it be guarded against.

§

We exist always in utter dependence on the Universal Mind. Man and God may meet and mingle in his periods of supreme exaltation, he may feel the sacred presence within himself to the utmost degree, but he does not thereby abolish all the distinctions between them absolutely. For he arrives at the knowledge of the timeless spaceless divine infinitude after a process of graded personal effort, whereas the World-Mind's knowledge of itself has forever been what it was is and shall be, above all processes and beyond all efforts.

§

There is some kind of a distinction between his higher individuality and the Universal Infinite out of which it is rayed, whatever the Vedantins may say. And this distinction remains in his highest mystical state, which is not one of total absorption and utter destruction of this individuality but the mergence of its own will in the universal will, the closest intimacy of its own being with the universal being.

§

Philosophy rejects decisively all those Vedantic pantheistic notions and Western mystical naïveties which would deify man and identify him with God. It asserts that the phrases in which these beliefs are embodied, such as the Indian "That thou art," the Persian "I am God," and the medieval European "union with God," are exaggerations of the truth, which is that God is immanent in us, that through realization of our higher self we become more *like* God, but that God never ceases to be the Unattainable, the Incomprehensible.

§

No mortal may penetrate the mystery of the ultimate mind in its own nature—which means in its static inactive being. The Godhead is not only beyond human conception but also beyond mystic perception. But Mind in its active dynamic state, that is, the World-Mind, and rather its ray in us called the Overself, *is* within range of human perception, communion, and even union. It is this that the mystic really finds when he believes that he has found God.

§

This condition is commonly said to be nothing less than "union with God." What is really attained is the higher self, the ray of the divine sun reflected in man, the immortal soul in fact—God Himself being forever utterly beyond man's finite capacity to comprehend. However the mystical experience is an authentic one and the conflict between interpretations does not dissolve its authenticity.

§

The mystic may indeed feel the very stuff of God in his rapture, but this does not supply him with the whole content of God's knowledge. If therefore he claims not only to be one with God but also to be one with God's entire consciousness, it is sheer presumption.

§

When, however, the content of this concept is subjected to critical analysis, we discover some disturbing facts. What mystic is or ever has been omnipresent, omniscient, and omnipotent? Such are the distinguishing characteristics of God. Yet how many mystics have asserted they were identical with God! Is it not an insult to common sense to make such an assertion? Yet every "paramahamsa" in India still makes it!

§

God, the World-Mind, knows all things in an eternal present at once. No mystic has ever claimed, no mystic has ever dared to claim, such total knowledge. Most mystics have, however, claimed union with God. If this be true, then quite clearly they can have had only a fragmentary, not a full union.

Philosophy, being more precise in its statements, avers that they have really achieved union not with God, but with something Godlike—the soul.

§

It is legitimate to say that something godlike is within me, but it is quite illegitimate to say "I am God." For the fragrance of a flower is after all not the same as the flower itself.

§

It is a fallacy to think that this displacement of the lower self brings about its complete substitution by the infinite and absolute Deity. This fallacy is an ancient and common one in mystical circles and leads to fantastic declarations of self-deification. If the lower self is displaced, it is not destroyed. It lives on but in strict subordination to the higher one, the Overself, the divine soul of man; and it is this latter, not the divine world-principle, which is the true displacing element.

§

There is metaphysically no such thing as a human appearance of God, as the Infinite Mind brought down into finite flesh. This error is taught as a sacred truth by the Bahais in their Manifestation doctrine, by the Christians in the Incarnation doctrine, and by the Hindus in their Avatar doctrine. God cannot be born in the flesh, cannot take a human incarnation. If He could so confine Himself, He would cease to be God. For how could the Perfect, the Incomprehensible, and the Inconceivable become the imperfect, the comprehensible, and the conceivable?

Yet there is some fire behind this smoke. From time to time, someone is born predestined to give a spiritual impulse to a particular people, area, or age. He is charged with a special mission of teaching and redemption and is imbued with special power from the universal intelligence to enable him to carry it out. He must plant seeds which grow slowly into trees to carry fruit that will feed millions of unborn people. In this sense he is different from and, if you like, superior to anyone else who is also inspired by the Overself. But this difference or superiority does not alter his human status, does not make him more than a man still, however divinely used and power-charged he may be. Such a man will claim no essential superiority over other men; on the contrary, he will plainly admit that they, too, may attain the same state of inspiration which he possesses. Hence Muhammed confessed, repeatedly: "I am only a human being like unto yourselves. But revelations are made to me." And the tenth Sikh guru declared, "Those who call me the Supreme Lord, will go to hell." No human temple can receive the Infinite Essence within its confining walls. No mortal man has ever been or could ever be the Incarnation of the all-transcending Godhead. No earthly flesh or human intelligence has the right to identify itself with the unknowable principle. Only minds untrained in the metaphysics of truth could accept the contrary belief. The widespread character of this belief evidences how few have ever had such a training, and the widespread character of the corruptions and troubles which have always followed in the train of such man-worship, evidences it as a fallacy.

§

In time his relation to the higher self becomes more intimate than any earthly friendship, closer than any human union could ever be. Yet it always remains a relation, never becomes an absorption; always a nearness, never a merger.

§

The downfall of every faith began when the worship of God as Spirit was displaced by the worship of Man as God. No visible prophet, saint, or saviour has the right to demand that which should be offered to the Unseen alone. It is not true reverence but ignorant blasphemy which could believe that the unattainable Absolute has put itself into mortal human form however beneficent the purpose may be. The idea that God can enter the flesh as a man was originally given to most religions as a chief feature for the benefit of the populace. It was very helpful both in their mental and practical life. But it was true only on the religious level, which after all is the elementary one. It was not quite true on the philosophical level. Those few who were initiated into the advanced teaching were able to interpret this notion in a mystical or metaphysical way which, whilst remote from popular comprehension, was closer to divine actuality. They will never degrade the Godhead in their thought of it by accepting the popular belief in personification, incarnation, or avatarhood. It is a sign of primitive ignorance when the humanity of these inspired men is unrecognized or even denied, when they are put on a pedestal of special deification. The teaching that Godhead can voluntarily descend into man's body is a misunderstanding of truth. The irony is that those who try to displace the gross misunderstanding by the pure truth itself are called blasphemous. The real blasphemy is to lower the infinite Godhead to being directly an active agent in the finite world.

Nothing can contain the divine essence although everything can be and is permeated by it. No one can personify it, although every man bears its ray within him. To place a limitation upon it is to utter a blasphemy against it. The infinite Mind cannot be localized to take birth in any particular land. The absolute existence cannot be personified in a human form. The eternal Godhead cannot be identified with a special fleshly body. The inscrutable Reality has no name and address. It cannot be turned into an historical person, however exalted, with a body of bones nerves muscle and skin. To think otherwise is to think materialistically. The notion which would place the Deity as a human colossus amongst millions of human midgets and billions of lesser creatures shows little true reverence and less critical intelligence.

We must acknowledge the ever-existence of Absolute mind, even though it is incomprehensible to the senses and inconceivable to the thoughts. We must deny that it can ever manifest itself within time and space and consequently deny also that it can ever show itself under a human form. We must deny that any man is right in arrogating to himself the sole channel through whom worship must be performed, communion achieved, or belief given.

The time has come to repudiate all this foolish worship of human beings and to transfer our reverence and obedience to the pure divine Being alone. The more metaphysical comprehension we develop, the less we shall look to the person of a teacher. We shall then regard the Teaching itself as the essential thing.

§

When duality is blended with, ***and within***, unity it is the true ***jivanmukta*** realization. The One is then experienced as the Two but ***known*** to be really the One.

§

The effects of enlightenment include: an imperturbable detachment from outer possessions, rank, honours, and persons; an overwhelming certainty about truth; a carefree, heavenly peace above all disturbances and vicissitudes; an acceptance of the general rightness of the universal situation, with each entity and each event playing its role; and impeccable sincerity which says what it means, means what it says.

§

When you awaken to truth as it really is, you will have no occult vision, you will have no "astral" experience, no ravishing ecstasy. You will awaken to it in a state of utter stillness, and you will realize that truth was *always* there within you and that reality was always there around you. Truth is not something which has grown and developed through your efforts. It is not something which has been achieved or attained by laboriously adding up those efforts. It is not something which has to be made more and more perfect each year. And once your mental eyes are opened to truth they can never be closed again.

§

We must learn to differentiate between the partial attainment of the mystic who stops short at passive enjoyment of ecstatic states and the perfect attainment of the sage who does not depend on any particular states but dwells in the unbroken calm of the unconditioned Overself. From his high point of view all such states are necessarily illusory, however personally satisfying at the time, inasmuch as they are transient conditions and do not pertain to the final result.

§

No announcements tell the world that he has come into enlightenment. No heralds blow the trumpets proclaiming man's greatest victory—over himself. This is in fact the quietest moment of his whole life.

§

There is some confusion on this point in the minds of many students. On attaining enlightenment a man does not attain omniscience. At most, he may receive a revelation of the inner operations of life and Nature, of the higher laws governing life and man. That is, he may also become a seer and find a cosmogony presented to his gaze. But the actuality in a majority of cases is that he attains enlightenment only, not cosmogonical seership.

§

There are varying degrees of spiritual illumination, which accounts both for the varying outlooks to be found among mystics and for the different kinds of Glimpse among aspirants. All illuminations and all Glimpses free the man from his negative qualities and base nature, but in the latter case only temporarily. He is able, as a result, to see into his higher nature. In the first degree, it is as if a window covered with dirt were cleaned enough to reveal a beautiful garden outside it. He is still subject to the activity of thinking, the emotion of joy, and the discrimination between X and Y. In the next and higher degree, it is as if the window were still more cleaned so that still more beauty is revealed beyond it. Here there are no thoughts to intervene between the seer and the seen. In the third degree, the discrimination is no longer present. In the fourth degree, it is as if the window were thoroughly cleaned. Here there is no longer even a rapturous emotion but only a balanced happiness, a steady tranquillity which, being beyond the intellect, cannot properly be described by the intellect.

Again, mental peace is a fruit of the first and lowest degree of illumination, although thoughts will continue to arise although gently, and thinking in the discursive manner will continue to be active although slowly. But concentration will be sufficiently strong to detach him from the world and, as a consequence, to yield the happiness which accompanies such detachment. Only those who have attained to this degree can correctly be regarded as "saved" as only they alone are unable to fall back into illusion, error, sin, greed, or sensuality.

In the second degree, there will be more inward absorption and cerebral processes will entirely fade out.

Freedom from all possibility of anger is a fruit of the third and higher degree.

§

To be the witness is the first stage; to be Witness of the witness is the next; but to BE is the final one. For consciousness lets go of the witness in the end. Consciousness alone is itself the real experience.

§

The difference between the intermediate and the final state is the difference between feeling the Overself to be a distinct and separate entity and feeling it to be the very essence of oneself, between temporary experience of it and enduring union with it.

§

Not until the light he has received becomes stabilized as a permanent thing can he be regarded as a master, and not until it is also full and complete can he be regarded as a sage.

§

A rare but complete illumination must not only pass from the first to the final degree of intensity, but must also contain a picture of the cosmic order. That is to say, it must be a revelation. It must explain the profounder nature of the universe, the inner meaning of individual existence, and the hidden relationship between the two.

§

The deeper one penetrates into the Void the more he is purified of the illusions of personality, time, matter, space, and causality. Between the second and third stages of insight's unfoldment there are really two further subsidiary stages which are wrapped in the greatest mystery and are rarely touched by the average mystic or yogi. For both of them are stages which lead further downwards into the Void. The yogi touches the edge of the Void, as it were, but not its centre. These two stages are purificatory ones and utterly annihilate the last illusions and the last egoisms of the seeker. They are dissolved forever and cannot revive again. Nothing more useful can and may be said about it here. *For this is the innermost holy of holies, the most sacred sanctuary accessible to man*. He who touches this grade touches what may not be spoken aloud for sneering ears, nor written down for sneering eyes. Consequently none has ever ventured to explain publicly what must not be so explained.

§

At long last, when the union of self with Overself is total and complete, some part of his consciousness will remain unmoving in infinity, unending in eternity. There, in that sacred glory, he will be preoccupied with his divine identity, held to it by irresistible magnetism, gladly, lovingly.

§

Where is the man who is free of the ego? To him we must bow in deep reverence, in wondering admiration, in enforced humility. Here is one who has found his true self, his personal independence, his own being. Here at last is a free man, someone who has found his real worth in a world of false values. Here at last is a truly great man and truly sincere man.

§

When he has fully accomplished this passing-over, all the elements of his lower nature will then have been fully eliminated. The ego will be destroyed. Instead of being enslaved by its own senses and passions, blinded by its own thoughts and ignorance, his mind will be inspired, enlightened, and liberated by the Overself. Yet life in the human self will not be destroyed because he has entered life in the divine Overself. But neither will it continue in the old and lower way. That self will henceforth function as a perfectly obedient instrument of the soul and no longer of the animal body or intellectual nature. No evil thought and no animal passion can ever again take hold of his mind. What remains of his character is therefore the incorruptible part and the immortal part. Death may rob him of lesser things, but not of the thing which he cherishes most. Having already parted in his heart with what is perishable, he can await it without perturbation and with sublime resignation.

§

The general idea in the popular and religious circles of India is that the highest state of illumination is attained during a trance condition (*samadhi*). This is not the teaching in the highest philosophic circles of India. There is another condition, "sahaja samadhi," which is described in a few little-known texts and which is regarded as superior. It is esteemed because no trance is necessary and because it is a continuous state. The inferior state is one which is intermittently entered and left: it cannot be retained without returning to trance. The philosophic "fourth state," by contrast, remains unbroken even when active and awake in the busy world.

§

I do not claim sahaja yields ultimate reality: I only claim that it yields the ultimate so far *known to man*.

§

When we comprehend what it is that must go into the making of a sage, how many and how diverse the experiences through which he has passed in former incarnations, we realize that such a man's wisdom is part of his bloodstream.

§

Of little use are explanations which befog truth and bewilder understanding. To inform a Western reader that an enlightened man sees only "Brahman" is to imply that he does not see forms, that is, the world. But the fact is that he *does* see what unenlightened men see—the physical objects and creatures around him—or he could not attend to the simplest little necessity or duty of which all humans have to take care. But he sees things without being limited to their physical appearance—he knows their inner reality too.

§

Sahaja samadhi is not broken into intervals, is permanent, and involves no special effort. Its arisal is instantaneous and without progressive stages. It can accompany daily activity without interfering with it. It is a settled calm and complete inner quiet.

There are no distinguishing marks that an outside observer can use to identify a sahaja-conscious man because sahaja represents consciousness itself rather than its transitory states.

Sahaja has been called the lightning flash. Philosophy considers it to be the most desirable goal.

This is illustrated with a classic instance of Indian spirituality involving a king named Janaka. One day he was about to mount his horse and put one foot into the stirrup which hung from the saddle. As he was about to lift himself upwards into the saddle the "lightning flash" struck his consciousness. He was instantly carried away and concentrated so deeply that he failed for some time to lift himself up any higher. From that day onwards he lived in sahaja samadhi which was always present within him.

Those at the state of achieved sahaja are under no compulsion to continue to meditate any more or practise yoga. They often do either because of inclinations produced by past habits or as a means of helping other persons. In either case it is experienced as a pleasure. Because this consciousness is permanent, the experiencer does not need to go into meditation. This is despite the outward appearance of a person who places himself in the posture of meditation in order to achieve something.

When you are engaged in outward activity it is not the same as when you are in a trance. This is true for both the beginner and the adept. The adept, however, does not lose the sahaja awareness which he has achieved and can withdraw into the depths of consciousness which the ordinary cannot do.

§

THE SAINT: has successfully carried out ascetic disciplines and purificatory regimes for devotional purposes.

THE PROPHET: has listened for God's voice, heard and communicated God's message of prediction, warning, or counsel.

THE MYSTIC: has intimately experienced God's presence while inwardly rapt in contemplation or has seen a vision of God's cosmogony while concentrated in meditation.

THE SAGE: has attained the same results as all these three, has added a knowledge of infinite and eternal reality thereto, and has brought the whole into balanced union.

THE PHILOSOPHER: is a sage who has also engaged in the spiritual education of others.

§

Philosophy uses the attained man not as a god for grovelling worship and blind obedience, but as an ideal for effectual admiration and reverent analysis.

§

We are asked: What is the interpretation of a sentence in that excellent little book *Light on the Path* by Mabel Collins, which runs "For within you is the light of the world—the only light that can be shed upon the Path. If you are unable to perceive it within you, it is useless to look for it elsewhere. It is beyond you; because when you reach it you have lost yourself. It is unattainable because it forever recedes. You will enter the light but you will never touch the flame."

The meaning of this mysterious sentence is that the sage refuses to claim the ultimate mergence which is his right because he refuses to desert "the great orphan Humanity." He stops short at the very threshold of Nirvana simply to remain here and help others reach that threshold. Thus by his altruistic activity, meditative power, and intellectual penetration he continuously earns a title to that utter absorption of his ego in the unutterable Absolute which is Nirvana, but by his continuous self-giving for suffering mankind he never actually attains this goal. This extraordinary situation may be represented mathematically by the asymptote—a line which is drawn on a graph to approach nearer and nearer to a given curve but which never actually touches it within a finite distance. Only a man who feels with and for his fellow creatures will dare to make such a tremendous sacrifice of the supreme peace which he has won. How much more generous, how nobly grander is this example of ever-active altruistic service than that of ever-idle meditative reclusiveness!

§

Light the lamp and it will spread out its rays by itself. We are indeed blessed by the presence of these great souls on this earth and doubly so if we meet in person. They deserve not merely our respect but our veneration. But even if we are never fortunate enough to meet one of these masters, the mere knowledge that such men do exist and live demonstrates the possibility of spiritual achievement and proves that the quest is no chimera. It should comfort and encourage us to know this. Therefore we should regard such a man as one of humanity's precious treasures. We should cherish his name as a personal inspiration. We should venerate his sayings or writings as whispers out of the eternal silence.

§

There is some confusion, as least in India, but also in the West, about the kind of life an enlightened man will live. It is popularly believed especially in the Orient, that he sits in his cave or his hut or his ashram sunk continually in meditation. The idea that he can be active in the world is not often accepted, especially by the masses who have not been properly instructed in these matters and who do not know the differences between religion and mysticism and between mysticism and philosophy. The truth is that the enlightened man may or may not practise meditation; but he has no dependence upon it, because his enlightenment being fully established will not be increased by further meditation. Whenever he does meditate, it is either for the purpose of withdrawing from the world totally for short periods, at intervals, either for his own satisfaction or to recuperate his energies, or to benefit others by telepathy. When it is said "for his own satisfaction," what is meant is that meditation in seclusion may have become a way of life in his previous incarnation. This generates a karmic tendency which reappears in this life and the satisfaction of this tendency pleases him, but it is not absolutely essential for him. He can dispense with it when needful to do so, whereas the unenlightened man is too often at the mercy of his tendencies and propensities.

§

Such rare peace stands out in poignant contrast against the burdens and fretfulness of our ordinary lives. Such rare goodness is needed by a generation accustomed to violence, atrocity, bestiality and horror, lunacy and hatred.

§

There is no classification into matter and spirit for the Sage. There is only one life for him. If a man can find reality only in trance, if he says that the objective world is unreal, he is not a Sage, he is a Yogi.

§

The true adept does not sell either the secrets of his knowledge or the use of his powers. There are several reasons for this. The most important is that he would harm himself for he would lose the link with the very source of his knowledge and power. He does not possess them in himself but by virtue of being possessed by the Higher Self. From the moment that he attempted to make them a means of worldly profit, It would gradually begin to desert him. Another reason is that he would lose his privileged position to speak the pure truth. To the extent that he had to rely upon purchasers of it, to that extent he would have to shape it or conform it to their tastes and prejudices; otherwise they would refuse to have it. He would have to use his powers to please them. He would have to accommodate his knowledge to their weaknesses. He could succeed in the profession of teaching truth only by failing in his own duty of realizing truth. For the truth being the one thing he got without price, is the one thing which he must give without price. This is the law governing its distribution. Anyone who violates it proves by this very violation that he does not possess truth in all its shining purity.

§

There are noteworthy differences between the genuine illuminate and the false one. But I shall indicate only a few of the points one may observe in the man who is truly self-realized. First of all, he does not desire to become the leader of a new cult; therefore, he does not indulge in any of the attempts to draw publicity or notice which mark our modern saviours. He never seeks to arouse attention by oddity of teaching, talk, dress, or manner. In fact, he does not even desire to appear as a teacher, seeks no adherents, and asks no pupils to join him. Though he possesses immense spiritual power which may irresistibly influence your life, he will seem quite unconscious of it. He makes no claim to the possession of peculiar powers. He is completely without pose or pretense. The things which arouse passion or love or hatred in men do not seem to touch him; he is indifferent to them as Nature is to our comments when we praise her sunshine or revile her storms. For in him, we have to recognize a man freed, loosed from every limit which desire and emotion can place upon us. He walks detached from the anxious thoughts or seductive passions which eat out the hearts of men. Though he behaves and lives simply and naturally, we are aware that there is a mystery within that man. We are unable to avoid the impression that because his understanding has plumbed life deeper than other men's, we are compelled to call a halt when we would attempt to comprehend him.

§

His inner state will not be easily discernible to others, unless they happen to be the few who are themselves sufficiently advanced and sufficiently sensitive to appreciate it. Yet it is his duty to announce the glorious news of its discovery, to publish the titanic fact of its existence. But he will do so in his own way, according to his own characteristics and circumstances. He will not need to announce it in a speech, or print it in a book; he will not publish the fact in daily newspapers or shout it from the housetops. His whole life will be the best announcement, the grandest publication.

§

Such is the wonderful infinitude of the soul that the man who succeeds in identifying his everyday consciousness with it, succeeds also in making his influence and inspiration felt in any part of the world where there is someone who puts faith in him and gives devotion to him. His bodily presence or visitation is not essential. The soul is his real self and operates on subconscious levels. Whoever recognizes this truth and humbly, harmoniously, places himself in a passive receptive attitude towards the spiritual adept, finds a source of blessed help outside his own limited powers.

§

Association with or proximity to such a man not only brings out what is best in them but also, when it ends, invokes the reaction of what is worst.

§

Those who have malignantly attacked the person or injured the work of such a man through whom the divine forces are working for the enlightenment of mankind, create for themselves a terrible karma which accumulates and strikes them down in time. He himself will endeavour to protect his work by appropriate means, one being temporarily to withdraw his love from them for the rest of his incarnation until their dying moments. Then he will extend it again with full force and appear to them as in a vision, full of forgiveness, blessing, and comfort.

§

We are asked why, if thought-transference be a fact, the hibernating hermit should not still represent the loftiest achievement, should not in fact be as antisocial as he superficially seems. He may be hidden away in a mountain cave, but is not his mind free to roam where it likes and has not its power been raised to a supreme degree by his mystical practices? We reply that if he is merely concerned with resting in his inner tranquillity undisturbed by the thought of others, then his achievement is only a self-centered one.

There is much confusion amongst students about these yogis who are supposed to sit in solitude and help humanity telepathically. It is not only yogis who sit in solitude who are doing so. Nor is it needful to be a solitary to be able to do so. The truth is that most yogis who live in solitude are still in the student stage, still trying to develop themselves. And even in the rarer cases where a yogi has perfected himself in meditation, he may be using the latter simply to bask egotistically in inner peace for his own benefit and without a thought for others. It is only when a man is a philosophic yogi that he will be deliberately using his meditational self-absorptions to uplift individuals and help humanity for their good. If the mystic *is* using his mental powers for altruistic ends, if he *is* engaged in telepathically helping others at a distance, then he has gone beyond the ordinary mystical level and we salute him for it.

The Adept will not try to influence any other man, much less try to control him. Therefore, his notion of serving another by enlightening him does not include the activity of proselytizing, but rather the office of teaching. Such service means helping a man to understand for himself and to see for himself what he could not see and understand before. The Adept does this not only by using the ordinary methods of speech, writing, and example, but much more by extraordinary method which only an Adept can employ. In this he puts himself in a passive attitude towards the other person's ego and thus registers the character, thought, and feeling in one swift general impression, which manifests itself within his own consciousness like a photograph upon a sensitized film. He recognizes this as a picture of the evolutionary degree to which the other person has attained, but he recognizes it also as a picture of the false self with which the other person identifies himself. No matter how much sympathy he feels for the other man, no matter how negative are the emotions or the thoughts he finds reproducing themselves within his own being, it is without effect upon himself. This is because he has outgrown both the desires and the illusions which still reign over the other man's mind. With the next step in his technique he challenges that self as being fearful for its own unworthy and ultimately doomed existence, and finally dismisses the picture of it in favour of the person's true self, the divine Overself. Then he throws out of his mind every thought of the other person's imperfect egoistic condition and replaces it by the affirmation of his true spiritual selfhood.

Thus, if the Adept begins his service to another who, attracted by his wisdom seeks counselling or by his godliness seeks his inspiration, by noting the defects in the character of the person, he ends it by ignoring them. He then images the seeker as standing serenely in the light, free from the ego and its desires, strong and wise and pure because living in the truth. The Adept closes his eyes to the present state of the seeker, to all the evidences of distress and weakness and darkness which he earlier noted and opens them to the real, innermost state of the seeker, where he sees him united with the Overself. He persists in silently holding this thought and this picture, and he holds it with the dynamic intensity of which he only is capable. The effect of this inner working sometimes appears immediately in the seeker's consciousness, but more likely it will take some time to rise up from the subconscious mind. Even if it takes years to manifest itself, it will certainly do so in the end.

We know that one mind can influence another through the medium of speech or writing: we know also that it may even influence another directly and without any medium through the silent power of telepathy. All this work takes place on the level of thought and emotion. But the Adept may not only work on this level: it is possible for him to work on a still deeper level. He can go into the innermost core of his own being and there touch the innermost core of the other man's being. In this way, Spirit speaks to Spirit, but without words or even thoughts. Within his innermost being there is a mysterious emptiness to which the Adept alone gains access during meditation or trance. All thoughts die at its threshold as he enters it. But when eventually he returns to the ordinary state and the thinking activity starts again, then those first series of thoughts are endowed with a peculiar power, are impregnated with a magical potency. Their echoes reverberate telepathically across space in the minds of others to whom they may be directed deliberately by the Adept. Their influence upon sympathetic and responsive persons is at first too subtle and too deep to be recognized, but eventually they reach the surface of consciousness.

This indeed is the scientific fact behind the popular medieval European and contemporary Oriental belief in the virtue of an Adept's blessing and the value of an Adept's initiation. The Adept's true perception of him is somewhere registered like a seed in the subconscious mind of the receptive person, and will in the course of time work its way up through the earth of the unconscious like a plant until it appears above ground in the conscious mind. If it is much slower in showing its effects, it is also much more effectual, much more lasting than the ordinary way of communicating thought or transmitting influence. In this way, by his own inner growth he will begin to perceive, little by little, for himself the truth about his own inner being and outer life in the same way that the Adept perceives it. This is nothing less than a passage from the ego's point of view to the higher one.

§

It is a mistake to believe that the mystical adepts all possess the same unvarying supernormal powers. On the contrary, they manifest such power or powers as are in consonance with their previous line of development and aspiration. One who has come along an intellectual line of development, for instance, would most naturally manifest exceptional intellectual powers. The situation has been well put by Saint Paul in the First Epistle to the Corinthians: "Now there are diversities of graces, but the same Spirit. And there are diversities of ministries but the same Lord. And there are diversities of workings but the same God who worketh all in all." When the Overself activates the newly made adept's psyche, the effect shows itself in some part or faculty; in another adept it produces a different effect. Thus the source is always the same but the manifestation is different.

§

The mystic who talks of giving love to all mankind has still not realized Truth. What he really means is that he, the ego, is giving the love. The Gnani, on the contrary, knows all men as himself and therefore the idea of giving them love does not arise, he accepts his identity of interest with them completely.

§

The realized man leaves no lineal descendants to take over his spiritual estate. Spiritual succession is a fiction. The heir to a master's mantle must win it afresh: he cannot inherit it.

§

There is no such act as a one-sided self-giving. Karma brings us back our due. He who spends his life in the dedicated service of philosophic enlightenment may reject the merely material rewards that this service could bring him, but he cannot reject the beneficent thoughts, the loving remembrances, the sincere veneration which those who have benefited sometimes send him. Such invisible rewards help him to atone more peacefully and less painfully for the strategic errors he has made, the tactical shortcomings he has manifested. Life is an arduous struggle for most people, but much more so for such a one who is always a hated target for the unseen powers of darkness. Do not hesitate to send him your silent humble blessing, therefore, and remember that Nature will not waste it. The enemies you are now struggling against within yourself he has already conquered, but the enemies he is now struggling against are beyond your present experience. He has won the right to sit by a hearth of peace. If he has made the greatest renunciation and does not do so, it is for your sake and for the sake of those others like you.

§

When he penetrates to the still centre of his being, the thoughts of this and that subside, either to a low ebb or into a temporary non-existence. Since thoughts express themselves in language, when they are inactive speech becomes inactive too. What he feels is quite literally too deep for thoughts. He falls into perfect silence. Yet it is not an empty silence. Something is present in it, some power which he can direct toward another man and which that man can feel and absorb temporarily—to whatever extent he is capable—if or when he is in a relaxed and receptive mood. The communication will best take place, if both are physically present, in total silence and bodily stillness, that is, in meditation.

§

The sage will not be primarily concerned with his own personal welfare, but then he will also not be primarily concerned with mankind's welfare. Both these duties find a place in his outlook, but they do not find a primary place. This is always filled by a single motive: to do the will, to express the inspiration of that greater self of which he is sublimely aware and to which he has utterly surrendered himself. This is a point whereon many students get confused or go astray. The sage does not stress altruism as the supreme value of life, nor does he reject egoism as the lowest value of life. He will act as the Overself bids him in each case, egotistically if it so wishes or altruistically if it so declares, but he will always act for its sake as the principal aim and by its light as the principal means.

§

His goodwill to, and sympathy for all men, rather empathy, enables him to experience their very being in his own being. Yet his loyalty toward his higher self enables him to keep his individuality as the inerasable background for this happening.

§

Despite all his psychical knowledge and personal attainment, the sage never loses his deep sense of the mystery which is at the heart of existence, which is God.

§

What is the sage's reaction to the cosmos? It is very different from that of the ignorant who have never asked the question "What am I?" and who may regard the calm visage of a Yogi as a "frozen face." The sage has no sense of conflict, no inner division. He has expanded his notion of self until it has embraced the universe and therefore rightly he may say "the universe is my idea." He may make this strange utterance because he has so expanded his understanding of mind. Lesser men may only say "the universe is an idea."

§

Bergson was right. His acute French intelligence penetrated like an eagle's sight beneath the world-illusion and saw it for what it is—a cosmic process of continual change which never comes to an end, a universal movement whose first impetus and final exhaustion will never be known, a flux of absolute duration and therefore unimaginable. And for the sage who attains to the knowledge of THAT which forever seems to be changing but forever paradoxically retains its own pure reality, for him as for the ignorant, the flux must go on. But it will go on here on this earth, not in the same mythical heaven or mirage-like hell. He will repeatedly have to take flesh, as all others will have to, so long as duration lasts, that is, forever. For he cannot sit apart like the yogi while his compassion is too profound to waste itself in mere sentiment. It demands the profound expression of sacrificial service in motion. His attitude is that so clearly described by a nineteenth-century agnostic whom religionists once held in horror, Thomas Huxley: "We live in a world which is full of misery and ignorance, and the plain duty of each and all of us is to try to make the little corner he can influence somewhat less miserable and somewhat less ignorant than it was before he entered it." The escape into Nirvana for him is only the escape into the inner realization of the truth whilst alive: it is not to escape from the external cycle of rebirths and deaths. It is a change of attitude. But that bait had to be held out to him at an earlier stage until his will and nerve were strong enough to endure this revelation. There is no escape except inwards. For the sage is too compassionate to withdraw into proud indifferentism and too understanding to rest completely satisfied with his own wonderful attainment. The sounds of sufferings of men, the ignorance that is the root of these sufferings, beat ceaselessly on the tympanum of his ears. What can he do but answer, *and answer with his very life*—which he gives in perpetual reincarnation upon the cross of flesh as a vicarious sacrifice for others. It is thus alone that he achieves immortality, not by fleeing forever—as he could if he willed—into the Great Unconsciousness, but by suffering forever the pains and pangs of perpetual rebirth that he may help or guide his own.

§

26

THE WORLD-IDEA

Divine order of the universe—
Change as universal activity—
Polarities, complementaries, and dualities of the universe—
True idea of man

Whatever we call it, most people feel—whether vaguely or strongly—that there must be a God and that there must be something which God has in view in letting the universe come into existence. This purpose I call the World-Idea, because to me God is the World's Mind. This is a thrilling conception. It was an ancient revelation which came to the first cultures, the first civilizations, of any importance, as it has come to all others which have appeared, and it is still coming today to our own. With this knowledge, deeply absorbed and properly applied, man comes into harmonious alignment with his Source.

§

All spiritual study is incomplete if it ignores the facts, truths, laws, and principles of cosmogony. To attempt to justify this neglect with the accusation that they belong to the world of illusion is silly and useless. For the accuser must still continue to live in an illusory body and use an illusory self governed by those laws. After every such attempt and for each violation of those laws—upon which the order and harmony of the universe depend—which his neglect brings about, he must pay the penalty in suffering.

§

When we gaze observantly and reflectively around an object—whether it be a microscope-revealed cell or a telescope-revealed star—it inescapably imposes upon us the comprehension that an infinite intelligence rules this wonderful cosmos. The purposive way in which the universe is organized betrays, if it be anything at all, the working of a Mind which understands.

§

To recognize that the order of the cosmos is superbly intelligent beyond human invention, mysterious beyond human understanding, and even divinely holy is not to lapse into being sentimental. It is to accept the transcendence and self-sufficiency of THAT WHICH IS.

§

He comes to see the whole cosmos as a manifestation of the Supreme Being. It follows that involuntarily, spontaneously, he brings himself—mind and body, heart and will—into harmony with this view.

§

The cosmic order is divine intelligence expressed, equilibrium sought through contrasts and complementaries, the One Base multiplying itself in countless forms, the Supreme Will established according to higher laws. The World-Mind is hidden deep within our individual minds. The World-Idea begets all our knowledge. Whoever seeks aright finds the sacred stillness inside and the sacred activity in the universe.

§

The World-Idea provides secret invisible patterns for all things that have come into existence. These are not necessarily the forms that our limited perceptions present to us but the forms that are ultimate in God's Will.

§

It is a paradox of the World-Idea that it is at once a rigid pattern and, within that pattern, a latent source of indeterminate possibilities. This seems impossible to human minds, but it would not be the soul of a divine order if it were merely mechanical.

§

At the centre of each man, each animal, each plant, each cell, and each atom, there is a complete stillness. A seemingly empty stillness, yet it holds the divine energies and the divine Idea for that thing.

§

What they may expect to find with intellect at most is the slow uncovering of little fragments of the World-Idea: but with intuition the subtler meanings and larger patterns are possible. These include but also transcend the physical plane. A few fated persons, whose mission is revelation, are granted once in a lifetime the Cosmic Vision.

§

The World-Idea is perfect. How could it be otherwise since it is God's Idea? If we fail to become a co-worker with it, nothing of this perfection will be lost. If we do, we add nothing to it.

§

The goal of life is to be consciously united with Life.

§

The World-Idea's end is foreordained from the beginning. This leaves no ultimate personal choice. But there's a measure of free will in a single direction—how soon or how late that divine end is accomplished. The time element has not been ordered, the direction has.

§

The management of human affairs, the values of human society, and the operations of human faculties are basic influences which necessarily shape human ideas or beliefs about divine existence which, being on a totally different and transcendental level of experience, does not correspond to those concepts. The biggest of these mistakes is about the world's creation. A picture or plan is supposed to arise in the Divine Mind and then the Divine Will operates on something called Matter (or, with more up-to-date human knowledge, called Energy) to fashion the world and its inhabitants. In short, first the thought, then, by stages, the thing is brought into existence. A potter works like this on clay, but his mind and power are not transcendental. The Divine Mind is its own substance and its own energy; its thoughts are creative of these things. Not only so but the number of universes possible is infinite. Not only this, but they are infinitely different, as though infinite self-expression were being sought. The human understanding may reel at the idea, but creation has never had a beginning nor an end: it is eternal. Nor can it ever come to an end (despite rhythmic intervals of pause), for the Infinite Being can never express itself fully in a finite number of these forms of expression.

§

Two points should be clearly understood. First, the world of external Nature, being eternal, is not brought into existence by an act of sudden creation out of nothing. Second, this world is rooted in the divine substance and is consequently not an empty illusion but an indirect manifestation of divine reality.

§

We may call it evolution if we wish but the actuality is not quite the same. The universe is being *guided* to follow the World-Idea—this is the essence of what is happening.

§

We reject all theories of the Divine Principle having a self-benefiting purpose—such as to know Itself or to get rid of its loneliness—in manifesting the cosmos. It is the Perfect and needs nothing. The cosmos arises of itself under an inherent law of necessity, and the evolution of all entities therein is to enable them to reflect something of the Divine; it is for their sake, not for the Divine's, that they exist.

§

To say that man is unconsciously seeking God, or rather his Higher Self, is the truth. To say that God is seeking man is an error based upon a truth. This truth is that in the divine idea of the universe, the evolutionary development of life-cells will bring them slowly up to an awareness of the diviner level; but the Higher Self, having no desire and no emotions, cannot be said to be seeking anything. Indeed, the evolutionary pattern being what it is, there is no need for it to seek, as the development of all beings from primitive amoeba to perfect spiritual consciousness is assured.

§

Jung's archetypes, as far as I know his thought (and I am not a student of much of it), apply to the unconscious of the human being. The archetypes of the World-Idea, if you wish to call them that, apply universally and are not concerned with the human species alone.

§

What is the universe but a gigantic symbol of God? Its infinite variety hints at the infinite endlessness of the Absolute itself.

§

It is not only man that is made in the image of God: the whole universe likewise is also an image of God. It is not only by coming to know himself that man discovers the divine life hidden deep in his heart: it is also by listening in the stillness of Nature to what she is forever declaring, that he discovers the presence of an infinite World-Mind.

§

If Nature keeps her lips inexorably shut to the questions of those who abuse her, she graciously opens them in perfect response to those who ask with a quieted, co-operative and harmonious ego.

§

Human beings have made too much fuss about themselves, their own importance in the cosmic scale. Why should there not be other forms of life superior to them, conscious intelligent beings higher in mentality, character, and spiritual knowledge, better equipped with powers and techniques?

§

There are beings not subject to the same laws as those governing mankind's physical existence. They are normally not visible to men. They are gods.

§

The Gods are both symbols of particular forces and beings dwelling on higher planes.

§

The inhabitants of each planet belong to different stages of evolution: some higher and some lower. This applies not only to the human inhabitants but also to the animal and even the plant inhabitants. They pass in great waves from one planet to another at certain stages of this evolution, going where they can find the most appropriate conditions either for expression of their present stage or for the stimulation of their next immediate stage. Consequently the stragglers and laggards who fall behind pass to a planet where the conditions are of a lower nature, for there they are more at home. On the other hand, the pioneers who have outstripped the mass and can find no conditions suitable for their further development pass to a planet in a higher stage.

§

These three cosmic forces—Attraction, Repulsion, and Rest—constitute the triune manifestation of the World-Idea. You will find them in every department of existence.

§

There is no stability anywhere but only the show of it. Whether it be a man's fortunes or a mountain's surface, everything is evanescent. Only the *rate* of this evanescence differs but the fact of it does not.

§

Energy radiates whether in the form of continuous waves or disconnected particles—"moment to moment," Buddha called it. It is this cosmic radiation which becomes "matter."

§

The idea of human perfection would mean the attainment of a static condition, but nowhere in nature do we find such condition. Everything, as Buddha pointed out, is in a state of becoming, or as Krishnamurti number two calls it: Reality is motion. Buddha never denied that there was anything beyond becoming. He simply refused to discuss the possibility, whereas persons like Krishnamurti two stop there and affirm it as being the ultimate. There were very good reasons why Buddha refused. He was living in a country where the intelligentsia were lost in speculations, fruitless and impractical, and where the emotional were lost in religion, endlessly ritualized and filled with superstition. The mystics were lost in that impossible task of making meditation their whole life. Nature forbade it and brought them back. Becoming and motion are processes, but Being, pure consciousness, is not. In the experience of a glimpse we discover this fact. Being transcends becoming, but it is only the Gods who live on the plane of Being; we humans may visit it, even for long periods, but we must return.

§

But if the universe has no internal purpose for the World-Mind, it has one for every living entity within it and especially for every self-conscious entity such as man. If there can never be a goal for World-Mind itself, there is a very definite one for its creature man.

§

A tension holds all things in equilibrium between coming together of their elements, temporary maintenance of their forms, and passing away into dissolution. This includes the mineral, the plant, the animal, and the human. But when we look at the last-named, a new possibility opens up which could not have happened to Nature's earlier kingdoms. All things dissolve in the end, I wrote, but man alone dissolves *consciously* into a higher Consciousness.

§

The course taken by each life-entity in its slow development is neither straight nor direct, but a winding one, going forward and backward upward and downward, curved like a series of interwoven spirals.

§

Why should the waves of life-entities take this spiral-like two-way course? Why do they not go along a direct single one? The answer is that they have to gather experience to grow; if this experience includes totally opposed conditions, *all* the parts of each entity can grow, all its latent qualities can be stirred into unfoldment. In the oppositions of birth and death, growth and decay, in-breathing and exhaling, youth and age, joy and suffering, introversion and extroversion, spirit-form and body-form, it fulfils itself.

§

Experience teaches human beings that life is governed by duality, that like Nature itself, it holds contrasts and oppositions within itself. Just as day and night are positive and negative poles, so are joy and sorrow. But just as there is a point where day meets night, a point which we call the twilight, so in our experience, human experience, the joys and sorrows have a neutral point—and in Nature, an equilibrium. So the mind must find its own equilibrium, and thus it will find its own sense of peace. To see that duality governs everything is to see why human life is one tremendous paradox.

§

The truth of paradox is possibly too deep for most persons to accept; apparently it is too self-contradictory. This is why the balanced mind is needed to understand that the contradiction is joined with complementary roles.

§

Every individual comes, in time, into possession of that very peace. The answer, so often summed up in one word, is paradox. For this is what sums up the world, life, and man.

§

What I learned from the Hindu texts about Brahma breathing out the universe into physical existence and then back into Himself, not only referred symbolically to the periodic reincarnations of the universe but also and actually to its moment-to-moment rhythm of interchange of contrasts, differences, and even opposites. It is this interchange which not only makes universal existence possible but which also sustains universal equilibrium. Without it there would be no world for man to behold, no experiences in it for him to develop, no conscious awareness in time and space.

§

It would be a mistake to believe that these two forces, although so very different from each other, are fighting each other. This is not so. They are to be regarded as complementary to one another. They are like positive and negative poles in electricity, and they must exist together or die together. They are inseparable, but the need between them is correct balance, or equilibrium.

§

Everything in Nature is included within this law of contrasting conditions. Nothing is excepted from it. Even the universe of definite, spherical forms exists in its opposite—formless space. We humans may not like the law; we would prefer light without shadow, joy without pain; but such is the World-Idea, God's thought. It is the product of infinite wisdom and as such we may trust and accept that it could not be otherwise.

§

One of the helpful notions which philosophy contributes to those who not only seek Truth through the intellect alone, but also seek to know how they are to live with that Truth in the active world itself, is the idea of the twofold view. There is the immediate view and there is the ultimate viewpoint. The first offers us a convenient way of looking at our activities in the world and of dealing with them whilst yet holding firmly to the Truth. The first tells us to act as if the world is real in the absolute sense. The second viewpoint, the ultimate, tells us that there can be only one true way of looking at everything, because there is only one Reality. Since it deals with the Absolute, where time and space disappear and there is no subject to view, no object to be viewed, there is no thought or complex of thoughts which can hold it; it transcends intellect. Therefore it could be said that philosophy uses duality for its practical viewpoint, but it stays in nonduality for its basic one, thus reconciling both.

§

Everything comes in pairs as death with life and darkness with light. Whatever seems to be necessary to existence is so only because its opposite is equally necessary. Duality is a governing factor of the world and everything within it including ourselves. That alone is outside the world, is nondual, which is untouchable Reality. This is the Chinese idea of yin and yang, and the *Bhagavad Gita*'s expression "the pairs of opposites" conveys the same idea. Duality is a fact. It is here. But it is also an illusion and the opposite truth which completes it is the nondual. We may deplore the illusory nature of our existence, but we need not get lost in it for it is fulfilled, completed, and finalized in its complement the Real.

§

The idea of man which exists in and is eternally known by the World-Mind is a master-idea.

§

The man that is made in the image of God is not physical man or desire-filled man or thought-breeding man but he who dwells behind all these—silent, serene, and unnoticed.

§

The World-Idea is self-existent. It is unfolded in time and by time; it is the basis of the universe and reflected in the human being. It is the fundamental pattern of both and provides the fundamental meaning of human life.

§

Though it seems entirely our own faculty, this thought-making power is derived from a hidden one, the Universal Mind, in which all other men's minds lie embedded. What he does with this power is a man's own concern, for better or worse, yielding him more knowledge or more ignorance.

§

The notion that God created this world spectacle for the benefit of man alone is an absurd and unwarranted anthropolatry, but the notion that life first attains individual self-consciousness in man is justified in philosophy and by experience. What is it of which he alone is conscious? It is of being himself, his ego. In all earlier stages of evolution, consciousness is entirely veiled in its forms and never becomes self-aware. Only in the human state does individual consciousness of being first dawn. There may exist on other planets creatures infinitely more intelligent and more amiable than human beings. We may not be the only pebbles on the beach of life. Nevertheless the piece of arrogance which places man highest in the scale of existence contains the dim reverberation of a great truth, for man bears the divine within his breast.

§

Students who have come finally to philosophy from the Indian Advaita Vedanta, bring with them the belief that the divine soul having somehow lost its consciousness is now seeking to become self-conscious again. They suppose that the ego originates and ends on the same level—divinity—and therefore the question is often asked why it should go forth on such a long and unnecessary journey. This question is a misconceived one. It is not the ego itself which ever was consciously divine, but its source, the Overself. The ego's divine character lies in its essential but hidden being, but it has never known that. The purpose of gathering experience (the evolutionary process) is precisely to bring it to such awareness. The ego comes to slow birth in finite consciousness out of utter unconsciousness and, later, to recognition and union with its infinite source. That source, whence it has emanated, remains untouched, unaffected, ever knowing and serenely witnessing. The purpose in this evolution is the ego's own advancement. When the Quest is reached, the Overself reveals its presence fitfully and brokenly at first but later the hide-and-seek game ends in loving union.

§

What is the use, ask many questioners, of first, an evolution of the human soul which merely brings it back to the same point where it started and second, of developing a selfhood through the long cycles of evolution only to have it merged or dissolved in the end into the unselfed Absolute? Is not the whole scheme absurdly useless? The answer is that if this were really the case, the criticism passed would be quite a fair one. But it is not the case. The unit of life emanated from the Overself begins with the merest glimmer of consciousness, appearing on our plane as a protozoic cell. It evolves eventually into the fullest human consciousness, including the intellectual and spiritual. It does not finish as it began; on the contrary, there is a grand purpose behind all its travail. There is thus a wide gulf between its original state and its final one. The second point is more difficult to clear up, but it may be plainly affirmed that man's individuality survives even in the divinest state accessible to him. There it becomes the same in quality but not identical in essence. The most intimate mental and physical experiences of human love cast a little light for our comprehension of this mystery. The misunderstanding which leads to these questions arises chiefly because of the error which believes that it is the divine soul which goes through all this pilgrimage by reincarnating in a series of earthly forms. The true teaching about reincarnation is not that the divine soul enters into the captivity and ignorance of the flesh again and again but that something emanated from the soul, that is, a unit of life that eventually develops into the personal ego, does so. The

Overself contains this reincarnating ego within itself but does not itself reincarnate. It is the parent; the ego is only its offspring. The long and tremendous evolution through which the unit of life passes from its primitive cellular existence to its matured human one is a genuine evolution of its consciousness. Whoever believes that the process first plunges a soul down from the heights into a body or forces Spirit to lose itself in Matter, and then leaves it no alternative but to climb all the way back to the lost summit again, believes wrongly. The Overself never descends or climbs, never loses its own sublime consciousness. What really does this is something that emanates from it and that consequently holds its capacity and power in latency, something which is finited out of the Overself's infinitude and becomes first, the simple unit of life and later, the complex human ego. It is not the Overself that suffers and struggles during this long unfoldment but its child, the ego. It is not the Overself that slowly expands its intelligence and consciousness, but the ego. It is not the Overself that gets deluded by ignorance and passion, by selfishness and extroversion, but the ego.

The belief in the merger of the ego held by some Hindu sects or in its annihilation held by some Buddhist ones, is unphilosophical. The "I" differentiated itself out of the infinite ocean of Mind into a distinct individuality after a long development through the diverse kingdoms of Nature. Having thus arrived at consciousness of what it is, having travelled the spiral of growth from germ to man, the result of all this effort is certainly not gained only to be thrown away.

Were this to happen then the entire history of the human race would be a meaningless one, its entire travail a resultless one, its entire aspiration a valueless one. If evolution were merely the complementary return journey of an involutionary process, if the evolving entity arrived only at its starting point for all its pains, then the whole plan would be a senseless one. If the journey of man consisted of nothing more than treading a circle from the time of his emergence from the Divine Essence to the time of his mergence back into it, it would be a vain and useless activity. It would be a stupendous adventure but also a stupid one. There is something more than that in his movement. Except in the speculations of certain theorists, it simply does not happen.

The self-consciousness thus developed will not be dissolved, extinguished, or re-absorbed into the Whole again, leaving not a trace behind. Rather will it begin a new spiral of evolution towards higher altitudes of consciousness and diviner levels of being, in which it will co-operate as harmoniously with the universal existence as formerly it collided against it. It will not separate its own good from the general good. Here is part of the answer to this question: What are the ultimate reasons for human wanderings through the world-process? That life matters, that the universe possesses meaning, and that the evolutionary agonies are leading to something worthwhile—these are beliefs we are entitled to hold. If the cosmos is a wheel which turns and turns endlessly, it does not turn aimlessly. Evolution does not return us to the starting point as we were. The ascent is not a circle but a spiral.

Evolution presupposes that its own possibility has always been latent within the evolving entities. Hence the highest form is hidden away in the lowest one. There is development from the blindly instinctive life of animals to the consciously thinking life of man. The blind instinctive struggles of the plant to sustain itself are displaced in the evolutionary process by the intelligent self-conscious efforts of the man. Nor does this ascent end in the Vedantic merger or the Buddhistic annihilation. It could not, for it is a development of the individuality. Everywhere we find that evolution produces variety. There are myriads of individual entities, but each possesses some quality of uniqueness which distinguishes it from all others. Life may be one but its multitudinous expressions do differ, as though difference were inherent in such expression.

Evolution as mentalistically defined by philosophy is not quite the same as evolution as materialistically defined by Darwin. With us it is simply the mode of striving, through rhythmic rise and fall, for an ever fuller expansion of the individual unit's consciousness. However, the ego already possesses all such possibilities latently. Consequently the whole process, although apparently an ascending one, is really an unfolding one.

§

The ideas in a man's mind are hidden and secret until he expresses them through actions, or as speech, or as the visible creations and productions of his hands, or in behaviour generally. Those ideas are neither lost nor destroyed. They are a permanent part of the man's memory and character and consciousness and subconsciousness, where they have been recorded as automatically and as durably as a master phonograph disc records music. Just as a wax copy may be burnt but the music will still live on in the master disc, so the cosmos may be annihilated or disintegrate completely but the creative idea of it will still live on in the World-Mind. More, in the same way a man's body may die and disintegrate, but the creative idea of him will still remain in the World-Mind as his Soul. It will not die. It's his real Self, his perfect Self. It is the true Idea of him which is forever calling to be realized. It is the unmanifest image of God in which man is made and which he has yet to bring into manifestation in his everyday consciousness.

§

No living creature in the kingdom of animals knows more than its immediate surroundings or cares for more than the sustenance of its immediate existence. It lives in an immense and varied universe but that fact is lost to its mentality and outside its interest. Only when the evolving entity attains the stage of developed human beings does this unconsciousness disappear. Then life takes on a larger meaning and the life-force becomes aware of itself, individualized, self-conscious. Only then does a higher purpose become possible and apparent.

§

There is not one cell in the whole organism of man which does not reflect in miniature the pattern, the proportions, and the functions of the immense cosmos itself.

§

There is no choice in the matter, ultimately, although there is immediately. The entire human race will have to traverse the course chalked out for it, will have to develop the finer feelings, the concrete intellect, the abstract intellect, the balance between the different sides. If men do not seek to do so now, it is only a question of time before they will be forced to do so later.

§

It is not possible to know what lies at the heart of the great mystery, but it is possible to know what it is not. The intellect, bound by the forms of logic and conditioned by the linkage between cause and effect, here enters a realm where these hold no sway. The discoveries of Germany's leading nuclear physicist, Professor Heisenberg, were formulated in his law of indeterminacy. The ancient Egyptian sages symbolized this inscrutability under the figure of the Veil of Isis. The ancient Hindu sages called it Maya, that is, the inexplicable. Argument and debate, ferreting and probing among all available facts, searching and sifting of records are futile here. This is the real truth behind the doctrine of agnosticism. Every man, no matter who he be, from the most knowledgeable scientist to the profoundest philosopher, must bow his head in acknowledgment of this human limitation. He is still a human being, he is not a god. Yet there is something godlike within him and this he must find and cling to for his true salvation, his only redemption. If he does this he will fulfil his purpose on earth and then only he finds true peace of mind and an end to all this restless, agitated, uncertain mental condition. Study what this planet's best men have given us. It is no truer message than this: "Seek for the divine within yourself, return to it every day, learn how to continue in it and finally *be* it."

§

27

WORLD MIND

God as the Supreme Individual—
God as Mind-In-Activity—As Solar Logos

All scientific evidence indicates that there is a single power which presides over the entire universe, and all religious mystic experience and philosophic insight confirms it. Not only is this so, but this power also maintains the universe; its intelligence is unique, matchless, incredible. This power is what I call the World-Mind.

§

In all these studies the principal concept should be returned to again and again: the entire universe, everything—objects and creatures—is in Mind. I hold all the objects of my experience in *my* consciousness but I myself am held, along with them, in an incredibly greater consciousness, the World-Mind's.

§

For us who are philosophically minded, the World-Mind truly exists. For us it is God, and for us there is a relationship with it—the relationship of devotion and aspiration, of communion and meditation. All the abstract talk about nonduality may go on, but in the end the talkers must humble themselves before the infinite Being until they are as nothing and until they are lost in the stillness—Its stillness.

§

We are frequently informed by religious and mystical sources that God is Love. It would be needful for those who accept this statement to balance and complete it by the affirmation that God is Pure Intelligence.

§

The World-Mind is a radiation of the forever incomprehensible Mind. It is the essence of all things and all beings, from the smallest to the largest.

§

If God were not a mystery He would not be God. Men who claim to know Him need semantic correction; this said, their experience may yet be exceptional, elevating, and immaterialistic. But let God remain God, incomprehensible and untouchable.

§

In the sense that the World-Mind is the active agent behind and within the universe, it is carrying the whole burden of creation; it is the real doer, carrying us and our actions too.

§

Swami Narayananda said, "God is the Subject of all subjects. In one sense He can never be known. It being the very Subject of all subjects how can we know it? To know means to objectify a thing, and the Supreme Subject can never become an object. In another sense, God is more than known to us. For it is our very Self. What proof do we want for our very existence?"

§

There has been so much friction and clash between the different religions because of this idea: whether God is personal or impersonal—so much persecution, even hatred, so unnecessarily. I say unnecessarily because the difference between the two conceptions is only an apparent one. Mind is the source of all; this is Mind inactive. Mind as World-Mind-in-manifestation is the personal God. Between essence and manifestation the only difference is that essence is hidden and manifestation is known. World-Mind is personal (in the sense of being what the Hindus call "Ishvara"); Mind is totally impersonal. Basically, the two are one.

§

Men of inferior intelligence quite naturally want a God who will be attentive to their requirements, interested in their personal lives, and helpful during times of distress. That is to say, they want a human God. Men of superior intelligence come in time to consider God as an impersonal essence that is everywhere present, and consequently embodied in themselves and to be communed with interiorly too. That is to say, they recognize only a mystical God. Men of the highest intelligence perceive that the "I" is illusory, that it is only ignorance of this fact that causes man to regard himself as a separate embodiment of the divine essence, and that in reality there is only this nondual nameless being. How impossible it is to get men of inferior intelligence to worship or even to credit such an Existence which has no shape, no individuality, no thinking even! Hence such men are given a figure after their own image as God, a deity that is a personal, human, five-sensed being.

§

All verbal definitions of the World-Mind are inevitably limited and inadequate. If the statements here made seem to be of the nature of dogmatic concepts it is because of the inadequacy of language to convey more subtle meaning. They who read these lines with intuitive insight allied to clear thinking will see that the concepts are flexible verbal frames for holding thought steady in that borderland of human consciousness where thinking verges on wordless knowing.

§

The Light of the World-Mind is the Source of the physical universe; the Love of the World-Mind is its structural basis.

§

The World-Mind is called Adi-buddhi in the Nepalese-Tibetan esotericism: meaning Divine Ideation, The First Intelligence, the Universal Wisdom.

§

The World-Mind eternally thinks this universe into being in a pulsating rhythm of thought and rest. The process is as eternal as the World-Mind itself. The energies which accompany this thinking are electrical. The scientists note and tap the energies, and ignore the Idea and the Mind they are expressing.

§

God-active, the Unseen Power, is (for us humans) the World-Mind. God-in-repose is Mind.

§

It would however be a mistake to consider the World-Mind as one entity and Mind as another separate from it. It would be truer to consider World-Mind as the active function of Mind. Mind cannot be separated from its powers. The two are one. In its quiescent state it is simply Mind. In its active state it is World-Mind. Mind in its inmost transcendent nature is the inscrutable mystery of Mysteries but when expressing itself in act and immanent in the universe, it is the World-Mind. We may find in the attributes of the manifested God—that is, the World-Mind—the only indications of the quality, existence, and character of the unmanifest Godhead that it is possible for man to comprehend. All this is a mystery which is and perhaps forever will remain an incomprehensible paradox.

§

It is the *presence* of the World-Mind which makes things happen according to the World-Idea: the former does not need to put forward each particular activity.

§

The point which appears in space is a point of light. It spreads and spreads and spreads and becomes the World-Mind. God has emerged out of Godhead. And out of the World-Mind the world itself emerges—not all at once, but in various stages. From that great light come all other and lesser lights, come the suns and the planets, the galaxies, the universes, and all the mighty hosts of creatures small and great, of beings just beginning to sense and others fully conscious, aware, wise. And with the world appear the opposites, the dual principle which can be detected everywhere in Nature, the yin and yang of Chinese thought.

§

Were the World-Mind beyond, because outside, the finite universe, then it would be limited by that universe and thus lose its own infinitude. But because *it includes* the universe completely within itself while remaining completely unlimited, it is genuinely infinite. World-Mind is neither limited nor dissipated by its self-projection in the universe. If World-Mind is immanent in the universe, it is not confined to the universe; if it is present in every particle of the All, its expression is not exhausted by the All.

§

The Intelligence which formulated the World-Idea is living and creative—in short, Divine. The so-called laws of nature merely show its workings.

§

Spinoza arrived at this truth by clear mathematical reflection, that "each particular thing is expressed by infinite ideas in infinite ways in the infinite understanding of God."

§

The World-Mind, however, has a double life. As Mind, it is eternally free but as the World-Mind, it is eternally crucified, as Plato said, on the cross of the world's body.

§

How does God "create" the universe? Since in the beginning God alone is, there is no second substance that can be used for such "creation." God is forced to use his own substance for the purpose. God is Infinite Mind, so he uses mental power--Imagination—working on mental substance—Thought—to produce the result which appears to us as the universe.

§

There is no power in the material universe itself. All its forces and energies derive from a single source—the World-Mind—whose thinking is expressed by that universe.

§

Can anything be derived from something that is essentially different from it? This is impossible. Therefore existence cannot be derived from non-existence. If the universe exists today, then its essence must have existed when the universe itself had not been formed. This essence needed no "creation" for it was God, World-Mind, Itself.

§

Manifestation implies the necessity of manifesting. But it might be objected that any sort of necessity existing in the divine equally implies its insufficiency. The answer is that the number One may become aware of itself as being one only by becoming aware of the presence of Two—itself and another. But the figure Nought is under no compulsion. Here we have a mathematical hint towards understanding the riddle of manifestation. Mind as Void is the supreme inconceivable unmanifesting ultimate whereas the World-Mind is forever throwing forth the universe-series as a second, an "other" wherein it becomes self-aware.

§

Thus make it. Unseen itself, its presence is seen in every earthly form; unthinkable though it be, its existence is self-manifested in every thought.

§

If it be true that absolute divine Mind knows nothing of the universe, nothing of mortal man, then it is also true that the World-Mind, which is its other aspect, does know them.

§

The visible cosmos has come into being out of the invisible absolute by a process of emanation. That is why the relation between them is not only pantheistic but also transcendent.

§

If the divine activity ceases in one universe it continues at the same time in another. If our World-Mind returns to its source in the end, there are other World-Minds and other worlds which continue. Creation is a thing without beginning and without end, but there are interludes and periods of rest just as there are in the individual's own life in and outside the body.

§

The one infinite life-power which reveals itself in the cosmos and manifests itself through time and space, cannot be named. It is something that *is*. For a name would falsely separate it from other things when the truth is that it *is* those things, all things. Nor would we know what to call it, since we know nothing about its real nature.

§

Modern man looks in all sorts of impossible places for an invisible God and will not worship the visible God which confronts him. Yet little thinking is needed to show that we are all suckled at the everlasting breast of Nature. It is easy to see that the source of all life is the sun and that its creative, protective, and destructive powers are responsible for the entire physical process of the universe. However it is not merely to the physical sun alone that the aspirant addresses himself but to the World-Mind behind it. He must look upon the sun as a veritable self-expression and self-showing of the World-Mind to all its creatures.

§

All the forces of the physical world are derived from a single source—the solar energy.

§

The statement "Light is God" is meant in two senses: first, as the poetical and a psychical fact that, in the present condition of the human being, his spiritual ignorance is equivalent to darkness and his discovery of God is equivalent to light; second, as the scientific fact that has verified in its findings that all physical matter ultimately reduces itself to waves of light, and since God has made the universe out of His own substance, the light-waves are ultimately divine.

§

28

THE ALONE

Mind-In-Itself—The Unique Mind—As Absolute

Philosophy understands sympathetically but does not agree practically with the Buddha's consistent refusal to explain the ultimate realization. His counsel to disciples was: "What word is there to be sent from a region where the chariot of speech finds no track on which to go? Therefore to their questions offer them silence only."

It is certainly hard to capture this transcendental indefinable experience in prosaic pen-and-ink notes. But is it really so impossible for the initiate to break his silence and voice his knowledge in some dim finited adumbration of the Infinite? To confess that intellectually we know nothing and can know nothing about the Absolute is understandable. But to say that therefore we should leave its existence entirely out of our intellectual world-view, is not. For although the exact definition and direct explanation of words are unable to catch the whole of this subtle experience within their receiving range because they are turned into ordinary human intellectual emotional and physical experience, they may nevertheless evoke an intuitive recognition of its beauty; they may suggest to sensitive minds a hint of its worth and they may arouse the first aspiration towards its attainment for oneself.

Why if this state transcends thinking, whether in words or pictures, have so many mystics nevertheless written so much about it? That they have protested at the same time the impossibility of describing the highest levels of their experience does not alter this curious fact. The answer to our question is that to have kept completely silent and not to have revealed that such a unique experience is possible and that such a supreme reality is existent would have been to have left their less fortunate fellow men in utter ignorance of an immensely important truth about human life and destiny. But to have left some record behind them, even if it would only hint at what it could not adequately describe, would be to have left some light in the darkness. And even though an intellectual statement of a super-intellectual fact is only like an indirect and reflected light, nevertheless it is better than having no light at all.

So long as men feel the need to converse with other men on this subject, so long as masters seek to instruct disciples in it, and so long as fortunate seers recognize the duty to leave some record—even if it be an imperfect one—of their enlightenment behind them for unfortunate humanity, so long will the silence have to be broken, despite Buddha, and the lost word uttered anew.

§

The topic with which all such metaphysical thinking should end after it has pondered on mentalism is that out of which the thinking principle itself arises—Mind—and it should be considered under its aspect as the one reality. When this intellectual understanding is brought within one's own experience as fact, when it is made as much one's own as a bodily pain, then it becomes direct insight. Such thinking is the most profitable and resultful in which he can engage, for it brings the student to the very portal of Mind where it stops activity by itself and where the differentiation of ideas disappears. As the mental muscles strain after this concept of the Absolute, the Ineffable and Infinite, they lose their materialist rigidity and become more sensitive to intimations from the Overself. When thinking is able to reach such a profound depth that it attains utter impersonality and calm universality, it is able to approach the fundamental principle of its own being. When hard thinking reaches a culminating point, it then voluntarily destroys itself. Such an attainment of course can take place deep within the innermost recesses of the individual's consciousness alone.

§

Mentalism is the study of Mind and its product, thoughts. To separate the two, to disentangle them, is to become aware of Awareness itself. This achievement comes not by any process of intellectual activity but by the very opposite—suspending such activity. And it comes not as another idea but as extremely vivid, powerfully compelling insight.

§

Thinking can, ordinarily, only produce more thoughts. Even thinking about truth, about reality, however correct it be, shares this limitation. But if properly instructed it will know its place and understand the situation, with the consequence that at the proper moment it will make no further effort, and will seek to merge into meditation. When the merger is successfully completed, a holy silence will pervade the consciousness which remains. Truth will then be revealed of its own accord.

§

If Mind is to be regarded aright, we must put out of our thought even the notion of the cosmic Ever-Becoming. But to do this is to enter a virtual Void? Precisely. When we take away all the forms of external physical existence and all the differences of internal mental existence, what we get is an utter emptiness of being which can hardly be differentiated after we have taken away its features and individualities, its finite times and finite distances. There is then nothing but a great void. What is the nature of this void? It is pure Thought. It is out of this empty Thought that the fullness of the universe has paradoxically evolved. Hence it is said that the world's reality is secondary whereas Mind's reality is primary. In the Void the hidden oneness of things is disengaged from the things themselves. Silence therefore is not merely the negation of sound but rather the element in which, as Carlyle said, great things fashion themselves. It is the supreme storehouse of power.

§

To attach oneself to a guru, an avatar, one religion, one creed, is to see the stars only. To put one's faith in the Infinite Being and in its presence within the heart, is to see the vast empty sky itself. The stars will come and go, will disintegrate and vanish, but the sky remains.

§

Mind is the essence of all manifested things as World-Mind and the Mystery behind unmanifest Nothing.

§

The term nonduality remains a sound in the air when heard, a visual image when read. Without the key of mentalism it remains just that. How many Vedanta students and, be it said, teachers interpret it aright? And that is to understand there are no two separate entities—a thing and also the thought of it. The thing is in mind, is a projection of mind as the thought. This is nonduality, for mind is not apart from what comes from and goes back into it. As with things, so with bodies and worlds. All appear along with the ultimately cosmic but immediately individual thought of them.

§

Nonduality simply means that there is nothing other than the unseen Power, nothing else, no universe, no creature.

§

What we need to grasp is that although our apprehension of the Real is gradual, the Real is nonetheless with us at every moment in all its radiant totality. Modern science has filled our heads with the false notion that reality is in a state of evolution, whereas it is only our mental concept of reality which is in a state of evolution.

§

He will have gone far intellectually when he can understand the statement that mind is the seeker but Mind is the sought.

§

He can find the nothingness within himself only after he has evaluated the nothingness of himself. The mystery of the Great Void does not disclose itself to the smugly satisfied or the arrogantly proud or the intellectually conceited.

§

IT is the Principle behind both consciousness and unconsciousness, making the first possible and the second significant. Yet neither consciousness nor unconsciousness, *as we humans know them, resembles it.*

§

He will arrive at the firm unshakeable conviction that there is an inward reality behind all existence. If he wishes he may go farther still and seek to translate the intellectual idea of this reality into a conscious fact. In that case the comprehension that in the quest of pure Mind he is in quest of that which is alone the Supreme Reality in this entire universe, must possess him. The mystery of Mind is a theme upon which no aspirant can ever reflect enough: first, because of its importance, and second, because of its capacity to unfold his latent spirituality. He will doubtless feel cold on these lofty peaks of thought, but in the end he will find a heavenly reward whilst still on earth. We are not saying that something of the nature of mind as we humans know it is the supreme reality of the universe, but only that it is more like that reality than anything else we know of and certainly more like it than what we usually call by the name of "matter." The simplest way to express this is to say that Reality is of the nature of our mind rather than of our body, although it is Mind transcending the familiar phases and raised to infinity. It is the ultimate being the highest state. This is the Principle which forever remains what it was and will be. It is in the universe and yet the universe is in it too. It never evolves, for it is outside time. It has no shape, for it is outside space. It is beyond man's consciousness, for it is beyond both his thoughts and sense-experience, yet all consciousness springs mysteriously out of it. Nevertheless man may enter into its knowledge, may enter into its Void, so soon as he can drop his thoughts, let go his sense-experience, but keep his sense of being. Then he may understand what Jesus meant when saying: "He that loseth his life shall find it." Such an accomplishment may appear too spectral to be of any use to his matter-of-fact generation. What is their madness will be his sanity. He will know there is reality where they think there is nothingness.

§

There is here no form to be perceived, no image born of the senses to be worshipped, no oracular utterance to be listened for, and no emotional ecstasy to be revelled in. Hence the Chinese sage, Lao Tzu said: "In eternal non-existence I look for the spirituality of things!" The philosopher perceives that there is no such thing as creation out of nothing for the simple reason that Mind is eternally and universally present. "Nothing" is merely an appearance. Here indeed there is neither time nor space. It is like a great silent boundless circle wherein no life seems to stir, no consciousness seems to be at work, and no activity is in sway. Yet the seer will know by a pure insight which will grip his consciousness as it has never been gripped before, that here indeed is the root of all life, all consciousness, and all activity. But how it is so is as inexplicable intellectually as what its nature is. With the Mind the last word of human comprehension is uttered. With the Mind the last world of possible being is explored. But whereas the utterance is comprehensible by his consciousness, the speaker is not. It is a Silence which speaks but what it says is only that it IS; more than that none can hear.

§

The absoluteness of the Godhead is complete and basic. It is not categorically identical with man any more than the ray is with the sun; they are different although not more fundamentally different than the ray from the sun. Hence there can be no direct communication and no positive relationship between them. A profound impenetrability, an existence beyond comprehension, is the first characteristic of the Godhead, when gazed at by human sight.

§

The Mind's first expression is the Void. The second and succeeding is the Light, that is, the World-Mind. This is followed by the third, the World-Idea. Finally comes the fourth, manifestation of the world itself.

§

Mind is the essence of all conscious beings. Their consciousness is derivative, borrowed from it; they could know nothing of their own power; whereas Mind alone knows all things and itself. When it knows them in time, it is World-Mind; when it knows itself alone, it is the unknown to man and unknowable Godhead.

§

The Supreme Godhead is unindividualized. The World-Mind is individuated (but not personalized) into emanated Overselves. The Overself is an individual, but not a person. The ego is personal.

§

As Mind the Real is static, as World-Mind it is dynamic. As Godhead It alone *is* in the stillness of being; but as God it is the source, substance, and power of the universe. As Mind there is no second thing, no second intelligence to ask the question why It stirred and breathed forth World-Mind, hence why the whole world-process exists. Only man asks this question and it returns unanswered.

§

What is the meaning of the words "the Holy Trinity"? The Father is the absolute and ineffable Godhead, Mind in its ultimate being. The Son is the soul of the universe, that is, the World-Mind. The Holy Ghost is the soul of each individual, that is, the Overself. The Godhead is one and indivisible and not multiform and can never divide itself up into three personalities.

§

When Mind concentrates itself into the World-Mind, it establishes a focus. However vast, it goes out of its own unlimited condition, it passes from the true Infinite to the pseudo-Infinite. Consequently the World-Mind, being occupied with its cosmos, cannot be regarded as possessed of the absolute character of Pure Mind. For what is its work but a movement of imagination? And where in the ineffable absolute is there room for either work or imagination? The one would break its eternal stillness, the other would veil its unchangeable reality. This of course it can never do, for Being can never become Non-Being. But it can send forth an emanation from itself. Such an emanation is the World-Mind. Through its prolonged contemplation of the cosmos Mind thus becomes a fragment of itself, bereft of its own undifferentiated unbroken unity. Nevertheless the World-Mind, through its deputy the Overself, is still for humans the highest possible goal.

§

Neither the senses nor the intellect can tell us anything about the intrinsic nature of this Infinite Mind. Nevertheless we are not left in total ignorance about it. From its manifestation, the cosmos, we may catch a hint of its Intelligence. From its emanation, the soul, we may catch more than a hint of its Beneficence. "More than," I say, because the emanation may be felt within us as our very being whereas the manifestation is outside us and is apart.

§

The Infinite Power can never become exhausted. It is self-sustaining.

§

Let us not deceive ourselves and dishonour the Supreme Being by thinking that we know anything at all about IT. We know nothing. The intellect may formulate conceptions, the intuition may give glimpses, but these are our human reactions to IT. Even the sage, who has attained a harmony with his Overself, has found only the godlike *within himself*. Yes, it is certainly the Light, but it is so *for him*, for the human being. He still stands as much outside the divine Mystery as everyone else. The difference is that whereas they stand in darkness he stands in this Light.

§

The chasm between the Real and man seems entirely impassable. The intellect is conditioned by its own finitude, by its particular set of space and time perceptions. It is unable to function where absolutes alone reign. The infinite eternal and absolute existence eludes the grasp of man's logical thought. He may form mental pictures of it but at best they will be as far off from it as a photograph is far off from flesh and blood. Idea-worship is idol-worship. Everything else is an object of knowledge, experienced in a certain way by ourself as the knower of it; but the Infinite Real cannot be an object of anyone's knowledge simply because it cannot be conditioned in any way whatsoever. It is absolute. If it is to be known to all it must therefore be in a totally different way from that of ordinary experience. It is as inaccessible to psychic experience as it is impenetrable by thought and feeling. But although we may not directly know Reality, we may know that it is, and that in some mysterious way the whole cosmic existence roots from it. Thus whichever way man turns he, the finite creature, finds the door closed upon his face. The Infinite and Absolute Essence is forever beyond his vision, unreachable by his knowing capacity and inaccessible to his experience and will forever remain so. The point is so subtle that, unless its development is expressed with great care here, it is likely to be misunderstood. Although man must pause here and say, with Socrates, "None knoweth save God only"—for with this conception he has gone as far as human thought can grasp such mysteries—nevertheless he may know that the seers have not invented an imaginary Reality. He has neither been left alone in his mortality nor abandoned utterly to his finitude. The mysterious Godhead has provided a witness to its sacred existence, a Deputy to evidence its secret rulership. And that Witness and Deputy *can* be found for it sits imperishable in the very heart of man himself. It is indeed his true self, his immortal soul, his Overself. Although the ultimate principle is said to be inconceivable and unknowable, this is so only in relation to man's ordinary intellect and physical senses. It is not so in relation to a faculty in him which is still potential and unevolved—insight. If it be true that even no adept has ever seen the mysterious absolute, it is also true that he has seen the way it manifests its presence through something intimately emanated from it. If the nameless formless Void from which all things spring up and into which they go back is a world so subtle that it is not really intellectually understandable and so mysterious that it is not even mystically experienceable, we may however experience the strange atmosphere emanating from it, the unearthly aura signifying its hidden presence.

§

Reason tells us that pure Thought cannot know itself because that would set up a duality which would be false if pure thought is the only real existence. But this is only reason's inability to measure what transcends itself. Although all ordinary experience confirms it, extraordinary experience refutes it.

§

In the moment that there dawns on his understanding the fact of Mind's beginninglessness and deathlessness, he gains the second illumination, the first being that of the ego's illusoriness and transiency.

§

The divine essence is Unknowable to the finite intellect, but knowable, in a certain sense, by the deepest intuition. And this sense can arise to the man previously prepared by instruction and purification, or by studied knowledge and purification, if he puts away thoughts, even those about the essence, or lets them lapse of their own accord, and awaits its self-disclosure patiently, reverently, lovingly—three conditions of high importance.

§

The inability of little man to enter into the knowledge of transcendent God does not doom him to perpetual ignorance. For God, being present in all things, is present in him too. The flame is still in the spark. Here is his hope and chance. Just as he knows his own personal identity, so God knows God in him as the Overself. This divine knowing *is continually going on, whether he is awake or asleep, whether he is an atheist or a saint.* He can share in it too, but only by consenting to submit his intellect to his intuition. This is not an arbitrary condition imposed by theocratic whim but one which inheres in the very nature of the knowing processes. By accepting it, he may put the whole matter to the test and learn for himself, in due time, his other nonpersonal identity.

§

The actual experience alone can settle this argument. This is what I found: The ego vanished; the everyday "I" which the world knew and which knew the world, was no longer there. But a new and diviner individuality appeared in its place, a consciousness which could say "I AM" and which I recognized to have been my real self all along. It was not lost, merged, or dissolved: it was fully and vividly conscious that it was a point *in* universal Mind and so not apart from that Mind itself. Only the lower self, the false self, was gone but that was a loss for which to be immeasurably grateful.

§

Every man credits himself with having consciousness during the wakeful state. He never questions or disputes the fact. He does not need anyone else to tell it to him, nor does he tell it to himself. It is the surest part of his knowledge. Yet this is not a knowing which he brings into the field of awareness. It is known differently from the way other facts are known by him. This difference is that the ego is absent from the knowledge—the fact is not actually perceived.

§

Mind has no second thing to know and experience, no world. Nor can anyone know and experience Mind and yet remain an individual, a person.

§

The final grade of inner experience, the deepest phase of contemplation, is one where the experiencer himself disappears, the meditator vanishes, the knower no longer has an object—not even the Overself—to know for duality collapses. Because this grade is beyond the supreme "Light" experience where the Overself reveals its presence visually as a dazzling mass, shaft, ball, or ray of unearthly radiance which is seen whether the bodily eyes are open or closed, it has been called the divine darkness.

§

(a) Awareness alone *is* whatever it turns its attention to, seems to exist at the time: only that. If to Void then there is nothing else. If to world, then world assumes reality. (b) What is it that is aware? The thought of a point of awareness creates, gives reality at the lowest level to ego, and at the highest to Higher Self but when the thought itself is dropped there is only the One Existence, Being, in the divine Emptiness. It is therefore the Source of all life, intelligence, form. (c) The idea held becomes direct experience for the personality, the awareness becomes direct perception.

§

The true union, completely authentic and completely beatific, where mind melts into Mind without the admixture of personal wish or traditional suggestion, cannot be properly described in words. For he who experiences it may know its onset or its end because of the enormous contrast with his ordinary self, but he will not know its full height simply because he will not even know that he is experiencing it. *For to do so would be to re-introduce the ego again and thus fall away from the purity of the union.* There would then be admixture—which is the fate of most unions.

§

If you believe that you have had the ultimate experience, it is more likely that you had an emotional, or mental, or mystic one. The authentic thing does not *enter* consciousness. You do not know that it has transpired. You discover it is already here only by looking back at what you were and contrasting it with what you now are; or when others recognize it in you and draw attention to it; or when a situation arises which throws up your real status. It is a permanent fact, not a brief mystic "glimpse."

§

After the last sermon has been preached, the last book written, Mind remains the Mystery behind all mysteries. Thought cannot conceive It, imagination cannot picture It, nor language express It. The greatest mystic's experience is only his own personal reaction to Its atmosphere, as from a distance. Even this blows him to pieces like a bomb, but the fact that he can collect them together again afterwards shows that it must have been present in some inexplicable supernormal way and was not lost, both to continue existence and to remember the event.

§

Only after he has worked his way through different degrees of comprehension of the world whose passing his own development requires, and even after he has penetrated the mystery beyond it, does he come to the unexpected insight and attitude which frees him from both. In other words he is neither in the Void, the One, or the Many yet nor is he not in them. Truth thus becomes a triple paradox!

§

In *The Hidden Teaching Beyond Yoga* and *The Wisdom of the Overself* I unveiled that portion of the hidden teaching which negated materialism and showed the world to be immaterial and spiritual. In this book I unveil the remaining portion which shows that the person himself is devoid of real existence, that the ego is a fiction, and that there is only the One Universal Mind.

§

The "Void" means void of all mental activity and productivity. It means that the notions and images of the mind have been emptied out, that all perceptions of the body and conceptions of the brain have gone.

§

Without keeping steadily in view this original mentalness of things and hence their original oneness with self and Mind, the mystic must naturally get confused if not deceived by what he takes to be the opposition of Spirit and Matter. The mystic looks within, to self; the materialist looks without, to world. And each misses what the other finds. But to the philosopher neither of these is primary. He looks to that Mind of which both self and world are but manifestations and in which he finds the manifestations also. It is not enough for him to receive, as the mystic receives, fitful and occasional illuminations from periodic meditation. He relates this intellectual understanding to his further discovery got during mystical self-absorption in the Void that the reality of his own self is Mind. Back in the world once more he studies it again under this further light, confirms that the manifold world consists ultimately of mental images, conjoins with his full metaphysical understanding that it is simply Mind in manifestation, and thus comes to comprehend that it is essentially one with the same Mind which he experiences in self-absorption. Thus his insight actualizes, experiences, this Mind-in-itself as and not apart from the sensuous world whereas the mystic divides them. With insight, the sense of oneness does not destroy the sense of difference but both remain strangely present, whereas with the ordinary mystical perception each cancels the other. The myriad forms which make up the picture of this world will not disappear as an essential characteristic of reality nor will his awareness of them or his traffic with them be affected. Hence he possesses a firm and final attainment wherein he will permanently possess the insight into pure Mind even in the midst of physical sensations. He sees everything in this multitudinous world as being but the Mind itself as easily as he can see nothing, the imageless Void, as being but the Mind itself, whenever he cares to turn aside into self-absorption. He sees both the outer faces of all men and the inner depths of his own self as being but the Mind itself. Thus he experiences the unity of all existence; not intermittently but at every moment he knows the Mind as ultimate. This is the philosophic or final realization. It is as permanent as the mystic's is transient. Whatever he does or refrains from doing, whatever he experiences or fails to experience, he gives up all discriminations between reality and appearance, between truth and illusion, and lets his insight function freely as his thoughts select and cling to nothing. He experiences the miracle of undifferentiated being, the wonder of undifferenced unity. The artificial man-made frontiers melt away. He sees his fellow men as inescapably and inherently divine as they are, not merely as the mundane creatures they believe they are, so that any traces of an ascetical holier-than-thou attitude fall completely away from him.

§

To keep this origin always at the back of one's mind because it is also the end of all things, is a necessary practice. But this can only be done if one cultivates reactionlessness to the happenings of every day. This does not mean showing no outward reaction, but it does mean that deep down indifference has been achieved—not an empty indifference, but one based on seeing the Divine essence in all things, all creatures, and a Divine meaning in all happenings.

§

There is but One God, One Life, One infinite Power, one all-knowing Mind. Each man individualizes it but does not multiply it. He brings it to a point, the Overself, but does not alter its unity or change its character.

§

The One Mind is experiencing itself in us, less in the ego-shadow and fully in the Overself, hardly aware in that shadow and self-realized in the light that casts it.

§

It is the unique not only because of what IT is but also because two statements concerning IT can be quite contradictory, yet each can still be correct!

§

First, remember that It is appearing as ego; then remember to think that *you* are It; finally cease to think *of* It so you may be free of thoughts to be It!

§

Absolute mind is the actuality of human life and the plenitude of universal existence. Apart from Mind they could not even come into existence, and separated from it they could not continue to exist. Their truth and being are in It. But it would be utterly wrong to imagine the Absolute as the sum total of all finite beings and individual beings. The absolute is not the integral of all its visible aspects. It is the unlimited, the boundless void within which millions of universes may appear and disappear ceaselessly and unendingly but yet leave It unaffected. The latter do not exhaust even one millionth of its being.

§

Awareness is the very nature of one's being: it *is* the Self.

§

We must never forget that the entire dynamic movement occurs inseparably within a static blessed repose. Becoming is not apart from Being. Its kinetic movement takes place in the eternal stillness. World-Mind is forever working in the universe whereas Mind is forever at rest and its still motionlessness paradoxically makes all activity and motion possible. The infinite unconditioned Essence could never become confined within or subject to the finite limited world-form. The one dwells in a transcendental timelessness whereas the other exists in a continuous time. There cannot be two eternal principles, two ultimate realities, for each will limit the other's existence and thus deprive it of its absolute character. There is only the One, which is beyond all phenomena and yet includes them. The manifestation of the cosmic order, filled with countless objects and entities though it be, does not in any way or to any extent alter the character of the absolute Reality in which it appears. That character is unvarying—is never reduced to a lower form, never confined in a limited one, never modified by conditions, never deprived of a single iota of its being, substance, amplitude, or quality. It always is what it was. It is the ultimate origin of everything and everyone in this universe, yet it remains as unchanged by their death as by their birth, by their absence as by their presence. Everything in the universe is liable to changes, because it was born and must die. We venerate God because He is not liable to change, being ever-existent and self-subsisting, birthless and deathless.

§

It would be completely false to regard the Void as being a nothing and containing nothing. It is Being itself, and contains reality behind all things. Nor is it a kind of inertia, of paralysis. All action springs out of it, all the world-forces derive from it.

§

"The Godhead is as void as though it were not," said Eckhart. "Pass from the station of 'I' and 'We' and choose for thy home Non-entity. For when thou hast done the like of this, thou shalt reach the supreme felicity," wrote Qurratulayn, a Persian poetess, nearly a century ago. We may begin to grasp the meaning of such statements by grasping the conception that Infinite Mind is the formless, matterless, Void, Spirit. Mortal error is mistaking forms for final realities instead of penetrating to their essence, Mind. Whatever can be said about the unnameable "Void" will be not enough at least and merely symbolic at most. The mystic's last Word is the Freemason's lost Word. It can never be spoken for it can never be heard. It is the one idea which can never be transferred to another mind, the one meaning which can never get through any pen or any lip. Yet it is there—the supreme Fact behind all the myriad facts of universal existence. To elevate any form by an external worship or an internal meditation which should be given only to the formless Void is to elevate an idol in the place of God. Muhammed is reported to have once said that the worship of any one other than the great Allah, that is, "the Beginningless, the Endless," was the first of major sins. Yet to honour the sublime No-thing by thought or rite is hard for the unmetaphysical. And it requires much metaphysical insight to perceive its truth. The cold impersonality of this idea is at first repelled by us with something like horror. A change in this attitude can come about only gradually at most. But if we perseveringly pursue our quest of truth we shall overcome our aversion in the end. If it be true that Truth is not something we can utter, that the Nameless cannot fitly be represented by any name, we may however continue to use any word we like, provided we keep its limitations clearly in our understanding of it. After all, although the thinking intellect creates its own image of truth, it is the Overself that starts the creative process working. But in the end we shall have to reserve our best worship not for a particular manifestation in time but for the Timeless itself, not for a historical personage but for the impersonal Infinite.

§

We are constantly faced by the hoariest of all problems which is "Why did the Universe arise out of the depth and darkness of the Absolute Spirit?" The Seer can offer us a picture of the way in which this Spirit has involved itself into matter and is evolving itself back to self-knowledge. That is only the *How* and not the *Why* of the world. The truth is not only that nobody has ever known, that nobody knows, and that nobody will ever know the final and fundamental purpose of creation, but that God himself does not even know—for God too has arisen out of the Absolute no less than the universe, has found himself emanated from the primeval darkness and utter silence. Even God must be content to watch the flow and not wonder why, for both God and man must merge and be absorbed when they face the Absolute for the last time. (In the symbolic language of the Bible, "For man cannot meet God face to face and live.")

§

That which both Greek Plato and Indian Vedantin called "the One" did not refer to the beginning figure of a series, but to "One-without-a-Second."

§

The Real is forever and unalterably the same, whether it be the unmanifest Void or the manifested world. It has never been born and consequently can never die. It cannot divide itself into different "realities" with different space-time levels or multiply itself beyond its own primal oneness. It cannot evolve or diminish, improve or deteriorate. Whereas everything else exists in dependence upon Mind and exists for a limited time, however prolonged, and therefore has only a relative existence, Mind is the absolute, the unique, the ultimate reality because with all its innumerable manifestations in the universe it has never at any moment ceased to be itself. Only its appearances suffer change because they are in time and space, never itself, which is out of time and space. The divisions of time into past present and future are meaningless here; we may speak only of its "everness." The truth about it is timeless, as no scientific truth could ever be, in the sense that whatever fate the universe undergoes its own ultimate significance remains unchanged. If the Absolute appears *to us* as the first in the time-series, as the First Cause of the Universe, this is only true from our limited standpoint. It is in fact only our human idea. The human mind can take into itself the truth of transcendental being only by taking out of itself the screens of time space and person. For being eternally self-existence, reality is utterly timeless. Space divisions are equally unmeaning in its "Be-ness." The Absolute is both everywhere and nowhere. It cannot be considered in spatial terms. Even the word "infinite" is really such a term. If it is used here because no other is available, let it be clearly understood, then, that it is used merely as a suggestive metaphor. If the infinite did not include the finite then it would be less than infinite. It is erroneous to make them both mutually exclusive. The finite alone must exclude the infinite from its experience but not vice-versa. In the same way the infinite Duration does not exclude finite time.

§

INDEX

A

B

H

Q

R

T

BOOKS OF RELATED INTEREST FROM NAB

MEDITATION FOR PEOPLE IN CHARGE:

Paul Brunton

MEDITATION FOR PEOPLE IN CHARGE: Paul Brunton

If your authority touches lives or influences minds—or if you're close to someone whose does—this book is a great gift. It's full of accessible, handy, and inspiring wisdom and anyone else who wants (or needs) to keep in mind the ultimate happiness of everyone affected by his or her decisions. Paul Brunton is admired throughout the world for his skill in adapting traditional wisdom teachings to modern conditions.

ISBN: 978-81-7822-345-2

MEDITATION FOR PEOPLE IN CRISIS:

Paul Brunton

MEDITATION FOR PEOPLE IN CRISIS: Paul Brunton

Considering the being itself as the centre of happiness, the author describes the stages of awakening that pave the way to fulfilment. He urges the troubled to shed off their gravest inhibitions and graciously acknowledge the self. Only we can attempt an opening to our hearts and mind. For those in Crisis or with someone close in turbulent times—help is at hand.

ISBN: 978-81-7822-341-4

THE NOTE BOOKS OF PAUL BRUNTON IN 16 VOLS.

Perspectives (Vol-1): An inspiring insight into the essence of East-West spiritual philosophy.

The Quest (Vol-2): The Quest gives timely, candid, immediately useful advice about the promises and pitfalls of spiritual seeking.

Practices for The Quest Relax and Retreat (Vol-3): The book goes directly to the heart of exercises, techniques, and mental attitudes useful for spiritual self-discovery and self-development.

Meditation (Vol-4, Part-1): Meditation is an inspiring invitation to the most adventure of human spirituality—the direct experience of one's own beloved soul.

The Body (Vol-4, Part-2): The body is a balanced course in perceiving and perfecting the physical body's potential to become an eloquent expression of the divine force within.

Emotions of Ethics; The Intellect (Vol-5): The book is a detailed guide to its spiritual development.

The Ego: From Birth to Rebirth (Vol-6): The ego is a unique and unprecedented contribution to the literature of self-realization.

Healing of the Self: The Negatives (Vol-7): The book treats the mind – body relationship and contrasts conventional, psychic and spiritual approaches to healing.

Reflections on My Life and Writings (Vol-8): The book contains Paul Brunton's reflections about himself through fifty years of research, practice and writing.

Human Experience: The Arts in Culture (Vol-9): It teaches us to convert our lives into a process of spiritual discoveries and explores causes and purposes of suffering, problems of marriage and other relationships.

The Orient: Its Legacy to the West (Vol-10): Providing a fascinating view of traditional and contemporary oriental life, the book highlights the colours from Himalayan countries.

The Sensitives (Vol-11): The Sensitives is a timely, informed evaluation of mysticism, "paranormal" experience, sects and cults.

The Religious Urge (Reverential Life) (Vol-12): The book distinguishes the heart's ineradicable religious instinct from traditional religious forms.

Relativity, Philosophy and Mind (Vol-13): The author explains the philosophy of the science of the deeper lev els of mind. There is a deep meaning associated with our sleep and dreams.

Inspiration and The Overself (Vol-14): The book explains the tests and methods to develop intuitions, making it a vitalizing power for our existence.

Advanced Contemplation the Peace Within You (Vol-15): The author believes that there is indeed no short path to peace within oneself and the book is an uplifting approach to the peace within, at the core of every human being.

Englightened Mind, Divine Mind (Vol-16): The book discovers a strong, controversial and definitive account of what "Enlightenment" is.